Mrs. J. Webb.

W. Rothenstein 1922

The Adventure of Living

A Subjective Autobiography

(1860–1922)

By

John St. Loe Strachey

Editor of *The Spectator*

" We carry with us the wonders we seek without us; there is all Africa and her prodigies in us; we are that bold and adventurous piece of Nature, which he that studies wisely learns in a compendium what others labour at in a divided piece and endless volume."
SIR THOMAS BROWNE

Illustrated

G. P. Putnam's Sons
New York and London
The Knickerbocker Press
1922

TO MY WIFE

You who know something of the irony of life in general, and still more of it in the present particular, will not be surprised that, having made two strict rules for my guidance in the writing of this book, I break them both in the first page! Indeed, I can hear you say, though without any touch of the satirical, that it was only natural that I should do so.

The first of my two rules, heartily approved by you, let me add, is that I should not mention you in my autobiography.—We both deem it foolish as well as unseemly to violate in print the freemasonry of marriage.—The second, not unlike the first, is not to write about living people. And here am I hard at it in both cases!

Yet, after all, I have kept to my resolve in the spirit, if not in the letter:—and this though it has cost me some very good "copy,"—copy, too, which would have afforded me the pleasantest of memories. There are things seen by us together which I much regret to leave unchronicled, but these must wait for another occasion. Many of them are quite suitable to be recorded in one's lifetime. For example, I should dearly like to set forth our ride from Jerusalem to Damascus, together with some circumstances, as an old-fashioned traveller might have said, concerning the Garden of the Jews at Jahoni, and the strange and beautiful creature we found therein.

I count myself happy indeed to have seen half the de-

iii

lightful and notable things I have seen during my life, in your company. Do you remember the turbulent magnificence of our winter passage of the Splügen, not in a snowstorm, but in something much more thrilling—a fierce windstorm in a great frost? The whirling, stinging, white dust darkened the air and coated our sledges, our horses, and our faces. We shall neither of us ever forget how just below the Hospice your sledge was actually blown over by the mere fury of the blizzard; how we tramped through the drifts, and how all ended in "the welcome of an inn" on the summit; the hot soup and the *Côtelettes de Veau*. It was together, too, that we watched the sunrise from the Citadel at Cairo and saw the Pyramids tipped with rose and saffron. Ours, too, was the desert mirage that, in spite of reason and experience, almost betrayed us in our ride to the Fayum. You shared with me what was certainly an adventure of the spirit, though not of the body, when for the first time we saw the fateful and well-loved shores of America. The lights danced like fireflies in the great towers of New York, while behind them glowed in sombre splendour the fiery Bastions of a November sunset.

But, of course, none of all this affords the reason why I dedicate my book to you. That reason will perhaps be fully understood only by me and by our children. It can also be found in certain wise and cunning little hearts, inscrutable as those of kings, in a London nursery. Susan, Charlotte, and Christopher could tell if they would.

If that sounds inconsequent, or, at any rate, incomprehensible, may I not plead that so do the ineffable Mysteries of Life and Death.

J. St. Loe Strachey.

PREFACE TO THE AMERICAN EDITION

IT is with great pleasure that I accept Major Putnam's suggestion that I should write a special preface to the American edition of my autobiography. Major Putnam, I, and the *Spectator*, are a triumvirate of old friends, and I should not be likely to refuse a request made by him, even if its fulfilment was a much less agreeable task than that of addressing an American audience.

I was born with a mind which might well be described as *Anima naturaliter Americana*. I have always loved America and the Americans, and, though I cannot expect them to feel for me as I feel for them, I cherish the belief that, at any rate, they do not dislike me instinctively. That many of them regard me as somewhat wild and injudicious in my praise of their country I am well aware. They hold that I often praise America not only too much, but that I praise her for the wrong things,—praise, indeed, where I ought to censure, and so "spoil" their countrymen. Well, if that is a true bill, all I can say is that it is too late to expect me to mend my ways.

During my boyhood people here understood America much less than they do now. Though I should be exaggerating if I said that there was anything approaching dislike of America or Americans, there were certain intellectual people in England who were apt to parade a kind of conscious and supercilious patronage of the wilder products of American life and literature. I heard exaggerated stories about Americans, and especially about the Americans of the Far West,—heard them, that is, represented as semi-barbarians, coarse, rash, and boastful, with bad manners and no feeling for the reticences of life. Such legends exasperated me beyond words. I felt as did the author of *Ionica* on re-reading the play of Ajax.

> The world may like, for all I care,
>   The gentler voice, the cooler head,
> That bows a rival to despair,
>   And cheaply compliments the dead.
>
> That smiles at all that's coarse and rash,
>   Yet wins the trophies of the fight,
> Unscathed in honour's wreck and crash,
>   Heartless, but always in the right.

.   .   .   .

There were my superior persons drawn to the life! When the complaisant judge would not acknowledge the rights of the noble Ajax, but gave to another what was due to him, the poet touched me even more nearly:—

> Thanked, and self-pleased: ay, let him wear
>   What to that noble breast was due;
> And I, dear passionate Teucer, dare
>   Go through the homeless world with you.

The poem I admit does not sound very apposite in the year 1922, but it well reflected my indignation some fifty years ago. The West might then be regarded as the Ajax of the Nations. Nowadays, not even the youngest of enthusiasts could think it necessary to show his devotion by wanting to "go through the homeless world" with the richest and the most powerful community on the face of the earth.

I am not going to make any show of false modesty by suggesting that Americans may not care to read about the intimate details of my life and opinions, or to follow "the adventure of living" of a journalist and a public writer whose life, judged superficially, has been quite uneventful. I read with pleasure the lives of American men and women when they were not people of action, and I daresay people across the Atlantic will pay me a similar compliment.

Yet—I should like to give a word or two of explanation as to the way in which I have treated my subject. At first sight I expect that my book will seem chaotic and bewildering, a mighty maze and quite without a plan. As a matter of fact, however, the work was very carefully planned. My sins of omission and of commission were deliberate and, as our forefathers would have said, matters of art.

My first object was a negative one; that is, to avoid the kind of autobiography in which the author waddles painfully, diligently, and conscientiously along an arid path, which he has strewn, not with flowers and fruits of joy, but with the cinders of the commonplace. My readers know such autobiographies only too well. They are usually based upon copious diaries and letters. The author, as soon as he gets to maturity, spares us nothing. We look down endless vistas of dinners and luncheon parties and of stories of how he met the celebrated Mr. Jones at the house of the hardly less celebrated Mr. Smith and how they talked about Mr. Robinson, the most celebrated of all of them. If I have done nothing else worthy of gratitude, I have, at any rate, avoided such predestinated dullness.

What I have made my prime object is the description of the influences that have affected my life and, for good or evil, made me what I am. The interesting thing about a human being is not only what he is, but how he came to be what he is.

The main influence of my life has been *The Spectator*, and, therefore, as will be seen, I have made *The Spectator* the pivot of my book, or, shall I say, the centre from which in telling my story I have worked backwards and forwards. But this is not all. Though I pay a certain homage to chronology and let my chapters mainly follow the years, I am in this matter not too strict. Throughout, I obey the instinct of the journalist and take good copy wherever I can find it. I follow the scent while it is hot and do not say to myself or to my readers that this or that would be out-of-place here, and must be deferred to such and such a chapter, or to some portion of the book giving an account of later years, devoted to miscellaneous anecdotes! In a word, I am discursive not by accident, but by design.

If I am asked why I make this apologia, I shall have no difficulty in replying. I desire to leave nothing unsaid which may bring me into intimate touch with the greatest reading public that the world has ever seen—and, to my mind, a public as worthy as it is great.

J. St. Loe Strachey.

May 5, 1922

Postscript to American Preface

While this book and preface is going through the press, I cannot resist adding a Postscript on a point suggested by my publisher. It is that I should say something which may inform the new generation as to "The Spectator's" position during the Civil War.

"The Spectator" was as strong a friend of America in past years as it is at present, and in those past years its friendship was the more useful because the need for a true understanding between all parts of the English-speaking race was

not realised by nearly so many people as it is now. That there was ever any essential bitterness of feeling here or in America I will not admit for a moment, but that there was ignorance, pig-headedness, and want of vision, is beyond all doubt. This want of vision was specially illustrated during the Civil War. "The Spectator," however, I am proud to say, without being unjust to the South, or failing to note its gallantry, and its noble sacrifices even in a wrong cause, was consistently on the side of the North. Moreover, it realised that the North was going to win, and ought to win, and so would abolish slavery. There is a special tradition at the "Spectator" office of which we are very proud. It is that the military critic of "The Spectator," at that time Mr. Hooper, a civilian but with an extraordinary flair for strategy, divined exactly what Sherman was doing when he started on his famous march. Many years afterwards General Sherman, either in a speech or on the written page, for I cannot now verify the fact, though I am perfectly certain of it, said that when he started with the wires cut behind him, there were only two people in the world who knew what his objective was. One was himself and the other, as he said, "an anonymous writer in the London 'Spectator.'" My American readers will understand why I and all connected with "The Spectator" are intensely proud of this fact. The fate, not only of America but of the whole English-speaking race, hung upon the success of Sherman's feat of daring. In turn that success hung upon the fact that Sherman's objective was the sea. To have divined that was a notable achievement in the art of publicity.

J. St. L. S.

CONTENTS

xii

Contents

ILLUSTRATIONS

xiii

The Adventure of Living

The Adventure of Living

CHAPTER I

HOW I CAME TO "THE SPECTATOR"

Sir Thomas Browne gave his son an admirable piece of literary advice. The young son had been travelling in Hungary and proposed to write an account of what he had seen. His father approved the project, but urged him strongly not to trouble himself about the methods of extracting iron and copper from the ores, or with a multitude of facts and statistics. These were matters in which there was no need to be particular. But, he added, his son must on no account forget to give a full description of the "Roman alabaster tomb in the barber's shop at Pesth."

In writing my recollections I mean to keep always before me the alabaster tomb in the barber's shop rather than a view of life which is based on high politics, or even high literature. At first sight it may seem as if the life of an editor is not likely to contain very much of the alabaster tomb element. In truth, however, every life is an adventure, and if a sense of this adventure cannot be communicated to the reader, one may feel sure that it is the fault of the writer, not of the facts. A dull man might make a dull thing of his autobiography even if he had lived through the French Revolution; whereas a country curate might thrill the world with his story, provided that his mind were cast in the right mould and that he found a quickening interest in its delineation. Barbellion's *Diary* provides the proof. The interest of that supremely interesting book lies in the way of telling.

But how is one to know what will interest one's readers? That is a difficult question. Clearly it is no use to put up a man of straw, call him the Public, and then try to play down to him or up to him and his alleged and purely hypothetical opinions and tastes. Those who attempt to fawn upon the puppet of their own creation are as likely as not to end by interesting nobody. At any rate, try and please yourself, then at least one person's liking is engaged. That is the autobiographer's simple secret.

All the same there is a better reason than that. Pleasure is contagious. He who writes with zest will infect his readers. The man who argues, "This seems stupid and tedious to me, but I expect it is what the public likes," is certain to make shipwreck of his endeavour.

The pivot of my life has been *The Spectator*, and so *The Spectator* must be the pivot of my book—the point upon which it and I and all that is mine turn. I therefore make no apology for beginning this book with the story of how I came to *The Spectator*.

My father, a friend of both the joint editors, Mr. Hutton and Mr. Townsend, was a frequent contributor to the paper. In a sense, therefore, I was brought up in a "Spectator" atmosphere. Indeed, the first contributions ever made by me to the press were two sonnets which appeared in its pages, one in the year 1875 and the other in 1876. I did not, however, begin serious journalistic work in *The Spectator*, but, curiously enough, in its rival, *The Saturday Review*. While I was at Oxford I sent several middle articles to *The Saturday*, got them accepted, and later, to my great delight, received novels and poems for review. I also wrote occasionally in *The Pall Mall*, in the days in which it was edited by Lord Morley, and in *The Academy*. It was not until I settled down in London to read for the Bar, a year and a half after I had left Oxford, that I made any attempt to write for *The Spectator*. In the last few days of 1885 I got my father to give me a formal introduction to the editors, and went to see them in Wellington Street. They told me, as in my turn I have had to tell so many would-be reviewers, what no doubt was perfectly true, namely that they had already got more outside reviewers than they could possibly find work for, and that they were sorry to say I must not count upon their being able to give me books. All the same, they would like me to take away a couple of volumes to notice,—making it clear, however, that they did this out of friendship for my father.

I was given my choice of books, and the two I chose were a new edition of *Gulliver's Travels*, well illustrated in colour by a French artist, and, if I remember rightly, the *Memoirs of Henry Greville*, the brother of the great Greville. I will not say that I departed from the old *Spectator* offices at 1 Wellington Street—a building destined to play so great a part in my life—in dudgeon or even in disappointment. I had not expected very much. Still, no man, young or old, cares to have it made quite clear that a door at which he wishes to enter is permanently shut against him.

However, I was not likely to be depressed for long at so small a matter as this; I was much too full of enjoyment in my new London life. The wide world affords nothing to equal one's first year in London—at least, that was my feeling. My first year at Oxford had been delightful, as were also the three following, but there was to me something in the throb of the great pulse of London which, as a stimulant, nay, an excitant, of the mind, even Oxford could not rival.

For once I had plenty of leisure to enjoy the thrilling drama of life—a drama too often dimmed by the cares, the business, or even the pleasures of the onlooker. A Bar student is not overworked, and if he is not rich, or socially sought after, he can find, as I did, plenty of time in which to look around him and enjoy the scene. That exhilaration, that luxury of leisurely circumspection may never return, or only, as happily in my own case, with the grand climacteric. Once more I see and enjoy the gorgeous drama by the Thames.

To walk every morning to the Temple or to Lincoln's Inn, where I was reading in Chambers, was a feast. Then there were theatres, balls, dances, dinners, and a thousand splendid sights to be enjoyed, for I was then, as I have always been and am now, an indefatigable sightseer. I would, I confess, to this day go miles to see the least promising of curiosities or antiquities. "Who knows? it may be one of the wonders of the world" has always been my order of the day.

I was aware of my good fortune. I remember thinking how much more delightful it must be to come fresh to London than to be like so many of my friends, Londoners born and bred. They could not be thrilled as I was by the sight of St. Paul's or Westminster Abbey, or by the scimitar curve of the Thames from Blackfriars to Westminster. Through the National Gallery or the British Museum I paced a king. The vista of the London River as I went to Greenwich intoxicated me like heady wine. And Hampton Court in the spring, *Ut vidi ut perii*—"How I saw, how I perished." It was all a pageant of pure pleasure, and I walked on air, eating the fruit of the Hesperides.

But though I was so fully convinced that the doors of *The Spectator* were shut against me, I was, of course, determined that my two reviews should, if possible, make the editors feel what a huge mistake they had made and what a loss they were incurring. But, alas! here I encountered a great disappointment. When I had written my reviews they appeared to me to be total failures! I was living at the time in an "upper part" in South Molton Street, in which I, my younger brother, Henry Strachey, and two of my greatest friends, the present Sir Bernard Mallet and his younger brother Stephen Mallet, had set up house. I remember to this day owning to my brother that though I had intended my review of *Gulliver's Travels* to be epoch-making, it had turned out a horrible fiasco. However, I somehow felt I should only flounder deeper into the quagmire of my own creation if I rewrote the two reviews. Accordingly, they were sent off in the usual way. Knowing my father's experience in such matters, I did not expect to get them back in type for many weeks. As a matter of fact, they came back quite quickly. I corrected the proofs and returned them. To my astonishment the review of Swift appeared almost at once. I supposed, in the luxury of depression, that they wished to cast the rubbish out of the way as quickly as possible.

My first intention was not to go again to *The Spectator* office, the place where I was so obviously not wanted, but I remembered that my father had told me that it was always the custom to return books as soon as the proofs were corrected or the articles had appeared. I determined, therefore, that I would do the proper thing, though I felt rather shy, and feared I might be looked upon as "cadging" for work.

With my books under my arm I walked off to Wellington Street, on a Tuesday morning, and went up to Mr.

Hutton's room, where on that day the two editors used to
spend the greater part of the morning discussing the
coming issue of the paper. I had prepared a nice little
impromptu speech, which was to convey in unmistakable
terms that I had not come to ask for more books; "I fully
realise and fully acquiesce in your inability to use my
work." When I went in I was most cordially received,
and almost immediately Mr. Hutton asked me to look over
a pile of new books and see if there was anything there I
would like. This appeared to be my cue, and I accordingly proceeded to explain that I had not come to ask for
more books but only to bring back the two books I had
already reviewed and to thank the editors. I quite understood that there was no more work for me.

Then, to my amazement, Mr. Townsend, with that
vividness of expression which was his, said something to
the effect that they had only said that when they didn't
know that I could write. The position, it appeared, had
been entirely changed by the review of *Gulliver's Travels*
and they hoped very much that I should be able to do
regular work for *The Spectator*. Mr. Hutton chimed in
with equally kind and appreciative words, and I can
well remember the pleasant confusion caused in my
mind by the evident satisfaction of my future chiefs. I
was actually hailed as "a writer and critic of the first
force."

To say that I returned home elated would not be exactly
true. Bewildered would more accurately describe my
state of mind. I had genuinely believed that my attempt
to give the final word of criticism upon *Gulliver's Travels*—
that is what a young man always thinks, and ought to
think, he is doing in the matter of literary criticism—had
been a total failure. Surely I couldn't be wrong about my
own work. Yet *The Spectator* editors were evidently not

mad or pulling my leg or even flattering me! It was a
violent mystery.

Of course I was pleased at heart, but I tried to unload
some of my liabilities to Nemesis by the thought that my
new patrons would probably get tired of my manner of
writing before very long. What had captured them for the
moment was merely a certain novelty of style. They
would very soon see through it, as I had done in my poignant self-criticism. But this prudent view was before long,
in a couple of days, to be exact, knocked on the head by a
delightful letter which Mr. Townsend wrote to my father.
In it he expressed himself even more strongly in regard to
the review than he had done in speaking to me.

I honestly think that what I liked best in the whole
business was the element of adventure. There was something thrilling and, so, intensely delightful to me in the
thought, that I had walked down to Wellington Street,
like a character in a novel, prepared for a setback, only to
find that Fate was there, "hid in an auger-hole," ready to
rush and seize me. Somehow or other I felt, though I
would not admit it even to myself, that the incident had
been written in the Book of Destiny, and that it was one
which was going to affect my whole life. Of course, being,
like other young men, a creature governed wholly by
reason and good sense, I scouted the notion of a destined
day as sentimental and ridiculous. Still, the facts were
"as stated," and could not be altogether denied.

Looking back at the lucky accident which brought the
right book, the right reviewer, and the properly-tuned
editors together, I am bound to say that I think that the
editors were right and that I had produced good copy.
At any rate, their view being what it was, I have no sort of
doubt that they were quite right to express it as plainly
and as generously as they did to me. To have followed

the conventional rule of not puffing up a young man with praise and to have guarded their true opinion as a kind of guilty secret would have been distinctly unfair to me, nay, prejudicial. There are, I suppose, a certain number of young people to whom it would be unsafe to give a full measure of eulogy. But these are a small minority. The ordinary young man or young woman is much more likely to be encouraged or sometimes even alarmed by unstinted praise. Generous encouragement is the necessary mental nourishment of youth, and those who withhold it from them are not only foolish but cruel. They are keeping food from the hungry.

If my editors had told me that they thought the review rather a poor piece of work, I should, by "the law of reversed effort," have been almost certain to have taken up a combative line and have convinced myself that it was epoch-making. When a man thinks himself overpraised, if he has anything in him at all, he begins to get anxious about his next step. He is put very much on his mettle not to lose what he has gained.

It may amuse my readers, if I quote a few sentences from the article, and allow them to see whether their judgment coincides with that of my chiefs at *The Spectator* on a matter which was for me fraught with the decrees of Destiny. This is how I began my review of Swift and his masterpiece:

"Never anyone living thought like you," said to Swift the woman who loved him with a passion that had caught some of his own fierceness and despair. The love which great natures inspire had endowed Vanessa with a rare inspiration. Half-consciously she has touched the notes that help us to resolve the discord in Swift's life. Truly, the mind of living man never worked as Swift's worked. That this is so is visible in every line, in every word he ever wrote. No phrase of his is like any other man's; no conception of his is ever cast in the common mould. It is this that lends something so dreadful and mysterious to all Swift's writings.

From this time I began to get books regularly from *The Spectator* and to pay periodical visits to the office, where I learned to understand and to appreciate my chiefs. But more of them later. The year 1886 was one of political convulsion, the year of the great split in the Liberal Party; the year in which Lord Hartington and Mr. Chamberlain finally severed themselves from Mr. Gladstone and began that co-operation with the Conservatives which resulted in the formation of the Unionist Party. I do not, however, want to deal here with the Unionist crisis, except so far as it affected me and *The Spectator*. While my father and my elder brother remained Liberals and followed Mr. Gladstone, I followed Lord Hartington, Mr. Chamberlain, and Mr. Goschen. My conversion was not in any way sought by my new friends and chiefs at *The Spectator* office, though they at once took the Unionist side. I have no doubt, however, that my intercourse with Hutton and Townsend had its effect, though I also think that my mind was naturally Unionist in politics. I was already a Lincoln worshipper in American history and desired closer union with the Dominions, not separation. I was for concentration, not dispersion, in the Empire. In any case, I took the plunge, one which might have been painful if my father had not been the most just, the most fair-minded, and the most kind-hearted of men. Although he was an intense, nay, a fierce Gladstonian, I never had the slightest feeling of estrangement from him or he from me. It happened, however, that the break-up of the Liberal Party affected me greatly at *The Spectator*. When the election of 1886 took place, I was asked by a friend and

Somersetshire neighbour, Mr. Henry Hobhouse, who had become, like me, a Liberal Unionist, to act as his election agent. This I did, though, as a matter of fact, he was unopposed. The moment he was declared elected I made out my return as election agent and went straight back to my work in London. Almost at once I received a letter which surprised me enormously. It was from Mr. Hutton, telling me that Mr. Townsend had gone away for his usual summer holiday, and that he wanted someone to come and help him by writing a couple of leaders a week and some of the notes. I, of course, was delighted at the prospect, for my mind was full of politics and I was longing to have my say. Here again, though it did not consciously occur to me that I was in for anything big, I seem to have had some sort of subconscious premonition. At any rate, I accepted with delight and well remember my talk at the office before taking up my duties. My editor explained to me that Mr. Asquith, who had been up till the end of 1885 the writer of a weekly leader in *The Spectator* and also a holiday writer, had now severed his connection with the paper, owing to his entry into active politics. It did not occur to me, however, that I was likely to get the post of regular leader-writer in his stead, though this was what actually happened.

I left the office, I remember, greatly pleased with the two subjects upon which I was to write. The first article was to be an exhortation to the Conservative side of the Unionist Party not to be led into thinking that they were necessarily a minority in the country and that they could not expect any but a minute fraction of working-men to be on their side. With all the daring of twenty-six I set out to teach the Conservative party their business. This is how I began my article which appeared on the 24th of July, 1886.

In their hearts the Conservatives cannot really believe that anyone with less than £100 a year willingly votes on their side. A victory in a popular constituency always astonishes them. They cannot restrain a feeling that by all the rules of reason and logic they ought to have lost. What inducement, they wonder, can the working-men have to vote for them? Lord Beaconsfield, of course, never shared such notions as these. . . . Yet his party never sincerely believed what he told them, and only followed him because they saw no other escape from their difficulties. The last extension of the franchise has again shown that he was right, and that in no conditions of life do Englishmen vote as a herd.

Here is how I ended it:

Conciliation or Coercion was the cry everywhere. And yet the majority of the new voters, to their eternal honour, proved their political infancy so full of sense and patriotism that they let go by unheeded the appeals to their class-prejudices and to their emotions, and chose, instead, the harder and seemingly less generous policy, based on reason rather than on sentiment, on conviction rather than on despair. As the trial was severe, so is the honour due to the new voters lasting and conspicuous.

The length of the quotation is justified by its effect on —my life. For me it has another interest. In re-reading it, I note that, right or wrong, it takes exactly the view of the English democracy which I have always taken and which I hold today as strongly as I did forty years ago.

The article had an instant reaction. It delighted Mr. Townsend, who, though he did not *know* it was by me, guessed that it was mine, and wrote at once to ask me whether, when Mr. Hutton went on his holiday, I could remain at work as his assistant. Very soon after, he suggested, with a swift generosity that still warms my heart, that if I liked to give up the Bar, for which I was still supposing myself to be reading, I could have a permanent place at *The Spectator*, and even, if I remember rightly, hinted that I might look forward to succeeding the first of the two partners who died or retired, and so to becoming joint editor or joint proprietor. That prospect I do admit took away my breath. With the solemn caution of youth, or at any rate with youth's delight in irony in action, I almost felt that I should have to go and make representations to my chief about his juvenile impetuosity and want of care and prudence. Surely he must see that he had not had enough experience of me yet to make so large a proposition, that it was absurd, and so forth. *O sancta simplicitas!*

CHAPTER II

EVEN the success chronicled in the preceding chapter did not exhaust the store of good luck destined for my first appearance as a political leader-writer. Fate again showed its determination to force me upon *The Spectator*. When I arrived at the office on the Tuesday morning following the publication of the number of the paper in which my first two leaders appeared, I found that the second leader had done even better than the first. Its title seemed appallingly dull, and, I remember, called forth a protest from Mr. Hutton when I suggested writing it. It was entitled "The Privy Council and the Colonies." I had always been an ardent Imperialist, and I had taken to Constitutional Law like a duck to the water, and felt strongly, like so many young men before me, the intellectual attraction of legal problems and still more the majesty and picturesqueness of our great Tribunals. Especially had I been fascinated by the Judicial Committee of the Privy Council and its world-wide jurisdiction. I had even helped to draw some pleadings in a Judicial Committee case when in Chambers. Accordingly, though with some difficulty, I persuaded Mr. Hutton to let me have my say and show what a potent bond of Empire was to be found therein. I also wanted to emphasise how further ties of Imperial unity might be developed on similar lines—a fact, I may say, which was not discovered by the practical politicians till about the year 1912, or twenty-seven years later.

Now it happened that Mr. Gladstone's Ministry, though beaten at the elections, had not yet gone out of office. It also happened that Lord Granville, then Colonial Secretary, was to receive the Agents-General of the self-governing Colonies, as they were then called, on the Saturday; and finally, that Lord Granville had a fit of the gout. The result of the last fact was that he had to put off preparing his speech till the last possible moment. When he had been wheeled in a chair into the reception-room—his foot was too painful to allow him to walk—he began his address to the Deputation in these terms:

In a very remarkable article which appears in this week's *Spectator* it is pointed out "that people are apt to overlook the importance of the Judicial Committee of the Privy Council as one of the bonds that unite the Colonies and the Mother Country."

He then went on to use the article as the foundation for his speech. I had talked about the Judicial Committee of the Privy Council being a body which "binds without friction and links without strain," and Lord Granville did the same.

But of this speech I knew nothing when I entered *The Spectator* office on my fateful second Tuesday. I was only intent to get instructions for new leaders. Besides, I had been away on a country-house visit from the Saturday to the Monday, and had missed Monday's *Times*. I was therefore immensely surprised when Mr. Hutton, from the depths of his beard, asked me in deep tones whether I had seen *The Times* of Monday, and what was said therein about my Privy Council article. I admit that for a moment I thought I had been guilty of some appalling blunder and that, as the soldiers say, I was "for it." However, I saw that I must face the music as best I could, and admitted that I had not seen the paper. "Then you ought to have," was Mr. Hutton's not very reassuring reply. He got up, went to a side-table, and, after much digging into a huge heap of papers, extracted Monday's *Times* and with his usual gruff good-temper read out the opening words of Lord Granville's speech. He was, in fact, greatly delighted, and almost said in so many words that it wasn't every day that the Editors of *The Spectator* could draw Cabinet Ministers to advertise their paper.

Certainly it was astonishingly good luck for a "commencing journalist" to bring down two birds with two articles, *i.e.*, to hit one of his own editors with one article, and to bag a Cabinet Minister with the other.

No doubt the perfectly cautious man would have said, "This is an accident, a mere coincidence, it means nothing and will never happen again." Fortunately people do not argue in that rational and statistical spirit. All my chiefs knew or cared was that I had written good stuff and on a very technical subject, and that I had caught the ear of the man who, considering the subject, most mattered—the Secretary of State for the Colonies.

Anyway, my two first trial leaders had done the trick and I was from that moment free of *The Spectator*. Townsend's holiday succeeded to Hutton's, and when the holidays were over, including my own, which not unnaturally took me to Venice,—"*Italiam petimus*" should always be the motto of an English youth,—I returned to take up the position of a weekly leader-writer and holiday-understudy, a mixed post which by the irony of fate, as I have already said, had just been vacated by Mr. Asquith. Here was an adventure indeed, and I can say again with perfect sincerity that for me the greatest delight of the whole thing was this element of the Romantic.

I was quite sensible that I had had the devil's own luck in my capture of a post on *The Spectator*. Indeed, I very much preferred that, to the thought that the good fortune that was mine was the reward of a grinding and ignoble perseverance. I was in no mood for the drab virtues. I hugged the thought that it was not through my merits but because I possessed a conquering star that I had got where I was.

Curiously enough, I had never dreamed of joining *The Spectator* staff or even of becoming its Editor. I had imagined every other sort of strange and sudden preferment, of frantic proprietors asking me at a moment's notice to edit their papers, or of taking up some great and responsible position, but never of carrying by assault 1 Wellington Street. But that, of course, made it all the more delightful. No one could have prepared me a greater or a more grateful surprise.

It is strange to look back and see how at this moment that mystery which we barbarously call "the force of circumstances" seemed to have determined not merely to drive in my nail but to hammer it up to the head. It happened that both Mr. Hutton and Mr. Townsend had great belief in the literary judgment of Canon Ainger, a man, it is to be feared, now almost forgotten, but whose opinion was looked upon in the 'eighties and 'nineties with something approaching reverence.

In 1886—my "Spectator" year, as I may call it—when I was acting as election-agent to Mr. Henry Hobhouse, I happened to be searching in the old library at Hadspen House for something to read, something with which to occupy the time of waiting between the issue of the writ and nomination-day. If there was to be no opposition it

did not seem worth while to get too busy over the elec-
torate. We remained, therefore, in a kind of enchanter's
circle until nomination-day was over. It was a time in
which everybody whispered mysteriously that a very
strong candidate, name unknown, would suddenly appear
at Yeovil, Langport, or Chard—I forget which of these
pleasant little towns was the place of nomination—and
imperil our chances. As was natural to me then, and, I
must confess, would be natural to me now, my search for a
book took me straight to that part of the library in which
the poets congregated. My eye wandered over the shelves,
and lighted upon *Poems in the Dorsetshire Dialect* by the
Rev. William Barnes. Hadspen House was quite close
to the Dorset border. I was interested and I took down
the volume. I don't think I had ever heard of Barnes
before, but being very fond of the Somersetshire dialect
and proud of my ability to speak in it, my first impulse
was rather to turn up my nose at the vernacular of a
neighbouring county. It was, then, with a decided inclination to look a gift-horse in the mouth that I retired
with Barnes to my den. Yet, as Hafiz says, "by this a
world was affected." I opened the poems at the enchanting stanzas, "Lonesome woodlands! zunny woodlands!"
and was transported. In a moment I realised that for me
a new foot was on the earth, a new name come down from
Heaven. I read and read, and can still remember how the
exquisite rhythm of "Woak Hill" was swept into my mind,
to make there an impression which will never be oblit-
erated while life lives in my brain. I did not know, in
that delirium of exaltation which a poetic discovery always
makes in the heart of a youth, whether most to admire the
bold artifice of the man who had adapted an unrhymed
Persian metre—the Pearl—to the needs of a poem in the
broadest Dorsetshire dialect, or the deep intensity of the

emotion with which he had clothed a glorious piece of prosodiac scholarship.

I recognised at once that the poem was fraught with a pathos as magnificent as anything in the whole range of classic literature—and also that this pathos had that touch of stableness in sorrow which we associate, and rightly associate, with the classics. Miserably bad scholar as I was, and am, I knew enough to see that the Dorsetshire schoolmaster and village parson had dared to challenge the deified Virgil himself. The depth of feeling in the lines—

> An' took her wi' air-reachen arm
> To my zide at Woak Hill

is not exceeded even by those which tell how Æneas filled his arms with the empty air when he stretched them to enfold the dead Creusa.

Upon the last two stanzas in "Woak Hill" I may as truly be said to have lived for a month as Charles Lamb lived upon "Rose Aylmer."

> An' that's why folk thought, for a season,
>   My mind were a-wandren
> Wi' sorrow, when I wer so sorely
>   A-tried at Woak Hill.

> But no; that my Mary mid never
>   Behold herzelf slighted,
> I wanted to think that I guided
>   My guide from Woak Hill.

Equally potent was the spell cast by what is hardly less great a poem than "Woak Hill," the enchanting "Evenen, an' Maids out at Door." There the Theocritus of the West dares to use not merely the words of common speech and primitive origin, but words drawn from Low Latin and of administrative connotation. Barnes achieves this triumph in words with perfect ease. He can use a word like "parish" not, as Crabbe did, for purposes of pure narration but in a passage of heightened rhetoric:

But when you be a-lost vrom the parish, zome more
    Will come on in your pleäzen to bloom an' to die;
An' the zummer will always have maidens avore
    Their doors, vor to chatty an' zee volk goo by.

For daughters ha' mornen when mothers ha' night,
    An' there's beauty alive when the fairest is dead;
As when one sparklen wave do zink down from the light,
    Another do come up an' catch it instead.

Rightly did the Edinburgh reviewer of the 'thirties, in noticing Barnes's poems—the very edition from which I was reading, perfect, by the way, in its ribbed paper and clear print—declare "there has been no such art since Horace." And here I may interpolate that the reviewer in question was Mr. George Venables, who was within a year to become a friend of mine. He and his family were close friends of my wife's people, and when after my marriage I met him, a common love of Barnes brought together the ardent worshipper of the new schools of poetry, for such I was, and the old and distinguished lawyer who was Thackeray's contemporary at the Charterhouse. Barnes was for us both a sign of literary freemasonry which at once made us recognise each other as fellow-craftsmen.

Bewildered readers will ask how my discovery of Barnes affected my position at *The Spectator*. It happened in this way. A couple of weeks after I had been established at *The Spectator* as a "*verus socius*" Barnes died, at a very great age. It was one of those cases in which death suddenly makes a man visible to the generation into which he has survived. Barnes had outlived not only his contemporaries but his renown, and most of the journalists detailed to write his obituary notice had evidently found it a hard task to say why he should be held in remembrance.

But by a pure accident here was I, in the high tide of my enthusiasm for my new poet. Needless to say I was only too glad to have a chance to let myself go on Barnes, and so was entrusted with the Barnes Obituary article for *The Spectator*.

The result was that the next week my chiefs showed me a letter one of them had received from Canon Ainger, asking for the name of the "evidently new hand" who had written on Barnes, and making some very complimentary remarks on his work. It was eminently characteristic of them that instead of being a little annoyed at being told that an article had appeared in *The Spectator* with an unexpected literary charm, they were as genuinely delighted as I was.

In any case, the incident served, as I have said, to drive the nail up to the head and to make Mr. Hutton and Mr. Townsend feel that they had not been rash in their choice, and had got a man who could do literature as well as politics.

Not being without a sense of superstition, at any rate where cats are concerned, and a devout lover of "the furred serpent," I may record the last, the complete rite of my initiation at *The Spectator* office. While I was one day during my novitiate talking over articles and waiting for instructions—or, rather, finding articles for my chiefs to write about, for that very soon became the routine—a large, consequential, not to say stout black Tom-cat slowly entered the room, walked round me, sniffed at my legs in a suspicious manner, and then, to my intense

amazement and amusement, hurled himself from the floor
with some difficulty and alighted upon my shoulder.   Mr.
Townsend, who loved anything dramatic, though he did
not love animals as Mr. Hutton did, pointed to the cat
and muttered dramatically, "Hutton, just look at that!"

He went on to declare that the cat very seldom honoured
"upstairs" with his presence, but kept himself, as a rule,
strictly to himself, in the basement.   Apparently, however,
the sagacious beast had realised that there was a new
element in the office, and had come to inspect it and see
whether he could give it his approval or not.   When it was
given, it was conceded by all concerned that the appointment had received its consecration.   Like "the Senior
Fellow" in Sir Frederick Pollock's poem on the College
Cat, I was passed by the highest authority in the office.

> One said, "The Senior Fellow's vote!"
> The Senior Fellow, black of coat,
>   Save where his front was white,
> Arose and sniffed the stranger's shoes
> With critic nose, as ancients use
>   To judge mankind aright.
>
> I—for 'twas I who tell the tale—
> Conscious of fortune's trembling scale,
>   Awaited the decree;
> But Tom had judged: "He loves our race,"
> And, as to his ancestral place,
>   He leapt upon my knee.
>
> Thenceforth, in common-room and hall,
> A *verus socius* known to all,
>   I came and went and sat,
> Far from cross fate's or envy's reach;
> For none a title could impeach
>   Accepted by the cat.

It was at this time that Mr. Townsend wrote me, on behalf of himself and his partner, a letter stating definitely that if I would devote myself to *The Spectator*, he and Hutton would guarantee me at once a certain salary, though I might still take any work I liked outside. But this was not all. The letter went on to say that the first of the partners who died or retired would offer me a half-share of the paper. It was pointed out that, of course, that might conceivably mean a fairly long apprenticeship, but that it was far more likely to mean a short one. It proved to be neither the one nor the other, but what might be called a compromise period of some ten years.

And so in the course of a very few weeks my fate had been decided for me and the question I had so often put to myself: Should I stick to the Bar or throw in my lot with journalism? was answered. A great wave had seized me and cast me up upon the shore of 1 Wellington Street. I felt breathless but happy. Though I did not fully realise how deeply my life had been affected by the decision or how strange in some ways was the course that lay before me, I had an instinctive feeling that I must follow whole-heartedly the path of Destiny. I determined to free my mind from all thoughts of a return to the Bar. I shut my eyes for ever to the vision of myself as Lord Chancellor or Lord Chief Justice—a vision that has haunted every young man who has ever embarked upon the study of English Law;—the vision of which Dr. Johnson, even at the end of his life, could not speak without profound emotion.

I acted promptly. I at once gave up my nice little room in the Temple. It was about eight foot square, furnished with one table, one arm-chair, one cane chair, and a bookcase, and dignified by the name of Chambers. I sometimes wonder now whether, if I could have looked down the long avenue of the years and seen the crowded, turbulent series of events which, as Professor Einstein has taught us, was rushing upon me like a tiger on its prey, I should have been alarmed or not. I should have seen many things exciting, many things sad, many things difficult, but above all I should have seen what could only have been described as a veritable snowstorm of written and printed pages.

I have sometimes, as every man will, reversed the process, looked back and reviewed the past. On such occasions I have been half inclined to make the reflection, common to all journalists, when they survey the monumental works of our brethren in the superior ranks of the literary profession: "Have I not cast my life and energy away on things ephemeral and unworthy? Have not I preferred a kind of glorified pot-boiling to the service of the spirit?" In the end, however, like the painter with the journalist's heart in Robert Browning's poem, I console myself for having enlisted among the tradesmen of literature rather than among the artists:

> For I have done some service in my time,
> And not been paid profusely.
> Let some great soul write my six thousand leaders!

It is, I admit, an appalling thought to have covered so much paper and used so much ink. But, after all, an apology may be made for mere volume in journalism analogous to that made for it by Dr. Johnson when he said that poets must to some extent be judged by their quantity as well as their quality. Anyway, I am inclined to be proud of my output. When an occasion like the present makes me turn back to my old articles, I am glad to say that my attitude, far from being one of shame, is more like that of the Duke of Wellington. When quite an old man, somebody brought him his Indian Despatches to look over.   As he read he is recorded to have muttered: "Damned good!   I don't know how the devil I ever managed to write 'em."

The tale of how I came to *The Spectator* is finished.   I must now describe what sort of a youth it was who got there, and what were the influences that had gone to his making.

CHAPTER III

MY PHYSICAL HOME, MY FAMILY, AND MY
GOOD FORTUNE THEREIN

THE autobiographer, or at any rate the writer of the type of autobiography on which I am engaged, need not apologise for being egotistical. If he is not that he is nothing. He must start with the assumption that people want to hear about him and to hear it from himself. Further, he must be genuinely and actively interested in his own life and therefore write about it willingly and with zest. If you get anywhere near the position of an autobiographer, "*invitus*," addressing a reader, "*invitum*," the game is up.

It would, then, be an absurdity to pretend to avoid egotism.

It would be almost as futile to apologise for being trivial. All details of human life are interesting, or can be made interesting, especially if they can be shown to be contributory to the development of the subject on the Anatomy-table. The elements that contributed to the building up of the man under observation are sure to be worth recording.

The autobiographer who is going to succeed with his task must set down whatever he believes went to the making of his mind and soul, and of that highly composite product which constitutes a human being. Nothing is

too small or too unimportant to be worthy of record.
But people to whom criticism is a passion and who love it
even more than life, and they are often very valuable
people, will say, "Are we not, then, to be allowed to dub
your book trivial, if we think so?" Of course they must
have that license, but they must make good the plea of
triviality, not in the facts but in the exposition. *There*
no man has a right to be trivial, or empty, or commonplace. Whatever is recorded must be recorded worthily.
Take a plain example. If I set forth to describe my crossing Waterloo Bridge on a particular day in a particular
year, I must not merely on that ground be attacked for
triviality. I may be able to show, in the first place, that
the crossing by that bridge and not, let us say, by using
Hungerford Bridge or Blackfriars Bridge, affected my
life. I may also be able to describe my walk or drive in
such a way that it will make a deep impress upon the
reader's mind. In a word, to get judgment against me,
the critic must demur, not on my facts but on a point of
literature, that is, on my method of presentation.

In considering the multitude of things which have gone
to make me what I am, which have drawn into a single
strand the innumerable threads that the Fates have been
spinning for me ever since they began their dread business,
what strikes me most of all and first of all is my good
fortune. I may, on a future occasion, complain that in
middle life and in later life I did not have good luck, but
bad luck, but I should be an ingrate to Destiny if I did
not admit that nothing could have been more happy
than the circumstances with which I was surrounded
at my birth—the circumstances which made the boy, who
made the youth, who made the man.

Above all, I was fortunate in my father and my mother.
Though I must put them first in honour on my record, as

View of North Front of Sutton Court, in the County of Somerset,
the Family House of the Stracheys.

first in time and in memory, I can show them best by touching in a preliminary study on those surroundings, moral and intellectual, into which I was born.

In the first place, I count myself specially happy in that my parents were people of moderate fortune. They were not too poor to give me the pleasures and the freedoms of a liberal education, and of all that used to be included in the phrase "easy circumstances." Ours was a pleasant and leisurely way of life, undisturbed by the major worries and anxieties of narrow means.

On the other hand, my home surroundings were not of the pompous, luxurious kind which makes nothing moral or physical matter very much, which drowns a man in security. I knew what it was to want a thing, and to be told that it was much too expensive to be thought of. I knew I should have to make my way in life like my ancestors before me, for not only was my family in no sense a rich one, but I was a second son, who could only look forward to a second son's portion,—an honourable distinction, this, and one of which my father and my mother were often wont to speak.

I had, in a word, all the pride of a second son, a creature devoted to carving his own way to fame and fortune. I will not say that my parents wanted to console me for being a second son and for seeing my elder brother inherit the estate and Sutton the beloved, for that was never thought of or dreamt of by them, or by me. On the contrary, I was told in all sincerity, and firmly believe now, as I did then, that though somebody must keep the flame alight on the family altar, where it was lighted so long ago, and though this duty fell to the eldest son, I need not envy him. He was tied. I as a younger son was left free, untrammelled, the world before me. If I was worthy of my fate, the ball was at my feet. Such was the policy of younger sons, and so it was handed on to me.

Again, I was fortunate in being brought up in the country, and not in London or near some great town;—in being, that is, the inmate of "an English country-house" in the accepted sense, a place to which a certain definite way of life pertains, especially when the house is not bought, but inherited, and is regarded with a peculiar veneration and admiration by all who live in it.

The love of some old "house in the country" constitutes a family freemasonry, of which those who have not actually experienced it can form no conception. It unites those who differ in opinion, in age, in outlook on life, and in circumstances. It is the password of the heart.

Call a dog-kennel Sutton, and I should love it. How much more so when it stands beside its sheltering elms and limes, with its terraces looking to the blue line of Mendip, its battlemented and flower-tufted fortress wall, and its knightly Tower built for security and defence.

In a word, I had the supreme good-luck to be born the second son of a Somersetshire squire and to be brought up in a Somersetshire country-house. If the reader would know what that means to a Somersetshire man, let him turn to Coryat's *Crudities* and see what the Elizabethan tourist says in his Introduction as to the possession of a Manor in the county aforesaid.

But I must be careful not to give a false impression. Sutton is no palace in miniature, no grandiose expression of the spacious days of Elizabeth, no pompous outcome of Vanbrugh's magnificent mind, no piece of reticent elegance by Adams. Instead, it may well seem to the visiting stranger little more than a fortuitous concourse of mediæval, Elizabethan, Jacobean, and modern atoms, which time and the country builder, too unlearned to be vulgar, have harmonized into a very moderate, though admittedly attractive, "country seat," of the smaller sort.

Just as the house had nothing grand about it, so the life lived in it was not in the least like that described in the old-fashioned sporting or Society novel, or in the Christmas Number of an Illustrated Paper or Magazine. Neither my home nor my family was by any means "typical," which so often means very untypical. This is specially true of the Family. They were not in my time, and, indeed, never have been, persons "complete with" foxhounds, racers, cellars of port, mortgages, gaming or elections debts, obsequious tenantry, and a brutal enforcement of the Game Laws, varied by the semi-fraudulent enclosure of the poor man's common. With such rural magnificoes, if they ever existed in that form, which I greatly doubt, we had nothing in common. Even when reduced to reasonable limits, the picture will not fit the majority of English country-houses and country gentlemen.

In the first place, the Stracheys could not afford the type of life depicted by the novelists and satirists, and, in the second place, they had not the opportunity. Their eldest sons always had to do something in the world, and even when in possession of the estate were by no means inclined to spend their lives as nothing but sportsmen. Certainly my ancestors never showed any inclination to vegetate, or to live gun in hand and spaniel at heel, like the squires in the old engravings and colour-prints.

Here I may say parenthetically that we have the good luck to possess many old family papers at Sutton. I used to read long and happily in these as a boy, and early saw the falsehood of the conventional, feudal view of the English squirearchy. When I worked back to the mediæval possessors of Sutton, I could find nothing to satisfy my youthful dreams of knights in armour doing deeds of prowess, or even of tyranny upon "the villagers crouching at their feet." Instead, I found, with some disappointment, I admit, that the very first record in regard to Sutton was that of a dispute in the law-courts with the local parson—a dispute which is, of course, perennial in all villages and "quiet places by rivers or among woods." It is as active now as it was in the twelfth century.

Whether Sir Walter de Sutton, with half a knight's fee, for that, apparently, was the proper legal description of the Sutton Court estate, got the best of the Vicar, or the Vicar of him, does not seem to have been recorded. Anyway, they went for each other, not with lance in rest, on the one side, and Holy Water, bell, book, and candle on the other, but with attorneys, and writs, and motions in arrest of judgment, and all the formulæ which can be seen at work in the Year Books of Edward II, for that was the date of the Tower, and of the aforesaid Walter de Sutton.

As I shall show later, when I come to deal with my ancestry, Sutton was never a "Heartbreak House." In each succeeding generation it held the place which it held when I was young, and which, Heaven be praised! it still holds. A small, comfortable, yet dignified manor-house, surrounded by farmhouses and cottages in which live still just the kind of people who have lived there throughout the period of legal or of literary memory—the period described as that to which "the memory of man runneth not to the contrary."

The village people were poor, but yet not dependent; people not, perhaps, very enterprising, and yet with a culture of their own; and people, above all, with natural dignity and good manners shown to those they like and respect, though often with a conventional set of bad manners to use, if required, as armour against a rough world.

These are always produced when they are inclined to suspect strangers of regarding them with patronage, ridicule, or contempt.

At this day I could show a rural labourer living in one of the Sutton Court cottages, aged eighty-three or so, who lived there when I was a boy and looked then, to my eyes, almost exactly as he does now. Tall, distinguished, with not merely good manners but a good manner, and with real refinement of speech, though a strong Somersetshire accent, Israel Veal would show nothing of himself to a stranger. Probably he would speak so little, though quite politely, that he would be put down as "one of those muddle-headed, stupid yokels with little or no mind," who, according to the townsman, "moulder" in country villages "till they become demented."

Yet when, a year ago, I introduced my son to him, though my son was, till then, unknown to him, he at once talked freely. He had got the password and knew all was safe and well. He proceeded at once to tell him what he had often told me—how he had "helped to put Sir Henry" (my father's uncle, whom he succeeded) "into his coffin." He then went on to describe how (in 1858) the coffin was carried on men's shoulders the whole way to Chew Magna to be buried there in the Strachey Chapel. The event set down in cold print does not sound of very great interest or importance. It will seem, indeed, at first hearing to partake a little too much of the country-man of the melodrama, or of the comic papers, who always talks about funerals and corpses. As a matter of fact, however, Israel Veal has so little self-consciousness and possesses such a gift for dignified narration that, told by him, the story, if indeed it can be called a story, always seems of real significance. There is something of the air of the prophet about the narrator, though he indulge in no prophecy. I found myself, indeed, saying to my son, "I am so glad you have heard that as I used to hear it," quite imagining for the moment that it was a piece of family lore of high import which was being sacramentally passed on by the old retainer.

At Sutton, though I was not brought up in a hunting-stable, or amid a crowd of gamekeepers, and so forth, we had the usual establishment of a country-gentleman of moderate means in the 'seventies. My mother had a comfortable, heavy landau, with a pair of quiet horses, still officially and in bills called "coach-horses." My father had a small brougham of his own for doing magistrate's work, drawn by a horse believed to be of a very fiery disposition, and called "Black Bess." I and my brothers had ponies on whose backs we spent many hours. My father had been an invalid most of his life, and, owing to a stiff knee, could not ride. But, though an anxious parent, he wisely realised that an Englishman must if possible know how to use the back of a horse. Ours was a bad riding country, owing to the great number of small fields, but we galloped up and down the roads with a youthful lack of consideration for our horses' legs. Curiously enough, there were no hounds near us, and therefore I never actually rode to hounds till I was forty. Happily, however, I was familiar with the saddle, and, though an exceedingly careless rider, had not, even after nearly twenty years' intermission of riding, to re-learn my grip.

Even now, to get on a horse and ride through woods and lanes and over Downs and Commons is an enormous pleasure, and if a mild jump or two can be added I am transported into the Seventh Heaven. To me the greatest of all physical enjoyments has always been the sensation produced by a horse with all four legs off the ground.

There was another aspect of the country-house, which I am sure was not without its effect. My father, though he knew little or nothing about agriculture, was to a great extent his own agent, and therefore the farmers and the cottage tenants were constantly coming to the house to consult him and to talk over small matters. There also came to him pretty frequently people on police and magistrate's business, to get warrants signed, so that the offenders could be legally held till brought before the Petty Sessions. At these interviews, whether economic, administrative, or constabulary, I and my brothers were permitted to attend. While my father sat at his table in what was called "the magistrate's room," or "Sir Edward's business room," and the other persons of the drama either sat opposite him, if they were merely on business, or stood if they were accompanied by a policeman, we children sat discreetly on a sofa on my father's side of the room and listened with all our ears.

It was always interesting and curious, and occasionally we had a real piece of dramatic "fat," in the shape of charges of witchcraft. Assaults or threatening language "likely to cause breaches of the Peace" were also regarded as highly diverting. Charges of witchcraft were usually levelled by one old lady against another. One might hear accounts of how intrepid men and women nailed down the footsteps of the witch, of how deadly-nightshade was grown over the porch of a cottage to keep off witches, and how evil spirits in the shape of squeaking chickens frequented the woman who was "overlooked." My father did his best to make peace and subdue superstition, but it was quite easy to see that his audiences, especially when they were women, regarded him as a victim of ignorance. "Poor gentleman, he don't understand a word about it." That was their attitude.

Lastly, my country home had what so many English country-houses have, a largish library. The hoary tradition that English squires are as a class illiterate, which they are not even when inordinately given to sport, has no foundation. In the Great Parlour, for so it was called, there were plenty of good books, and I was early turned loose among them. My father would have thought it a crime to keep books from a boy on the plea that he might injure the bindings or lose the volumes or get harm from unlicensed reading. I did exactly what I liked in the library and browsed about with a splendid incoherence which would have shocked a pedant, but delighted a true man of letters. Now I would open the folio edition of Ben Jonson, now Congreve's plays and poems printed by Baskerville; now a volume of "Counsel's Brief delivered in the defence of Warren Hastings Esqre. at his impeachment," which we happened to possess; now *Travels to the Court of Ashanti;* now *Chinese Punishments;* now Flaxman's Illustrations to the *Iliad*, the *Odyssey*, or *Dante*.

Those were glorious days, for one had real leisure. One varied the turning over of books in the Great Parlour with a scamper on one's pony, with visits to the strawberry-bed, and with stretching oneself full-length on a sofa, or the hearth-rug in the Hall, reading four or five books at a time. In such an atmosphere it was easy to forget one's proper lessons and the abhorred dexterity of Greek and Latin grammarians.

If the physical "aura" of Sutton Court was delightful and stimulating to mind and body, still more stimulating and of still happier chance was the mental atmosphere. I may class myself as thrice-blessed in being brought up in Whig ideas, in a Whig family, with Whig traditions, for in spite of the stones, intellectual and political, that have been thrown at them, salvation is of the Whigs.

When I speak thus of the Whigs I do not, of course, mean Whiggism of the Whig aristocracy as represented by modern Tory historians, or by the parasitic sycophants of a militant Proletariat. I mean true Whig principles—the principles of Halifax, of Somers, of Locke, of Addison, and of Steele—the principles of the Bill of Rights and of "the Glorious Revolution of 1688";—the Whiggism which had its origin in the party of Cromwell and of the Independents, of John Milton and of Richard Baxter, the party which even in its decadence flowered in England in Chatham and William Pitt, and in America in Washington, John Adams, and the founders of the Republic. Whig principles to me mean that the will of the majority of the nation as a whole must prevail, and not the will of any section, even if it is a large section and does manual work. These are the principles which are in deadly opposition to Jacobinism and Bolshevism. Under Jacobinism and Bolshevism, as their inventors proclaim, true policy must be made to prevail by force, or frand, if necessary. Privilege is claimed for the minority. Oligarchy, and a very militant form of oligarchy, thus takes the place of true democracy.

But though the will of the people, be it what it may be, must prevail, the Whig claims absolute liberty in all matters of personal opinion and of conscience, and advocates the greatest amount of liberty procurable in social action. He will not sanction direct action in order to secure even these things, but he asserts the right of free speech in order to convert the majority, when it needs converting, to his views, and will not rest till he obtains it. Never persecute a man for his opinions as long as he does not proceed to lawless action. Maintain freedom against a lawless crowd as steadfastly as against a lawless crown. Never refuse a man an impartial hearing, and never judge a man guilty till he has been proved so. These are the true Whig principles, and in these I was brought up.

It is true that my father, yielding not unnaturally to the fashion of his day,—the fashion of decrying the Whigs —would always call himself a Liberal rather than a Whig, and, indeed, Whiggism in his youth was often little better than a specially bad type of Toryism. As soon, however, as I began to study history in any detail, that is not in handbooks, but in the originals, I soon saw that he was one of the best of Whigs, whether in matters of State or Church. Moderation, justice, freedom, sympathy with suffering, tolerance, yielded not in the form of patronage but in obedience to a claim of right which could not be gainsaid—these were the pillars of his mind.

Who will deny that it was good fortune to be brought up in these views and by such an expounder? As I looked at the pictures that hung on the walls in the Great Hall (not very great, in fact, though bearing that name), I remembered with a glow of pride that it was on these principles that my family had been nourished. William Strachey, the first Secretary to the Colony of Virginia, would, I felt, have been a true Whig if Whig principles had been enunciated in his time, for the Virginia Company was a Liberal movement. John Strachey, his son, stood at the very cradle of Whiggism, for was he not the intimate friend of John Locke? Locke in his letters from exile and in his formative period writes to Strachey with affection and admiration.

To my glowing imagination John Strachey thus became the unknown inspirer of Locke, and therefore, perhaps, the inspirer and founder of the Whig philosophy. The son of Locke's friend, though the West Country was, as a rule, hopelessly Tory and full of Squire Westerns, stood firm by William and Mary and George I. As a Fellow of the Royal Society, the second John Strachey must have been a friend of Sir Isaac Newton, the mighty Whig of Science.

There were also Cromwellian ancestors on the distaff side. Indeed, though once more not in the ordinary conventional sense, the aura of Sutton was a Whig aura.

Though the aura of Sutton Court had a strong effect upon me morally and intellectually, the emotional side of me was even more deeply touched. The beauty and fascination of the house, its walls, its trees, and its memories, made, as I have already said, so deep an impression upon me that to this hour I love the place, the thought of it, and even the very name of it, as I love no other material thing. By nature I am not among those who become permanently attached to objects. It is true that I love my own home in Surrey, a house which I built, as it were, with my own hands. I love the scenery; I love it also as the place where my wife and I went as young people, and as the place where my children were born, but the thought of it does not touch me emotionally as does the thought of Sutton. What I have felt about Sutton all my life, I shall feel till I feel no more on earth. But that will not be all. I am convinced that I shall in some sense or other feel it in some other place. The indent on my soul will not be effaced.

I have touched on some of the chief things, natal and prenatal, which went to the making of my mind before I began to shape that mind for myself. Every man must do this, for whatever be the stars in his horoscope or the good fairies who preside over his cradle, they can only give, as it were, "useful instructions" and a good plan of the route. They leave him also plenty of opportunities for muddling those instructions and plunging into every kind of folly that they showed him how to avoid. In the last resort, a man is his own star and must make his own soul, though, of course, he has a right, nay, a duty, to give thanks for all good chances and happy circumstances. At any rate, I must now approach the time at which I took control of myself, and of the magic boat that had been built and equipped for me by others. Had I been fully conscious when I started on my own voyage, it should have been with a devout gratitude that my ship, at any rate, had not been rigged in the eclipse, and that I set sail under so bright a sky and with so prosperous a gale behind me.

CHAPTER IV

MY FATHER

I DELAY too long the picture of my father. Perhaps unconsciously I have been trying to avoid describing him, for I know the difficulty of the task and dread producing something unworthy. Important as were our home and traditions, our family, our friends, and our mode of life, they are as nothing in my making when compared to the influence of such a man as he was.

I shall not attempt to describe my father's physical appearance, for that has been done with sympathy, felicity, and power of presentation in my brother's portrait here reproduced. I will say only that he was slight of build and short of stature. He is standing in the little Great Hall at Sutton, in his black overcoat and hat, ready for one of those walks on the terrace which he took from his earliest childhood. He was born in the old house in 1812. It was not, however, till the year 1819 that he first came to live at Sutton. His earliest recollection was, as he used to tell us, playing on the terrace with the great ginger-coloured tom-cat, "King George." We always supposed this feline magnifico to have derived from some stock imported by the first Sir Henry when he was Master of the Household to George III. As my readers will see, King George's successor, in the true "mode" of his race, sits in a purely detached manner in the middle of the polished oak floor near, but in no special relation to his master, or rather, dependent, for no cat has a master though many have dependents.

But unstinted, unconditional eulogy is bound to end in flattery, and my father was much too good a man and too simple a man to be exposed to even the hint of such a taint. Though he would take sincere praise and sympathy with the pleasure of a wholly unaffected nature, the best courtier in the world would have found it impossible to flatter him.

I shall, therefore, be particular to draw clearly such faults as he had. Also I shall tell them first, though I know they will have a tendency to change into eulogy as I proceed. In truth, his faults, such as they were, endeared him only the more to people who understood him.

He did not always show complete equity in judgment, though I admit, and I think the majority of mankind would admit, that there was something essentially noble, if unpractical, in the way in which this want of equity was shown. So tender was his heart, so passionate his hatred of cruelty, so profound his chivalry, that he was apt to have his intellectual balance unduly affected by any tale of suffering inflicted by the strong on the weak, or by any accusation of wrong done to women or to children. When he heard such a tale he was too little inclined to show the worldly wisdom of the man who says, "Let us wait and hear all the facts. It may be a mere cock-and-bull story."

Instead, his attitude always reminded me of that of some eager knight-errant, on fire to accomplish his duty and to succour helpless damsels and all persons in distress. He always assumed that a call for succour came from a deserving object, if only it was agonising enough. He would post off, as it were, lance in rest and vizor down,

Sir Edward Strachey in the Hall at Sutton Court
with his Favourite Cat.

(From a picture by his son, Henry Strachey.)

upon the slightest rumour of wrong or cruelty. No woman suffering, or alleged to be suffering, from the cruelty of a husband, would ever call for his sympathy in vain. It was, however, cases of cruelty to little children that most tended to overwhelm his judgment. His burning horror at the mere idea of such deeds knew no bounds. A wife might to some extent be able to protect herself from the brutalities of her husband, but what chance had a helpless, friendless, terrified child, incapable even of running away from its tormentors, or of making an appeal for protection to outsiders? Those who have lived on unkindness and terror ever since they became conscious, cannot even console their poor little hearts with imaginary visions of happiness.

The unhappiness of a tortured child is a thing not to be thought of. It scorches the mind like a blast of sulphur.

Not only as a magistrate was my father's voice always raised on the side of the women and children. He would always listen to any mother who came to protest against the cruelty of the village schoolmistress to her offspring. The cruelty of the teacher was almost as unendurable to him as that of a bad father or husband. He would not hear of any justification for rapping school-children over the knuckles with a ruler. If one ventured to say that there were such things as demon-children and that they had a power to probe and prod even the best of good people into a kind of frenzy in which they were hardly accountable for their acts, the plea roused his deepest indignation. Indeed, it was only at some sort of suggestion like this that I ever saw my father really angry. Then, and only then. he would flare up and reply that this was the sort of excuse that people always made to cover cruelty, wickedness, and injustice. Grown-up people were much too ready to invent plausible grounds for the oppression of children..

"Serve you right," was never heard to fall from his lips by any child.

That he was justified in the general, if not in the particular, case, I fully realise. Indeed, I and all his children, I think, look back now with the sense that even if we sometimes criticised him (I admit, only very slightly) on this point, we were and remain proud that he was *splendide in-judex*.

Let no one suppose that because my father was a saint, as undoubtedly he was, his general attitude towards life was of the priggish or puritanical kind. It was nothing of the sort. Was not one of his favourite characters in Shakespeare the immortal Mrs. Quickly?

He was a very fastidious and reticent man in matters of the spirit, unless you approached him definitely and in earnest on a particular point. Then he would talk freely, and showed a marked liberality of soul. A courtly eighteenth century divine, though probably nobody would in reality have had less in common with my father, might have described him as "a thoroughly well-bred man in matters of religion." In spite of the fact that he was brought up amongst the Evangelicals and understood them and shared their better side, nothing, I feel sure, disgusted him more than their way of living in their spiritual shirtsleeves.

I can imagine his horror at the habit of the Clapham sect of "engaging" (*i.e.*, engaging in prayer), in season and out of season. "Shall we engage?" the Evangelical Pietist, whether a clergyman or a layman, would say at the end of some buttered-toast-and-pound-cake tea-party, and then everyone would be expected to flop down on their knees and listen to an extemporary appeal to their Maker!

My father was full of stories of the men of his own time

and of the men of former times, of historical allusions and analogies. He abounded in pregnant sayings culled from English, from Greek and Latin, and also from Persian, for he had learned the French of the East when he was at Haileybury studying for the Civil Service of the Honourable East India Company. Also he was fairly well-read in some branches of French literature and knew enough Italian to translate a quotation from Dante or from Tasso. He was also deeply read and deeply interested in Biblical criticism and in the statecraft of the Old Testament. His book on "Hebrew Politics" was hailed by theological students of liberal views as a real contribution to Biblical exegesis.

This all sounds like the record of a scholar. Yet he was not a scholar but a man with a most active and creative interest in his own world and his own time. Politics was his master-passion in things secular, and he followed every turn of the political wheel, not merely with the interest of a spectator, but with that of a man whose heart and mind were both deeply concerned. He was a Party Liberal, and also a liberal in the very best sense, and full of the most earnest zeal for the people's cause. My only quarrel with him here—if it was a quarrel—was that in his anxiety to support what he believed to be the cause of the people he was in effect anti-democratic.

On this point I was wont to chaff him, for there was no man with whom you could more easily argue without hurting his feelings. I would put it like this:

You think of the people and your duty to them in too much of a *grand seigneur* manner for me. You seem to want to find out what they want, and then do it, whether it is right or wrong, out of a patronising sense of moral benevolence. I, on the other hand, am a true democrat because I regard myself as one of the people—a creature with just as many rights as they have. Their opinion, if it is the opinion of the majority, will of course prevail, and ought to prevail, and I shall loyally acquiesce in it. But I am not going to do what I think unwise, as you appear to think I should, because somebody has put a ticket on the back of a certain view and declared it to be the popular view. It may quite well turn out that the alleged popular view is not popular at all, but is scouted by the majority.

That, of course, was, and was meant to be, a parody of his attitude, but it was one which he never resented, though he would not admit its nearness to the truth.

I shall not give the supreme characteristic impression of the man if I do not tell something about his stories, and give some specimens of his table-talk, especially as I have felt very strongly, though it may be difficult to transfer the impression, that his general talk, quite apart from his example and direct teaching, had a potent influence upon my character, and so upon my life.

To begin with, he was an ideal talker to children and young people, because, besides leisure, he had an innate kindliness and sympathy with the young which made him always anxious to put himself and his mind and heart at their disposal. He was in a perpetual mood to answer any questions, however tiresome and however often repeated. As he was a man of wide reading, of good memory, and almost an expert in many kinds of knowledge, we as children had something of that incomparable advantage for which I have always envied royalty. They are able to learn by the simple process of talking to people who know. That is not only the easiest road to knowledge, but if your teacher is no charlatan a more vivid impression is made upon the mind than is made by books.

If you went to my father and asked him who Aurung-zebe was, or Hereward the Wake, or Masaniello, or Edward

Keen, or Callimachus, or Titus Oates, or Dr. Chalmers, or Saint Januarius, he would tell you at once something vivid and stimulating about each of them, something which remained in your mind. Often his answer would lead to other fascinating and delightful discoveries for the questioner. I will take a couple of examples at random. When I asked him about Masaniello, he not only told the story of the insurrection among the *lazzaroni* at Naples, but he launched out into accounts of his own experience of Naples in the 'forties and of the crowds of picturesque and starving beggars and banditti who in those days still infested the city and its horrible and putrescent lanes and alleys. The Naples of the Bombas, in which he had spent two or more winters, was always a delightful source of anecdote. I could fill a book with his talk about Neapolitan nobles who let two apartments in their Palaces with only one set of furniture, and of the Neapolitan boatmen who formed the crew of the boat which he kept in the Bay, for he was too great an invalid to walk. Especially did we love to hear of how he was carried up Mount Vesuvius in a "litter"—a word which he always used. It thrilled me. It seemed to make the whole scene Roman and magnificent. One thought of Pliny going to observe the great eruption, of Cicero, of Pompey, of Seneca, carried down to Baiæ in their curtained chairs. My other example is Callimachus, the Greek, or rather, Alexandrine poet of the Decadence. The mention of his name brought in its train an excellent story derived from my father's uncle, the second Sir Henry Strachey, the squire whom he succeeded at Sutton. The story runs as follows. When the said great-uncle, as a boy just come out to India, went to dine with the great Orientalist, Sir William Jones, in his house in Calcutta (*circa* 1793), Sir William quoted to him a couple of lines out of Callimachus' Hymn

to Apollo, which he had hurled at the head of Burke
when the great Whig tribune threatened that he would get
him (Sir William Jones) recalled if he continued to support
Warren Hastings.   The lines quoted from the obscure
Greek poet he translated to the young civilian, Henry
Strachey.   "In reply, I reminded Burke," he said, "of the
lines in the Hymn to Apollo: *'The Euphrates is a noble
river, but it rolls down all the dead dogs of Babylon to the sea.'"*

My father was wont to point out that, as a matter of
fact, Jones's memory was not quite accurate.   If you
look at the Burke correspondence, you will see the dignified letter in which Jones replied to Burke.   In it he makes
no direct reference to the orator's threat, and only uses the
first line of Callimachus, which he turns into a compliment.
He is sure, he declares, that the mighty torrent of Burke's
eloquence will always be used in the defence of a friend.
Perhaps he thought that, if Burke looked up the passage,
he would be snubbed as it were automatically.

When, however, Jones told the story twelve years afterwards he did what we are all inclined to do in such circumstances.   He imagined himself much more valiant and
much more ready to take a great man by the scruff of his
neck and shake him, than he really was.   We are all
heroes in our memories.   By the way, it was Callimachus
who wrote the epigram on the death of Heraclitus which
was made immortal by the translation of the author of
"Ionica."   It is, I hold, the best poetic translation in the
English tongue.

Of the distinguished people with whom my father was
personally acquainted in his earlier days, among the most
memorable were Carlyle and Edward Irving.   Carlyle
was tutor to my father's first cousin, Charles Buller, later
to be known as "the young Marcellus of the Whig Party."
Of Carlyle he had many stories.   Curiously enough, I

might have seen Carlyle myself, for when I was about fifteen or sixteen he was still alive, and my father offered to take me to see him in Chelsea. With the cheery insolence of youth, I weighed the question in the balance and decided that I did not want to trouble myself with the generation that was passing away. I can still remember, however, that what almost moved me to accept my father's proposal was the fact that Carlyle was actually born in the 18th century, and before Keats. Edward Irving had made a vivid impression upon my father, though he only saw him, I believe, at the age of seven or eight. He could distinctly remember Irving taking him upon his knee, holding him at arm's length, looking into his face, and saying, in his deep, vibrant orator's voice: "Edward, don't ye long to be a mon?" Evidently the impression made upon my father by the words, or rather the way in which they were spoken, was profound. The incident always reminded me of that wonderful story told by Crabbe Robinson the Diarist. As a young man, Crabbe Robinson went to see one of the trials in which Erskine was engaged as Counsel. All he could remember of the speech was Erskine leaning over the jury-box and in low tones, full of meaning and tremulous with passion, uttering the commonplace words: "Gentlemen of the Jury, if you give a verdict against my client I shall leave this court a miserable man!" So profound was the influence of the orator that Crabbe Robinson tells us that for weeks afterwards he used to wake with a start in the middle of the night, saying over to himself the words: "I shall leave this court a miserable man."

Another contemporary well known to my father was Peacock, the novelist, for Peacock was also an official in the India House and so a colleague of my grandfather, Edward Strachey.

Of my father's religious views, though they deeply affected my own, I shall speak only very shortly. He was, above all, a devout man. Pure in heart, he earned the promised blessing and saw God throughout his days on earth. The fatherhood of God and the imminence of the Kingdom of Heaven were no empty words for him. But, though he was so single-minded a follower of Christ and His teachings, he was no Pharisee of the New Dispensation; the sacerdotalism of the Christian Churches was as hateful to him as the sacerdotalism of the Jews was to Christ. He was concerned with the living spirit, not with ritual, or formularies, or doctrinal shibboleths. His mind was open to all that was true, good, and generous. He asked for free and full development of the soul of man. "The cry of Ajax was for light," was one of his best-loved quotations.

He welcomed the researches of scholarship in the foundations of religion, as he did of science in the material world, and of philosophy in the things of the mind. Though he loved to worship with his fellows, and was a sincere member of the Church of England, the maxim *nulla salus extra ecclesiasm* filled him with horror. It was the worst of blasphemies.

His teacher was Frederick Maurice, but in certain ways he went further than that noble-hearted, if somewhat mystical, divine. It would have been an absurdity to ask my father whether it would not be better to give up Christianity and try instead the faith of Christ. That was always his faith. For him religion meant a way of life, a spiritual exaltation—not going to church, or saying prayers, or being sedulous in certain prescribed devotions. His creed was a communion with, and a trust in, God, through Christ. Above all, he had an overmastering sense of duty.

My Father 51

He was sensitive in body and mind to a high degree, and so may have *seemed* to himself and other observers to be like Mr. Fearing in Bunyan's Dream. But I remember that when Mr. Fearing came to the Valley of the Shadow of Death, no man was happier or braver. The river had never been so low as when he crossed it. The Shining Ones had never made an easier passage for a pilgrim. So it was with my father. He had all his life dreaded the physical side of dissolution. Yet, when Death came he was wholly calm and untroubled. It is designedly that I do not say he was resigned. Resignation implies regret. He had none.

I do not think I can more fitly sum up the impression made by my father than by quoting the epigram of Martial on "Felix Antonius."

> To-day, my friend is seventy-five;
>   He tells his tale with no regret;
>   His brave old eyes are steadfast yet,
> His heart the lightest heart alive.
>
> He sees behind him green and wide
>   The pathway of his pilgrim years;
>   He sees the shore and dreadless hears
> The whisper of the creeping tide.
>
> For out of all his days, not one
>   Has passed and left its unlaid ghost
>   To seek a light for ever lost,
> Or wail a deed for ever done.
>
> So for reward of life-long truth
>   He lives again, as good men can,
>   Redoubling his allotted span
> With memories of a stainless youth.

The version I have taken is that by Sir Henry Newbolt, and undoubtedly it is one of the best examples extant of the transference of the spirit of a Latin poem into English. My readers, however, will no doubt remember that this epigram was also translated into English by Pope. Though the modern poet's version is to be preferred, the older translation contains one of the most felicitous lines written even by Pope.

It is needless to say that I realise the essential inappropriateness of joining my father's name with that of Martial. It is, indeed, a capital example of the irony of circumstance that I am able to do so. But, after all, why should we be annoyed instead of being thankful, when bright flowers spring up on a dunghill? Certainly, my father would not have felt any indignity. He was the least superstitious and also the least sophistical of men. If a thing was worthy in itself he would never call it common or unclean on a punctilio.

If, while dealing with my father's influence on my life, I were not to say something about the influence of my mother, I should leave a very false impression. My mother was a woman of a quick intelligence and of a specially attractive personality. To her we children owed a great deal in the matter of manners. My father gave us an excellent example in behaviour and in that gentleness, unselfishness, and sincerity which is the foundation of good breeding. My mother, who was never shy, and very good at mental diagnosis, added that burnish without which good manners often lose half their power. What she particularly insisted on was the practice of that graciousness of which she herself afforded so admirable an example. Naturally, like a good mother, she always reproved us for bad manners, or for being unkind to other children, or selfish, or affected, or oafish, or sulky. Her direst thunders, however, were kept for anything which approached ill-breeding. Giving ourselves airs, or "posing," or any other form of juvenile vulgarity, were well-nigh unforgivable sins.

But she did not content herself with inculcating the positive side of good manners. She was equally strong on the negative side. For example, if there was a party of farm tenants, or cottagers, a school-feast, or anything of the kind, both when we were small and half grown-up, she insisted that we must never dream of keeping in a corner by ourselves. We must go and do our duty in entertaining our guests. No excuses of shyness or not liking to talk to people one didn't know, or suggestions that they would think us putting on side if we went up to them, were allowed for a moment. The injunctions we received were that, at a party in our own house, we must never think of our own pleasure or enjoyment, but must devote ourselves wholly and solely to the pleasure of our guests. The sight of anyone sitting moping in a corner and looking bored or unhappy was the destruction of a party. Such persons, if seen, must be pounced upon at once, amused, and made much of, till they were perfectly happy, as "the guests who got more attention than anybody else." In a word, we were taught that the strength of the social chain is its weakest link. It was quite safe to leave the big people, or the big people's children, to look after themselves. The people to be made much of and treated like royalty were those who looked uncomfortable or seemed to feel out of it. The result was that my mother's parties were never a failure. Though her ill-health never allowed her to be a hostess on a big scale, her parties, whether in Somersetshire or at Cannes, were always voted delightful. Everyone, from Somersetshire farmer or clergyman, to the notables of a Riviera winter resort, owned her social charm. As an example of it, I remember how one winter, which we spent at Bournemouth, for my mother's health, the invalid's drawing-room became at once the centre of a memorable little society, consisting, as far as I remember, of people whom we had never known before. There was a delightful old Mr. Marshall, of the Marshalls of the Lakes, who used to come and play whist with her, and with whom we boys sometimes rode. Though he was about eighty, he kept up his riding and liked to have a boy to ride with him. Another old gentleman, attractive in his manner, in his dress, and in his kindly, old-fashioned dignity, was Lord Suffolk. He dressed like "the Squire" in the old *Punches*. He wore a low-crowned, broadish-brimmed hat, Bedford cord breeches and gaiters, and a light-brown or buff cloth coat and waistcoat. He had two invalid daughters, and these, if I remember rightly, were the cause of the family having a villa at Bourne-mouth.

It was, however, either at the house-parties at Chewton or at Strawberry Hill, which were hardly considered complete by Lady Waldegrave without my mother, or else again at Cannes in her own villa that she made her main impression upon people of the greater world. Though of good parts, she was not in any sense intellectual. I never heard her attempt to say brilliant things or epigrammatic things, or to talk about books or historic people.

She was, like so many charming women, perfectly natural and perfectly at her ease, and full of receptive interest. When she talked it was always to draw out her interlocutor and never to show off her own cleverness. She was quite as popular, indeed I had almost said more popular, with women as with men, and had as great a fascination for young people as for old. I remember well our pleasure in being told of a letter written by one of the

big London hostesses who had come out to Cannes, made
my mother's acquaintance, and fallen a charm to her
winning voice, her warm regard, and her gracious eyes.
She had written to a friend, saying, in effect,

What on earth did you mean by not telling me more about
your cousin, Lady Strachey? She turns out to be one of the
most delightful people I have ever met, and yet you never
breathed a word about her. Why did you want to keep her to
yourself? Through your selfishness I have missed three or four
weeks of her.

It is notoriously difficult to describe charm, and I shall
make no attempt, except to say that my mother's spell
did not consist in good looks in the ordinary sense of the
word. She had a witching expression, an exceedingly
graceful carriage of her head and body, and a good figure;
but her face was so mobile and so entirely governed by
her smile that photographs and pictures were always
pronounced as "impossible" and "utterly unlike."

Though she was in no sense nervous, the attempt to sit
for her picture seemed at once to break the spell and destroy that *"beau regard"* which was, I feel sure, the secret
of the pleasure she spread around her. No doubt she took
trouble to please, but she had the art of concealing her art.
No one ever criticised her as "theatrical" or "artificial."

Her children fully felt her charm. Looking back, I can
now see that she, most wisely, took as much trouble to
fascinate us as she did the rest of the world. She would
not mind this remark, for she was no naturalist, but held
that you ought to take as much trouble to be polite and to
give pleasure to your nearest and dearest as to strangers.
Anyway, we were never allowed to be rude or careless
to her, or to anybody else merely because they were well-
loved relations. We never failed to get up from our

chairs when she entered the room, or to open doors for her, or to show her any other physical form of politeness. But she did not inculcate this by anything approaching harshness, or by a sharp tongue. All she did was to make us feel that we were uncouth bores, to be pitied rather than condemned, if we failed in the minor politenesses.

No doubt she was assisted here by the fact of being an invalid, and also by the good example which my father set us. He was one of the best-bred of men as well as one of the noblest and most simple-hearted. I shall never forget the patient courtesy with which he would treat some old village woman who was positively storming at him in regard to alleged grievances. His politeness, however, never had in it any studied element. Nobody could ever have said that he was overdoing it. Again, there was no inverted snobbishness about him. He was quite as polite to a great lady as to a cottager's wife.

I will undertake to say that in his whole life he had never shown off—a thing which could be said of very few men, but which, after all, is the secret of all good breeding.

But to return to my mother. She also never showed off, though with her the art of pleasing and being pleased was very carefully studied. She inherited this quality from her father, Dr. Symonds. She also found in him her example for the exact conduct of the social code. I remember her saying that, though her father was a very hard-worked doctor, and often had to take meals quickly and at odd times, he made it an absolute rule, no matter how busy he was, never to get into a rush, or be fussed, or do things in a huggermugger way. If he came in late and tired, he would eat his dinner as quietly and decorously as if he had got several hours before him. Everything had to be done decently and in order. He would not dream of getting up from his chair if he wanted an extra spoon or fork in a hurry, but would either send one of his children to get it for him or else ring the bell for the butler.

This was not an attempt at grandeur, but due to a feeling that if he once got into chaotic ways he would go to pieces. Probably he felt the necessity all the more from the fact that he was a widower and might the more easily have dropped into untidy and slovenly household ways.

I have no time to dwell on my mother's most intimate friendship with Lady Waldegrave and with their habit of writing daily letters to each other, and of the social and political life which my mother shared with her friend as well as her health would permit. For my present purposes, what matters, though it sounds abominably egotistical to say so, is the effect of my mother upon my character and life. Unquestionably the fact of her being an invalid was a great lesson. In the first place, it did a great deal to educate her children to be unselfish. It was a rule of the house that everything was to be sacrificed to my mother's comfort, for she was often not only in great pain but dangerously ill. My father was, in any case, the most unselfish of men, but we might have regarded that, as children often will, as a kind of personal quality of his own, like a lame knee, or a dislike of draughts, or a fondness for cold mutton, or other simple forms of living. When we saw his daily and hourly sacrifice of himself to my mother and that tenderness of heart which never failed him, we must have been made of rock or oak not to be inspired by an example so noble and fraught with so magnificent a pathos. We showed badly in comparison with our father, but still we had him always before us, and if we were ever tempted to exhibit selfishness or want of consideration to my mother, his devotion was a standing, though never an open, rebuke, and brought the bitterest remorse.

My mother maintained the true dignity of the sick-room. She never complained either of the hard fate which chained one who loved the world and its amusements so much to her bed, nor, again, did she ever cherish or show the slightest grievance if we had seemed unkind or had not done what she would have liked us to do. It is needless to say that the effect of this was exactly what she would have desired, though not admitted even to herself, for she was not a person at all self-conscious or self-analytical in these matters.

The fact remains that people who are brought up in a house with an invalid, where that invalid has the love, respect, and devotion of the head of the home, get a valuable lesson. There is more than that. The sight of pain and suffering and the imminence of sorrow and danger, if it be not too terrifying, is good for children. It makes them early acquainted with the realities of life and its essential sternness. Then, when death or sorrow makes its inevitable descent, the child is prepared to meet it, or knows, at any rate, the spirit in which it ought to be met. Those who have never seen Death or heard the swing of his scythe, till he suddenly bursts upon them, or upon those they love dearly, are greatly to be pitied. They have not learnt the art of quietening the soul in face of an inexorable command.

Timor mortis is a reality, and we can be, and ought to be, prepared for it. The sick-room, if children are made to understand its significance in a wise and kindly spirit, and through the conduct of such people as my father and my mother, is a teacher of no mean order.

CHAPTER V

MY FATHER'S STORIES OF THE STRACHEY FAMILY

DELIGHTFUL as were my father's literary and historical stories and observations, already described, I liked them best when they dealt with our own family and its traditions. My father, though without a trace of anything approaching pride of birth, knew his own family history well, and was never tired of relating stories of "famous men and our fathers that begat us." As a great Shakespearian devotee, he specially delighted to tell us of our direct ancestor, William Strachey, "the friend of Ben Jonson," for so we knew him.

The said ancestor married the Widow Baber, niece of a famous seafarer, Sir Richard Cross, who commanded the *Bonaventura* at the Siege of Cadiz, and so brought Sutton into the family. This William Strachey almost certainly knew Shakespeare. It is now generally admitted that the storm in *The Tempest* was based upon Strachey's account of the shipwreck of Sir George Somers's fleet on the Bermudas—the Isle of Devils so greatly dreaded by seamen. They provided in this case, however, a haven of refuge. Strachey was first Secretary to the Colony of Virginia. Thus we have an ancestor who gives us the right, as a distinguished American scholar once said to me, to consider ourselves "Founders' kin to the United States"—a piece of family pride which no man can deem snobbish or ridiculous.

59

William Strachey wrote a very remarkable letter describing the shipwreck, or rather tempest. The letter was addressed to the Lady Willoughby de Broke of that day, a woman of ability and greatly interested in the Virginia Company, as were all the liberal spirits of the age, including Elizabeth herself. This letter was handed about in manuscript, as was so often the case in those times, and Shakespeare, in all human probability, must have seen it, detected good copy for the theatre—he had a never-failing instinct in that direction—and used it for his famous last play. Shakespeare must have met and talked with Strachey on his return from America, for recent investigations have shown that Shakespeare had many communications with the men who founded the Virginia Company, and was very likely a member.

Here I may interpose that I have always been specially interested in the fact that in the letter to Lady Willoughby de Broke, Strachey notes a circumstance that was often observed in the war. He tells us that the young gallants, when every hand was required to work at the pumps, had to exert themselves to the very utmost, and to work as long and as hard as the professional seamen. To the astonishment of himself and everyone else, they were able to do as much work and to keep at it as strenuously as the old mariners.

Another reason for feeling pretty sure that William Strachey must have known Shakespeare is the fact, of which we have ample proof, that Strachey was well known to the men of letters of the day. To begin with, he was a friend of Ben Jonson and wrote a set of commendatory verses for the Laureate's "Sejanus." These appear in the folio edition of Jonson's works. Probably this sonnet— it has fourteen lines—is one of the most cryptic things in the whole of Elizabethan literature. No member of our

John Strachey, the Friend of Locke.

family or any other family has ever been able to construe it. Yet it is a pleasure to me to gather from the concluding couplet that the author had sound Whig principles:

> If men would shun swol'n Fortune's ruinous blasts,
> Let them use temperance; nothing violent lasts.

An even more interesting proof of William Strachey's literary connections is to be found in the fact that when he, Strachey, went to Venice he took with him a letter of introduction from the poet, Dr. Donne, to the then Ambassador with the Republic, Sir Henry Wotton, also a poet. The letter is witty and trenchant. After noting that Strachey was "sometime secretary to Sir Thomas Gates," he adds, "I do boldly say that the greatest folly he ever committed was to submit himself and parts to so mean a master." The rest of the letter is pleasantly complimentary and shows that Donne and Strachey were fast friends.

This William Strachey, as my father used to point out to us, had a very considerable amount of book-writing to his credit. There were two or three pamphlets written by him and published as what we should now call Virginia Company propaganda. One of these gives a very delightful example of the English and American habit of applying a "get-civilisation-quick" system for the native inhabitants of any country into which they penetrate. Strachey's book, which was reprinted by the Hakluyt Society, was entitled "Articles, Lawes and Orders, Divine, Politique, and Martiall, for the Colony of Virginia," and was printed in 1610.

One of these pamphlets was sold at auction in London just before the war, and went—very naturally and, in a sense, very properly—to America. The volume in question contained, besides the ordinary letter-press, several

poems by William Strachey and an autograph inscription
written in the most wonderfully neat and clear handwriting
—a standard in handwriting to which no member of the
family before or since has ever attained.   But besides the
handwriting the dedication has other claims on our attention.   It is charmingly worded.   It shows, amongst other
things, how natural was the cryptic dedication to the
Shakespeare Sonnets.   It runs as follows:

> To his right truly honoured, and
> best beloved friend, sometymes
> a Personall Confederat and
> Adventurer, and now a
> sincere and holy Beadsman
> for this Christian prose-
> cutiō Thomas Lawson, Esq.
> William Strachey wisheth
> as full an accomplishment of his best Desires,
> as devoutly as becoms the Dutie of a
> Harty Freinde.   January /21.

"This Christian prosecutiō" was the Virginia Company
and its system of colonisation.   There is also in one of the
show-cases in the Bodleian an interesting short dictionary
of the language of the Chesapeake Indians compiled by
Strachey.   In a note attached thereto Strachey says that
he thinks it will be useful to persons who wish to "trade or
truck" with the Indians.

Another memorable fact in regard to William Strachey I
may mention here, though it was not known to my father.
I lately discovered that Campion, the poet-musician, who,
like Strachey, was a Member of Gray's Inn, wrote a short
Latin poem to Strachey.   It is addressed "Ad Guillielmus
Strachæum."   In it Campion tells Strachey that although
he has very few verses to give to his "old comrade," the

man "who rejoiced in and made many competent verses,"
he will always be dear to him. He ends by calling him
"summus pieridem unicusque cultor." The poem con-
cludes almost as it began: "Strachæo, veteri meo sodali"
—*To Strachey, my old comrade.*

Evidently Strachey did not keep his verses entirely for
dedication. As far as I know, the best of his verses
dedicatory are those addressed to Lord Bacon in his
"Historie of Travaile into Virginia." They run:—

> Wild as they are, accept them, so we're wee;
> To make them civill will our honour be;
> And if good worcks be the effects of myndes,
> Which like good angells be, let our designes,
> As we are Angli, make us Angells too;
> No better worck can state—or church-man do.

The Campion connection interests me personally because Campion was the protagonist of unrhymed lyrical
verse—my special metrical hobby. I like to think that
William Strachey may have supported Campion in his
controversy with Gabriel Harvey, who, by the way, lived
at Saffron Walden, from which town came also William
Strachey. There is danger, however, in such speculation.
Before long someone may prove that it was not Bacon who
wrote Shakespeare but Strachey who wrote both Bacon
and Shakespeare.

The following example of my father's family lore was
still more interesting and exciting to us. John Strachey,
son of William Strachey, married a Miss Hodges of Wedmore, an heiress in the heraldic sense, through whom we
can proudly claim to represent the Somersetshire family
of Hodges, whose arms we have always quartered. This
lady's grandfather, or great-grandfather—I am not quite
sure which—was of the very best type of Elizabethan

soldiers-errant.   He was killed at the Siege of Antwerp in 1583.

He had the good fortune to be commemorated in one of the most spirited epitaphs of his age.   On the wall of Wedmore Church in Somersetshire is a brass tablet bearing a heart surrounded by a laurel-wreath.   The inscription of the memorial runs thus:

Sacred to the memory of Captain Thomas Hodges, of the County of Somerset, esq., who, at the siege of Antwerp, about 1583, with unconquered courage won two ensigns from the enemy; where, receiving his last wound, he gave three legacies: his soule to the Lord Jesus, his body to be lodged in Flemish earth, his heart to be sent to his dear wife in England.

> Here lies his wounded heart, for whome
> One kingdom was too small a roome;
> Two kingdoms therefore have thought good to part
> So stout a body and so brave a heart.

I have often wondered how a poet could have been found in Somersetshire in those days to produce such spirited verse.   The Elizabethan age, so splendid in great poetry, was apt to be tortured and affected in what Dr. Johnson called "lapidary inscriptions."

Little did I think when, as a boy, I first read those lines how closely linked England was to remain with the soil where Thomas Hodges fell, how many thousand stout bodies and brave hearts would again be laid in Flemish earth, and how many true soldiers would in my own day deserve my forbear's epitaph.

It seems most likely that Thomas Hodges's armour was preserved by the Hodges and brought to Sutton by Miss Hodges.   In an old Hodges inventory which is still among the papers at Sutton there is mentioned "an armour of proof." My father also used to tell us how he had seen two or three sets of armour hanging on the brackets which supported the Minstrels' Gallery in the Hall at Sutton. My father's uncle, alas, was born in the eighteenth century and bred in India till about 1820. He was therefore little affected by Scott and the Gothic revival. When he came back to England, though full of interest in his house and family, he not only removed the Minstrels' Gallery from the Hall, but allowed the armour that had hung on it for some hundred and fifty years to be destroyed. The Estate mason was seen mixing mortar in the breastplate, and the coachman washed the carriage with his legs in the Cromwellian jack-boots. Oddly enough, when we were quite small children, my eldest brother, by pure accident, discovered half a steel helmet behind one of the greenhouses.

Two swords, however, were allowed to remain at Sutton, and are there to this day. They are, however, probably Cromwellian and not Elizabethan.

We know very little of what happened to the Stracheys during the Civil War, for at the crisis of the conflict John Strachey was only a boy. He was born in 1634 and therefore was only twenty-six at the end of the Commonwealth, and would have been only fifteen years old at the time of the King's execution. That the family were good Roundheads, however, cannot be doubted, for John Strachey when he grew up became a close friend of John Locke. Further, Captain Thomas Hodges, whose daughter was later married to John Strachey, raised a troop of horse to fight on the side of the Commonwealth. My father was always very proud of the fact that the intellectual father of the Whigs was so closely united with our ancestor. A propos of a deferred visit to Spain, Locke says in one of his letters that he is glad he is not going, because he will now be able to pay his visit to Sutton Court; "a greater rarity than my travels have afforded me, for, believe me, one may go a long way before one meets a friend."

Of all my father's stories those which delighted and thrilled us most were his anecdotes of Clive. Clive, one might almost say, was the patron saint of the family, and some day I hope to make a further and better collection of legends in regard to him and other relations and connections of my family with India.

But first I must explain why we Stracheys regard Clive as our patron saint. It will be remembered how, after Clive had won Plassey, he came home full of riches and honours, obtained his peerage and bought his unique collection of rotten boroughs. He did not, however, remain long at home. He was soon sent out to India again to reform the Civil Service and to place the affairs alike of the Company and of the King, *i.e.* the British Government and Parliament, on a sound basis. The moment Clive left India, the Company's government had begun to degenerate on all sides, military, naval, and civilian. In two years corruption was destroying what Clive's statesmanship and military genius had won.

Clive, when he agreed to return to Bengal was a Member of Parliament, and like a wise man he knew that anyone who has to deal with great affairs must be sure of a good Private Secretary. He looked round, therefore, for an able and trustworthy young man, and lighted upon Henry Strachey, who had just reached years of discretion. But I had better quote Clive's own ringing words in regard to his selection. They will serve to show, among other things, that Clive was not the kind of inspired savage that he is sometimes portrayed, but a man with an extraordinary command of the English language. In the speech in

The Close, Sutton Court, Somerset.

the House of Commons in which Clive flung back the accusations made against him in regard to the grants and presents which he took from Meer Jaffir, not only after the Battle of Plassey but in the final settlement which concluded his Indian career, he described the members of his official family—the men whom he had taken out to India with him on that occasion. As Strachey had become a Member of the House of Commons he could not refer to him by name. Here are Clive's actual words:

Another gentleman was my Secretary, now a Member of this House. He was recommended to me by one of the greatest men in this Kingdom, now no more, Mr. Grenville. Many and great are the obligations I have been under to him (Grenville), but the greatest of all the obligations was his having recommended to me this gentleman. Without his ability and indefatigable industry I could never have gone through my great and arduous undertaking, and in serving me he served the Company.

Curiously enough, we have no idea how Henry Strachey came across George Grenville, or why George Grenville was able to give him so high a character. In any case, Clive was a shrewd judge of men, and though very good to his subordinates, would never tolerate inefficiency. His approval meant much.

But Clive did more for us as a family than merely appoint Henry Strachey to be his private secretary. It happened that at the time of his appointment Henry Strachey was very much in the position in which Clive was when he first went out to India. Henry Strachey was the eldest son of a hopelessly embarrassed country gentleman of old family. John Strachey, the friend of Locke, had been very well off, and so had his son John, the Fellow of the Royal Society. Besides Sutton and an estate at

Elm and Buckland, near Frome, he owned a considerable amount of property in Westminster. There are many interesting and amusing things to tell of him, but here I will only say that the said John Strachey the second had two wives and nineteen children, consequently at his death the family estates were heavily "dipped." His son, Hodges Strachey, who succeeded him, added to these pecuniary troubles, and then died; the property descended to a younger brother, Henry Strachey. Though he married into a rich Edinburgh family, the Clerks of Penny-cuick, and so was kinsman not only of the Clerks but of the Primroses, he did nothing to redeem the fortunes of the family. Indeed, things had gone so far by his time that the Strachey estates had actually passed to the mortgagees in discharge of a sum of twelve thousand pounds. A year's grace was, however, given. If the £12,000 could not be paid within the twelve months, Sutton, and the whole of the land, would have passed for ever from the family.

When Clive heard of this predicament, he, with extra-ordinary generosity, advanced the money in anticipation of the remuneration which Strachey was to receive for his services in India. Thus Sutton Court was saved. Thanks to Clive there are still Stracheys at Sutton and I am here to tell the tale. In those days twelve thousand pounds was a very big sum of money indeed to an impecunious country gentleman, and a considerable sum even to a man as rich as Clive. The modern equivalent would be over £30,000. But Clive was not a man who hesitated to do things in a big way, and he was well repaid. Henry Strachey was not only devoted to him throughout his life, but acted as his executor and as the guardian to his infant son and heir.

One of three or four pictures which Dance, the portrait-painter, painted of Clive hangs to this day in the Hall at Sutton. It always thrilled me to look at this picture, when a boy, because of the background, where, surrounded by the smoke of battle, a company of horsemen with drawn swords charge an invisible Oriental foe. If I remember rightly, the British Cavalry played no part at Plassey, but probably the artist thought that historical accuracy might quite legitimately be subordinated in this instance to the demands of art.

I could fill this book with stories of Clive which my father had heard from his father and from his uncle and from other contemporaries. I will only mention one here, however, and I choose it because it further illustrates the wonderful power of Clive's prose style, a power which always impressed me, even as a boy. Just before Clive died by his own hand, he addressed a letter to Henry Strachey, who had now become a close friend as well as an ex-secretary, and who had married Lady Clive's first cousin. He was thus a member of the actual as well as of the official family of his Chief. Here are the words which Clive addressed to Strachey:—

How miserable is my condition! I have a disease which makes life insupportable, but which my doctors tell me won't shorten it one hour.

If ever man conveyed the sense of physical suffering, deep melancholy, and utter despair by the medium of the written word, it was Clive in this passage. He had, it will be remembered, attempted suicide before, as a young man. When the pistol refused to go off, he considered it an omen that he was reserved for greater things.

My father used to tell us (whether on good medical evidence or not I do not know) that it was supposed that Clive suffered from a very painful form of dyspepsia accompanied by vertigo, and that when these attacks came on they depressed him beyond measure. He lived in constant dread of their recurrence, and it was upon a sudden sense that an attack was impending that he cut his throat. He could not face again what might have been an agony of three or four months' duration.

It was natural that, as boys, we liked especially to hear the story of the suicide in Berkeley Square. There was plenty of blood and mystery in the tale.

Some eight years before his death, I got my father, who was a very accurate and careful man, to put down, partly from family papers and partly from memory, as exact an account as he could of the actual suicide. This, the authentic version of the suicide, I published in the *Spectator*.

My father's stories of the first Sir Henry, as we were wont to call him, Clive's Private Secretary, were many, and all of them poignant or amazing. As a child, however, though I always delighted in them I did not fully realise their historical interest. They gave a vivid picture of the mind and actions of a Whig Member of Parliament from about 1770 to 1812, the period during which Henry Strachey was continuously in Parliament. In the course of his forty years of public life, Henry Strachey held a number of important offices, for he was a much-trusted man. He played, indeed, a part more like that of one of the great permanent officials of the present day than that of a politician. I take it that he had not a powerful gift of speech and that he was not a pushing man, otherwise, considering his brains and the way in which he was trusted, he would have gone a good deal higher than he did. A story which testifies to his influence is curious. When Burke began his attacks in the Commons upon Warren Hastings, he tried to enlist support from Henry Strachey, who does not seem to have thrown in his lot especially with Hastings. All he would do, however, was to tell

Burke that he would be neutral—provided that, in the course of the attacks on Hastings, Burke cast no aspersions upon the name and fame of Lord Clive. If Clive's memory was assailed he, Strachey, would hit back. Whether it was due to this fact or to some other, it is certain that Burke was always careful to draw a clear distinction between the cases of Clive and of Hastings.

Perhaps the most vivid story of all is the following. Strachey had been in office in the ill-starred Coalition under Fox and North. When the Ministry broke up, the King sent for Lord Shelburne, a member of the Coalition, who, it will be remembered, at once formed a Government of his own. While the Ministry was in the making, Henry Strachey met Fox on Hay Hill, that minute yet "celebrated acclivity" which runs from the corner of Berkeley Square into Dover Street. The smiling demagogue, who, by the by, was a fellow member of Brooke's, hailed his ex-colleague with a—

"Hullo, Strachey, what's going to happen to you?"

"Oh, Lord Shelburne says he wants me to keep my office."

"Then, by God, you're out!"

Nobody, at that time, believed in Shelburne's good faith. He was alleged by both sides to be a man on whose word no dependence could ever be placed—a man who would tell you that he wanted your assistance on the very day he had struck your name out of the list of his Cabinet.

Things, however, turned out differently in Strachey's case, and Shelburne kept his word. In all probability, indeed, he was a man who was very much maligned.

In any case, Shelburne trusted Strachey, and when he began the negotiations for the Peace of Versailles which ended the war with America, and recognised the United States, Strachey was sent as a negotiator. Originally a

Member of Parliament named Oswald had been employed at Paris, but he had not proved to be a match for the able American delegates, Franklin, Jay, and Adams. Accordingly Strachey was sent over to give tone and vigour to the British Delegation. As a family we are exceedingly proud of the account of Strachey given by that great man, John Adams, later President of the United States. It is contained in his secret report sent to Washington from Paris:

Strachey is as artful and insinuating a man as they could send; he pushes and presses every point as far as it can possibly go; he has a most eager, earnest, pointed spirit.

That is a certificate of character of which any statesman or diplomat might be proud.

But Strachey, I am glad to say, was more than a mere skilful agent. It is now fully recognised by Canadian historians who have made a special study of the question, that Strachey was the one man at Paris who stood up for the United Empire Loyalists and did his very best to get for them proper recognition and proper compensation. Unfortunately the British Ministry was tired and callous, and Strachey's efforts did not prevail, but he fought for the United Empire Loyalists to the end. Without his help, things would have been worse than they were.

One thing that helped to make Strachey a good peace negotiator was the fact that a year before he had gone to America as Secretary to Lord Howe and Admiral Howe when they were sent out either to carry on the war by sea and land, or else to make peace with the insurgent colonies.

As a result of this official visit to America, Strachey had a very large number of confidential papers left in his possession, and some of these have escaped the burning which was the fate of most of his correspondence. He was one of the men who made it a practice to destroy private

papers as soon as they were done with.   The story of these
American papers is, again, one which must be reserved for
another occasion.   But, though the time has come to cut
Henry Strachey off at the main, and though I must
reluctantly forego the account of his dealings with George
III, when he, Strachey, was Master of the Household, I
cannot resist giving one family document which my father
was very fond of reading to us and which was, I honestly
think, regarded by the family as the most priceless of all
the papers kept in the strong-room at Sutton Court.   It
went by the name of the "Head Munky" letter.

Lady Strachey, the first Sir Henry's wife, was a widow
with children when she married.   She also had children by
her second marriage and, as several of these married, she
had at the end of her life a large number of grandchildren.
Anyway, she was evidently a lady who thoroughly understood what children want at a children's party.   She fully
appreciated, that is, the value of bears, monkeys, croco-
diles, and Punch as entertainers of the young—witness the
letter which follows:

WATER MARK 1804.

To Lady Strachey,
  9 hill street
    Berkeley square.

MY LADY,

   agreebel to order James Botton and Company will attend
Tomorrow evening at 8 But begs to inform That the Bear
being Laim am afeard cant perform But the doggs and mun-
kees is in good condishon and will I hopes be aprooved with
the music
   my tarms is as follers pr nite

Bear	...	10.	6.
8 doggs for kotillin ⎱ at pr dogg 2 ⎰	...	...	16

musick	5
Drum and orms	7
head munky	7
3 others	9
keeper	2. 6

Punch is a seprit Consarn and Cums high but Can order him at sam time though not in that line since micklemass he belongs to Mr valentine Burstem at the marmaid

14 Princess Court
holborn—
I am
my Lady
your most dutiful
humbel servant

tuesday   JAMES BOTTEN.

19 Piccadilly

P.S.   Please Let the head munky Jacko Cum down The airy on account not making no dirt in the haul

The Jentleman says consarning tubb for the crocodile but I never Lets her out nor the ostriges as I explained to him for your satisfaction—

My father always said, and no doubt with truth, that the "Jentleman" alluded to at the end of the letter was the butler.   He had evidently been sent to "The Mermaid" or some other hostelry to negotiate for the appearance of "Jacko."   When I read the letter I always see a vivid picture of "Jacko" coming over and down the area railings, hand over hand, and wiping his paws on the doormat!

Evidently Mr. James Botten was an artist in his way and, like his employer, understood the infant mind, for does he not put the bear at the very top of his list and charges for him at the highest rate?   Why children so delight in bears and have such a firm belief that they are kind, gentle, and grandfatherly animals is a piece of psychology which I have never been able to fathom. As to the existence of the feeling, there can be no possible doubt. My grandchildren, budding Montessorians though they be, have the same absolute and unlimited confidence in bears that I had at the age of three.

There is another story of this Lady Strachey which I may as well put in here, because it is with such amazing clearness the characteristic of a vanished age. My father used to say that when the second Sir Henry Strachey came back from India, for he was there only ten years, his father was still in Parliament. Henry Strachey was only just thirty, and therefore there was the usual desire felt by his family to find something for the young man to do— something "to prevent him idling about in town and doing nothing or worse." In order to provide this necessary occupation his mother offered him £4,000 with which to buy a seat in Parliament. She thought that a seat would keep him amused and out of mischief! In spite of the fact that he was a strenuous Radical, Sir Henry's only remark in telling the story was: "I refused, because I did not like the idea of always voting in the opposite lobby to my father." The first Henry Strachey, though a staunch Whig in early life, was a supporter of William Pitt and later, of Lord Liverpool. Therefore the second Henry Strachey, if he had got into the House, when he first came home, would no doubt have voted with the Radical Rump.

There are many stories I could tell of the second Sir Henry, who lived on at Sutton till the year '58, when my father succeeded, but these again must be kept for another book—if I ever have time to write it. I must say the same of my own grandfather, my father's father, Edward Strachey, and his memorable wife. Of both of them plenty is to be found in Carlyle's account of his early years. I shall only record of Edward Strachey here the fact that after he returned from India he became an official at the India House on the Judicial side, and was called the Examiner, his duties being to examine the reports of important law-cases sent from India to the Board of Directors. When one day I asked my father for his earliest recollection of any important event, he told me that he could well remember his father coming back from the India House (which was by a Thames wherry, for the Examiner lived at Shooter's Hill and had to cross the river) and saying to his mother: "The Emperor is dead." That was in the year 1822, and the Emperor was, of course, Napoleon. Strachey was one of the first people to hear of the event because St. Helena was borrowed by the Government for prison purposes from the East India Company. The East Indiamen, however, still used it as a house of call. Therefore it happened that the East India Company, by the actual appearance of one of the ship's captains at the India House, heard of the great event an hour or two before the Government to whom the despatches were forwarded. My father must have been ten years old at the time, as he was born in 1812.

CHAPTER VI

MY CHILDHOOD AND SOME PSYCHOLOGICAL INCIDENTS

AND now for the child who was so happy in his surroundings, and, above all, in those who were to care for him.

There were naturally certain nursery traditions about me of the magnifying kind, but, taken as a whole, I don't think I can claim to have been anything but a normal child, with health fair to moderate and an intelligence which was reasonably quick and responsive. I had, however, no educational precociousness; I did not read till I was nearly nine, and even then did not use the power of reading. The book habit did not come till I was twelve or thirteen—though then it came, as far as poetry was concerned, with a rush. By fifteen I had read all the older English poets and most of the new. In reading poetry I showed a devotion which I am thankful to say I have always maintained. In this matter at least I am the opposite of Darwin. He confessed that the power to read poetry left him entirely in middle life. The older I grow, the more I love verse.

The actual study of metre was a source of acute satisfaction. It is said of me, indeed, that when, at a little more than two and a half years old, we were starting for a long journey to Pau, where my mother had been ordered to winter, I insisted on my father not packing, but taking with him in his hand, Spenser's *Faerie Queen*. He had been

77

reading it to us that autumn. I did not know what a journey meant, but I was determined the readings should not be broken. I also could not have known what Spenser meant, but his stanza fed ear, and heart, and mind with melody.

It was at this age, too, that I seem to have made two theological observations which greatly amused my family. I was discovered one day digging with tempestuous energy in the garden. When asked what I was doing, I replied, "Digging for hell-fire!" That was especially curious because my father, as a strong Broad Churchman and a devoted friend and disciple of Frederick Maurice, was a wholehearted disbeliever in hell and its flames. He had "dismissed Hell with costs," as Lord Westbury said, ever since he came to man's estate. How I derived my knowledge on this point was never cleared up. Demons with three-pronged forks and curly tails are, of course, universally regarded as "the friends of little children" by natural right, and my preference I must suppose was transferred to their flaming home.

My other early piece of theological criticism was characteristic. Either my father or my mother, I forget which, was explaining to me the story of the Crucifixion and our Lord's arrest by the armed men of the High Priest. Greatly surprised and perturbed by the fact that Christ did not resist and make a fight of it I energetically enquired, "Hadn't He a gun?" I was told No. "Hadn't He a sword?" No. And then: "Hadn't He even a stick with a point?" Though not naturally combative, I have always been a strong believer in the virtue of the counter-attack as the best, or, indeed, the only efficient form of self-defence.

I was, I believe, an easy-going, contented child, with no tendency to be frightened either by strangers, by imagi-

nary terrors, or by the dark. I jogged easily along the
Nursery high-road. There was, however, a family tradition that, though as a rule I was perfectly willing to let
other children have my toys, and would not take the
trouble to do what nurses call "stand up for myself," I
did occasionally astonish my playmates and my guardians
by super-passionate outbursts. These, however, were
very rare indeed, for all my life I have had a great dislike
or even horror of anything in the shape of losing my
temper, an unconscious recognition, as it were, of the wisdom of the Roman saying, "Anger is a short madness."
Instinctively I felt with Beaumont and Fletcher:

> Oh, what a beast in uncollected man!

My general psychology, as far as I can tell from memory, was plain and straightforward when a child. I have
no recollection of feeling any general depression or disappointment, of thinking that I was misunderstood, *i.e.*
of entertaining what is now called "an inferiority com-
plex." I never gave way to any form of childish melancholy. I did not even have alarming, or mysterious, or
metaphysical dreams! What makes this more curious
is the fact that I very much outgrew my strength, about
the age of nine or ten. I was not allowed to play active
games, or run about, or do any of the things in which I
delighted.

Though without great physical strength, I was all my
life exceedingly fond of the joys of bodily exercise, whether
swimming, rowing, riding, walking, mountaineering, skat-
ing, playing tennis or racquets or whatever game was
going.

In none of these pastimes did I reach anything approaching excellence, but from all of them I got intense
enjoyment. I tasted, indeed, almost every form of

athleticism and genuinely smacked my lips at the flavour of each in turn, yet never bothered about the super-pleasure which comes from doing such things as well as they can be done.

Though my bodily health did not give me an unhappy or depressed childhood, or make me suffer from any sort of morbid reaction, I had occasionally a very curious and somewhat rare experience—one which, though it has been noted and discussed, has never, as far as I know, been fully explained by physicians either of the body or of the soul.

The condition to which I refer is that which the musician Berlioz called *"isolement"*—the sense of spiritual isolation, which seizes on those who experience it with a poignancy amounting to awe. Wordsworth's *Ode to Immortality* affords the *locus classicus* in the way of description:

> Fallings from us, vanishings,
> Blank misgivings of a creature
> Moving about in worlds not realised.

I once amused myself by getting together a large number of descriptions of *"isolement,"* and found that, though they may differ considerably, they have in common the characteristics enumerated by the Ode.

The first thing to be noted about the sense of *isolement* is that it comes, not in sleeping, but in waking hours, and that, whether truly or not, it brings with it the feeling that it is the result of some external impulse. The best form of explanation, however, is to describe as exactly as I can my own sensations. Though the sense of *isolement* has been experienced by me as a little child, as a lad, as a young man, and even up to the age of forty or forty-five, the recollections of my first visitation, which occurred when I could not have been more, at the very most, than six years of age, are very much more vivid and keener-edged than those of the later occasions.

Outside the two doors of the nurseries at Sutton Court there is a long passage, and in this is something unusual—a little fire-place and grate. I was one day standing in that passage, quite close to the grate, and expecting nothing in particular. Then suddenly there came over me a feeling so strange and so different from anything I had ever felt before as to be almost terrifying. It was *overwhelming* in the true meaning of the word. Incredible as it seems in the case of so small a child, I had the clearest and most poignant feeling of being left completely, utterly alone, not merely in the world, but in something far, far bigger—in the universe, in a vastness infinite and unutterable.

As with Wordsworth, everything seemed to vanish and fall away from me, even my own body. I was literally "beside myself." I stood a naked soul in the sight of what I must *now*, though of course did not then, call for want of better explanatory expressions, the All, the Only, the Whole, the Everlasting. It was no annihilation, no temporary absorption into the Universal Consciousness, no ingression into the Divine Shadow, that the child experienced. Rather it was the amplest exaltation and magnification of the Ego which it is possible to conceive. I gained, not lost, by discarding the "lendings" of life. Something that was from one point of view a void, and from another a rounded completeness, hemmed me in.

Here I should perhaps interpolate yet another caveat. I did not, of course, as a child, use or even know of the vocabulary of the metaphysicians. I did, however, entertain thoughts which I could not then express, but which the words given above most nearly represent. There is one exception. In talking about "a naked soul"

6

I am not *interpreting* my childish thrill of deep emotion into a later vocabulary. I have always remembered the emotion in those very words. It is so recorded on my memory. Of that I am sure.

The effect on me was intensely awe-inspiring—so awe-inspiring, indeed, as to be disturbing in a high degree. Though it did not in the least terrify me or torture me, or make me have anything approaching a dread of its repetition, I experienced a kind of rawness and sensitiveness of soul such as when, to put it pathologically, a super-sensitive mucous membrane surface is touched roughly by a hand or instrument. One is not exactly pained, but one quivers to the impact. So quivered my soul, though not my brain or my body, for there was no suggestion of any bodily faintness, or of any agitation of "grey matter," in the experience. For example, I was not in the least dizzy. I was outside my bodily self and far away from the world of matter.

In addition to this awe and sensitiveness, and what one might call spiritual discomfort, there was something altogether curious and unexpected, something that still remains for me as much the most vivid and also much the most soul-shaking part of the experience, something which many people will regard as impossible to have occupied the mind of a child of six. I can best describe it, though very inadequately, as a sudden realisation of the appalling greatness of the issues of living. I avoid saying "life and death" deliberately, for Death was nowhere in the picture. I was confronted in an instant, and without any preparation, or gradation of emotion, not only with the immanence but with the ineffable greatness of that whole of which I was a part. Though it may be a little difficult to make the distinction clear, this feeling had nothing to do with the sense of isolation. It was an entirely separate experience. I felt, with a conviction which I know not how to translate into words, that what I was "in for" by being a sentient human being was immeasurably great. It was thence that the sense of awe came, thence the extraordinary sensitiveness, thence the painful exhilaration, the spiritual sublimation. "Oh! what a tremendous thing it is to be a living person! Oh, how dreadfully great!" That is the way the child felt. That was what kept ringing in my ears.

Though I was isolated, I had no sense of smallness or of utter insignificance in face of the Universe. I did not feel myself a miserable, fortuitous atom, a grain of cosmic dust. I felt, though, again, I am interpreting rather than recording, that I was fully equal to my fate. As a human being I was not only immortal, but *capax imperii*,—a creature worthy of a heritage so tremendous.

From that day to this, talk about the unimportance, the futility of man and his destiny has left me quite cold.

Though, as a small child, I was by no means without religious feeling, and had, as I have always had, a deep and instinctive sense of the Divine existence, I had not the least desire to translate my vision of the universal into the terms of theology.

That is a very odd fact, but a fact it is. The vision remained, and remains, isolated, immutable, and apart. Though I had perfect confidence in my father and mother, and often talked to them of spiritual matters, I did not at the time feel any impulse to relate my experience either to them or to anyone else. I had no desire to unload my mind—a remarkable thing for so eager a talker and expounder as I have always been. This reticence, I am sure, came not from a fear of being laughed at, or of shocking anyone, or again from a fear of a repetition of the experience. It simply did not occur to me to talk. The experience was solely mine, I was satisfied and even a little perturbed by the result. Probably some sense of the great difficulty of finding words to fit my thoughts also held me back.

It was only after two or three similar visitations that I casually told the story of this "ecstasy" to my younger brother. I was then about twenty-four and he twenty. I was much surprised to find that he had never had any experiences of this particular kind, for I supposed them common. He, however, became much interested, and some little time after showed me the passage to which I have referred in Berlioz' *Memoirs*.

This set me investigating, and I soon found examples of states of ecstasy similar to, if not exactly like, my own. Tennyson supplied one in the visional passages in the *Princess*. Kinglake had a visitation akin to *isolement*. Wordsworth, however, came nearest to my sensations. Indeed, he describes them exactly.

My later manifestations of *isolement* were similar to my first, though not so vivid. As I write at the age of sixty-two, my impression is that the last occasion on which I experienced the sense of *isolement* was about twenty years ago. How welcome would be a repetition! I do not, however, expect another ecstasy, any more than did Wordsworth, and for very much the same reasons. I do not think that the vision was due to any morbid or irregular working of the brain, or to any other pathological or corporeal mal-functioning. I believe that the experience was purely an experience of the spirit. That is why I attribute to it a psychological and even metaphysical value.

At any rate, it corresponds with my personal metaphysic of existence. Further, I think with Wordsworth that in all probability the fact that it was most vivid in early

childhood and gradually ceased when I grew up, is a proof
that in some way or other it was based on a spiritual
memory. Wordsworth, after the description I have
already given, goes on :—

> High instincts, before which our mortal nature
> Did tremble like a guilty thing surprised;
>   But for those first affections,
>   Those shadowy recollections,
>   Which, be they what they may,
> Are yet the fountain-light of all our day,
> Are yet a master-light of all our seeing;
>   Uphold us—cherish—and have power to make
> Our noisy years seem moments in the being
> Of the eternal silence; truths that wake
>   To perish never;
> Which neither listlessness, nor mad endeavour,
>   Nor man nor boy,
> Nor all that is at enmity with joy,
> Can utterly abolish or destroy!

That seems to me the explanation which can most reasonably be applied to the mental phenomena which I have
described. It satisfied me completely. Wordsworth
struck the exact balance between mental exaltation and
the trembling "like a guilty thing surprised," of which I
have given a more prosaic account.

I must add here that the *Ode to Immortality* is not a
poem which my father used to read to us as children, and
as far as I can remember I did not take to reading it, or
know anything about it, till I was seventeen or eighteen;
that is, ten or twelve years later. Even when it became a
favourite with me, for some reason or other I did not dwell
upon the *isolement* part of it, but rather upon the earlier
passages. Curiously enough, it was a quotation in

Clough's *Amours de Voyages* which first made me realise that Wordsworth was dealing with *isolement*.

I hope no one will think that in describing my experiences of *isolement* in my own mind I was exaggerating the importance of the incident.   I know that similar waking trances are very common.   I also know that modern psychology, or, I should say, certain schools of modern psychology, regard them merely as manifestations or outcrops of the unconscious self.   If I understand the argument rightly, they hold that just as in dreams the unconscious self gets possession of one's personality and the consciousness is for a certain time deposed or exiled, the same thing may happen, and does happen in our waking hours.   Therefore *isolement* must not be regarded as anything wonderful or mystic, but merely as a day-dream. I admit that this seems at first sight a plausible explanation.   Yet I can say with Gibbon, "this statement is probable; but certainly false."

Anyone who has experienced the feeling as I experienced it would think it by no means unlikely that it represented something far deeper, and was due to some impulse external to oneself.   Certainly to me the feeling was essentially one of revelation, of being suddenly made to see and understand things which before had been dark or unknown.   I realised that what I should now call the materialistic hypothesis would not help me to a solution.   No "fanciful shapes of a plastic earth" were in my vision.   My *Ego*, whatever it was or was to be, was, I perceived, a spirit and not a creature of flesh-and-blood, and also not a hypothesis, but a reality.

Since it is appropriate to my account of the phenomenon of *isolement*, I may add a curious passage in Walt Whitman's *Specimen Days and Collect*, which shows that the poet knew this form of ecstasy:

Even for the treatment of the universal, in politics, meta-physics, or anything, sooner or later we come down to our single, solitary soul. There is, in sanest hours, a consciousness, a thought that rises, independent, lifted out from all else, calm, like the stars, shining, eternal. This is the thought of identity —yours for you, whoever you are, as mine for me. Miracle of miracles, beyond statement, most spiritual and vaguest of earth's dreams, yet hardest basic fact, and only entrance to all facts. In such devout hours, in the midst of the significant wonders of heaven and earth (significant only because of the Me in the centre), creeds, conventions fall away and become of no account before this simple idea. Under the luminousness of real vision, it alone takes possession, takes value. Like the shadowy dwarf in the fable, once liberated and look'd upon, it expands over the whole earth and spreads to the roof of heaven. The quality of BEING, in the object's self, according to its own central idea and purpose, and of growing therefrom and thereto—not criticism by other standards and adjustments thereto—is the lesson of Nature.

Who knows whether this may not be Walt Whitman's "secret," or, at any rate, the spiritual experience of which the poet's latest biographer, Mr. Emory Holloway, writes? His interesting account of Walt Whitman's Manuscript Note-Books is preceded by the following statement:

The first of these (The MS. Note-Books) begins with a sense of suppressed, half-articulate power in the language of a novel ecstasy. Some mystical experience, some great if not sudden access of intellectual power, some enlargement and clarifying of vision, some selfless throb of cosmic sympathy, has come to Walt Whitman. At first he can only ejaculate his wonder, and pray for the advent of a perfect man who will be worthy to communicate to the world this new vision of human-ity. Then, like the prophet Isaiah, whose great book he is wont to carry in his pocket to Coney Island, he suddenly realises that a vision is itself a commission; and from this moment he dedicates himself to a life task as audacious as it seems divine.

Though the subject, I admit, fascinates me, I must say no more on it, lest my autobiography should become "a sort of a commentary" on "the ecstasy," featuring Plotinus!

Though always intensely interested in things psychical, and a copious reader of all the phenomena of the unseen world, I have only had one other psychic adventure in the whole of my life, and that an insignificant one. It is, however, worth recording shortly. It happened that in the early autumn of the year 1920, while my son was away from home, learning French in a family at Versailles, I went to my dressing-room to sleep, at about three o'clock in the afternoon. I woke up at four o'clock —an hour's sleep is my ration—with a start and the recollection that I had just dreamt a dream of a very alarming kind. In my dream my wife had come to me with a telegram in her hand, and had told me that our son had been killed in a hunting accident in France. The impression was extremely vivid, and for a moment I was greatly perturbed. This, however, did not last. A little reflection soon made me feel that it could be nothing but a bad dream—a nightmare. People do not hunt in August, or at Versailles, and therefore there was no reason whatever to regard the dream seriously. Still, as a faithful member of the Psychical Society, I thought I must take notice of the incident, even though it seemed ridiculous. No scientific investigator ever dares to say that any "odd" observed fact is not worth considering.

Accordingly I sat down and wrote to my son, mentioning the dream and asking whether between three and four on that day he was in any kind of mental trouble or anxiety—anything that by an imperfect telephonic message might have got through to me as a hunting accident. To my astonishment, I received by return a letter from Versailles telling me that about three-fifteen on the day in question he had been in a small railway accident, which, though not resulting in any deaths, had injured several people, and had given him a fairly severe shaking.

Considering how seldom I dream, and if I do dream, how seldom the dream concerns anybody else, it is difficult to account for this as a mere coincidence. My dreams, when I have them, are practically all of the pure nightmare description and of the usual sealed-pattern. I am worried by the sense of not being able to pack in time to catch my train, or else I am compelled to go back to Oxford and try to pass an examination under impossible and humiliating conditions. Indeed, I don't think I can ever remember a dream, except this one about my son, which was of a non-egotistical kind, that is, in which somebody else speaks, and of which I am not the centre. In a word, it seems to me that, though my son had no recollection of thinking of me (the accident was not important enough for that), his unconscious self got busy and, as I was in a light sleep, it was able to telephone an excited message to its nearest relation, my unconscious self.

CHAPTER VII

MY CHILDHOOD (*Continued*)

IT must not be supposed that either my childhood or boyhood was a psychic or poetic affair, or that in any way I was a cranky and abnormal child. I was nothing of the kind. In spite of what I had better call my metrical precociousness, which I deal with in detail in a later chapter, I was exceedingly fond of outdoor sports of all sorts. Though never a very strong swimmer, I loved particularly what Dr. Johnson might have called the "pleasures of immersion," whether in the icy cold of our Somersetshire streams or in the bland waters of the Mediterranean. The back of the horse and the buffet of the wave still remain for me the intensest of physical delights. Next in my affections comes mountain-climbing, though here I must not write of it. Instead, I would record two memories—one of the very beginning, and one of the very end, of my childhood. My very first memory is concerned with the American Civil War—a conflict which has always exercised a great influence over my mind. To me the struggle between the North and the South stands for one of the pivotal facts in the history of the English-speaking race. I have a clear recollection of my mother showing me a full-page picture, probably in the *Illustrated London News*, entitled "The Last Shot in the War." It was, if my memory serves, a darkish picture, with a big piece of artillery dimly por-

Sutton Court, Somerset.

trayed in the foreground, and a still dimmer background, in which one seemed to catch sight of shadowy armies, warring in the gloom. Or were they only trees and clouds? I cannot remember my mother's words, but I have a recollection, firm though so distant, that she told me how the great war had come about, and how this was the end of all the misery and slaughter. The year, I think, must have been '65, that is, when I was five years old.

As soon as my father began to talk to us of great events, which was when I was about six, and to expound, as fathers should, the merits of the struggle, I became an intense Northerner. All my father's sympathies were with the North, both on the imperative duty of maintaining the Union and on the slavery issue. He was an intense abolitionist. As a lad of sixteen or seventeen, he had given up sugar, at the end of the 'twenties, because in those days sugar was grown by slaves on the West Indian plantations. He would not support a slave industry, and until the slaves were freed he did not go back to sugar.

Curiously enough, though my father greatly admired Mr. Lincoln, he did not put into my mind that passionate devotion to the saviour of the Union which I developed later. By this I do not mean that he was critical of Lincoln, but merely that Lincoln was not one of his special heroes. This fact, however, made a sounder foundation for my feelings about America and the American people than would the mere cult of the individual. I learned first to understand the greatness of the separation issue, to realise the magnificence and the significance of the American nation.

Another point of interest in the context is worth noting. My American readers must not run away with the idea that there was anything strange in a Somersetshire squire being on the side of the North. It is quite a delusion to suppose that all the people of education and position in England were Southerners. They were nothing of the kind. I cannot, of course, remember those times myself, but I often talked them over with men like Lord Cromer, who not only was on the Northern side, but paid a visit to the Northern Armies as a young artillery officer, and heard the guns at Petersburg. He pointed out how strong Conservatives such as his uncle, Tom Baring, were convinced Northerners, as was also, of course, Disraeli.

No doubt the man who did the harm in England and made Americans believe that we rejoiced in the rebellion, was Mr. Gladstone. Partly through want of information and partly through a curious mental twist, he persuaded himself that the South was fighting for freedom like the Italians in Naples or Lombardy. He not only believed in "the erring sister, go in peace" policy, but considered that for "erring sister" should be substituted "good and gallant sister." Mr. Gladstone's influence was, unfortunately, at that time very great, and he misled an enormous number of people on the merits of the quarrel. Happily my father, though a keen admirer of Gladstone, did not follow him here. He maintained the Northern view against all comers, as did the Duke of Argyll, Lord Houghton, and dozens of other men of light and leading, including, I am glad to say, my future chiefs, the Editors of *The Spectator*.

Of another combative memory I can be more specific, for my recollection of it is positively photographic. I can see myself, a little creature in a straw hat, playing on what the nurses used to call "the libery lawn"—a beautiful stretch of sward, upon which the Great Parlour window opened. This lawn is half surrounded by an old red sandstone battlement wall, with a long, terrace-like mound in front of it. Suddenly, in the middle of our play, I saw the Great Parlour window open and my father, with his hand held to shelter his eyes from the glare, stepping on to the gravel path. He called to my elder brother and me that if we liked he would read us an account of a great battle that had just been fought in Austria. It was the Battle of Sadowa. My father held in his hand a copy of the *Daily News*, to which he was a fairly frequent contributor. The paper contained Forbes's vivid account of the action which humbled the Austrian Empire before its Hohenzollern rivals. I was always glad to hear about a fight, and was very soon tucked up at the end of my father's green sofa. Owing to his stiff knee he always used a sofa to rest and read on rather than sat in an armchair. He began to read at once, for he was as eager as we were to devour the story of how "Our Special Correspondent" climbed the church-tower and saw men and armies battling in the plain below.

I did not, of course, understand the nature of the war, but my father was greatly moved and read with such emotion that the encounter lived before my eyes. Here I should note that my father, though the most humane of men, was intensely fond of stories of war, and in a layman's way understood a good deal about strategy. For example, he knew not only, like Sir Thomas Browne, all the battles in Plutarch, but also all the big Indian battles and those of the Peninsula. He was a special student of Waterloo, for he had talked with plenty of men and officers who had been in the Belgian Campaign.

Another recollection of my childhood will come in aptly here, for it concerns a Waterloo veteran. He lived at Chew Magna, and kept a small shop. Like many of the combatants on the British side, he was probably only about fifteen or sixteen years old at Waterloo. Half the regiments there were Militia regiments, and notoriously were composed of lads. Therefore, in '69 or '70, when I used to ride over to see him, my soldier was only about seventy-one or seventy-two. At his shop could be bought pencils, pens, and little books of most attractive appearance, seal-ing-wax and many other objects fascinating to the schoolboy. However, the real attraction was the seller, and not the things sold. As soon as I discovered that the man had been at Waterloo, I loved to go in, pull over the old man's stock, and then gossip with him about the Battle. Unless my recollection plays me false, he was distinctly a good talker. This is how he told the story of the 18th of June:

Our regiment was marched out into a cornfield. The officers told us to lie down on the ground and wait, because the enemy had got their artillery playing on us. Cannon-balls kept coming over pretty close to the ground. If we kept flat, how-ever, there was not much risk. Every now and then the artillery fire would cease entirely, and then our officers called us to get up as quick as ever we could, and form square. The front rank lay down, the second rank knelt, the third stooped low, and the rear rank stood up. Our bayonets were fixed and our muskets loaded. There was not much time. As soon as we had got into place we heard the cavalry thundering up. Then, all of a sudden and as if they had sprung up from the ground (there was a little hollow in front), they were riding round us, riding like mad, cursing and swearing and shouting, waving their swords, and trying to force their horses on to our bayonets. We kept shooting at 'em all the time. But the bullets used to bound off their steel coats. (They were, of course, cuirassiers.) We soon found out, however, that if we aimed under their arm-pits, or at their faces, or the lower part of their bodies, we could kill them, or at least damage them. Our square was never really broken, but every now and then one of the Frenchmen would drive his horse right through our bayonets and into the middle, where we killed him. Of course, their idea was that if one got in, the others could follow him, but we never let them do that. We always closed up and held fast. Then, all of a sudden, the cavalry would go back as quick as they came, and in a minute there was not one of them to be seen. They had all utterly disappeared. As soon as ever they were gone, the guns began to fire again, and down we all went flat to the ground, and this went on all the morning, first up and then down.

From a private soldier's point of view, this was, I expect, a very accurate description of the battle.

I, of course, wanted to know more, and especially whether he had seen the Duke. He declared that he had, but it was a dim picture. According to my friend, he saw the Duke and his staff riding by at the back of the square, and heard him say something to an officer, but what he did not catch. If he had only known, he was describing a particular characteristic of the Duke. Wellington, when in action, was the dumbest of dumb things, and it would have required a moral earthquake to get more than some curt order out of him. Even a "tinker's curse" or "a tuppenny damn" would have seemed loquacious in him on such an occasion. The not very sensational "*Up Guards and at 'em!*" was in later life disputed by the Duke. Under great pressure, the most he would admit was that he might possibly have said it, though he did not believe he ever did.

The kind of battle remark he favoured was one which my father used to tell me he had heard from Mountstewart Elphinstone, his father's bosom friend. Elphinstone rode with the Duke at the Battle of Assaye. When some hundred Mahratta guns were in full blast against the British line, Elphinstone asked Sir Arthur Wellesley—it was Elphinstone's first battle—whether the fire was really hot. "Well, they're making a good deal of noise, but they don't seem to be doing much damage," was the reply of the Duke, after he had carefully looked up and down the line.

By a curious piece of luck, we boys were in touch not only with a Waterloo veteran, but also with a man who had been at Trafalgar. At Lady Waldegrave's house, Strawberry Hill, one of the men in the garden had been, as a boy, on the *Victory*. My brother Harry remembers speaking to him, but, though I must have seen him, I have no recollection of him, and probably did not talk to him. If I had, I am sure I should have questioned him, and would probably have remembered the answers.

I will end the stories of my childhood by relating an incident which always seems to me to belong to the earlier epoch, though it really happened when I was about thirteen, and therefore no longer a child. The scene is Sutton, and therefore it must have been during the holidays, for I am sure I was living at our tutor's at Chewton at the time. I had gone out for a country walk by myself, for I was fond of roaming about the fields, and especially of tracing to their sources the wooded gullies abounding in our Somersetshire country. On such solitary rambles I was always accompanied by a poet, in my pocket. On the occasion I am going to describe, Swinburne in his *Poems and Ballads* was my guest of honour.

I emerged from my riverine exploration on to a hillside where the stream rose—near a place with the delightfully rustic name of Hinton Belwit. Here the springtime and the bright sun invited me to sit upon a stile and to read of Dolores or Faustine, or *The Garden of Proserpine*,— I know not which. While thus absorbed and probably muttering verses aloud, I did not notice a typical Somersetshire farmer of the 'seventies who was approaching the stile. When, therefore, I heard his voice and looked up, it was as if the man had dropped from the clouds. What he was saying was quite as unexpected as his appearance. It ran something like this: "It be all craft, craft. You men be as full of craft as hell be of tailors." Needless to say, I was enchanted. This looked like the beginning of an adventure, for the old gentleman was puffing hard and in the condition which Jeremy Taylor describes as "very zealously angry."

I, however, was too much interested to learn what he meant to resent his abuse, and politely invited an explanation. He went on to declare with great vehemence what a curse this book-learning and education were to the working-men and how they filled them with "craft"—that was the refrain of all his remarks. It made them unfit to work and to serve honest men like himself, who had never had anything to do with that evil thing—book-learning. When I gently asked why the sight of me had made him think about it, he explained, with a look of infinite slyness, that he saw I was reading a book. Then came an amusing disclosure. At fourteen I was a very much overgrown lad, almost as tall as I am now, and weighing almost as much and he had mistaken me for one of the ordination pupils of a Roman Catholic priest who lived in the valley close by. They were wont to walk about the country breviary in hand, not merely reading, but actually reciting the office to themselves. My green book was taken for a breviary, or for a book of hours, and my mouthings of *Dolores* or *The Garden of Proserpine* for "the blessed mutter of the Mass"! Assured by me that I was not a priest, he asked me who I was. I told him my name and he instantly stretched out a huge and grimy hand, and shook mine with a hearty violence, and insisted that I should come home with him and drink a mug of cider, I accepted with avidity. It was all in the adven-

7

ture. Who knows? I might go to his house and find the most delightful maiden in disguise! In fact, anything and everything was possible. So I went, expecting and hoping for great things, though quite willing to be content with small things and "a mug o' zyder" if I could not get anything bigger.

As soon as we got into the farm kitchen and saw the farmer's wife, the old gentleman began to explain his mistake. "And to think, Mother, that this be young Mr. Strachey, after all. You can mind, carn't you, wife, how we used to see him and his brothers riding by with their ponies and their long hair? It is just like King Arthur and the cakes, it is." At this his good wife, with a toss of her head, said, "Don't you be so ignorant, maaster, talking about what you don't know. It's King Henry you means." "That I don't. I mean King Arthur. You go down and get the young maaster a mug o' zyder, and don't you say no more."

Then he slowly closed one pig-like eye and aimed it in my direction. That was his idea of winking. Patting me on the knee, he added, "The women be always like that— bain't they?—always trying to think they know better. It was just like King Arthur and the cakes, weren't it?" I, of course, assented and, I am sorry to say, with the magnificent pedantry of boyhood, reflected that he was not the first person to make the mistake. Did not Mrs. Quickly piously ejaculate that the dead Falstaff was "in Arthur's bosom"? Besides, it was proof that the Somersetshire people still remembered King Arthur—a point treasured by me for my father, who was a keen student and great lover of the Arthurian legends. It was he who edited for Macmillan the *Morte d'Arthur* in the Globe series. According to my father, and I expect quite rightly, Arthur was the last of the British kings to stand up against the

Saxons, and really did inhabit that most magnificent of ditch-defended hills, Cadbury Castle.

Cadbury, as the village at its foot, Queen's Camel, shows, is quite possibly a broken-down form of Camelot. But there is better proof than that. Till forty years ago, and possibly even now, the people round Cadbury told tales of King Arthur, and firmly believed he would come again. For example, the rector of Queen's Camel told my father that a local girl, a housemaid in the Rectory, told him, as if it were a matter of course, that every night of the full moon the King and his Knights rode round the castle hall and watered their horses at the Wishing-Well. She had seen them herself. Another man told the rector that his father had one day seen a sort of opening in the hill, and had looked in. "There he zeed a king sitting in a kind of a cave, with a golden crown on his head and beautiful robes on him."

The best Arthurian story of all was the following. The rector, as an archæologist, did a little excavation on his own on the flat place at the very top of the hill—a place in which there were what looked like rough foundations. He used to take with him a local labourer to do some of the spade-work. One day they dug up a Quern. The labourer asked what it was. The clergyman explained that it was a form of hand-mill used in the olden days for grinding corn. In reply he was met with one of the most amazing remarks ever made to an antiquarian. "Oh, a little hand-mill be it! Ah, now I understands what I never did before. That's why they fairies take such a lot of corn up to the top of the hill. They be taking it up for to grind."

Anticipating Kipling, the rector might well have exclaimed, "How is one to put that into a 'Report on Excavations on Cadbury Hill submitted to the Somersetshire Archæological Society by the Rector of Queen's Camel'?"

Anyway, I was delighted to have actually heard a man speak the words "King Arthur," and also went home chuckling at the thought of being mistaken for a Roman priest—an event which particularly amused my mother.

Soon after I was eleven, we went to Chewton Vicarage for the first time as "private pupils." Then my mother's health became worse, and we had to go to Cannes more or less regularly. In order that our education should be continued, we then reverted to the plan of tutors in the house. We had two of these in succession, both Balliol men. Though they were able men, they were not successes as educationalists. My father always used to say that he thought both of them had been badly overworked at Oxford and had been advised to take tutorial posts as a rest-cure—a very pleasant rest-cure when it took the form of wintering in the South of France.

But, though my brothers and I effectually resisted the efforts made to teach us, we learnt during our winters in France a great many things indirectly. Unfortunately, French was not one of those things. My father would have liked us to speak and write French. He had it, however, so strongly impressed upon him by his advisers that if we were to go to Oxford we must above all things get a sufficient knowledge of Latin and Greek to pass Responsions that, though we had an occasional lesson in French, our sojourn on the Riviera, as far as learning French was concerned, was thrown away.

We lived entirely with the boys and girls of the rest of the British colony, and regarded the French inhabitants literally as part of the scenery, and largely as a humorous part thereof. We got on well enough with them, and knew enough French to buy endless sweets at Rumpelmeyer's or *chez Nègres*, to get queer knives and "oddities" at the fairs, or to conduct paper-chases along the course of the

Sutton Court, Somerset.

Canal or in Pine Woods bordering it. We refused, however, to take the French or their language seriously.

However, my father did contrive to instil a little French politics into us. He was a fervent admirer of Gambetta and the Third Republic, and used to read us extracts from Gambetta's organ, *La République Française*. It thus happened that I early became a staunch adherent of the great Democratic leader and was full of zeal against first the Comte de Chambord and then the Comte de Paris. I still remember the excitement we all felt over Marshal MacMahon's rather half-hearted efforts to play the part of a General Monk.

We had, further, the excitement of seeing a famous General immured close to us in a fortress prison for the crime of treason. The Ile de Ste. Marguerite, opposite Cannes, with its picturesque Vauban fortifications, became, while we were at Cannes, the prison of Marshal Bazaine, the man who surrendered Metz to the Germans. He occupied, besides, the very rooms which had been occupied by "The Man with the Iron Mask." Can it be wondered that when we had a picnic-party on the island, or rowed under the walls of the fortress in a boat, we used to strain every muscle in order to get a glimpse of the prisoner? On one occasion we saw somebody's hat or head moving along a parapet, and were told it was the Marshal taking his daily exercise on the terrace of the fort, but whether it really was or not, who can say? At any rate, the Marshal escaped from his imprisonment during our stay, probably to the relief of his jailers. That was a source of great excitement in itself, and it was heightened by rumours that an English girl had assisted the prisoner to break out.

We were not personally in favour of Bazaine, but regarded him with distinct repulsion for surrendering at

Metz. Still, an escape was an escape; and, besides, the fat old Marshal had let himself down by a rope into an open boat!

The epoch of tutors came to an end soon after the birth of my sister, which happened at Marseilles, when my mother was on her way to Cannes. After the event, my mother was pronounced by the doctors to be able to winter in England, and I and my two brothers, therefore, went back to Chewton Mendip and became private pupils of Mr. Philpott, for the second time. Here we remained till I went first to a tutor at Oxford—Mr. Bell—and then to live with my uncle and aunt, Professor T. H. Green (Mrs. Green was my mother's sister). There I was "coached for Balliol" by two of the best scholars in the University. One of them was Professor Nettleship, who a couple of years later was made Professor of Latin, and the other is now Sir Herbert Warren, President of Magdalen. They were both delightful expounders of the classics, and, though I was an unaccountably bad scholar, I am proud to say that they both liked me and liked teaching me. However, I need say no more on this point, as all that is worth saying about it is supplied by Sir Herbert Warren in the letter which I have included in my Oxford Chapter.

CHAPTER VIII

THE FAMILY NURSE

In the families of the well-to-do few influences have a greater effect upon the child, and so upon the man, than that exercised by the servants of the household in which he or she is brought up. And of those influences, upstairs or downstairs, none, of course, is so potent as that of the nurse. That is what Goethe would call one of the secrets that are known to all. Why it should ever be regarded as a secret Heaven knows; yet it must be so considered, for it is very seldom spoken of except in the case of nurses.

Anyway, I and my brothers, and in our earlier years my sister, were quite as fortunate in our nurse as we were in our parents and in our home. Her name was Mrs. Leaker. She was not married, but bore the brevet rank always accorded to upper servants of her position. She played many parts in our family household, and always with a high distinction. She began as nurse; she next became cook; then housekeeper; then reverted for a time to nurse, and then became something more than housekeeper because she ruled over the nursery as well as over the kitchen, the store-room, and the housemaids' room. But whatever her name in the household, and whatever her duties, she was always in fact head-nurse. She loved children, and they loved her, though not without a certain sense of awe. She had a fiery temper; but that fieriness was reserved

103

almost entirely for grown-up people. A child, if it knew the proper moment for action, could do anything it liked with her.

Taken altogether, she was one of the most remarkable women, whether for character or intellect, that I have ever come across. In appearance she had, what can be best described as, the gipsy look, though she did not believe herself to have gipsy blood. Her complexion was swarthy, her hair was black, and her eyes dark and full of an eager and scintillating brightness which made her face light up and change with every mood of her mind and radiate a vivid intelligence. If anyone who knew her was asked to state the most memorable thing about her, I am sure the answer would be, "mobility," both of mind and body. There was a quickness as well as a lightness in her step— I hear it as I write—in the gestures of her hands and her head, and indeed in everything she did.

Let nobody suppose for a moment that this was a case of *paralysis agitans*, or St. Vitus' Dance. There was nothing involuntary in her unrest. It was all part of an intense vitality and an intense desire for self-expression. When she was in one of her worst tempers, she would pace up and down a room, turning at each wall like a lion in a cage, in a way which I have only seen one other person effect with equal spirit and unconsciousness. That was an eminent statesman, in the moment of great political crisis. Her nature was so eager and so active, and seemed to be so perpetually fretting her body and mind, that anyone seeing her in middle life would have been inclined to prophesy that such agitations must wear her out prematurely and that she had only a short life before her, or else an imbecile's end.

Yet, as a matter of fact, she lived in good health till over eighty, and to the last moment retained the full control

Mrs. Salome Leaker,—"The Family Nurse."

of her faculties. She died, as might any other old person, of bronchitis. In truth, she was an example of Sir Thomas Browne's dictum that we live by an invisible flame within us. As a matter of fact, her flame was anything but invisible. It was remarkably visible. It leapt, and crackled, and gleamed, and took on, like the witch's oils, every colour in the spectrum. Now crimson, now violet, now purple, now yellow, glowed and flashed the colours of her mind.

Mrs. Leaker was brought up in a poor household, in an age when illiteracy, alas! seemed the natural fate of the poor. But you could no more have kept education from her than you could have kept food from a hungry lioness. She was determined to get it somehow, and get it she did. She taught herself to read before she had reached womanhood, and taught herself by pure force of her will, adopting, curiously enough, what would now be described as the Montessori method. She opened books and read them somehow or other till she understood the meaning of the words. Her letters her mother had taught her. She often told me that nobody had taught her to read. When she had attained the power of reading, self-education was easy enough. It led to results of an amazing kind—results which at first sight seem to prove all the lore of the educationalists at fault. People, we are told, must be trained to like and understand good literature. Without that training they will never know the good from the bad.

Now read this story of an innate appreciation of good literature which she told me with her own lips. I asked her once, when I was a lad, what she thought of "Junius," who had begun to exercise a great influence over my rhetorical instincts. It was as natural to consult her on a point of literature as on one of domestic surgery. Her reply was perhaps the strangest ever made by a woman over sixty

to a boy of undergraduate age.   It ran in this way, for I
recall her words.

When I was a girl, and a young housemaid in my first place
at Mrs. Lloyd's, in Clifton, I used to have as part of my work
to dust the library.   When I was dusting, I used to take down
the books and look at what was in them, and often got through
a page or two with my duster in my hand.   Once I took down
a volume marked "Junius," and read a page or two, and as I
read I began to feel as if I was drunk.   In those days I had
never heard of the Duke of Grafton or Lord Sandwich, or any
of the other people he talks about, and I did not know what it
all meant, but the words went to my head like brandy.

Now, I ask anyone with a sense of literature whether it
would be possible to give a better lightning criticism of
"Junius" and his style than that conveyed in Leaker's
words.   She had got the exact touch.   "Junius," in truth,
is not only empty for her, but empty for the whole world
except as regards his style.   There he is unquestionably
great.   Tumid, exaggerated, and monotonous as it often
is, his style does affect one like wine.   That is certainly
how it affected, and still affects, me.   Even at an age when
I did not really know much more about the Duke of
Grafton than did Leaker, and probably cared less, I had
got the peroration of the first letter to the Duke of Grafton
by heart.   I used to walk up and down the terrace, or
across the meadows that led to the waterfall, shouting to
myself, or my bored companions, that torrent of lucid,
thrilling invective.   I mean the passage in which "Junius" gives advice to the University of Cambridge.   They
will, he hopes, take it to heart when they shall be "perfectly recovered from the delirium of an Installation,"
and when that learned society has become "once more a
peaceful scene of slumber and thoughtless meditation."

How the waterfall gave me back the reverberating words! How the lime-trees rocked to the final crack of the whip over the unhappy Grafton! "The learned dullness of declamation will be silent; and even the venal Muse, though happiest in fiction, will forget your virtues."

But that was by no means her only achievement of literary diagnosis and the power to get hold of books somehow or other. When in the 'twenties she came to Bristol from Dartmouth, which was her home, with her mother and brothers (her father was dead), she travelled, as did all people with slender means in those days, in the waggon. These vehicles proceeded at the rate of about three or four miles an hour. All she could tell about her journey was that she lay in the straw, in the bottom of the waggon, and read Wordsworth's *Ruth*, *The White Doe of Rylstone*. She was, throughout her life, very fond of *Ruth* and this was her first reading. I have often thought to myself how much the great apostrophe must have meant to the lion-hearted, vehement, imaginative girl:

> Before me shone a glorious world,—
> Fresh as a banner bright, unfurled
> To music suddenly.

In later life she had the poem by heart, and I venture to say that there was not a word of it that she did not understand, both intellectually and emotionally. But though she loved books and literature, it must not be supposed that she was indifferent to other forms of art. Anything beautiful in nature or art made a profound impression upon her. When Leaker first went to Paris, on our way to Pau or Cannes, I forget which, my mother sent her to the Louvre and told her specially to look at the Venus of Milo. She gave her directions where to find the statue; when she came back, she said to my mother:

I couldn't find the statue you told me about, but I saw another which is the most lovely thing in the world. I never thought to see anything so beautiful, and the broken arm did not matter at all, for she stood there like a goddess.

She had found the Venus for herself, although some fault in the directions had made her feel sure that it could not be what she had been sent to look at. Later on, when we took to going to France regularly for my mother's health, she every year did her homage to the Venus. What is more, when she went for the first time to Florence, she fully realised how poor a thing the Venus de Medici was in comparison.

But though, as I have said, all beautiful things appealed to her, literature was her first love and the element in which she lived. But literature did not in her case only mean Shakespeare, Milton, and the Bible, as it does to so many English people. She cropped all the flowers in the fields of literature, prose and verse. She was as intense an admirer of Shakespeare as was my father, and a greater lover of Milton. Shakespeare she lived on, including, curiously enough, *Timon of Athens*, who was a great favourite. When any lazy member of my family wanted to find a particular line or passage in Shakespeare, he or she would go to Leaker rather than trouble to look up the quotation in a concordance; Leaker was certain to find you at once what you wanted. There was no pedantry about her and no mere *tour de force* of the memory. She entered into the innermost mental recesses of Shakespeare's characters. What is more, she made us children follow her.

Though we were kept clean and well looked after, there was no nonsense in her nursery as to over-exciting our minds or emotions, or that sort of thing. She was quite prepared to read us to sleep with the witches in *Macbeth*, or the death-scene in *Othello*. I can remember now the exaltation derived, half from the mesmerism of the verse and half from a pleasant terror, by her rendering of the lines: "Put out the light, and then put out the light." I see her now, with her wrinkled brown face, her cap with white streamers awry over her black hair beginning to turn grey. In front of her was a book, propped up against the rim of a tin candlestick shaped like a small basin. In it was a dip candle and a pair of snuffers. That was how nursery light was provided in the later 'sixties and even in the early 'seventies. As she sat bent forward, declaiming the most soul-shaking things in Shakespeare between nine and ten at night, we lay in our beds with our chins on the counterpanes, silent, scared, but intensely happy. We loved every word, and slept quite well when the play was finished. We were supposed to go to sleep at nine, but if there was anything exciting in the play, very little pressure was required to get Leaker to finish, even if it took an extra half-hour—or a little more. In truth, she was always ready to read to us by night or day.

Though no Sabbatarian, she had a tendency to give *Paradise Lost* a turn on Sundays. As far as I remember, she never read *Paradise Regained*. *Comus* and the short poems, especially *Lycidas*, were great favourites with her. One might have supposed that she would not like Wordsworth. As a matter of fact, she loved him and thoroughly understood him and his philosophy of life. She did not merely read the lyric and elegiac poems like *Ruth*, but had gone through and enjoyed *The Excursion* and many of the longer poems. Coleridge she loved, and Southey, and Crabbe, and Gray, and Dr. Johnson, and indeed the whole of English poetic literature. In modern poetry she read freely Tennyson and Robert Browning, and admired them both.

Byron was a special favourite of hers, and here again she showed her intellect and her taste, not by worshipping the Eastern Tales or the sentimentalities of *Childe Harold*, but by a thorough appreciation of *Don Juan*. Her taste, indeed, was almost unfailing. Take a simple example. She used frequently to chant the delightful lines to Tom Moore, which begin:

> My boat is on the shore,
> And my barque is on the sea,
> But ere I go, Tom Moore,
> Here's a double health to thee.

Having a great deal of sympathy for scorn and indignation, she, of course, loved the last verse and implanted it deeply in my mind by constant quotation in tones of scathing intensity:

> Here's a tear for those who love me,
> And a smile for those who hate,
> And whatever sky's above me,
> Here's a heart for every fate.

That was her own spirit. Truly she had a heart for every fate. She was quite fearless.

Although she was not in the least a prejudiced person, I remember once, in the excitement of my own discovery of Swinburne, trying to create an equal enthusiasm in her mind. She returned me the book, however, without enthusiasm and with the trenchant remark that it made her feel as if she was in an overheated conservatory, too full of highly-scented flowers to be pleasant! She was not in the least shocked by Swinburne, and if you produced a good line or two you could win her approval, but the atmosphere was not sympathetic. Of Rossetti she was a little more tolerant, but she felt, I think, that there was not enough scope and freedom.

It is unnecessary to dwell upon the educational advantages of such a nurse, and of having the very best part of English literature poured into one's mouth almost with the nursery-bottle, and certainly with the nursery mug. If my friends find me, as I fear they sometimes do, too fond of making quotations, they must blame Mrs. Leaker, for when at her best she threw quotations from the English Classics around her in a kind of hailstorm. Some of the lines that had stuck in her mind were very curious, though she had forgotten where they came from. One specially amusing piece of Eighteenth-Century satirical verse I have never been able to trace. Perhaps if I put it forth here I shall find out whence it comes—very likely from some perfectly obvious source. The lines which were used to calm us in our more grandiose and self-conceited moods ran as follows:

> Similes that never hit,
> Vivacity that is not wit,
> Schemes laid this hour, the next forsaken,
> Advice oft asked, but never taken.

She had a couplet which she often produced when the newspapers came out with some big social scandal or the coming to financial grief of some great family name. On such occasions she would mutter to herself:

> Debts and duns
> And nothing for my younger sons.

Another verse, though I quote it not the least to show her literary taste but because it was exceedingly characteristic of her, was in the spring-time always on her lips:

The broom, the broom, the yellow broom,
The ancient poets sung it,
And sweet it is on summer days
To lie at ease among it.

I could fill a book, and perhaps some day I will do so, with Leaker's reflections on men and things, and her epigrammatic sayings, and still more with her wonderful old sea-stories, especially of the press-gang, which she could almost remember in operation. Her father was, as she always put it, "in the King's Navy," and he had been "bosun" to a ship's "cap'n." He was at the Mutiny of the Nore, but was not a mutineer.

She was, however, full of stories about the Mutiny, which we found extremely exciting. She used to sing, or rather "croon" to us some of the mutineers' songs. One that I specially remember began with this verse:

Parker was a gay young sailor,
Fortune to him did not prove kind;
He was hung for mutiny at the Nore,
Worse than him were left behind.

After declaiming that verse to us, she would add in low tones that made one's blood run cold, "Men have been hung at the yardarm for singing that song. It was condemned throughout the Fleet."

That in itself seems a link with the past, but through Leaker I had a much more remarkable example of what, in spite of the smiles of the statistician, fascinated us all. Leaker, when about the age of sixty, brought her old mother, who was then ninety-four or ninety-five, to whom she was devoted, to live in one of the cottages at Sutton, the year being, as far as I can recollect, 1868 or 1869. I can distinctly recall the old lady. She was very thin and faded, but with all her wits about her, though weak and shy.

Leaker told us, with pride, that her mother, when she was a little girl, had sat upon the knee of an old soldier who had fought at Blenheim. This is quite possible. If old Mrs. Leaker was, as I think, only five years short of a hundred in 1869, she could easily have been in the world at the same time as a lad who had been at Blenheim in his eighteenth year. Old Mrs. Leaker was, I calculated, born about 1774. She would therefore have been six years old in 1780. But a man who was ninety-five in 1780 would have been born in 1685, and so twenty-nine in 1714, the year of Blenheim. Possibly some historical calculator will despoil me of this story. Meantime, I am always thrilled to think that I have seen a woman who had seen a man who had been in action with the great Marlborough at his greatest victory.

Before I leave my old nurse I must say something about a very curious and interesting attempt which, at my request, she made at the end of her life. It was to put down her recollections and reflections. Unfortunately, I made this request rather too late, and so the result, as a whole, was confused and often unintelligible. Still, the two little MS. books which she wrote contain some very remarkable and characteristic pieces of writing, and show the woman as she was. Although in her day she had read plenty of autobiographies, she makes no attempt to imitate them, or to write in a pedantic or literary style. As far as she can, she shows us what she really was. Leaker's heart beats against the sides of the little books just as I used to hear it when I was a child in her arms, either in need of consolation, with toothache or growing-pains, or else trying to give consolation, for she was often, like all fierce people,

8

melancholy and depressed after her own fierce outbursts of anger.

Here is the very striking and characteristic exordium to her autobiography:

I have not had an unpleasant life, although I was an old maid, and was a servant for fifty years. I was a nurse and no mother could have loved her children more than I loved those I nursed. I had three dear, good mistresses, two of whom I left against their will.

The third and last was my mother, whom the old nurse outlived for many years.

Here is her account of the miseries endured by the poor after Waterloo—miseries which I often think of in these days, when I note the foolish, the demented way in which we are approaching our economic difficulties and dangers:

I am writing of the time a little after Waterloo. We were living at Dartmouth. Everything was very dear. We lived mostly on barley bread. We children were so used to it that we did not mind it, but my poor mother could never eat it without repugnance, and we always tried to make her get white bread, not knowing that she could not properly afford it. Many a time (so she told me in after-years) she made her supper off a turnip rather than let her children go hungry to bed. The cheapest sugar was then tenpence a pound, and the very cheapest tea quite as much as five shillings, but what I had to get for my mother was in very small quantities. We children never had it, nor, as far as I remember, cared for it. It was a treat when we could get milk to dip our bread in.

But though their poverty was so dire it did not kill the girl's joy in life or, wonderful to say, in literature:

Though we were very poor, my childhood seems pleasant to me as I look back, for my mother did all she could to make us

happy. She went out sewing very often, and we were glad she
should go, for she got better food than she could get at home,
and what was, I believe, as much good to her, she sometimes
got food for her mind. But, poor dear, she was always having
a struggle with her conscience, and her love of what is called
light reading, as being a Methodist she thought it wrong to
read such books. She told me that when she was married she
was given a new edition of all the Elizabethan plays, twenty-
five volumes, beautifully bound. (I heard afterwards that a
new edition was published at that time.) However, about the
year 1818 she thought it right to burn them, although she was
so fond of them. Yet when I was sitting at work with her she
would tell me tales out of the plays. How vexed I used to be
with her for burning them, poor dear loving mother! She
taught me to read out of my father's large old Bible, and the
Apocrypha was a book of wonder to me. She was fond of
Young's *Night Thoughts*. Milton she read often; my father
gave it to her; poor man, he thought it would please her. He
was a sweet-tempered man, easy and kindhearted, but not
clever like my mother. He once said to her when she laughed
at him for some blunders, "Well, my dear, what can the
woman with five talents expect from the man with one?"

Leaker had plenty of stories of the press-gang. Though
she never herself saw it in operation, people not very much
older told her of how they were "awakened in the night by
people crying out that they had been taken."

Her mother, too, used to tell her heartrending stories
about these times.

"I can hardly even now bear to think of the dreadful
things done by the press-gang in the name of the law. I
never hated the French as I hated them."

Needless to say, I inherited her hatred of the press-gang,
and have maintained it all my life. It was the very worst
and most oppressive form of national service ever invented,
and I think with pride that my collateral ancestor, Cap-

tain George St. Loe (*temp*. William & Mary) was the first man in England who urged in his writings that the only fair way of making the nation secure was compulsory universal service.

Leaker's mother was early in her married life converted to Methodism. Some of her reflections on the smuggling that went on in and around the little Devonshire port give the lie to those foolish, ignorant, and shameless people who allege that because people are poor they cannot be expected to have any idea of what is called conventional morality in regard to "mine and thine." They will naturally and excusably, it is asserted, break any law, moral or divine.

That is not how it struck Leaker's mother:

There was a good deal of smuggling going on in the town when I was a girl, and one day a member of my mother's chapel brought some gay things for her to buy. Oh, how I did long for her to get me a pretty neckerchief, but she said, "No, my dear, I cannot buy it for you, as I do not see any difference in cheating a single man or a government of men. I believe that in the sight of God both are equally sinful."

Leaker says of her mother, "She had a large share of romance, and loved a tale of witches, or a love-story"— and so did her daughter. The supernatural gained fresh interest from her skilful story-telling, and the art of the *raconteur* still lives in her pages. Here is one of the best of her stories. Even now it gives a delightful sense of fear:

This story was told me by the mother of a friend of mine— Mrs. Jackson was her name, a ladylike woman, but who appeared to me to be very old when I was a girl. Her husband was sailing master on board a man-of-war, and this is what took place once when she was on board with him. They were in port, and there was a large party of friends and officers spending the evening on the ship, when a sudden storm arose, and no one could go on shore. They were going to amuse themselves with music, and a violin was brought, but a string broke before the instrument had been touched. "Never mind," said the captain, "I have a man on board who is a first-rate hand at deceiving the sight." Everyone was pleased at the idea of conjuring, and the man was sent for, and asked to show some of his tricks; but he said, "No, I can't tonight, as it is not a good time." Said the captain, "What is to hinder you?" "Well, sir, I do not like doing it this stormy weather." "That is all stuff and nonsense," replied the captain; "you must try. Come, set to work." So the man asked for a chafing dish, which was brought to him. There was a fire of charcoal in it. He said and did something (Mrs. Jackson did not tell us what), and after a while there appeared in the dish, coming out of the fire, a tiny tree, with a tiny man holding a hatchet. The tree seemed to grow from the bottom, and the little man chopped at it all the time. The performing man was greatly agitated, and asked one of the ladies to lend him her apron (ladies wore them in those days). Mrs. Jackson took off hers and handed it to him. He tied it on, and ran round the table on which the chafing-dish stood, catching the chips, and apparently in great alarm lest one of them should fall to the ground. She used to say it was painful to see the poor man's agony of fear. While this was going on the storm grew much worse, so that the people on board were afraid that the ship would be driven from her anchorage. At last the tree fell under the tiny man's hatchet, and nothing was left on the table but the chafing-dish. The conjuror gave back the apron, and then, turning to the captain, said, "Never from this night will I do what I have done tonight. You may believe me or not, but if one of those chips had fallen to the ground, nothing could have saved the ship, and everyone on board would have gone down with her."

When the old lady told this story she would say that she had distinctly seen the chips fly, and heard the noise of the chopping. She used to show the apron, which she never wore again,

but kept, carefully put away, to be shown to anyone who liked
to see it.

Can one wonder that the little man with his little axe
and the little tree, and the unknown peril of death that
came up from the sea, made a deep impression upon my
mind, though not in any sense a haunting or unpleasant
one? I longed to see the chips fly and the tiny tree bow to
the sturdy strokes of the weird woodman.

Leaker's stories of ordinary witchcraft were many and
curious, and though they cannot be set out here I must
quote one or two lines in regard to them:

I do not think there was a place in the land so full of witches,
white and black, as Dartmouth. My mother was, for her time
and station, pretty fairly educated, yet she seemed to me to
believe in them firmly.

The autobiography shows that when she was sitting
alone, thinking and writing, the old nurse felt acutely the
solitude and weariness of an old age that had outlived
contemporaries as well as bodily faculties. When, however, the friends of another generation were with her,
she never seemed too tired or too sad to enter keenly into
all the interests of their lives. After a hopeful consultation with an oculist she writes:

Is it not strange, that when the most terrible trouble is a
little better, what looked light in comparison with want of
sight comes back as heavily as ever? How I wish I could be
more thankful for the mercies I have and not be always longing
for the unattainable.

Everyone who has lived through a great crisis has probably shared the old nurse's surprise at finding that smaller

troubles, which for a while were reduced to nothingness, soon revive with our own return to ordinary life.

However [as she says] I will not go into reflections, but write of my young days. How all these things come back to me, a lone old woman who longs for, and yet is afraid of death. If I could only be sure, be sure! Is it possible there is no other state of being? Oh, God, it is too dreadful to think of.

Then she would turn to *Paradise Lost*, and how often have we not heard her repeat the lines:

> And, in the lowest deep, a lower deep
> Still threatening to devour me, opens wide,

finding, as Aristotle would have said, relief and even comfort in the "purgation" through poetry, of the passions of pity and terror.

I will end my account of Leaker with one of her memories of happier moods in which we can feel the magic of spring laying hold on the vivid imagination of the bright-eyed Devonshire girl:

One early spring day I heard my eldest brother tell my mother that he had seen a primrose. She said, "Do not tell Salome, for if she knows there will be no keeping her at home." But I had heard, and that was enough. Early next morning away I went, rambling all day from field to field, picking primroses. First a handful of the common yellow ones, then some coloured ones, and did ever a Queen prize jewels as I did those coloured flowers? But the joy in them only lasted a little while. I would next see some white ones, and then the coloured ones were thrown away, and I would set to work to gather the pale ones. Oh, how beautiful they looked! I can see them now, and almost feel the rapture I felt then. It makes me young again—almost. My dear mother used to say, "What do you do with all the flowers you pick? You never bring any home." I do not know what I did with them, but the joy of picking them was beyond expression. Have I ever felt such joy or happiness since?

CHAPTER IX

BOYHOOD: POETRY AND METRE

IF I am to be exact, this chapter should have the subtitle of "Poetry and Metre," for poetry, other people's and my own, and an impassioned study of the metrical art, were the essential things about my boyhood. Between the ages of twelve and eighteen, at which time I may be said to have become grown-up, Poetry was my life.

My schoolboy period was not passed by me at school, except a term and a half at an excellent private school— one which still flourishes—the MacLaren School at Summertown. Rather reluctantly, for he was horrified by the bullying and cruelty which went on during his own day at English schools, my father consented to my mother's desire that we should go to school. After he had taken many precautions, and had ascertained that there was no bullying at Summertown, my elder brother and I were despatched to the school in question.

I was quite happy, got on well with the schoolmasters and with Mrs. MacLaren, the clever Scotswoman who ran the school, and gave satisfaction in everything except learning. In this matter I developed an extraordinary power of resistance, partly due, no doubt, to my bad eyesight. I was pronounced, in reports, to be a boy who gave no trouble and who was always happy and contented, and appeared to have good brains, and yet who, somehow or other, was easily surpassed at work by boys with inferior mental capacity.

My schoolfellows, I believe, thought me odd; but I made friends easily, and kept them. Though I could be "managed" by anyone who wanted to get something out of me, I was never put upon or bullied, because if attempts were made to coerce me, I was, like the immortal Mr. Micawber, not disinclined for a scrap. I stood erect before my fellow-boy, and when he tried to bully me I punched his head. Mr. Micawber's comment is too moving not to be recorded. "I and my fellow-man no longer meet upon those glorious terms." I and my fellow-schoolboy did occasionally meet upon those glorious terms, greatly to my enjoyment.

It happened, however, that there was an outbreak of scarlet fever in the school, and my father became anxious, and removed us at once—somewhat, I think, to my regret, but probably for my good. It was ultimately decided that my brother and I, instead of returning to MacLaren's, should, as I have already mentioned, go to the house of a clergyman, Mr. Philpott, who was the vicar of a neighbouring village, Chewton Mendip. The Vicarage was close to Chewton Priory, the house of my mother's closest friend, Lady Waldegrave.

Though Mr. Philpott was not an educational expert, in the modern sense, he was a man of good parts, fond of the arts, and something of a man of the world. His wife was a woman of great nobility of character and also of considerable mental power. She combined the qualities of a self-sacrificing and devoted mother with a certain ironic, or even sardonic, touch. She was a daughter of Mr. Tattersall, the owner of Tattersall's sale-rooms, and at her father's house she had become acquainted in the latter part of the 'fifties and the early 'sixties with all the great sporting characters of that epoch. Of these she used to tell us boys plenty of strange and curious anecdotes.

Chewton Mendip was only seven miles from Sutton, and so while there we were in constant touch with our own home life. We had also the amusement of seeing my father and mother when they went over, as they often did, to dine and sleep, or stay for longer visits, at the Priory. Lady Waldegrave was a great entertainer, and the house was thronged, not only with her country neighbours but with numbers of smart people from London—people such as Hayward, Bagehot, Lord Houghton, on the literary side, and men like Sir Walter Harcourt on the political. Again, picturesque figures in the European world, such as the Comte de Paris, the Duc d'Aumale, were often guests, and there were always members of the Foreign Embassies and Legations. For example, it was at the Priory that I first saw a real alive American, in the shape of General Schenk, the United States Minister to the Court of St. James. I remember well his teaching the whole house-party to play poker—a game till then quite unknown in England.

It was in the interval between leaving school and going to Chewton to the Philpotts that I began to read poetry for myself. Before, I had only loved it through my father's and Leaker's reading to us from Shakespeare, Scott, Byron, Spenser, Coleridge, Southey, and the old Ballads. When, however, I discovered that I could read poetry for myself, I tore the heart out of every book in the library that was in verse. Though my parents would have thought it an unforgivable crime to keep books from a child of theirs, for some reason or other I used to like in the summer-time to get up at about five or six o'clock (I was not a very good sleeper in those days, though I have been a perfect sleeper ever since), dress myself, run through the silent, sleeping house, and hide in the Great Parlour. There in absolute quietness and with a great sense of grandeur I got out my Byron or my Shelley, and raced though their pages in a delirium of delight. I can recall still, and most vividly, the sunlight streaming into the Great Parlour window, as I opened the great iron-sheathed shutters. Till breakfast-time I lolled on the big sofa, mouthing to myself explosive couplets from *Don Juan*. I am proud to say that, though I liked, as a boy should, the sentimentalism of the stanzas which begin

'Tis sweet to hear the watchdog's honest bark

I was equally delighted with

> Sweet is a legacy, and passing sweet
> The unexpected death of some old lady.

The ironic mixture of emotion and sarcasm fascinated me.

No sooner were Byron, Shelley, and Keats explored than I fell tooth and nail upon Swinburne, Morris, and Rossetti, and every other possible poet of my generation. I forget the exact date on which I became enamoured of the Elizabethan dramatists, but it was some time between fourteen and sixteen, and when I did catch the fever, it was severe.

As everyone ought to do under such circumstances, I thought, or pretended to think, that Marlowe, Beaumont, Fletcher, Ben Jonson, Webster, and Ford were the equals, if not indeed the superiors, of Shakespeare.

That was a view with which my father by no means agreed, but with his kindly wisdom he never attempted to condemn or dispute my opinions. He left me to find out the true Shakespeare for myself. This I ultimately did, and ended by being what, as a rule, is wrong in literature, but, I think, right in the case of Shakespeare, a complete idolator.

But though hand-in-hand with Charles Lamb I wandered through the Eden of the Elizabethan playwrights, I by no means neglected the Eighteenth Century. Quite early I became a wholehearted devotee of Pope and at once got the *Ode to the Unfortunate Lady* by heart. I dipped into *The Rape of the Lock,* gloried in the Moral Essays, especially in the *Characters of Women* and the epistle to Bathurst on the use of riches. Gray, who was a special favourite of Leaker's, soon became a favourite of mine, and I can still remember how I discovered the *Ode to Poesy* and how I went roaring its stanzas through the house. Such lines as

> Where each old poetic mountain
> Inspiration breathes around

or

> Hark, his hands the lyre explore,

were meat and drink to me. The *Elegy in a Country Churchyard* quickly seized my memory.

Nobody could avoid knowing when I had made a poetic discovery. I was as noisy as a hen that has laid an egg, or, to be more exact, I felt and behaved like a man who has come into a fortune. For me there were no coteries in Literature, or if there were, I belonged to them all. If I heard somebody say that there were good lines in the poems of some obscure author or other, I did not rest satisfied till I had got hold of his *Complete Works*. For example, when Crabbe was spoken of, I ran straight to *The Tales of the Hall* and thoroughly enjoyed myself. I even tasted *The Angel in the House* when I heard that Rossetti and Ruskin, and even Swinburne, admired

Coventry Patmore.   Though largely disappointed, I even
extracted honey from *The Angel*, though I confess it was
rather like a bee getting honey out of the artificial flowers in
the case in a parlour window.   Still, if I could only find
two lines that satisfied me, I thought myself amply
rewarded for the trouble of a search.   It is still a pleasure
to repeat

> And o'er them blew
> The authentic airs of Paradise.

I felt, I remember, about the epithet "authentic" what
Pinkerton in *The Wrecker* felt about Hebdomadary—
"You're a boss word."

I have no recollection of what made me take to writing
verse myself.   It was the old story.   "I lisped in numbers,
for the numbers came."   My first lisp—the first poem I
ever wrote—of all the odd things in the world was a
diminutive satire in the style of Pope.   Throughout my
boyhood I was an intense romanticist, and full of
Elizabethan fancies, imaginings, and even melancholies—I
use the word, of course, in the sense of Burton, or of
Shakespeare.   Yet all the time I read masses of Pope.
The occasion for my satire was one which must be
described as inevitable in the case of one eager to try his
hand at imitations of Pope.   By this I mean that the
satiric outburst was not provoked by any sort of anger.
I merely found in some of the circumstances of the life
around me good copy.   One of the things I liked particularly in Pope was the Epistle describing the Duke
of Chandos's house, the poem which begins—

> At Timon's villa let us pass a day,
> Where all cry out what sums are thrown away.

And there, straight in front of me, was the Priory, Lady
Waldegrave's grandiose country-house.   I heard plenty of
criticism of the house.   Its nucleus was a Carpenter's
Gothic villa, built originally by a Dean of Wells, bought
by Lord Waldegrave in the 'thirties or 'forties, and
then gradually turned by Frances, Lady Waldegrave,
into a big country-house, but a house too big for the piece
of ground in which it was set.   The skeleton of the
roadside villa was alleged by the local critics to show
through the swelling flesh that overlaid it.   Here was a
chance for the satirist, and so I sharpened my pencil and
began:

> Oh, stones and mortar by a Countess laid
> In sloping meadows by a turnpike glade,—
> A Gothic mansion where all arts unite
> To form a home for Baron, Earl or Knight.

The rest is lost!   Considering that I was only twelve, and
that Pope was little read by the youth of the 'seventies,
my couplets may fairly claim to be recognised as a literary
curiosity.

It is hardly necessary to say that the moment I found I
could write, and that metre and rhyme were no difficulty
to me, I went at it tooth and nail.   The more I wrote the
more interested did I become in metre, and it is not too
much to say that within a couple of years from my first
attempt, that is by the time I was about fourteen and a
half, I had experimented not only in most of the chief
measures, but in almost all the chief stanzas used by the
English poets.   To these, indeed, I added some of my own
devising.   In this way Prosody early became for me what
it has always been, a source of pleasure and delight in
itself.   I liked discovering metrical devices in the poets,

analysing them, *i.e.* discovering the way the trick worked, and in making experiments for myself. The result of this activity was that I had soon written enough verse to make a little pamphlet. With this pamphlet in my pocket and without consultation with anybody—the young of the poets are as shy as the young of the salmon—I trudged off to Wells, the county town, five miles distant across Mendip. How I discovered the name of the local printer I do not know, but I did discover it, and with beating heart approached his doors. After swearing him to secrecy, I asked for an estimate. He was a sympathetic man, and named a price which even then seemed to me low, and which was in reality so small that it would be positively unsafe to name to a master-printer nowadays.

As far as I remember, I did not receive a proof, but my delight at seeing my verses come back in print was beyond words. I remember, too, that I received a flattering note from my first publisher, prophesying success for future poetic ventures. But, though very happy, I believe, and am indeed sure, that I did not entertain any idea that I was going to become a poet. Possibly I thought the trade was a bad one for a second son who must support himself. It is more probable that I instinctively felt that although it was so great a source of joy to me, poetry was not my true vocation. Perhaps, also, I had already begun to note the voice of pessimism raised by the poets of the 'seventies, and to feel that they did not believe in themselves. I distinctly remember that Tennyson's "Is there no hope for modern rhyme?" was often on my lips and in my mind. His question distinctly expected the answer "No." It is little wonder, then, that I did not want to be a poet, and I never envisaged myself as a Byron, a Shelley, or a Keats.

The thing that strikes me most, on looking back at my little volume of verse, is its uncanny competence, not merely from the point of view of prosody, but of phraseology and what I may almost term scholarship. The poems did not show much inspiration, but they are what 18th-century critics would have called "well-turned." That would not be astonishing, in the case of a boy who had been well-educated and had acquired the art of expression. But I had not been well-educated. Owing to my ill-health my teachers had not been allowed to press me, and I was in a sense quite illiterate. I could hardly write, I could not spell at all, and nobody had ever pruned my budding fancies or shown me how to transfer thoughts to language, as one is shown, or ought to be shown, when one learns the Greek and Latin grammars and attacks Latin prose or Latin verse. My teaching in this direction had been more than sketchy. The only schoolroom matter in which I had made any advance was mathematics. Euclid and algebra fascinated me. I felt for them exactly what I felt for poetry. Though I did not know till many years afterwards that when Pythagoras discovered the forty-seventh proposition he sacrificed a yoke of oxen, not to Pallas Athene but to the Muses, I was instinctively exactly of his opinion. I can remember to this day how I worked out the proof of the forty-seventh proposition with Mr. Battersby, a young Cambridge man who was curate to Mr. Philpott and who took us on in mathematics. The realisation of the absolute, unalterable fact that in every right-angled triangle the square of the side subtending it is equal to the squares of the sides containing it, filled me with the kind of joy and glory that one feels on reading for the first time Keats's *Ode to a Nightingale* or one of the great passages in Shakespeare. I saw the genius of delight unfold his purple wing. I was transfigured and seemed to

9

tread upon air. For the first time in my life I realised the determination of an absolute relationship. A great window had been opened before my eyes. I saw all things new. My utter satisfaction could not be spoiled by feeling, as one does in the case of the earlier propositions of Euclid, that I had been proving what I knew already—something about which I could have made myself sure by the use of a foot-rule or a tape-measure. I had acquired knowledge, by an act of pure reasoning and not merely through the senses. I felt below my feet a rock-bed foundation which nothing could shake. Come what might, $a^2 = b^2 + c^2$. No one could ever deprive me of that priceless possession.

At that time I did not see or dream of the connection which no doubt does exist between mathematics and poetry—the connection which made the wise Dryden say that every poet ought to be something of a mathematician. Needless to say, my teachers did not see the connection. They were simply amazed that the same person should become as drunk with geometry and algebra as with poetry. Probably they consoled themselves by the thought that I was one of the people who could persuade themselves into believing anything!

It is of importance to record my precocity in the use of measured language, from the point of view of the growth of my mind. It will, I think, also amuse those of my readers who have written poetry for themselves in their youth (that, I suppose, is the case with most of us) to observe my hardihood in the way of metrical experiment. Here is the Invocation to the Muses which served as an Introduction to my little book. It will be noted that I have here tried my hand at my favourite measure, the dactylic. Towards anapæsts I have always felt a certain coldness, if not indeed repulsion.

To the Muses

(1874)

Come to my aid, Muses love-laden, lyrical:
Come to my aid, Comic, Tragic, Satirical.
   Come and breathe into me
Strains such as swept from Keats' heaven-strung lyre,
Strains such as Shelley's, which never can tire.
   Come then, and sing to me,
Sing me an ode such as Byron would sing,
Passionate, love-stirring, quick to begin.
   Why come you not to me?
Then must I write lyrics after vile rules
Made by some idiot, used by worse fools—
   Then the deuce take you all!

                      (*Ætat.* 14.)

I have to thank Mr. Edmund Gosse for inspiring this attempt. I hope he will forgive even if he does not forget. I had made a shopping expedition into Bristol, and went to tea or luncheon at Clifton Hill House where lived my mother's brother, John Addington Symonds. It happened that Mr. Gosse was a visitor at the house on the day in question, and that to my great delight we all talked poetry. I saw my chance, and proceeded to propound to these two authorities the following question: "Why is it that nobody has ever written an English poem in pure dactyls?" Greatly to my surprise and joy, Mr. Gosse informed me that it had been done. Thereupon he quoted the first four lines of what has ever since been a favourite poem of mine, Waller's lines to Hylas:

    Hylas, O Hylas! why sit we mute,
      Now that each bird saluteth the spring?
   Tie up the slackened strings of thy lute,
      Never may'st thou want matter to sing.

I hope I am not quoting incorrectly, but it is nearly fifty years since I saw the poem and at the moment I have not got a Waller handy.   With the exactitude of youth I verified Mr. Gosse's quotation the moment I got home. I took my poetry very seriously in those days.   I rushed to the Great Parlour, and though then quite indifferent to such a material thing as fine printing, I actually found the poem in one of Baskerville's exquisite productions.

The poem next to my dactylic Introduction was a dramatic lyric, partly blank verse and partly rhymed choruses, in the Swinburne manner.   In my poem the virtuous and "misunderstood" Byron is pursued and persecuted by the spirits of Evil, Hypocrisy, Fraud, and Tyranny, but is finally redeemed by the Spirit of Good, whose function it is to introduce the triumphant poet to Shelley.

There follows another dramatic lyric on Shelley's death, which takes the form of the death-bed confession to his priest of an old sailor at Spezzia.   The old man, according to a story published in 1875, was one of the crew of a small ship which ran down the boat containing Shelley and Williams, under the mistaken impression that the rich "milord Byron" was on board, with lots of money.   Here the style is more that of Browning than of Swinburne.   A few lines are quite sufficient to show the sort of progress I was making in blank verse.

> What noise of feet is that? Ah, 'tis the priest.
> Here, priest, I have a sin hangs heavy. See
> There by the fishing-nets that lovely youth,
> I killed him—oh, 'twas fifty years ago,
> Only, tonight he will not let me rest,
> But looks with loving eyes, making me fear.
> Oh, Father, 'twas not him I meant to kill,
> 'Twas the rich lord I coveted to rob,
> He with the bright wild eyes and haughty mien.

Imitation of Browning was by no means a passing mood with me. A year before I tackled my Shelley and Byron poems, I had written a piece of imitation Browningese which is not without its stock of amusement, considering what was to be the fate of the versifier.

JEAN DUVAL'S LAST WORDS

Jean Duval has presented himself at a Paris newspaper office, asking for employment; this being refused him he makes a last request, offering to sell his muse, which he had hoped to keep unhired. This also being refused, his want of bread overcomes him, and he curses the Editor and dies.

> A plague on all gold, say I,
> I who must win it, or die.
> Here goes, I'll sell my Muse.
> You may buy her for twenty sous.
> No, I'll write by the ream,
> Only give me your theme,
> And a sou more for a light
> To put in my garret at night.
> Garret!—ah, I was forgetting,
> My present's a very cheap letting
> Under the prison wall,
> Just where it grows so tall.
> Why don't I steal, you say?
> Oh, I wasn't brought up that way.
> Will you give me the twenty sous?
> Come, it isn't much to lose.
> You won't? Then I die. Ah, well,
> God will find you a lodging in hell.

(*Ætat.* 14.)

The melancholy which belongs to the young poet, a melancholy which had to be feigned in my case, was reserved for sonnets of a somewhat antinomian type. Here is an example.

SONNET

(1875)

O why so cruel, ye that have left behind
  Life's fears, and from draped death have drawn the veil?
  Oh, why so cruel? Does life or death avail?
Why tell us not?—why leave us here so blind,
To tread this earth, not sure that we may find
  Even an end beyond this worldly pale
  Of petty hates and loves so weak and frail?
O why not speak?—is it so great a thing
  To cross death's stream and whisper in the ear
  Of us weak mortals some faint hope or cheer?
Or tell us, dead ones, if the hopes that spring
  From joyous hours when all seems bright and clear
Have any truth. O speak, ye dead, and say
If that in hope of dying, live we may.

                    (*Ætat.* 15.)

A metrical essay of which I am more proud is a poem
written at the end of 1874, or possibly at the beginning of
1875. With a daring which now seems to me incredible I
undertook to write in that most difficult of measures, the
Spenserian stanza. The matter of the composition is by no
means memorable, but I think I have a right to congratu-
late myself upon the fact that I was able at that age to
manage the triple rhymes and the twelve-syllable line at
the end of each stanza without coming a complete cropper.
I could not do it now, even if my life depended on it.

To the Powers of Song

I

  Spirit, whose harmony doth fill the mind,
  Deign now to hear the wailing of a song

That lifts to thee its voice, and strives to find
Aught that may raise it from the servile throng
Who seek on earth but living to prolong.
For them no goddess, no fair poets reign,
They hear no singing, as the earth along
They move to their dull tasks; they live, they wane,
They die, and dying, not a thought of thee retain.

II

Thou art the Muse of whom the Grecian knew,
The power that reigneth in each loving heart;
From thee the sages their great teachings drew.
Thou mak'st life tuneful by the poet's art.
Without thy aid the love-god's fiery dart
Wakes but a savage and a blind desire,
Where nought of beauty e'er can claim a part.
Without thee, all to which frail men aspire
Has nothing good, is but of this poor earth, no higher.

III

Unhappy they who wander without light,
And know thee not, thou goddess of sweet life;
Cursed are they all that live not in thy sight,
Cursed by themselves they cannot drown the strife
In thee, of passion, of the ills so rife
On earth; they have no star, no hope, no love,
To guide them in the stormy ways of life;
They are but as the beasts who slowly move
On the world's face, nor care to look for light above.

IV

I am not as these men; I look for light,
But none appears, no rays for me are flung.
I would not be with those that sit in night;
I fain would be that glorious host among,
That band of poets who have greatly sung.

But woe, alas, I cannot, I no power
Of singing have, all my tired heart is wrung
To think I might have known a happier hour,
And sung myself, not let my aching spirit cower.

(*Ætat.* 14.)

A bad poem, though interesting from the number of poets mentioned, is a satiric effort entitled *The Examination*. It supposes that all the living poets have been summoned by Apollo to undergo a competitive examination. The bards, summoned by postcards, which had just then been introduced, repair to Parnassus and are shown to the Hall. Rossetti and Morris, however, make a fuss because the paper is not to their taste. Walt Whitman, already a great favourite of mine, "though spurning a jingle," is hailed as "the singer of songs for all time." Proteus (Wilfrid Blount) is mentioned, for my cult for him was already growing. Among other poets who appear, but who have since died to fame, are Lord Lytton, Lord Southesk, Lord Lorne, Mrs. Singleton, and Martin Tupper. In the end Apollo becomes "fed up" with his versifiers, and dismisses them all with the intimation that any who have passed will receive printed cards. The curtain is rung down with the gloomy couplet:

Six months have elapsed, but no poet or bard,
So far as I know, has yet got a card

Another set of verses, written between the ages of fourteen and fifteen, which are worth recalling from the point of view of metre include some English hexameters. I was inspired to write them by an intense admiration of Clough's *Amours de Voyage*, an admiration which grows greater, not lesser, with years.

As I have started upon the subject of verse, I think I

had better pursue the course of the stream until, as the old geographers used to say about the Rhine, its waters were lost in the sands, in my case not of Holland but of Prose.

From 1877 to the time when I actually entered Balliol, at eighteen and a half, I went on writing verse, and was fortunate enough to get one or two pieces published. Besides two sonnets which were accepted by *The Spectator* —sonnets whose only *raison d'être* was a certain competence of expression—was a poem entitled *Love's Arrows*, which was accepted, to my great delight, by Sir George Grove, then the Editor of *Macmillan's Magazine*, a periodical given up to *belles-lettres*. The poem may be best described as in the Burne Jones manner. I shall not, however, quote any part of it, except the prose introduction, which I still regard with a certain enthusiasm as a successful fake. It ran as follows:

At a league's distance from the town of Ponteille in Provence and hard by the shrine of Our Lady of Marten, there is in the midst of verdant meadows a little pool, overshadowed on all sides by branching oak-trees, and surrounded at the water's edge by a green sward so fruitful that in spring it seemeth, for the abundance of white lilies, as covered with half-melted snow. Unto this fair place a damsel from out a near village once came to gather white flowers for the decking of Our Lady's chapel; and while so doing saw lying in the grass a naked boy; in his hair were tangled blue waterflowers, and at his side lay a bow and marvellously wrought quivers of two arrows, one tipped at the point with gold, the other with lead. These the damsel, taking up the quiver, drew out; but as she did so the gold arrow did prick her finger, and so sorely that, starting at the pain, she let fall the leaden one upon the sleeping boy. He at the touch of that arrow sprang up, and crying against her with much loathing, fled over the meadows. She followed him to overtake him, but could not, albeit she strove greatly;

and soon, wearied with her running, fell upon the grass in a swoon. Here had she lain, had not a goatherd of those parts found her and brought her to the village. Thus was much woe wrought unto the damsel, for after this she never again knew any joy, nor delighted in aught, save only it were to sit waiting and watching among the lilies by the pool. By these things it seemeth that the boy was not mortal, as she supposed, but rather the Demon or Spirit of Love, whom John of Dreux for his two arrows holdeth to be that same Eros of Greece.— MSS. *Mus. Aix. B. 754.*

Needless to say, it was a pure invention and not a copy, or travesty of an old model. I was egregiously proud of the scription at the end which, if I remember rightly, my father helped me to concoct. A certain interest has always attached in my mind to this piece of prose. To read it one would imagine that the author had closely studied the translations of Morris and other renderers of the French romances, but as far as I know I had not read any of them. The sole inspiration of my forgery were a few short references in Rossetti and Swinburne. This shows that in the case of literary forgeries one need not be surprised by verisimilitudes, and that it is never safe to say that a literary forger could not have done this or that. If he happens to have a certain flair for language and the tricks of the literary trade, he can do a wonderful amount of forgery upon a very small stock of knowledge. After all, George Byron forged Sonnets by Keats which took in Lord Houghton—a very good judge in the case of Keats.

CHAPTER X

OXFORD

My introduction to Oxford and its life was somewhat chaotic. Out of that chaos, as I shall show later, I achieved both good and evil. But I must first explain how the chaos arose. By the time I had reached seventeen it had become obvious to my father—or, rather, to the people at the University, who so advised him—that if I was to be able to matriculate at Balliol I must set my intellectual house in order and learn something of the things upon which alone one could matriculate. The irony of accident had designed my mental equipment to be of a kind perfectly useless for the purposes of the preliminary Oxford examinations. It was no doubt true that I knew enough poetry and general literature to confound half the Dons in Balliol. I also knew enough mathematics, as, to my astonishment, a mathematical tutor at Oxford in an unguarded hour confessed to me, to enable me to take a First in Mathematical Mods. But knowledge of literature, a power of writing, a not inconsiderable reading in modern history, and the aforesaid mathematics were no use whatever for the purposes of matriculation.

In those days Latin and Greek Grammar, Latin Prose and "Latin and Greek Unseen," and certain specially-prepared Greek and Latin Books were essentials. It is true that these alone would not have matriculated me. In addition to them the writing of a good essay and of a good general paper were required, to obtain success.   Still, the *sine qua non* was what the representative of the old Oxford in Matthew Arnold's *Friendship's Garland* calls "the good old fortifying classical curriculum."   I could by no possibility have reached the heights of "Hittal," who, it will be remembered, wrote "some longs and shorts about the Caledonian boar which were not bad."   Though English verses came so easily, Latin verses did not come at all.

After many family councils it was decided that I should accept the invitation of my uncle and aunt (Professor T. H. Green and his wife) and take up my residence with them in their house in St. Giles's.   There I read for Responsions.   If it had not been for some extraordinary power of resistance in the matter of Latin and Greek I ought to have found the task easy, for, as I have said elsewhere, I had two of the most accomplished scholars in the University to teach me.   One was Mr. Henry Nettleship, soon to become Regius Professor of Latin.   The other was a young Balliol man who had just won a Magdalen Fellowship and who was destined to become President of that famous college over which he still presides so worthily and so wisely.   But, alas! I was Greek and Latin proof, and all I really gained from my learned teachers was two very close and intimate friends, and the privilege of meeting at the house of the one and in the rooms in the College of the other, a good many of the abler Dons, young and old, and getting on good terms with them.   In the same way, I used to see at my uncle's house the best of Oxford company, and also a certain number of Cambridge men.

It must not be supposed, however, that I was not learning anything.   I was getting a priceless store of knowledge,

J. St. Loe Strachey. Ætat. 16.
(From a photograph done at Cannes, about 1876.)

nay, wisdom from my uncle, who was kindness itself and
who was, I am sure, fond of me. He was almost as ready
to talk and to answer questions as my father. In him, too,
I saw the working of a great and good man and of a noble
character.

Though in a different, but equally true, way, Green was
as religious a man as my father. If my father felt the
personal relationship between God and His children more
than Green did, that was chiefly because Green's mind
could take nothing which had not the sanction of reason, or,
to be more accurate, of an intuition guarded so closely by
Reason that very little of the mystic element in Faith
remained unchallenged. No one could live with Green
without loving him and feeling reverence for his deep
sincerity and his instinct for the good.

Though foolish people talked of him as a heretic, or even
an infidel, he was in truth one of the most devout of men.
That noble passage in Renan's play fits him exactly. The
Almighty, conversing as in Job with one of His Heavenly
Ministers as to this Planet's people, says:

Apprends, enfant fidèle, ma tendresse pour ceux qui doutent
ou qui nient. Ces doutes, ces négations sont fondés en raison;
ils viennent de mon obstination à me cacher. Ceux qui me
nient entrent dans mes vues. Ils nient l'image grotesque ou
abominable que l'on a mise en ma place. Dans ce monde
d'idolâtres et d'hypocrites, seuls, ils me respectent réellement.

Understand, faithful child, my tenderness for those who
doubt and who deny. Those doubts, those denials are founded
on reason; they come from my obstinate resolve to hide myself.
Those who deny me enter into my plans. They deny the
grotesque or abominable image which men have set up in my
place. In a world of idolators and hypocrites, they alone really
respect me.

But what I gained from my uncle and his friends, from Nettleship and from Warren, and also from the people I used to meet at the house of my great-uncle, Dr. Frederick Symonds, was not all that I achieved in the year before I matriculated. The air of Oxford did not repress but greatly stimulated my love of verse and *belles-lettres*, and I careered over the green pastures of our poetry like the colt let loose that I was. Elizabethan plays were at the moment my pet reading, and without knowing it I emulated Charles James Fox, who is said while at Oxford to have read a play a day—no doubt out of the Doddesley collection. I even went to the Bodleian in search of the Elizabethans, and remember to this day my delight in handling the big and little books mentioned by Lamb in his Dramatic Selections. I recall how I turned over the leaves of such enchanting works as Inigo Jones's designs for *The Tempest* played as a Masque. Though I do not happen to have seen it since, and so speak with a forty years' interval, the pen-and-ink drawing of Ariel, portrayed exactly like a Cinquecento angel, is fixed in my mind. It has all the graciousness and gentleness of Bellini and all the robust beauty of Veronese or Palma Vecchio. To tell the truth, I was in the mood of the lady of the Island over which Prospero waved his wand. I could say with Miranda, "O brave new world, that has such men and women in it!" Indeed, though I still stood outside the gates, as it were, I had already felt the subtle intoxication of Oxford.

The result of all this was that when I at last got through Responsions and entered Balliol, with the understanding that directly I got through Pass Mods. I was to abandon the Classics and read for the History School, I knew, as it were, too much and too little. This knowledge of some things and want of knowledge of others produced a result which was highly distasteful to the normal academic mind. In a word, I was in the position of Gibbon when he went up to Magdalen. His ignorance would have astonished a schoolboy and his learning a professor, and no doubt he seemed to the greater part of the High Table an odious and forward young man.

All the same, and though no one then believed it, I was extraordinarily innocent, if not as to my ignorance, as to my learning. When I met a Don who, I was told, was "unsurpassed" in the Greek or Latin classics and could probably appreciate them as well as if he had been a Greek or Roman of the best period, I was tremendously excited. I felt sure that being so highly endowed in this direction he could not possibly have neglected English literature, and must know all about that also, and so would be of the greatest help to me. I was inclined, therefore, to rush at these scholars with the perfect assurance that I could get something from them. When, however, they either evaded my questionings or told me curtly that they had never heard of the people about whom I asked, I felt sure that this was only said to get rid of me. For some reason unknown to me I had managed, I felt, to offend them as Alice offended the creatures in Wonderland.

I can recall a specific example. I found a certain learned scholar who had never even heard of, and took no interest in, Marlowe's *Dido and Æneas*, and could not be drawn into expressing an opinion as to whether the translations were good or bad. In other cases I found that even the names of men like Burton of the *Anatomy of Melancholy* produced no reaction. Yet, wretched Latinist as I was, I had been thunderstruck with delight when, rummaging the Cathedral after a Sunday service, where, by the way, I heard Pusey preach his last sermon, I came upon Burton's tomb, and read for the first time the immortal epitaph which begins:

Paucis notus, paucioribus ignotus,

I can see now that what I thought was the pretended ignorance of the Dons, and their fastidious unwillingness to talk to an uneducated schoolboy, as I believed myself to be, was nothing of the kind. I have not the slightest doubt now that they regarded me as a cheeky young ass who was trying to show off in regard to things of which he was totally ignorant and of which, needless to say, they were ignorant too, for, alas! the minute study of the Classics does not appear to necessitate a general knowledge of literature. A scholar fully *en rapport* with Aristophanes or Juvenal and Martial may never have read Ben Jonson's *Alchemist*, or Beaumont and Fletcher's *Knight of the Burning Pestle;* or studied Charles Churchill, or Green on *The Spleen.*

There was a mental attitude which the typical Don, full of the public-school spirit and its dislikes, could never forgive. Except for the few intimate friends who were devoted to me—Nettleship and Warren, T. H. Green and, later, curiously enough, Mr. A. L. Smith, the present Master of Balliol,—I was, I expect, universally regarded as the most intolerable undergraduate they had ever beheld.

Jowett, the Master of Balliol, evidently felt the Stracheyphobia very strongly, or perhaps I should say felt it his duty to express it very strongly. He had not, I think, a great natural instinct in regard to the characters of young men, but he was naturally anxious to improve those with whom he came in contact. His method was to apply two or three fixed rules. One of these was—and a good one in suitable cases—that if you got hold of a boy who thought too much of himself, the best thing was to stamp upon him upon every possible occasion, and so help him to reform his ways. No doubt it saved a great deal of trouble to give this rule a universal application, and it was often successful. Every now and then, however, the generalisation failed.

Fortunately for me, I was not only of a contented nature, but so happy—and also so happy-go-lucky—that I was not the very least worried by the opinion of my educational superiors. I should have been genuinely pleased to have pleased them, but as I had clearly failed in that, I did not trouble about it further. I could always console myself with the thought that schoolmasters and dons were notoriously narrow-minded people, and that when one got out into the big world their opinions would matter very little.

In a word, I accepted the situation with a cheerful and genuine acquiescence. The Master did not like me, but then, why should he? I was obviously not a model undergraduate. This acquiescence was soon buttressed by a reasoned if somewhat unfair estimate of the Master's character. I very soon began to hear plenty of Oxford gossip about him and his failings—chief among them being his supposed favouritism. He was very generally called a snob, which no doubt, in a superficial sense, he was, and I soon got my nose well in the air in regard to his worship of dukes and marquesses and even of the offscourings of Debrett and his willingness to give special privileges to their errant progeny. I had, however, to give the Master credit for the way in which he would often shower his partial favours on some boy who had climbed the ladder of learning and risen from a Board School to become a Scholar or Exhibitioner of Balliol. My general feeling,

10

however, was that of the idealist who despises the school-master or the scholar who becomes worldly in his old age, and even goes so far as to follow the shameless maxim, "*Dine with the Tories and vote with the Whigs*."

Of course I know now that Jowett's apparent worldli-ness and snobbishness were calculated. He was very anxious to get good educative influences exerted over the men who were to rule the country. This, translated into action, meant getting the big men of the day, the *Optimates* of British politics and commerce, to send their sons to Balliol. He also, no doubt, liked smart society for itself. Men of the world, especially when they were politicians or persons of distinction, greatly interested the translator of Plato, Thucydides, and Aristotle. Though he was not the kind of man to inflate himself with any idea that he was "*Socrates redivivus*," I have no doubt that he found the worldlywise malice of Lord Westbury as piquant as the Greek philosopher did the talk of Alcibiades.

Young men, however, do not make excuses, and, as I have said, I was inclined to be much scandalised, and to feel complacently self-righteous over stories of the Master's "love of a lord."

The feeling which I engendered in the minds of the rest of the Balliol Dons differed very little from that enter-tained by the Master. I can say truthfully that I never received a word of encouragement, of kindly direction, or of sympathy of any sort or kind from them in regard to my work or anything else. The only exception was Mr. A. L. Smith. The reason, I now feel sure, was that they believed that to take notice of me would have only made me more uppish. I daresay they imagined I should have been rude or surly, or have attempted to snub them. Still, the fact is something of a record, and so worthy of note.

If I had been at a public school and had learned there to

understand the ways of teachers and masters, as the public-school boy learns to understand them, as an old fox learns to understand the cry of the hounds and of the huntsmen, I should have had no difficulty whatever in getting on good terms with the College. As it was, I misunderstood them quite as much as they misunderstood me. Each of us was unable to handle the other. Yet I think, on a balance of accounts, I had a little more excuse on my side than the Dons had. I was very young, very immature, and with-out any knowledge or experience of institutional social life. They, on the other hand, must have had previous know-ledge of the exceptional boy who had not been at a public school. Therefore they should quite easily have been able to adjust their minds to my case. They should not have allowed themselves to assume that the "uppishness" was due to want of that humility which they rightly ex-pected in their pupils.

Curiously enough, my undergraduate contemporaries at Balliol were far more successful in their efforts at under-standing somebody who had not been at a public school. They appeared to have no prejudices against the home-bred boy. I was never made in the least to feel that there was any bar or barrier between me and my fellow-freshmen. As proof of this, I may point to the fact that every one of my intimate friends at Balliol were public-school boys. I have no doubt I was considered odd by most of my con-temporaries, but this oddness, and also my inability to play football or cricket, never seemed to create, as far as I could see, any prejudice. Indeed, I think that my friends were quite discerning enough and quite free enough from con-vention to be amused and interested by a companion who was not built up in accordance with the sealed pattern.

In spite of the Dons, about whom I troubled singularly little, in spite of my being ploughed twice for Mods., sent

down from my college, made to become an unattached
student, and only reinstated at Balliol after I had got
through Mods. and was guaranteed to be going to do
well in the History Schools, I can say with absolute truth
that I was never anything but supremely happy at Oxford
—I might almost say deliriously happy.

I may interpolate here that when I went back to Balliol
after my year as an unattached student, the only thing
that the Master said, on readmitting me, was something of
this kind: "The College is only taking you back, Mr.
Strachey, because your history tutor says that you are
likely to get a First." I was appropriately shocked at
this, for I had become well aware that Jowett was looked
upon by a good many people in the University as simply
a hunter for Firsts, a Head who did not care much what
kind of people he had in his College, or how their minds
were developed in the highest sense, so long as they came
out well in the Schools List. He was alleged, that is, to
take a tradesman's view of learning. These kinds of gibe
I naturally found soothing, for I was able to imagine
myself as a scholar, though not as a winner of a First.
Incidentally, also, though I did not acknowledge it to
myself, I think I was a little hurt by the Master's want of
what I might call humanity, or at any rate courtesy in his
treatment of the shorn lamb of Moderations. However, I
have not the least doubt that he thought he was stimulating me for my good. This, indeed, was his constant
mood. I remember at Collections his telling me that I
should never do anything except, possibly, be able to write
light trifles for the magazines. On another occasion he
asked me what I was going to do in life. I told him that I
wanted to go to the Bar, which was then my intention.
To this he replied oracularly, "I should have thought you
would have done better in diplomacy."

That tickled me. It was clearly a back-hander over an ingenious attempt which I had made a day or two before to prove how much better it would be for me to get off three days before Collections and so obtain another whole week in the bosom of my family at Cannes! No doubt Jowett's system of controlling the recalcitrant portions of the College through sarcasm was well meant and occasionally fairly successful. Taking it as a whole, however, I felt then, as I feel now, that sarcasm is the one weapon which it is never right or useful to use in the case of persons who are in the dependent position when compared with the wielder of the sarcastic rapier;—persons *in statu pupillari*, persons much younger than oneself, persons in one's employment, or, finally, members of one's own family. Sarcasm should be reserved for one's equals, or, still better, for one's superiors. The man who is treated with sarcasm, if he cannot answer back either because it is true, or he is stupid, or he is afraid to counter-attack a superior, is filled, and naturally filled, with a sense of burning indignation. He feels he has had a cruel wrong done to him and is in no mood to be converted to better courses. That to which his mind reacts at once is some form of vengeance, some way of getting even with his tormentor. The words that burn or rankle or corrode are not the words to stimulate. No doubt Socrates said that he was the gadfly of the State and stung that noble animal into action, but what may be good for a sluggish old coach-horse is not necessarily good for a thoroughbred colt with a thin skin.

To return to my general feeling about Oxford while I lived there. Instinctively I seem to have realised what I came to see so clearly in my post-Oxford days, that the great thing that one gets at a University is what Bagehot called the "impact of young mind upon young mind." Though there must be examinations and lectures, and discipline and hard reading, nothing of all this matters a jot in comparison with the association of youth with youth and the communion of quick and eager spirits. I have lived my life with clever people, men and women who thought themselves masters of dialectic, but I can say truthfully that I have never heard such good talk as in my own rooms and in the rooms of my contemporaries at Oxford. There, and there only, have I seen practised what Dr. Johnson believed to be an essential to good talk, the ability to stretch one's legs and have one's talk out. It may be remembered that Dr. Johnson, in praising John Wesley as a talker, sadly admitted that his great qualities in this respect were all marred because Wesley was always in a hurry, always had some pressing business in hand which cut him short when at his best.

The happy undergraduate never has to catch a train, never has an editor or a printer waiting for him, never has an appointment which he cannot cut, never, in effect, has money to make. He comes, indeed, nearer than anybody else on earth to the Hellenic ideal of the good citizen, of the free man in a free state. If he wants to talk all through the night with his friends, he talks. The idea of his sparing himself in order that he may be fresh next morning for Mr. Jones's lecture never enters his head for a moment. Rightly, he considers that to talk at large with a couple of friends is the most important thing in the world. In my day we would talk about anything, from the Greek feeling about landscape to the principles the Romans would have taken as the basis of actuarial tables, if they had had them. We unsphered Plato, we speculated as to what Euripides would have thought of Henry James, or whether Sophocles would have enjoyed Miss ———'s acting, and felt that it was of vital import to decide these matters. But I must stop, for I see I am beginning to make most dangerous admissions. If I go on, indeed, I am likely enough to become as much disliked by the readers of the present day as I was by the Oxford Dons of forty years ago.

I could fill this book with stories of my life at Oxford, of its enchantment, of my friendships, of my walks and rides and of my expeditions up the river; for, not being a professional athlete, I had time to enjoy myself. It would be a delight also to recall my associations, the first in my life, with young men who were writing verses, like myself, such men as Beeching, Mackail, Spring Rice (our Ambassador during the War, at Washington), Rennell Rodd, Nicolls, and a dozen others. But space forbids. I can only quote Shenstone's delightful verses on Oxford, in his *Ode to Memory*, verses which I have quoted a hundred times:

> And sketch with care the Muses' bow'r,
>   Where Isis rolls her silver tide,
> Nor yet omit one reed or flow'r
>   That shines on Cherwell's verdant side,
> If so thou may'st those hours prolong
> When polish'd Lycon join'd my song.
>
> The song it 'vails not to recite—
>   But, sure, to soothe our youthful dreams,
> Those banks and streams appear'd more bright
>   Than other banks, than other streams;
> Or, by thy softening pencil shown,
> Assume they beauties not their own?
>
> And paint that sweetly vacant scene
>   When, all beneath the poplar bough,
> My spirits light, my soul serene,
>   I breathed in verse one cordial vow
> That nothing should my soul inspire
> But friendship warm and love entire.

I do not mean to inflict upon my readers the tiresome record of my failure to pass Moderations, or the description of how I did eventually get through by a process which came very near to learning by heart English translations of Xenophon's *Memorabilia*, a portion of Livy's History, and Horace's Epistles.   To do so would be both long and tedious.   The circumstances have, however, a certain interest considered from one point of view, and that is the use and misuse of the classics for educational purposes.

CHAPTER XI

A CLASSICAL EDUCATION

THOUGH I made such a hash of classical studies and was apparently so impermeable to Latin and Greek literature, I am not one of those people who are prepared to damn the Greek and Latin classics, either with faint praise or with a strenuous invective. I am not prepared to say with Cobden that a single copy of *The Times* is worth the whole of Thucydides, or to ask, as did the late Mr. Carnegie, what use Homer was either in regard to wisdom or human progress. I believe that in all the things of the soul and the mind the stimulus of the Greek spirit is of the utmost value. The Romans, no doubt, excelled the Greeks on the practical side of law—though not in the pure jurisprudential spirit. Again, the Hebrews did incomparable service to mankind in their handling of such vital matters as the family, the place of women and children in the State, and the position of the slave. On the moral issues, in fact, the Jewish prophet is far the safer teacher:

> As men divinely taught, and better teaching
> The solid rules of Civil Government
> In their majestic, unaffected style
> Than all the oratory of Greece and Rome.
> In them is plainest taught, and easiest learnt,
> What makes a Nation happy, and keeps it so,
> What ruins Kingdoms, and lays Cities flat.

In what concerns the intellectual rather than the moral side of life the Greek is, of course, supreme. It is hardly too much to say that intellectual progress has only pursued a steady and consistent course when men's minds have been in touch with the Greek. The sense of beauty in all the arts, intellectual and figurative, was the prerogative of the Hellenic communities, or, rather, of Athens, for only in Athens was perfection in the arts achieved. The Greek was the best, as he was the first, director and teacher. It is true that the artists of Florence, Umbria, Lombardy, and Venice equalled the Greeks in some of the arts and excelled them absolutely in the new art of painting. In Greece, painting, though it had a beauty of its own, was hardly more than exquisitely-coloured sculpture in the lowest conceivable relief. In painting the Italians were guided by a wholly different series of visual conceptions. Their understanding and use of atmosphere and mass was something of which the Greeks had formed no conception. Apart, however, from painting, the Greeks were the first to light and feed the sacred flame of Beauty.

There is a charming story of the way in which Renan emphasised this fact. Some thirty-five years ago—I well remember the period—it was the fashion, just as, in a sense, it is the fashion now, to say that the Egyptians were the real masters of sculpture, wall-painting, and metal work, that the Greeks learnt from them, and in the fine arts originated nothing. At that time it happened that the Keeper of the Egyptian antiquities at the Louvre was running this theory for all it was worth. One day he showed Renan and a party of distinguished visitors a special exhibition illustrating his contention. Notable examples of Egyptian art were produced, as proving how perfectly and finally the Egyptians treated the human figure in the round, in bas-relief, in the bronze statue, in the wooden

statue, and even in earthenware.   And to all the treasures
displayed was added the chorus of the Professor: *"And
so, you see, the Greeks invented nothing."*   Renan assented.
"Nothing.   Nothing," he echoed, but added as an after-
thought: *"Seulement le Beau."*

I have sometimes thought that these words, *"Seulement
le Beau,"* might do as the commemorative epitaph of the
Greek race. But of course the Greek was a great deal more
than the exponent of the beautiful.   I only tell this story
to make it quite clear how deep is my reverence and
admiration for the Greeks, and how strongly I feel that
their philosophers and their poets are lively oracles from
which the human spirit may still draw perennial draughts
of inspiration.

But if this is so, it will be asked, "How comes it that,
with these views, you proclaim yourself an opponent to
compulsory Greek and compulsory Latin in schools and
universities?"   My answer is, it is just because I am such
an intense believer in the quickening power of the Greek
mind and in the immense advantages secured by getting
into touch with the Greek spirit that I desire the abolition
of compulsory Greek.   No civilised man should ever be
out of touch with it at first hand.   But this means, translated into action, no compulsory Greek grammar, no
compulsory drudgery in acquiring the things which do not
really belong to the Greeks but to the vapid pedants of
vanished ages.   I passionately desire that as many people
as possible should enjoy Hellenic culture. I want to clear
away the smoky mist of grammatical ineptitude which
keeps men from the great books and great minds of an-
tiquity and prevents the soul of the Greek and the soul of
the Englishman—natural allies, for some strange reason
—from flowing together.

It is appropriate that I should testify.   Owing to having

been forced to try to learn the Greek Grammar instead of reading the books written by the Greeks in a language which I could understand, I very nearly made an intellectual shipwreck. Indeed, it was only by a series of lucky accidents that I escaped complete ignorance of the Greek spirit, though retaining a certain knowledge of the grammar.

It was only after I had miserably squirmed my way through Mods., as a man may squirm through some hole in a prison wall, that I had the slightest idea of what was meant by the Greek spirit.

I closed my grammar, with all the miserable and complicated stuff about $\tau\acute{v}\pi\tau\omega$ and its aorists, the enclitic and the double-damned Digamma, to open my Jowett's Plato, my Dakyns' Xenophon, and, later, Gilbert Murray's Dramatists and Mackail's Anthology. It is true that in the squirming process I have described I had to read a portion of the *Anabasis* and of the *Odyssey* and *Memorabilia*, as well as books of Cæsar, Livy, Horace, and Virgil.

In the case of these books I acquired nothing but a distaste so deep that it has only just worn off. Only after an interval of forty years could I bear to read these kill-joys in translation. No doubt some of the fault was mine. Possibly I was born with an inability to learn languages. But if that is so it is a misfortune, not a crime for which one should be put on the rack!

By the time I realised fully the glory of Greek letters, I was a very busy man, and bitter indeed was the thought that the well-meaning persons who maintain our university system had actually been keeping me all those years from the divine wells of grace and beauty. But for them, how many more years of enjoyment might I have drawn from the Socratic *Dialogues*, from the *Apology*, and from the *Republic!* Think of it! It was not till four years ago that I read Thucydides and had my soul shaken by the supreme wickedness, the intellectual devilry of the Melian controversy. How I thrilled at the awful picture of the supreme tragedy at Syracuse! How I saw! How I perished with the Greek warriors standing to arms on the shore, and watching in their swaying agony the Athenian ships sink one by one, without being able to lift a hand, or cast a long or short spear to help them! Yet the watchers knew that the awful spectacle on which they gazed meant death, or a slavery worse than death, for every one of them!

Almost worse to me than the denial of Plato, the dramatists Thucydides and Homer, was the refusal to allow me to walk or hunt with Xenophon, and to saunter through his kitchen or his grounds. And all because I could not show the requisite grammatical ticket. Could anything be more fascinating than the tale of Xenophon's prim yet most lovable young wife, or the glorious picture of the boy and girl lovers with which Xenophon closes his *Symposium?*

My sense of a deprivation unnecessary and yet deliberate was as great in regard to Latin literature. It was only in 1919, owing to what I had almost called a fortunate illness, that I took to reading Cicero's Letters and came under an enchantment greater than that cast even by Walpole, Madame de Sévigné, or Madame du Deffand.

For forty years I was kept in ignorance of a book which painted the great world of Rome with a touch more intimate than even that of St. Simon. Cicero in his Letters makes the most dramatic moment in Roman history, the end of the Oligarchic Republic, live before one. Even Macaulay's account of the Revolution of 1688 seems tame when called in comparison.

I know that by the time some Greek or Latin scholar has got as far as this he will ask with a smile,

Why is this self-dubbed ignoramus making all this pother about being deprived of the classics? Surely he cannot have failed to realise that it is impossible to understand and appreciate the classics properly without having learnt Latin and Greek? But you cannot learn Latin and Greek without learning the grammar. He not only on his own showing has no grievance, but is giving support to those who desire that the classics should remain the centrepiece of our educational system.

For all such objections I have one, and I think a final, argument. When people ask me how I propose to enjoy Plato without knowing Greek, I ask them to tell me, in return, how they manage to enjoy reading one of the greatest poets in the world, Isaiah, without knowing Hebrew. How have they found consolation in the Psalms; how have they absorbed the worldly wisdom of Proverbs and Ecclesiastes; how have they read the lyric choruses of the Song of Solomon; how have they followed the majestic drama of the Book of Job? *They read them in translations*. That is the way in which they have filled their minds with the noble deeds and thoughts of the Hebrew history and Hebrew literature. That is the answer, the true answer, and the only answer.

A good, practical, commonsense proof of what I am saying is to be found in the fact that the ordinary man and also the man of brains who has gone through the good old fortifying classical curriculum, to quote Matthew Arnold once more, and who *theoretically* can read the great Greek and Latin authors in their own languages, and without translations, hardly reads them at all. Those who know that it is a translation or nothing will be found to be far

closer and more constant readers of Plato and Thucydides.
Certainly that is my case.   To this day I find myself reading the Greek and Latin authors in translation when many
of my friends, who took Honours Mods. and Honours
Greats, would no more think of opening books which they
are supposed to have read than they would attempt to
read Egyptian hieroglyphics. The man with a classical
education will still worry himself over an accidental
false quantity or a wrongly-placed Greek accent, but it is
extraordinary how seldom, unless he is a schoolmaster, you
hear of him enjoying the classics or applying knowledge
drawn from the classics to modern literature or to modern
politics.

A further proof of this view, which I admit sounds
strange, may be registered.   The only man I have known
who habitually read Greek in the original was Lord
Cromer, and he had not had a classical education.   He left
a private day-school in London to go straight to Chatham,
where he was prepared for entry into the artillery.   And at
Chatham they did not teach Greek.   Therefore when, as a
gunner subaltern, he went to the Ionian Islands on the
staff of Sir Henry Storks, he was without any knowledge
of Greek.   He wanted, however, as he told me, to know
modern Greek, as the language of the islands.   Also, like
the natural Englishman he was, to be able to talk with the
Albanian hunters with whom he went shooting in the hills
of the mainland.   But when he had mastered enough
modern Greek to read the newspaper and so forth, he began to wonder whether he could not use his knowledge to
find out what Homer was like.

He very soon found out that he could read him as one
reads Chaucer.   From this point he went on till he made
himself—I will not say a Greek scholar, but something
much better—a person able to read Greek and enjoy it in

the original. Throughout the period of my friendship with him, which lasted for nearly a quarter of a century, he was constantly reading and translating from Greek authors and talking about them in an intimate and stimulating way.

Once more, it is because I want people to study and to love classical literature and to imbibe the Greek spirit that I desire that the ordinary man should not be forced to grind away at Greek grammar when he might be getting in touch with great minds and great books. I am not blind, of course, to the gymnastic defence of the classics, though I do not share it. All I say is, do not let us make a knowledge of the Greek and Latin languages a *sine qua non* in our educational system, on the ground that such knowledge brings the ordinary man into touch with the Greek spirit. It does nothing of the kind.

But though Greek and Latin literature had thus been temporarily closed to me, I still, Heaven be praised, could enjoy the glories of my own language. When I began to read for the History School, I not only felt like a man who had recovered from a bad bout of influenza, but I began to realise that academic study was not necessarily divorced from the joys of literature, but that, instead, it might lead me to new and delightful pastures. Even early Constitutional History, though apparently so arid, opened to me an enchanting field of study. The study of the Anglo-Saxon period brought special delights. It introduced me to the Anglo-Saxon Chronicle and to Bede, both of them books which deserve far greater fame than they have yet received. Again, I can quite honestly say that the early part of Stubbs's Excerpts from the Laws, Charters, and Chronicles proved to be for me almost as pleasant as a volume of poetry. To my astonishment *Magna Charta* and the *Dialogus de Scaccario* were thoroughly good reading. The answer to *"Quod est murdrum"* was a thrilling revelation of what the Norman Conquest was and was not. I understood; and what is more delightful than that? There were even good courses, I found, in such apparently univiting a feast as "The Constitutions of Clarendon." I shall not easily forget my pleasure in discovering that the quotation *"Nollumus leges Angliæmutari,"* on which Noodle relied in his immortal oration, is to be found in the record of the Barons' great "Palaver."

II

CHAPTER XII

AN OXFORD FRIENDSHIP

THOUGH it is the rule of these memoirs not to deal at any length or detail with living people, I feel I must make an exception in regard to Sir Bernard Mallet, the first friend I made at Oxford, the closest friend of my college days, and the dearest friend of my after-life. Of course, even in his case I cannot say all that I should like to say, for I don't want to expose myself to the gibe of the wit who, reading a sympathetic notice of a living man, declared that he did not care for funeral orations on the living! Another advocate of ascetic reticence in similar circumstances is said to have remarked that it was hardly decent to use such favourable expressions except in the case of a dead man! But, though I am not going to expose myself to the accusation of gushing, I cannot give a true picture of myself without dwelling upon Mallet's influence upon me. My friendship with him was my first experience of real friendship—the relation which it is in the power of youth to establish and maintain, a relation akin to the tie of brotherhood, and one which may have, and ought to have, in it an element of devotion.

Friendship between two young men, keen on all things political, intellectual, and literary, is rightly and necessarily founded upon talk. My friend and I were eager to know not only about each other but about everything else in the universe. Mallet's influence became at once very great upon me at a point where I much needed it. He was deeply interested, and very well-read for a boy of his age, in Political Economy. His father, Sir Louis Mallet, was not only one of the most famous and most enlightened of Civil Servants, but had made a scientific study of the theory of economics. Besides that he had acted as Cobden's official secretary when Cobden negotiated the Commercial Treaty with France, and had become deeply attached to the great Free Trader and his policy. From his father Mallet had learnt what was infinitely more important than anything he could learn in textbooks. He had learnt to look upon Political Economy not as something to be applied only to trade, but something which concerned our morals, our politics, and even our spiritual life. Though it, no doubt, involved Free Trade, what both the Mallets pleaded for was "the policy of Free Exchange"—a policy entering and ruling every form of human activity, or, at any rate, everything to which the quality of value inured, and so the quality of exchangeability.

At the time when I went up to Balliol and sat down beside Mallet at the Freshmen's table in the Hall, wild and eager, shy and forthcoming, bursting with the desire to talk and to hear talk, and yet not exactly knowing how to approach my fellow-novices, I was an ardent, if theoretical, Republican and Socialist. I was, while only a schoolboy of fourteen or fifteen, a passionate admirer of Arch, the man who formed the first Agricultural Labourers' Union, and a regular reader of his penny weekly organ. It was the first paper to which I became an annual subscriber. Now, though I had noted some of the extravagances of the extremists, I was on the edge of conversion to full-blown Socialism or Communism. We did not much distinguish in those days between the two.   I was especially anxious, as every young man must be, to see if I could not do something to help ameliorate the condition of working-men and to find a policy which would secure a better distribution of wealth and of the good things of the world.

Very soon, at once indeed, I confided my views to my new friend.   Our conversation is imprinted upon my mind. Though, of course, I did not realise it at the time, it was destined to have a great effect upon my life.   I told Mallet that I was so haunted by the miseries of the poor and the injustice of our social order that, however much I disliked it for other reasons, and however great the dangers, I was growing more and more into the belief that it would be my duty to espouse the cause of Socialism; then, be it remembered, preached by Mr. Hyndman in full and Mr. Henry George, the single-tax man, in an attenuated form. I was a Free Trader, of course, but if, as a result of the Free Trade system, the poor were getting poorer, and the rich richer, as, alas! it seemed, I was prepared to fight to the death even against Free Trade.

On this Mallet, instead of growing zealously angry with my ignorant enthusiasm, asked me very pertinently what right I had to suggest that the principles of Political Economy and Free Trade had been tested and had failed. He admitted that if to maintain them would prevent a better distribution of wealth, they must be abolished forthwith.   He went on to agree also that if everything else had been exhausted, it would be right to try Socialism, *provided one was not convinced that the remedy would prove worse than the disease.*   But he went on to explain to me, what I had never realised before, that the enlightened economists took no responsibility for the existing system. They held, instead, that the present ills of the world came, not from obeying but from disobeying the teachings of

J. St. Loe Strachey as an Oxford Freshman.   Ætat. 18.

Political Economy. Everywhere Free Exchange was interfered with and violated, on some pretext or another. Even in England it would not be said that Free Exchange had been given a complete trial. It was, he went on to show, because they believed that the ills of human society could be cured, *and only cured*, by a proper understanding and a proper observance of the laws of economics that men like his father advocated Free Exchange so strongly and opposed every attempt to disestablish it.

We want as much as any Socialist to get rid of poverty, misery and destitution, and we believe we have got the true remedy, if only we were allowed to apply it. There would be plenty of the good things of the world for everybody, if we did not constantly interfere with production, and if we did not destroy capital, which would otherwise be competing for labour, not labour for it. By the madness of war and the preparation for war, we lay low that which prevents unemployment. We are always preventing instead of encouraging exchanges, the essential sources of wealth. Yet we wonder that we remain poor.

But the policy of Free Exchange, he went on, must not be regarded merely as a kind of alternative to Socialism. True believers in economics were bound to point out that the nostrum of the Socialists, though intended to do good, would do infinite harm if applied to the community. There was a possibility of release from the prison-house and its tortures by the way of Free Exchange, but none by the way of Socialism. That could only deepen and increase the darkness and bring even greater miseries upon mankind than those they endured at the present moment.

I listened greatly moved, and asked for more instruction. I soon realised that economics were a very different thing to what I had supposed. My father was a strong Free Trader and had talked to me on the subject, but without any great enthusiasm. He was an idealist, and in his youth had strong leanings, first to the Socialism of Owen, and then to the Christian Socialism of Maurice, Kingsley, and their friends. Though later he had dropped these views and had become a convinced supporter of Cobden and Bright in the controversy over the Factory Acts (and let me say that in this I still believe he was perfectly right), he had taken the Shaftesbury rather than the Manchester view. Right or wrong in principle, any proposal to protect women and children would have been sure to secure his support. He would rather be wrong with their advocates than right with a million of philosophers. Again, though he liked Bright, I don't think he ever quite forgave him for talking about the "residuum." My father had no sympathy with insult, even if it was deserved. With him, to suffer was to be worthy of help and comfort, and here, of course, he was right. Again, though he read his Mill, he was not deeply interested. He understood and assented to the main arguments, but he had never happened to get inspired by the idea that the way to accomplish his essential desire to improve the lot of the poor, and so to save society, was by discovering a true theory of applying the principles of Free Exchange. As Sir Louis Mallet used to say, a great deal of this misunderstanding came from the unfortunate fact that we called our policy Free *Trade*, and so narrowed it and made it appear sordid. If, like the French, we had called it Free Exchange, we should have made it universal and so inspiring.

Mallet's words, then, came to me like a revelation. I saw at once, as I have seen and felt ever since, that Political Economy. properly understood and properly applied, is not a dreary science, but one of the most fascinating and mentally stimulating of all forms of human knowledge.

Above all, it is the one which gives real hope for making a better business of human life in the future than was ever known in the past; far better than anything the Communist theorisers can offer. Let their theories be examined, not with sentimental indulgence but in the scientific spirit, and they fade away like the dreams they are.

My teacher was as keen as myself. But when two young minds are striking on each other, the sparks fly. It was not long, then, before I believed myself to have mastered the essential principles of Free Exchange—principles simple in themselves, though not easy to state exactly. To apply them in a lazy and sophistically-minded world is still more difficult. Even business men and traders, who ought to know better, ignore the science on which their livelihood is wholly founded.

Thus, with a halo of friendship and intellectual freedom round me, I learned what Economics really meant, and what might be accomplished if men could only understand the nature of Exchange, and apply their knowledge to affairs.

When I see some public man floundering in the morasses of sophistry, often a quagmire of his own creation, I say to myself, "There, but for Bernard Mallet, goes John St. Loe Strachey." I should, indeed, be an ingrate if I did not acknowledge my debt.

Here is Sir Bernard Mallet's account of me at Oxford in the year 1878.

SIR BERNARD MALLET'S MEMORANDUM

I can find no diaries—or any of the letters which I must have written to my people about Oxford, so I must do what I can without their help. I daresay they would not have been much use, as I never wrote good letters, and my recollections of our first meeting are still pretty fresh. It would be odd if they were not, for our Oxford alliance was far the biggest and most important influence in my life there.

I think it must have been within two or three days of my arrival at Balliol as freshman, in October, 1878, that I found myself sitting beside you at dinner in Hall. No doubt we soon found out each other's names. Yours at once fixed my attention because, as my father was then Under Secretary of State for India and in intimate relations with your two uncles, the great Indian statesmen, Sir John and General Richard Strachey, it had long been familiar to me. This seemed to place us at once, and give me a topic to begin on. Not that conversation was ever lacking in your company! I remember to this hour the vivid, emphatic way you talked, and your appearance then—your rather pale face and your thin but strongly-built figure. I was at once greatly impressed, but I am not sure that the first impression on a more or less conventional public-schoolboy (such as I suppose I must have been) was altogether favourable! Certainly I have always thought of you as a reason for distrusting my first impression of a man! Luckily for me, however, we continued to meet. You were so alive and unreserved that you very soon posted me up in all the details of your life and family, and drew the same confidences from me; and we soon found that we had so much in common that in a very few days we fell into those specially intimate relations which lasted through our Oxford days and long after. It is not easy to analyse or account for the rapid growth of such a friendship, but on my part, I think, it was the fact of your being so different from others which at first slightly repelled, and then strangely attracted me. To begin with, you had never been at school; you knew nothing of Greek or Latin as languages, nor of cricket or football! But the want of this routine education or discipline was no disadvantage to you (except for certain serious misadventures in "Mods.!") because your personality and strong intelligence enabled you to get far more out of exceptional home surroundings than you could have got out of any school. You had kept all your intellectual freshness and originality. In English literature, from the Elizabethan downwards, you had read widely and deeply, and your wonderful memory never failed you in quotation from the poets. You ought really, with those tastes and that training, to have become a poet yourself! and till politics and journalism drew you off I often thought that pure literature would be your line. But your political instincts were even then quite as strong; you came of a family with political interests and traditions; and as a boy you had met a good many Liberal statesmen—either at the house of Lady Waldegrave, your mother's friend and country neighbour, or at Cannes, where your family used to spend the winter. But your politics had rather a poetical tinge! Shelley, Swinburne, Walt Whitman coloured your ideas—you were a democrat and republican, with a great enthusiasm for the United States and for the story of Abraham Lincoln. But you were never faddist or doctrinaire, and your practical bent showed itself in the keen interest you took in the noticing of political economy in which I used to dabble, and which we used to discuss by the hour. You seemed, without having studied text-books, to have an intuitive grasp of economic and fiscal truths which astonished me and others much better qualified to judge than I was. The real truth is that, though there were, no doubt, gaps in your mental equipment which may have horrified the dons, you were miles ahead of most of us in the width and variety of your interests, in your gift of self-expression and, in a way, in knowledge of the world. Every talk with you seemed to open up new vistas to me. I was perhaps more receptive than the usual run of public-schoolboy, as I too had had interests awakened by home surroundings and tradition. We both of us, in fact, owed a very great deal to our respective fathers, and it was a real pleasure and guide to me to be introduced later to your father and home at Sutton Court—as I know it was to you to get to know and appreciate my father.

But I must not wander from my subject, which is to try and give a faithful account of how you struck me in those days. I have said nothing yet of one of your characteristics which I think weighed with me, and impressed me more than anything else, and that was the remarkable power you had, and have always retained, of drawing out the best in others. Intellectual power or force of character (or whatever you like to call it) is so often self-centred as to lose half its value. With you, however, it was different. You always appeared to be, and I think genuinely were, quite as much interested in other people's ideas or personalities as in your own—or even more interested. You listened to them, you questioned, you put them on their mettle, you helped them out by interpreting their crude or half-impressed thoughts, and all this without a trace of flattery or patronage. By this, and by your generous over-appreciation of them, you inspired your friends with greater confidence in themselves than they would otherwise have had. In your company they were, or felt themselves, really better men. To one of my disposition, at all events, this was a source of extraordinary encouragement and help. I felt it from the first, and I cannot omit mentioning it in my attempt to describe what you were like when we met at Oxford. I am afraid it is a poor attempt, and wanting in details which contemporary records, if they had existed, could alone have supplied. But I hope you may find something in it which will suit your purpose. I don't think, after all, you have changed as much as most people in the forty-odd years I have known you!

CHAPTER XIII

OXFORD MEMORIES (*Concluded*)

EVEN at the risk of making my autobiography open to accusation that it is a kind of Strachey Anthology, I should be giving a false impression of myself and my life at Oxford if I did not say something about my poetical life at the University, for there, as in my childhood and my boyhood, poetry played a great part. I did not leave the Muses till I left their bower on the Isis. Every mood of my Oxford life was reflected in my verse. I can only record a very few of those reflections, and here, again, must look forward to some day making a collection of my poems and letting them tell their own tale—an interesting incursion, I venture to say, for those who are interested in the evolution of English verse from 1870 to 1890.

The first thing to be recorded in this epitome of my *biographica poetica* is my intense delight at finding in Oxford people of my own age who cared for poetry as I did, and the same kind of poetry. It is true that most of my friends with a poetic bent wore their rue with a difference, but that did not matter. Though they practised a different rite, they were all sworn to the great mystery of the Muses. Men like Beeching, Mackail, Nichols, Warren, and also Willie Arnold, who, though not an undergraduate, very soon became one of my close friends, never failed, and this is the test, to be delighted in any new discovery in verse with which I was for the moment intoxicating myself.

I was always irregular in my tastes.   If I liked a piece of verse, I liked it with passion and praised it inordinately; again I was apt to be as absolute in my dislike.   I was a kind of poaching gipsy of literature.   I had not only a willingness to eat any wild thing from a hedgehog to a beechnut or a wild raspberry, but also an uncanny power of finding out literary game, raising it, and trapping it, not by the stately methods of the scholar but by some irrational and violent intuition.   Instead of reading slowly, patiently, and laboriously, as no doubt I ought to have read, *i.e.*, as my tutors would have liked me to read, I used to dive headlong into some poet, old or young.   Even if I could only "get at him" for an odd half-hour, I could bring back with me something worth keeping, something which would sing in my head and be forced into the ears of my friends for many days, and sometimes many weeks.

This habit of what one might call random and sudden quotation was amusingly hit off by a friend of mine, Fry, son of the late Lord Justice Sir Edward Fry.   In a neat little verse after the manner of Beeching's and Mackail's celebrated verses on the Balliol Dons—verse modelled, it may be noted, on the pageant of Kings and Queens in Swinburne's *Poems and Ballads*, Fry thus delineated me:

> I am Strachey, never bored
> By Webster, Massinger or Ford;
> There is no line of any poet
> Which can be quoted, but I know it.

In the first couplet I have to own a true bill.   Even if my friends were bored, though I was not, which I now feel must have often been the case, they certainly never showed it.   I seemed to be given a kind of privilege or license to quote as much as ever I liked.

I expect, however, that the Dons were not quite as easy-going. If I quoted something that seemed to me apposite at the end of a lecture, or when I was seeing my tutor over an essay, I noticed with an innocent wonderment that they were apt to appear shocked. Probably I made them feel nervous. Either they had not heard the lines before, and, therefore, very likely thought that I was trying to get a score off them by inventing some tag of rhymes which I could afterwards say they took for genuine, or, on the other hand, if they did know the lines, I made some blunder in quoting them which painfully added to a conviction already formed that I was a wild, inconsequent, and shallow-minded boy whose only idea was to "show off" and strut about in borrowed plumes. After all, even if that was a mistaken diagnosis it was not an unnatural one.

I was an unsettling and unclassifiable influence in a place that liked orderly classification. The Dons, I make no doubt, felt about me as did Lance about his dog. He who undertakes to be an undergraduate should be an under-graduate in all things, and not a kind of imitation Bohemian verse-writer, bawling his creaking couplets through the College Hall. They knew the type of scholar who could write good Greek verse, and even English verse. They also knew, and in a way respected, the athlete, the hunting man, or "the magnificent man" who kept two hunters and a private servant, and spent at the rate of a couple of thousands a year. But here was a creature who did not fit into any of these categories, and who was painfully irregular without being vicious or extravagant, or drunken, or abnormally rowdy. I was, in fact, a mental worry. I could not be fitted neatly into Oxford life.

I have mentioned Fry's rhyme about me. I must also mention Beeching's verse, or at any rate the first couplet—the rest, though friendly enough, was not worthy of the opening:

Spoken jest of Strachey, shall it
Fail to raise a smile in Mallet?

I was, of course, pleased to be thus associated with my
friend, though honesty compels me to say that I laughed
quite as much, or even more, at Mallet's jests than he did
at mine. Still for the rhyme's sake (I have always
sympathised with the rhymer's difficulties), it was necessary to put the joke on the other leg.

At Balliol in the late 'seventies' and early 'eighties' we
were a nest of singing-birds. I well remember the present
Sir Rennell Rodd coming into my rooms when I was a
freshman and asking me whether I would contribute to a
little collection of poems which he and a group of his
friends were bringing out, the group, by the way, including
the present Lord Curzon. I shyly assented; but there
was a difficulty. They wanted something short and
lyrical, and most of my verses were either too long, or else,
I thought, too immature to be published. In the end,
Rodd carried off with him the following lyric—a work in
regard to which I felt no pride of parentage either then or
now, and only quote because it was made the occasion for
a very neat parody by Mackail. Here is the poem:

My lute
Lies mute,
My lyre is all unstrung,
And the music it once flung
Dies away.
In the day
I have no power to sing,
Nor doth the night-time bring
Any song.
All is wrong,
Now my lady hath no care
For my heart and for my prayer.

The parody was quite delightful, and I can well remember
the intense joy with which I heard of it and my surprise
that the author thought it necessary to apologise for it.
He apparently thought I might be hurt.   It ran something
like this:

> My scout
> Is out.
> My scout is never in.
> I am growing very thin,
> And pale—
>
> etc., etc.

Our verse efforts, though not very good in themselves, had
a good result.

A rival clique of poets, led by Mackail and Beeching,
put forward a little pamphlet of their own, full of what
was really exquisite verse of the Burne-Jones, Morris,
Swinburne type.   In the following term, however, the
two poetic schools amalgamated under a common editorship, adopting the name of *Waifs and Strays* as their
title.   To almost every issue of the *Waifs and Strays* I
contributed, though I think my Editors sometimes were
rather horrified at my sending in so much blank verse, and
blank verse of what the Elizabethans called a "licentious"
type, that is, not governed by strict rules.

Besides this, my poems were apt to be too long.   I had
a friendly conflict over them with Beeching.   It showed,
however, the open-mindedness of the Morrisean editors that
my poetry, though so entirely different to their own, was
not only accepted but that they showed great sympathy
with my experiments in unrhymed measures.

Oxford memories are among the pleasantest things in
the world; they are the last chapter, or last chapter but
one, in the book of youth.   But I must soon roll up the

enchanted manuscript, come to sterner things, and leave many serene hours unnumbered. Especially do I regret to pass over the long days spent on the river in a four, with a cox and a good luncheon and tea hamper in the stern, and a sixth man in the bows. Those, indeed, were sweet hours and the fleetest of time. Mallet, I, and Warren were usually the nucleus of the party. To ourselves we added another three. Among these was sometimes Grant Duff, sometimes Horatio Brown, who, though he had left Oxford at that period, was often "up for a month or two"; sometimes, too, Portsmouth Fry, and one or other of Mallet's Clifton College friends. Again, sometimes Mallet's brother Stephen, or my brother Henry, joined the pursuit of the golden fleece.

I was always for pushing on in order to experience something or discover something. As Pepys used to say, "I was with child to see something new." Once, by incredible exertion, I managed to get my boatload as far up the river as Lechlade. The place, I need hardly say, was chosen by me not for geographical reasons or because of the painted glass, but solely and simply because of Shelley's poem. I longed to go to the actual source of the river, to Thames-head itself, but in this I never succeeded. Mallet was always for milder measures, and for enjoying the delights of the infant Thames at Bablock Hythe, or some place of equal charm and less exertion. Like the poet in Thomson, as I frequently reminded him, he

> Would oft suspend the dashing oar
> To bid his gentle spirit rest.

He would demand, or take, an "easy" on the slightest pretext. A water-lily, the dimness of his eyeglass, the drooping of the sunlight in the West, the problem of whether some dingy little bird was a kingfisher or a crested wagtail, demanded consultation and a pause in our toil. Occasional rests, he proved, were a wise, nay, necessary precaution with a heavy old tub manned by indifferent oarsmen. I, on the other hand, would have violently explored the Thames in a man-o'-war's barge if I could have done it no other way.

We talk of the charm of the open road, but what is it to the charm of the open river, especially when the stream gets narrow? There, if anywhere, reigns the Genius of the Unexpected. You push your boat round some acute angle of water, with willows and tall rushes obscuring your course, and then suddenly shoot out into the open, with a view, perhaps, of an old church or manor-house, or of stately fields and trees—things which a boy feels may be the prelude to the romance of his life. So strong with me, indeed, was this feeling that fate was waiting round the corner, not to stick a knife into me, but perhaps to crown me, that when I wrote my unfinished novel, I began with a boatload of undergraduates shooting out of the Thames up a tunnel of green boughs made by a canalised brook, into a little lake in front of an exquisite grey Elizabethan house. There the heroine and an aged parent or guardian were surprised taking tea upon a bank studded with primroses and violets. How an aged parent or guardian consented to have tea out-of-doors in violet-time was not explained! But if I do not take care I shall go the way of those orators who take up the whole of their speeches in explaining that they have not time to say anything. Therefore, farewell to the glories and delights of the Thames.

Whether, in point of fact, I was a bad son of Oxford, or she a disdainful, indifferent, or careless mother, I neither know nor desire to know. It is enough for me, as I have said already, that I loved her young and love her now, love her for her faults as much as for her virtues, but love her

12

most of all for her beauty and her quietness, and for the golden stream of youth which runs a glittering torrent through her stately streets and hallowed gardens, her walks between the waters, and her woodlands. The punctual tide of young hearts ebbs and flows as of yore in a thousand college rooms—true cells of happiness. It informs and inspires every inch of Oxford. It murmurs in her libraries and in her galleries and halls. The pictures of the men of the past—often England's truest knights of the eternal spirit—look gravely from their deep-set frames.

But what is the use of a biography if it is general and not particular? I may too often yield, like most people, to the temptations of a vague rhetoric, but not here. Every loving thought of Oxford has for me stamped upon it a specific and an originating example. When I think of the faces looking down on me from the walls, and of how ardently I used to wish that I might call my academic grandsires "my home and feast to share," I picture myself back in Oxford, listening to a lecture in the Hall of University. I see above me and above the wainscot Romney's (or is it Gainsborough's?) picture of "the generous, the ingenuous, the high-souled William Wyndham." I recall the delight with which I thought of that fascinating and impulsive creature. He had sat where I was sitting, and had dreamed like me in that very Hall the dreams of youth.

I keep in mind yet another specific example of how I linked myself to the past. I remember, when dining in Christ Church Hall with a friend, that I had the good luck to find myself opposite Lawrence's picture of Eden, afterwards Lord Auckland, the young diplomatist. He is dressed, if I remember rightly, in a green velvet coat of exquisite tint and texture. I daresay if by chance a reader looks up the two pictures he will find that under the spell of memory they have assumed

beauties not their own. But what does that matter?
They were to me, at twenty, an inspiration. They are still,
at sixty, a dream of delight.

Yet, intense as was my joy, when I return to Oxford and
see my son sharing the old pleasures, though with a difference, I can honestly say, "*Non equidem invideo miror
magis,*"—"I do not envy, but am the more amazed." I
hope, nay, am sure that my son can retort with sincerity
from this shepherd's dialogue turned upside down,
"*O fortunate senex; ergo tua rura manebunt.*"—"Oh, happy
old man; therefore your little fields and little woodlands at
Newlands shall still flourish and abound."

As my father taught me by his example long ago, I can
be supremely happy in my remembrances, and yet even
happier at my own end of the continuum. One has a right
to be Hibernian in an Einstein world. After all, have I
not a right to be? I, who have always been an explorer at
heart, am getting near the greatest exploration of all.
There are only two or three more bends of the stream, and
I shall shoot out into that lake or new reach, whichever it
may be. I may have a pleasant thrill of dread of what is
there, but not of fear. The tremendous nature of that
magnificent unknown may send a shiver through my limbs,
but it is stimulating, not paralysing.

Therefore, though I enjoy the past in retrospect, I open
my arms with a lover's joy to the future that is rushing to
meet me. The man who cannot enjoy that which is in
front of him has never really enjoyed the past. He is so
much engaged in whimpering over what he has lost, that he
misses the glory of what is to come. Heaven be praised
that sons have morning when fathers have night, and may
the fountain of perpetual youth always send its best, its
clearest, its most musical rivulets through the High, the
Broad, and the Corn.

But, though my memories of Oxford are so vivid and so happy, they are also, as must in the end be all things human, enwoven with tears. It was there that my eldest son died. I cannot do more than record the bare fact. Yet I cannot write of Oxford as if he had never been. The shadow that falls across my page could not be gainsaid.

CHAPTER XIV

PRESS WORK IN LONDON

BEFORE I come to the period when I became, not only Editor, but Proprietor, of *The Spectator*, I must give an account of some of my experiences with other newspapers. My first newspaper article appeared in *The Daily News*. It gave an account of the bonfires lighted on the hill-tops round Cortina, in the Tyrol, at which place we spent the summer of 1880, on the birthday of the Austrian Emperor. I was an undergraduate at the time and was much delighted to find myself described as "a correspondent" of *The Daily News*. I expect I owed the acceptance of my descriptive article to the first sentence, which began, "While the Austrian Kaiser is keeping his birthday with the waters of the Ischl in his kitchens, we at Cortina, etc., etc." The paper, however, for which I wrote chiefly during the time I was at Oxford and in my first year after leaving Balliol was *The Saturday Review*. The *Saturday* in those days was famous for its "middles," and I was very proud to be able to get articles of this kind accepted. I also wrote for *The Academy* and for *The Pall Mall*, which at that time was being edited by Lord Morley. I remember that when going with a letter of introduction to him, he asked me whether I had had any former experience of journalism. I told him that I was writing "middles" for the *Saturday*. His reply was characteristic. "Ah!

When I was a young man I wrote miles of 'middles' for them"—stretching out his hands to show the unending chain. Some of my work also appeared in *The Academy*, then a paper manfully struggling to represent the higher side of English literature. One article I recall was a review of a reprint of the poems of Gay—a poet who has come back into public notice owing to the delightful art of Mr. Lovat Fraser, combined with the talent of the ladies and gentlemen who so admirably represent Macheath and his minions male and female. On looking at the article the other day, I was glad to see that I drew attention to Gay's peculiar handling of the couplet and also to his delight in every kind of old song and ballad. I quoted in this respect, however, not from "The Beggar's Opera" but from the song as sung by Silenus in Gay's Eclogues. One of these songs I have always longed to hear or to read, owing to the fascination of its title— "The grass now grows where Troy town stood."

After I went to *The Spectator* the newspaper world widened in my view. I left off writing for the *Saturday* and the *Pall Mall* and the *Academy*. Instead, and after I married, I took a regular post as leader-writer on the staff of the *Standard*. I also wrote a weekly leader for the *Observer* for the best part of a year. Of the *Observer* I have only one thing to note, and that is a saying of the Editor, Mr. Dicey, brother to my old friend, Professor Dicey—a man for whom I have great veneration, though my lips are happily closed in regard to him by the fact that he still lives. At our first interview Mr. Dicey told me that in writing for the *Observer* I must remember that I was not writing for a weekly paper, like the *Spectator*, but for a daily paper which, however, only happened to come out on one day in the week. That, I always thought, was a very illuminating and instructive remark, and it is one which should be observed, in my opinion, by all writers in Sunday papers. At present Sunday papers are in danger of becoming merely weekly magazines. What the world wants, or, at any rate, what a great many people want, is a daily paper to read on Sundays, not a miscellany, however good. But perhaps Mr. Dicey and I were old-fashioned. Anyway, there was a sort of easy-going, old-fashioned, early-Victorian air about the *Observer* Office of those days which was very pleasant. Nobody appeared to be in a hurry, and one was given almost complete freedom as to the way in which to treat one's subject. I was also a contributor to the *Manchester Guardian*. For that distinguished paper I wrote Notes for their London Letter and also a number of short reviews.

I should add that from that time till I became Editor and Proprietor of the *Spectator* I wrote a weekly article for *The Economist*—a piece of work in which I delighted, for the Editor, Mr. Johnstone, was not only a great editor, but a very satisfactory one from the contributor's point of view. He told you exactly what he wanted written about, and then left you to your own devices. As it happened, I generally was in entire agreement with his policy, but if I had not been, it would not have mattered, because he made it so very clear to one, as an editor should, that one was expressing not one's own views, but the views of the *Economist*. Whether they were in fact right or wrong, they certainly deserved full consideration. Therefore, full exposition could never be regarded as taking the wrong side.

Though *The Economist* was less strongly Unionist than I was, I cannot recall any occasion on which my leaders were altered by the Editor. I can only recall, indeed, one comment made by Mr. Johnstone in the course of some nine years.   It was one that at the time very greatly interested and amused me.   It happened that Mr. Johnstone, though so great a journalist and so sound a politician, was not a man who had paid any attention to literature.   Possibly, indeed, he did not consider that it deserved it.   When, however, the complete works of Walter Bagehot, for many years Editor of *The Economist*, were published, Mr. Johnstone asked me to review them for the paper.   Needless to say I was delighted.   How could a young man in the 'nineties, full of interest in the Constitution, in Economics, and in *belles-lettres*, have felt otherwise than enthusiastic about Bagehot?

It was, therefore, with no small zest that I undertook an appreciation of Bagehot in his own paper.   I was always an immense admirer of Bagehot's power of dealing with literary problems, and still more of that perfection of style for which, by the way, he never received full credit. I sought to say something which would make people "sit up and take notice" in regard to his place in literature on this special point.   Accordingly, in praising his style, I said that it was worthy to be compared with that of Stevenson, who at the time was held to be our greatest master of words.   Mr. Johnstone, with, as I fully admitted, a quite unnecessary urbanity of manner, apologised to me for having altered the article.   He had, he explained, left out the passage about Stevenson.   But mark the reason!   It was not because he thought the praise exaggerated, but because he thought, and thought also that Mr. Bagehot's family might think, that one was not properly appreciative of Bagehot's work if one compared it to that of Stevenson!   I have always been a lover of the irony of accident in every form; but here was something which was almost too bewilderingly poignant.   I had thought, as I wrote, that people might think I was

going a good deal too far in my praise of Bagehot, but lo
and behold! my purple patch was "turned down," not
because of this but because it was held to be too laudatory
of Stevenson, and not laudatory enough of my hero!

I was, nevertheless, quite right. Bagehot's style was
inimitable, and I think if I were writing now, and with a
better perspective, I should have said not less but a good
deal more in its praise. The humorous passages in
"The English Constitution" are in their way perfect,
and, what is more, they are really original. They owe
nothing to any previous humorist. They stand somewhere between the heartiness of Sydney Smith and the
dainty fastidiousness of Matthew Arnold, and yet imitate
neither. They have a quality, indeed, which is entirely
their own and is entirely delightful. One of the things
which is so charming about them is that they are authoritative without being cocksure. What could be more admirable than the passage which points out that Southey,
"who lived almost entirely with domestic women, actually died in the belief that he was a poet"? The pathos
of the situation, and the Olympian stroke delivered in
such a word as "domestic" cannot but fill any artisan of
words with admiration. The essay, "Shakespeare and
the Plain Man," is full of such delights.

If I am told that I digress too much and that I seem to
forget that I am writing my autobiography and not an
estimate of Walter Bagehot, I shall not yield to the criticism. There is method in my madness. No, I am prepared to contend, and to contend with my last drop of
ink, that I am justified in what I have done. If this book
is worth anything, it is the history of a mind, and Bagehot
had a very great effect upon my mind, largely through
his skill in the art of presentation. Therefore it cannot
be out of place to say something about Bagehot's style.

In truth, instead of my being unduly discursive I have not really said as much as I ought to have said on the subject.

I was also for rather more than a year a leader-writer on the *Standard*—my only experience of true daily journalism. Of this work I can only say that I enjoyed it very much while I was in direct contact with Mr. Mudford, one of the greatest of English publicists, and the man who made the *Standard* what it was from 1874 till about 1894, one of the most important papers in the country. In those days the *Standard*, though strongly conservative, was in no sense a capitalist organ, nor in the bad sense a mere party organ. While it supported the fixed institutions of the country, the Church, the Crown, the House of Lords, and the City, it, at the same time, did it with reason and moderation. In fact, though it was called a Tory paper, and rejoiced in the name, it would have been called "left-centre" in any other country. It was, it need not be said, strongly Unionist. I, therefore, had no difficulty whatever in writing for it.

Oddly enough, it was said, and I think with truth, that Mr. Gladstone always read the leaders in the *Standard* and that it was his favourite paper. He had, no doubt, a strong vein of Conservatism in his nature. Though he thought it his duty to be a Liberal, when he gave himself a holiday, so to speak, from party feelings, what he reverted to was almost exactly the *Standard* attitude towards the great institutions I have just named. A propos of this I cannot resist a most illuminating story of Mr. Gladstone, which I once heard told by Mr. George Wyndham, the Irish Secretary. Mr. Wyndham commanded the Cheshire yeomanry, after Mr. Gladstone had gone into retirement, and had his regiment under canvas for training at the Park at Hawarden. Being an old

House of Commons friend, he went several times to dine. On one of these occasions he was alone with Mr. Gladstone after dinner. While sipping his port, the great man unbosomed himself on the political situation of the future in language which, as Mr. Wyndham pointed out, approximated to that of an old country squire—language which seemed astonishing from the mouth of one who had only a few months before been the leader of the Liberal and Radical Party.

Mr. Gladstone began with a panegyric of the English squires and landlords, and then went on to say that he feared that in the coming time the country-gentlemen of England who had done so much for her would have a hard and difficult time. "But," he went on, "I pray Heaven, Mr. Wyndham, that they will meet these trials and difficulties with a firm and courageous spirit. They must not weakly yield the position to which they have attained and which they deserve." I can remember no more of Mr. Gladstone's speech, but it was all to the effect that the country-gentleman must stand up against the rising tide of democracy. No wonder, then, that Mr. Gladstone liked the *Standard*, even though it very often attacked him in the strongest language.

Another person said to be a regular reader of the *Standard*, and I should add rightly said to be, was Queen Victoria. The Queen, as Lord Salisbury said at the time of her death, understood the English people exactly, and especially the English middle-class. Therefore she would have been wise to have read the *Standard* as the representative and interpreter of that class even if she had not liked the paper on its merits. As a matter of fact, however, its note happened to be pitched exactly to suit her. Her admiration was not politic, but personal.

Here I may note an interesting example of how little

the person who has had no first-hand experience of journalism understands the journalist's trade and how often he or she is amazed at what I may call our simple secrets. It happened that while I was writing leaders for the *Standard*, which was twice a week, *i.e.*, on Wednesday nights and on Sunday nights, the news came in of the death of Lady Ely, a lifelong personal friend of the Queen. Lady Ely had been with her almost from girlhood and held up to the last, if not actually a Court appointment, a position which brought her into constant personal contact with the Queen. She was, in fact, the last of the Queen's women contemporaries who were also close friends. This fact was common knowledge, and Mr. Mudford in one of his notes, which were written in a calligraphy the badness of which it is almost impossible to describe without the aid of a lithographic print, wrote to me shortly, telling me of the death and asking me to write that night a leader on Lady Ely. He pointed out how great the loss was to the Queen, and how much, therefore, she must stand in the need of sympathy. I don't suppose I had ever heard of Lady Ely before, for ever since I came to London she was living in retirement, and was not only not written about in the press, but was very little talked about in general society. Further, I had only the ordinary knowledge about the Queen, at that time much scantier than it is now. It might be supposed that with this amount of ignorance it would have been impossible to write a column and a half on the death of an old lady who may be said to have had no public life at all, and whose private life, even if it had been known, would have been either too trivial or too intimate to be written about in a newspaper.

All the same, the task was not one which any journalist worth his salt, that is, any journalist with imagination,

would find difficult to accomplish. What I did, and all
it was necessary to do, was to envisage a great lady devoted to the Queen from the time the Queen was married,
and also receiving in exchange the Queen's devotion to
her. These two women, now grown old, one in the service
of her country and the other in the service of her friend,
had gradually seen, not only their nearest and dearest
drop away, but almost the whole of their own generation.
Thus they stood very much alone in the world. Sovereigns by their nature are always lonely, and this loneliness was intensified in the case of the Queen by the pre-
mature death of Prince Albert and by that inability of
sovereigns to make intimate friends, owing, not only to
the seclusion which life in a palace entails, but to the
busy-ness of their lives. This being so, the breaking by
death of a friendship formed when life was easier to
Queen Victoria than it was after the death of the Prince
Consort was an irreparable loss. In a very special degree
the Queen needed sympathy of all who had minds to
think or hearts to feel.

Such considerations were as easy to put on paper
as they were true. To draw a picture of the unknown
Lady Ely seems more difficult, but, after all, one felt sure
that to have remained the intimate and trusted friend of
the Queen she must have had great qualities, for the Queen
did not give her confidence lightly. The separation of
the two friends and the intensification of the Queen's
loneliness was therefore bound to touch the heart of anyone who heard "the Virgilian cry" and felt "the sense of
tears in mortal things."

I am not ashamed to say that though by nature little
disposed towards the attitude of the courtier, I wrote my
modest tribute of regret *ex animo*. I was not only not
writing a conventional article of condolence, not even

writing dramatically, but sincerely. When, however, the leader was finished, I, of course, thought very little more of the matter, but passed on to consider, after the way of my profession, subjects so vital or so trivial as the best means of supporting Mr. Balfour in his law-and-order campaign in Ireland, maintaining the cause of Free Trade (the *Standard* was always a Free Trade paper), or discussing such topics as "Penny Fares in Omnibuses," or "The Preservation of the Ancient Monuments of London," or "Should Cats be Taxed?" It was therefore with some astonishment that I received a message from Mr. Mudford saying that the Queen had sent one of her Private Secretaries to enquire on behalf of Her Majesty the name of the writer of the article on Lady Ely. The Queen, said her Envoy, had been very touched and struck by the article and felt sure that it must have been written by someone who knew Lady Ely. It exactly represented her life and character, and her special devotion to the Queen. The Queen also appeared much struck by the representation of her own feeling towards her friend.

Mr. Mudford, of course, gave my name. I have often thought with some curiosity that the Queen must have been rather bewildered to find the complete remoteness of the writer from her friend and herself. The Queen had a very limited literary sense and, we may be sure, failed altogether to realise how the nerves and sinews work in that strange creature the journalist. She can hardly have been otherwise than disappointed in finding that it was not some old friend of her own, or some friend of her friend, but a person of whom she knew nothing—and with a name which must have left her quite cold, even though with her knowledge of India and her own family that name was not actually unfamiliar. My uncle, Sir John Strachey, after the murder of Lord Mayo, was for six or seven months Viceroy of India, pending the appointment of a successor. She also, no doubt, had known the name of another Indian uncle, Sir Richard Strachey.

But though Mr. Mudford was very sympathetic to the new journalist on his staff, the arrangement did not last long. After I had been there about six months, Mr. Mudford went into greater retirement than even before, and practically left the whole conduct of the paper to his subordinate, Mr. Byron Curtis, a journalist whom I can best describe by saying that he was of the kind delineated by Thackeray. Though we had no open quarrel I found it difficult to work with Mr. Curtis, and he, on the other hand, was by no means satisfied with my work. He used to say to me, "Please do remember, Mr. Strachey, that we don't want academic stuff such as you put into the *Spectator* and as they appear to like. What we want is a nice flow of English." "A nice flow of English" with Mr. Curtis meant what I may call the barrel-organ type of leader— something that flowed like water from a smooth-running pump. This I admit I could never manage to produce. Mr. Curtis's standard of style was solely governed by the question of the repetition of the same word. It was an unforgivable sin to repeat a substantive, adjective, or verb without an intervening space of at least four inches. This, of course, leads to that particular form of "journalese" in which a cricket-ball becomes a "leathern missile" and so forth. A propos of this I remember a good Fleet Street story. An Editor, enraged with a contributor, tore up an article on grouse, with the exclamation, "Look here! You have actually used the word 'grouse' twenty times in your first paragraph! Why cannot you call them something else?" "But," said the contributor, "what else can I call them? They are grouse, and that is the only name they have got. What would you want me to say?"

"Oh! hang it all! Don't make excuses. Why, can't you call them 'the feathered denizens of the moor'?"

In any case, Mr. Curtis and I found it impossible to work together. The process of separation was speeded up by the fact that I did not find night-work suit me. All the same, I very much liked going down to the policeman on night-duty. What was trying was to be up all night for two nights in the week, and to lead a normal life during the other five. That tended to throw one's working days quite out of gear. To adopt two ways of life was a failure. All the same, I am always glad when I pass down Fleet Street to be able to say to myself, "I too once lived in Arcadia," and knew the pleasant side of the life. There was something peculiarly delightful, when one's leader was finished, in lighting a pipe or a cigar and stretching out one's legs and feeling really at leisure. There is only real leisure in the middle of the night, that is between one and five. There are no appointments, no meals, no duties, no plans, no dependence on other people's arrangements. One is as free in one's complete isolation as a Trappist monk. If one sees a friend in Fleet Street or Shoe Lane at three, he will be as free as you.

Such a friend was Mr. Joseph Fisher, then the understudy of Mr. Byron Curtis. Mr. Fisher, who is an Ulsterman, later became the Editor of *The Northern Whig*, and I am happy to say is still alive. He has done excellent work in defending the interests of the Loyalists and Protestants of the North.

That, I think, is the full record of my regular newspaper activities, except for one particular. I have not mentioned the fact that I edited the official organ of the Liberal Unionist Party for about two years—a monthly, entitled *The Liberal Unionist*. The paper was started during the election of 1886. The work was interesting, if not particularly well paid, and brought me into contact with most of the leaders of the Unionist Party—Lord Hartington, Mr. Chamberlain, Mr. Goschen, the Duke of Argyll, Mr. Arthur Elliot, and Mr. Henry Hobhouse, to name only a few of my colleagues on the Liberal Unionist Central Committee.   I never had any difficulties with them.   They gave me a free hand, and in return I gave them what I think was good value.   As my work enlarged I found I wanted help in *The Liberal Unionist*, and secured an admirable helper in Mr. C. L. Graves.   This was the beginning of our private and journalistic friendship, and, though I must not break my rule of not dealing with living people, I may say here what a kind and loyal helper he has always been to me, not only in *The Liberal Unionist* but for many years in *The Spectator*.   All who know him, and especially his associates on *Punch*, will, I feel sure, agree with me that no man was ever a more loyal colleague.   No man has ever succeeded better than he in combining scholarship and vivacity in humorous and satiric verse.

While carrying on the activities I have mentioned above, I also from time to time wrote for the magazines— for the *Edinburgh Quarterly*, for the *National*, the *Nineteenth Century*, the *Contemporary*, and once or twice, I think, in the *Fortnightly*.   I even perpetrated a short story in a magazine now deceased—a story which, by the way, if I had time to adapt it, might, I think, make an excellent cinema film.   The title was good—"The Snake Ring."   It was a story of a murder in the High Alps, when the High Alps were not so much exploited as they are now. There were adventures in sledging over mountain passes in mid-winter, and wonderful mountain Palazzi, with gorgeous seventeenth-century interiors, in lonely snowed-up villages in inaccessible valleys.   As a rule, however,

13

my contributions to the magazines were of a serious kind.
Very soon after I left Oxford, I wrote my first article in the
Quarterly. This was followed by several more, for the
old Editor, Dr. Smith, took a strong liking to my work.
Dr. Smith was a man of real learning and a true journalist. Though it was the custom to laugh at his "h's," or
rather, his occasional want of them, he was very much
liked in society. As a boy I had made his acquaintance, I
remember, at Lady Waldegrave's, though this chance
meeting had nothing to do with the acceptance of
my first article. Henry Reeve of the *Edinburgh* also on
several occasions asked me to write the political article
in the *Review*. That was a pleasure. I was given a free
hand, and I had the agreeable sense that I was sitting in
the seats of the mighty, of Sydney Smith and of Macaulay.

CHAPTER XV

THE "CORNHILL"

My editorship of the *Cornhill*, to which I always look back with great pleasure, came as a complete surprise to me. Among the many new friends my marriage brought me was Mr. George Smith, the head of the firm of Smith & Elder, a man very well known in the London of the 'fifties, 'sixties, and 'seventies as the most enterprising of publishers, the discoverer of Charlotte Brontë, the friend and adviser of Thackeray, and, above all, the founder of the first cheap, popular, literary magazine, the *Cornhill*. It was in the editorship of the *Cornhill* that Thackeray found pecuniary if not editorial ease, and during the first ten years of its life it was the natural home of much of the best writing of the time. Tennyson on one side of the republic of Parnassus and Swinburne on the other were contributors to its pages. But pre-eminently it was the place to which was drawn the best fiction of the age. The planning, the enterprise, and very often the inspiration of the *Cornhill* came from Mr. George Smith. Though primarily a man of business, he had an extraordinary *flair* for literature. He was the last person in the world to have claimed the title of a man of letters, or, again, that of critic, and yet he had an appreciation of good literature and a capacity for finding it in unlikely places which was sometimes almost uncanny. Just as some of the greatest connoisseurs in the Arts know a good picture or an important piece of china when they see it, though they are often ignorant of the history or of the technique of any art, so Mr. George Smith had an almost unfailing eye for good copy when it came his way.

Nowadays, there is comparatively little difficulty in running a literary monthly on sound lines either here or in America. But that is because the world has learnt Mr. George Smith's lesson. All can raise the flower now, for all have got the seed, but at the beginning of the 'sixties the *Cornhill* had the quality of originality. It exactly hit the popular taste, and in a very short time it was selling by the hundred thousand, a tremendous achievement at that epoch. But though the *Cornhill* did so well and though Mr. George Smith's energies remained as great as ever up till his death, the magazine had to own the fate of many publications of its kind before and since. It met with competition, and I cannot help thinking that it also suffered from its proprietor getting interested in other things, especially in his magnificent and public-spirited venture—for such it was, rather than a business venture—the National Dictionary of Biography. Mr. George Smith himself always looked upon the National Dictionary as a piece of public service, and he put a great deal of his own time and energy into it. The *Cornhill*, though always maintaining a high literary standard, greatly altered its character after Mr. Leslie Stephen's editorship came to an end. Its price was altered to six-pence, and for a time it was purely a magazine of fiction, in which the firm of Smith & Elder ran in serial form novels of which they had bought the book rights. There were, besides the two serial novels, only a few short stories and light essays, but these were only a kind of stuffing for the fiction.

In the year '96, however, it occurred to Mr. Smith that it would be interesting to revive the *Cornhill* and show that there was still life and force in the magazine which had published some of Thackeray's best essays, and his later novels—the magazine in which had appeared novels like *Romola*, with Leighton's illustrations, and in which Louis Stevenson had given to the world those first and most delightful of his essays, afterwards collected in *Virginibus Puerisque*. Once more, determined George Smith, it should become the home of good literature as a whole, and not merely of readable fiction.

For his new series—the price reverted to sixpence—Mr. Smith wanted a new editor. He was not one of those people who waste time over that mysterious process known as "sounding" people, a process that seems to connote a great deal of farsightedness, caution, and discrimination in the sounder, but which, as a matter of fact, is almost always a cloak for indecision. That was not Mr. George Smith's way. He wrote me a plain, straightforward letter, telling me what his plans for the *Cornhill* were, adding without any flummery that he thought I was the man to give what he wanted, and asking me whether I would become Editor. I got the letter during my first visit to Cairo, in November, 1895. I at once replied that if my chiefs at *The Spectator* saw no objection, I should be delighted to try my hand. My chiefs saw no objection, and I set to work.

When I say "delighted," I am using the term in no conventional sense. My head had long been filled with plans for the editing of a literary magazine, and here was the chance to bring them to fruition. Besides, as every young man should, I longed for something in which I should have a show of my own and be able to try every sort of experiment—a thing which you can only do when you are either starting a new paper, or making, as was to be the case with the new series of the *Cornhill*, an entirely new departure.

If I remember rightly, I actually stipulated with Mr. George Smith for a free hand, but the stipulation was quite unnecessary.   I saw during my first talk with him that a free hand was exactly what he intended to give me. No editor ever had a more delightful proprietor.   Though he was, I suppose, very nearly forty years my senior, he was as young as I was, quite as full of enterprise, quite as anxious to make new departures, and quite as willing to run risks and to throw his cap over the hedge.   Nominally I had to deal with Mr. Reginald Smith, one of the partners in the firm and the son-in-law of Mr. George Smith.   (It was a mere accident that a Smith had married a Smith.) Reginald Smith was a good scholar, had done very well at Eton, at Cambridge, and had gone to the Bar, but he had not got his father-in-law's fire or his *flair* for literature, nor, again, his father-in-law's boldness.   I was on the best of terms with him and he was the most kind and friendly of publishers.   It often happened, however, in going over my plans for the new *Cornhill*, he thought this or that proposal on my part might prove too expensive, too risky, too radical, or too unconventional.   In such cases he always said that we had better take the decision to Mr. George Smith.   On the first occasion I was a little alarmed as to what the result might be.   I felt that Mr. Smith might naturally support his son-in-law in the direction of caution, and that the appeal to Cæsar might go against me.   The first example, however, was enough to convince me that my anxieties had no foundation.   I remember well how Mr. Smith at once out-dared my daring, saying that he entirely agreed with me, and not only thought that I ought to have my way, but enthusiastically declared that it was the best way. After that I had no more trouble, and it was I who in future suggested an appeal to the head, for I knew that the result would always be a decision on the side of enterprise. Mr. George Smith was never the man to be frightened by such phrases as "dangerous innovation which might be very much resented by the readers." Dangerous innovations were just what he liked, the things out of which he had made his fame and his money, and he backed them to the end like the true sportsman that he was.

There is nothing, perhaps, more interesting and more attractive than the planning and putting together of the first number of a magazine. I had a blank sheet of paper upon which to draw up my Table of Contents, except for an instalment of a novel. What I was determined to make the *Cornhill* under my editorship was a place of *belles-lettres*. And besides good prose, if I could get it, I wanted good poetry. In the prose I naturally aimed at short stories, memoirs (as long as these were really worth having) and inspiring literary and historical criticism. I always felt that there was very good copy to be found in anniversary studies, that is, studies of great men whose births or deaths happened to fall within the month of publication and so might reasonably be supposed to be in the public mind. Another direction in which I felt sure there was good copy, if I could get the right man to do it in the right way, was in the great criminal trials of former ages. Every journalist knows that a trial sells his paper better than any other event. The daily newspaper could always forestall the magazine in the matter of trials of the day, but there remained open to me the whole field of State trials.

Besides these features, I realised how much the ordinary Englishman likes natural history, if it is dealt with in the proper way, and likes also to hear of what is newest and most taking in the worlds of science and philosophy and in the things of the spirit generally. These, perhaps, were fairly obvious features, but there was one other in which I may claim a certain originality. In the 'nineties we were all talking and writing about "human documents," by which we meant memoirs, autobiographies, and, above all, diaries which, when written, were not meant to see the light, and in which the naked human heart was laid bare for inspection. It occurred to me that, though I could not get, except by some accident, a human document of this kind, it might be rather fun to manufacture one. I could not get a Marie Bashkirtseff to intrigue my readers as the young Russian lady in question had intrigued Mr. Gladstone and the rest of us, but I thought I could get hold of some one who could write a similar sort of diary, which, though it might not be so introspective, would be a good deal more witty. I therefore turned over in my mind the people I could ask to write a "journal intime." While I was in bed, experiencing the mental state that Sir Walter Scott used to call "simmering," *i.e.*, thinking about my work in a half-hypnotic condition, I remember that the idea occurred to me. The man to do what I wanted was, I suddenly felt, the wisest and wittiest of my Balliol contemporaries, Dean Beeching. But he was not then a Dean, or even a Canon or a Reader at Lincoln's Inn, but simply a country clergyman. I wrote at once to him, telling him that I had become Editor of the new *Cornhill*, and asking him to write for me, under the seal of secrecy, a monthly article in Diary form, which was to be called "Pages from a Private Diary." In it he was to put all the best things he could think of in the way of good stories, criticism of matters old and new, comments upon life, literature, and conduct, accounts of historical figures and historical events, all informed with *verve* and interest and all presented in that inimitable style, half-serious, half-quizzical, of which Beeching was a master.

Beeching wrote back to tell me how much he liked the idea, and how sure he was that he could not do anything of the kind worth my taking. It was quite beyond him. I replied that this was nonsense, that I was quite sure from his answer that he understood exactly what I wanted, that he could do it, and that I should want the first instalment by the middle of May. I further charged him solemnly that he was not to write the thing like an essay but that he must make it a real diary, writing it day by day, and making it in this way genuine reality and not an essay with dates in it. In the end he consented to try his best. He realised at once that it would be quite necessary to keep the diary as a true diary—that is, write it spasmodically. I then again enjoined the utmost secrecy upon him, saying that it was not only a case of "*omne ignotum pro magnifico*," but also that secrecy was the best possible advertisement. I knew that his copy would be extraordinarily attractive, and I wanted people at London dinner-parties and in club smoking-rooms to ask each other, "Have you guessed yet who the *Cornhill* diarist is?" I may say that my prophecy was exactly fulfilled, for not only did the Private Diary get a great deal of praise on its merits, which were truly memorable, but also on what I may call "guessing competition" grounds,—a vice or a virtue of human nature which I was quite determined to exploit for all it was worth. I still recall my excitement when Beeching's copy arrived. It was written in a beautifully neat hand (we did not type much in those days) and accompanied by a heart-broken letter in regard to the author and his supposed failure. I had only to read two pages to see that, with his wonderful

instinct for humour as well as his scholarship and knowledge of English and classical literature, he had given me
exactly what I wanted. I wrote at once to him, telling
him what I thought of the Diary and that there was to be
no talk of his abandoning it. I should expect it regularly once a month, for at least nine months or a year.
Once more I enjoined secrecy. The "Pages from a Private
Diary" were, of course, afterwards republished and did
exceedingly well as a book. They may still be read with
pleasure by anyone who cares for good literature and a
good laugh. All I need add about the Diary is that I
told Beeching to envisage himself, not as a country clergyman, for that would give away the secret, but as a retired
Anglo-Indian who had come to live in a village in the
south of England. This kind of man might be as interested in the villagers as he was in history and literature,
and would be able to look upon them with new eyes.
A little anti-clericalism might, I suggested, put the
reader off the track and help maintain the secret. In a
word, I rather suggested the idea of a Berkshire Xenophon, a man who had fought battles in his own day, but
was now studying economics or philosophy amid rural
scenes. Nobly did Beeching respond. I think in the
first instalment, if not, in the second, he told a delightful
story of a Berkshire labourer looking over a sty at a good
litter of Berkshire grunters and remarking, "What I do
say is this. We wants fewer of they black parsons and
more of they black pigs." Be that as it may, no person of
discernment ever wanted fewer Beechings, or fewer pages
from his Private Diary.

Another innovation which I was very keen to follow
up, and in which I was backed by Mr. George Smith, was
the habit of placing an editorial note to most of the articles,
in which I said something as to what the writer was at and

conveyed a suggestion (a very proper thing for an editor
to do) that the article was of unusual merit and deserved
looking into, and so on.   For example, in the case of the
"Pages from a Private Diary" I put the following:

There are as good private and "intimate" journals being
kept at this moment as any that were kept in the last century.
Unfortunately, however, the public will not see them, in the
course of nature, till forty or fifty years have elapsed; till, that
is, half their charm has evaporated.   The *Cornhill* has been
lucky enough, however, to secure one of the best of these, but
only on conditions.   The chief of these is absolute anonymity.
But, after all, anonymity only adds the pleasure of guessing.
All that can be said of the *Cornhill* Diarist is that he lives in
the country, and that, like the author of *The Anatomy of
Melancholy*, he is *paucis notus paucioribus ignotus*.

As a proof of the delightful things which Beeching wrote
in his Diary, out of his own head, as children say, I may
quote the following:

8th.—My old gardener has at last condescended to retire.
He has been on the place, I believe, for sixty years man and
boy; but for a long time he has been doing less and less; his
dinner-hour has grown by insensible degrees into two, his
intercalary luncheons and nuncheons more and more numerous,
and the state of the garden past winking at.   This morning he
was rather depressed, and broke it to me that I must try to
find someone to take his place.   As some help, he suggested the
names of a couple of his cronies, both well past their grand
climacteric.   When I made a scruple of their age, he pointed
out that no young man of this generation could be depended
upon; and, further, that he wished to end his days in his own
cottage (*i.e.* my cottage), where he had lived all his life, so
that there would be a difficulty in introducing anyone from
outside.   I suppose I must get a young fellow who won't mind
living for the present in lodgings.   I make a point, as far as

possible, of taking soldiers for servants, feeling in duty bound
to do so; besides, I like to have well set-up men about the place.
When they are teetotallers they do very well. William, my
coachman, is a teetotaller by profession, but, as the phrase
goes, not a bigot. He was a gunner, and the other night—I
suppose he had been drinking delight of battle with his peers—
he brought me home from ——, where I had been dining, in
his best artillery style, as though the carriage was a field-
piece.

He was equally delightful when raking in with both
hands from old and new sources good stories and good
sayings. Take, for example, though this was not in the
first number, the following story of a young Presbyterian:

Jack has a Scotch cousin, Donald, who is of a more metaphysical turn of mind, as becomes a Shorter Catechumen.
The following little dialogue will show that he inherits the
faith of his fathers:

Donald:　Mother, was Jesus Christ a Jew?
Mother:　Yes, Donald.
Donald:　But how could He be, when God the Father is a
Presbyterian?

The "Pages from a Private Diary" were a very great
success, in spite of their author being ultimately discovered by Mr. Bain, the well-known bookseller. Partly
by accident and partly from a printer friend, who told
him where the proofs went, he guessed that Beeching was
the author.

But proud as I was of the Diary, I am not sure that
my greatest find was not a wonderful short series entitled
"Memoirs of a Soudanese Soldier." It happened that
while I was up the Nile I came across an old Soudanese
soldier—a lieutenant who had just risen from the ranks,

and so avoided having to leave the Soudanese regiment to which he belonged on a rather exiguous pension. The officer in question, Ali Effendi Gifoon, was a typical Soudanese in face and figure. He looked like a large, grave, elderly monkey, but he was as brave as a lion and as courteous, as chivalrous, and as loyal as an Arthurian knight-errant. All the time there was in him a touch of the pathos that belongs to some noble animal. Slavery made him sad just as freedom made him loyal and grateful. I have seen many strange and picturesque people in my time, but of them all Ali Effendi Gifoon was the strangest. To begin with, he was a slave-soldier, which seemed to carry one back to Xerxes or some other of the great Babylonian or Persian rulers and their armies. He was caught when a young man high up the Nile by one of the great Arab slave-dealers and raiders of Egypt. The dealer sold him to Mehemet Ali the Pasha. He, like most tyrants of Turkish extraction, believed in slave-soldiers if you could get the right breed, and, therefore, he was always ready to buy the right type of man for his Soudanese battalions. In order to keep his ranks full, the dealers caught young Soudanese for him as one might catch young badgers or any other fighting animal "for a gent what wanted them very particular." A village was surrounded, and the children and young men pounced upon, and the rest who were not wanted were either killed or allowed to die of starvation.

His origin was strange enough, but still stranger was a fact which I soon learnt after I made the acquaintance of Gifoon, and travelled up the Nile with him for three days. We sat talking late into the night, on the top deck of the stern-wheeler mail boat, with a British officer acting as interpreter. Gifoon knew only two cities besides Cairo. They were Paris and the City of Mexico. It makes one's head whirl, but it is the truth. It reminds me of a New Zealand patient in our War Hospital. He made from our house his visit to London, and our Sister-in-charge warned him of the dangers and temptations of the metropolis. He assured her that he was all right, for he knew Wollaranga (his native town) and Cairo intimately, and that he was "salted" to the life of great cities.

Gifoon's knowledge of Mexico came about in this way. Napoleon III had no sooner entered upon his Mexican campaign than he found that his French troops died like flies in the piece of swampy country between the coast and the City of Mexico. Yet that fever-haunted track must be held, or communication would have been cut between the French troops on the Mexican plateau and the sea. In his difficulty Napoleon III appealed to his brother tyrant, the Khedive of Egypt. Ismail, wishing to please the Emperor, who could influence the French financiers, from whom he was always borrowing, instantly produced a battalion of Soudanese soldiers who were warranted to stand anything in the way of climate, or, if not, it did not much matter. There would be no complaints if they all died in Mexico, because they would leave nobody behind them with any right to complain. Slaves have no relations. Accordingly the Soudanese were shipped off to Vera Cruz, and there fought for the French. When the war came to an end the remaining Africans were brought back to Paris to grace Napoleon's spectacular effort to get out of his failure. Just as Napoleon gilded the dome of the Invalides when he came home from Russia in order to keep people's tongues off Borodino, so Napoleon III showed a sample of his black contingent on the Boulevards, and awarded Gifoon, the leading black hero, a medal given under the same conditions as the Victoria Cross.

When Gifoon got back to Cairo, one of those strange
things happened to him which happen only in Eastern
countries. The Khedive made the black man of valour
his coachman—partly to show what esteem he had for the
French ruler, partly to show how small was any achievement compared with the honour of doing personal service
to "Effendina," and partly, perhaps, in order to show off
his picturesque hero to stray European visitors, for Ismail
on the one side of his head had the instinct of the company-
promoter. He liked, as it were, good human copy for his
Prospectuses. When, however, Ismail's troubles ending,
abdication began and the re-making of the Egyptian
Army, the coachman V. C. drifted back to the army and
was found there by the British officers who were turning
the Soudanese soldiers into some of the best fighting
troops in the world.

Captain Machell, who was foremost in the making of
the Soudanese, by a lucky accident happened upon Gifoon,
saw his worth, made a friend of him, and brought him
forward. When I saw Machell in Egypt he not only told
me his friend's history, but added that in the leisure of a
desert camp he had got Gifoon to write down the story of
his life. The old man talked, and the young English
soldier, who knew Arabic, or, rather, the broken-down form
which Gifoon talked, translated into English, giving the
meaning of what was said as clearly as possible, not in
literary English but in the straightforward style in which
an English officer in the wilds makes out his Reports.
For example, when Gifoon talked about regiments, or
battalions, or corps, using in his Arabic dialect the nearest
word, Machell put down the expression which was most
appropriate, such, for example, as "*cadre*." This fact
gave rise to a very curious example of how easily plain
people get bemused in matters of style.

It happened that at the time my first number came out, I had a friend at the Reform Club who, as a Civil Engineer, had spent a good deal of time in the 'fifties and 'sixties in the Turkish Empire, and knew, or thought he knew, the East by heart. He was fond of me and greatly interested in my venture in the *Cornhill*, and also in all I told him about my good luck in getting the memoirs of a genuine Soudanese fighting-man. When I saw him after my new number had come out, I hastened to ask his verdict on the memoirs. I found him very sad and distracted. "Strachey, you have been 'had'—entirely taken in. The memoirs are not genuine. I assure you they are not. They are the most obvious fake. Anyone who has been in the East can see that at a glance." "But," I replied, "I know they are not a fake. I have seen the man myself, and talked with him for hours. I know also that Machell is a perfectly straight man and took down exactly what Ali Effendi Gifoon said. The idea of his trying to take me in is impossible." But he would not be moved. He was certain that the thing was a fake, and said he could convince me. As an infallible proof he pointed to a passage in which Gifoon used the regular military technical language to describe the organization of the troops under the Khedive. For example, the translator made the Soudanese soldier in the British version talk about "military operations," "regimental *cadres*," "seconded," and so forth. "You don't know the Orientals as I do," said the old gentleman over and over again. "They would no more be able to talk like that, Strachey, than you could talk like the Khoran." It was no use for me to point out that nobody suggested for a moment that he used the English words in dispute. How could he? He knew no English. The phrases which were supposed to show the fake were simply

Machell's rough-and-ready method of getting through to English readers the ideas that the Soudanese soldier intended to convey. He used some Arabic or Central African phrase which meant "war," or "a body of men," and so forth, and Machell fitted them with the nearest technical phrase at his command. No doubt a more artistic effect would have been produced by using the Arabic word, or finding some primitive Anglo-Saxon equivalent, and then explaining in a note that what was meant was, in fact, a "battalion," "company," or "section." But Machell, not being able to write in what the Americans call the "hath doth" style, boldly used the only language he knew—the language of the Reports, Schedules, and Forms of the British Army. To my mind, and to the mind of anyone with literary instinct, the very fact that made my old friend think the memoirs were a fake made me sure that they were genuine. If Machell had written like Walter Scott, or still more like Kipling, I should have had great doubts as to whether he was not making things up and taking me in. As it was, I felt perfectly happy.

The memoirs, though they never attracted the public attention they deserved, were full of extremely curious and interesting things, and showed, indeed, not only the oriental, but primitive tribesman's mind with a wonderful intimacy. The most curious thing in the memoirs was a prophecy made by a Mohammedan saint. Though I cannot quite expect people of the present generation to realise the full poignancy of this prophecy, I think I can make the chief point clear. The memoirs, which were written down in 1895 and published in 1896, contained the following prophecy:

I remember the great Sayid Hassan el Morghani of Kassala uttering the prophecies which were generally ridiculed then,

14

but which are rapidly being justified as events go on. Sayid Hassan was the father of Sayid Ali el Morghani, who was at Suakin with us, and who is now so greatly respected as the representative of this powerful sect of Moslems.

Sayid Hassan was undoubtedly possessed of second-sight and I implicitly believe him to have been a Ragil Kashif, *i.e.*, a man who could penetrate the mysteries of the future. Wild and improbable as his prophecies must have appeared to most of those who heard them at Kassala, yet his every utterance was received with profound respect, and gradually we saw one after another of his statements borne out by facts.

The burden of the Morghani's prophecies was that evil times were in store for the Soudan. He warned us all "El marah illi towlid me takhodhash" (Take not unto thyself a wife who will bear thee children), for a crisis was looming over the near future of the Soudan, when those who wish to support the Dowlah, or Government, must fly, and they will be lucky if they escape with their lives. Kassala would be laid waste four times, and on the fourth or last occasion the city would begin to live once more.

Mahomed Noor, who was Emir of Kassala at that time, openly ridiculed these prophecies; upon which the Morghani replied that all he had foretold would undoubtedly come to pass, but that, as Mahomed Noor had but a very short time to live, and would die a violent death, he would not have an opportunity of seeing it himself. Being pressed to say upon what he based his prophecies regarding the Emir's death, he said that his end was near, and that Mahomed Noor and his son would shortly be killed by the Abyssinians on the same day. The flame of *fitna*, or insurrection, would not first appear in the Soudan, but the fire would be kindled in Egypt itself. Then the whole Soudan would rise, and the people would not be appeased until the land had been deluged in blood and entire tribes had disappeared off the face of the earth. The work of re-conquest and re-establishment of order would fall upon the Ingleez, who, after suppressing the revolt in Egypt, and gradually having arranged the affairs of that country, would

finally occupy the Soudan, and would rule the Turk and the
Soudanese together for a period of five years. The idea of the
Turk being ruled by anyone was received with special incredul-
ity, and on his being pressed to explain who and what these
mighty Ingleez were, he said they were a people from the
North, tall of stature and of white complexion. The English
regeneration would place the Soudan on a better footing than
it had ever been on before, and he used to say that the land of
Kassala between El Khatmieh and Gebel um Karam would
ultimately be sold for a guinea a pace. The final struggle for
the supremacy in the Soudan would take place on the great
plain of Kerrere, to the north of Omdurman; and, pointing to
the desert outside Kassala, which is strewn with large white
stones, he said: "After this battle has been fought, the plain of
El Kerrere will be strewn with human skulls as thickly as it is
now covered with stones." When the Soudan had been
thoroughly subdued, the English occupation would be extended
to Abyssinia. Then there would no longer be dissension between the people of that country and the Egyptians, who
would intermarry freely, and would not allow the difference in
their religion to remain a barrier between them.

The passage about the Ingleez in this prophecy, though
striking and picturesque, might be explained away by the
fact that the Effendi later became so strongly impressed
by the power of the English that everything in his mind
was tinctured by this fact. Any vaticinations of changes
to be wrought by some great and mysterious external
power would, after our occupation of Egypt, naturally
suggest the English.

What, however, is much more striking is the prophecy
that the final struggle for the supremacy of the Soudan
would take place on the great plain of Kerrere, to the
north of Omdurman. When I first read that prophecy
in proof, the great plain outside the north of Omdurman
meant nothing to me. Not only did the re-conquest of

the Soudan appear anything but imminent, in the spring of 1896, but one was inclined to believe that the advance to Khartoum would very probably be made by water, or, again, would come from Suakin and the Red Sea. Lord Kitchener, as it happened, made the advance by the Nile Valley, *i.e.*, by land and rail, and so had to cross the plain to the north of Omdurman.

Though the plain of El Kerrere was in fact strewn first with the white djibbas, or tunics, of the dead Soudanese, and later with their skulls and bones, as thickly as a piece of sandy desert with stones—Lord Kitchener's army had not sufficient men to bury the vast mass of dead Dervishes till several years after—this might be put down as the commonplace of picturesque prophecy. It was, however, a distinctly good hit on the prophet's part to suggest that the Dervish rule would literally be swallowed up by the casualties in one great battle at the point indicated. That was exactly what happened. I remember well, years after the prophecy, reading in the account of the special correspondents that the field of Omdurman some few days after the battle looked exactly like a plain covered with patches of white snow. Anyway, though interested by the prophecy, it seemed to me at the time to be much too remote and too vague to take much interest in it. When, however, two years later, I read the passage about the patches of snow, I suddenly remembered the prophecy, looked it up, and was greatly impressed.

One of the things which I am proudest of as regards the *Cornhill* is the fact that I was able to discover three or four new writers who later made names for themselves. One of these was Mr. Patchett Martin, who, in a series of books, *Deeds that Won the Empire*, showed himself extraordinarily adept at carrying on the Macaulay tradition of readableness and picturesqueness in the handling of historical events. Another "find" was Mr. Bullen, a man really inspired with the spirit of the sea, and a man with a sense of literature. I remember, for example, early in my acquaintance with him,—an acquaintance due solely to the fact that I accepted his MS. on its merits and without knowing the least who he was—talking to him about Herman Melville's *Moby Dick*—the story of the mysterious White Whale which haunts the vast water spaces of the South Pacific—a story about which I note with interest that of late certain American and English writers have become quite mystical, or, as the Elizabethans would have put it, "fond."

The story of how Bullen's MS. was accepted, and, therefore, how Bullen became within a very few months, from an absolutely unknown ex-seaman struggling to keep himself and his family from starvation, a popular writer and lecturer, is worth recording. It shows how great a part pure luck plays in a man's life, and especially in the lives of men of letters. It is more agreeable, no doubt, to think that we are the sole architects of our careers, but the facts are often otherwise. We are as much, if not more beholden to luck than skill.

After the first number of the *Cornhill* had been got out, we became so snowed under with copy that I had to give instructions that, though all the MSS. should be gone through, none could be accepted. I told my staff that they must harden their hearts even to good short stories and good essays, as we had already accepted enough stuff to carry us on for three or four months. I was determined that I would not start water-logged, or, rather, inklogged! "All we can do is to send the MSS. back, but give a word of blessing and encouragement to the good ones."

Somewhat to my annoyance, as I was about to leave the

office one evening, Mr. Graves, who was my chief helper, forced a MS. upon me with the words, "I know what you said about showing you nothing more; but I simply won't take the responsibility of rejecting this. You must do it, if anyone has to. It is too good a piece of work for anyone except an Editor to reject." When I got home I very unwillingly began to read it. I felt I should be in a difficulty, whatever happened. If it was as good as Graves said, I should have to take it. But that would mean dislodging somebody else whose MS. I had already accepted. I had, however, only to read four or five pages to see that Mr. Graves was perfectly right and that, whatever else happened, this MS. had got to be accepted.

Happily, I did not wait, but wrote at once a letter of congratulation to the unknown Mr. Bullen, and told him I would take his story, which proved to be the first instalment of a book. Smith & Elder, when acquainted with what had happened, saw the value of the copy, got in touch with Bullen at once, and very soon agreed to publish his first Whaling book. He told me afterwards that when the letter arrived he was in the direst of straits. He had practically no money on which to keep himself, his wife, and his children alive. His health was in a bad state, as was that of his wife, and he was in the hands of a money-lender who was pressing for payment and was about to sell him up. He had, of course, put nothing of this into his covering letter, but somehow or other I had an instinct that the man was in trouble. Somehow or other, his emotional struggle had transferred itself to me along the wire of the letter. Subconsciousness spoke to subconsciousness. Curiously enough, a similar impulse founded on no evidence has come to me on one or two other occasions, and they have always proved substantial. Anyway, I think I either sent Bullen a cheque in advance, or asked him whether he would like to have one, and so the situation was saved.

The discovery of Bullen was always a pleasure, but still greater was my delight in the discovery of one of whom I may now say without exaggeration that he has become one of the leading men of letters of our time. The author I mean is Mr. Walter De La Mare. My friend, Mr. Ingpen, who was then on the staff of Smith & Elder, and was detailed to help me in getting up and getting out the *Cornhill*, came to me, after I had been in office for about three weeks, and asked me whether as a personal favour I would look at an article by a relation of his called De La Mare, a youth who was then on the staff of a business house in the City, but who had literary leanings and was married to Mr. Ingpen's sister. I told him that I should, of course, be delighted, but that I had outrun the constable terribly in the way of accepting MSS., as he knew, for he wrote most of the letters of acceptance. I was afraid, therefore, that however good his brother-in-law's work, I could only give one verdict. He told me that he fully realised the situation, but that he would be glad if I would read the MS. all the same, and tell him what I thought of it.

Accordingly I stuck the MS. in my pocket. With a certain feeling of dread that I might be forced to accept it, I took it out on the following Sunday, at Newlands, and began to read. I shall never forget my delight. I had been pleased at the Bullen find, but here was something quite different. When I laid down Mr. De La Mare's MS. —signed Walter Ramal, an anagram of De La Mare—I am proud to say that I fully realised that a new planet had swum into my ken. I had had the good luck to be the literary astronomer first to notice that the Host of Heaven had another recruit. That is an experience as thrilling as it is rare.　The story was entitled "A Mote," and I am delighted to think I had the prescience to pass it on to my readers with the following note, for, as I have said before, I insisted, somewhat to the horror of conventional people, in decorating the contributions of any new writer with an explanation or comment.　Here was my guess at De La Mare's story.　I do not mean to say that it contains the whole truth, but, at any rate, it was a good shot considering the facts before me.　Here it is:

Those who hold the doctrine of transmigration will hardly fail, after they have read this story, to think that the spirit of Edgar Allan Poe is once more abroad.—Ed. *Cornhill*.

Here I may add that these notes had a curiously irritating effect upon the older and more rigid readers of the magazine.　Mr. Reginald Smith, for example, was quite terrified by the passionate way in which old gentlemen at his club attacked him on the way in which the pages of the *Cornhill* were defiled by the Editor's "horrible little notes."　Nobody wanted to read them.　They were either futile or patronising, or both.　They utterly spoilt the magazine, and so forth and so on.　Mr. Reginald Smith, though kindness itself in the matter, was inclined to yield to the storm and to think that I had perhaps made a mistake in breaking away from the established custom. I appealed to Mr. George Smith, quite certain that he would support me and the innovation.　He did so; and I continued, though, perhaps, with a little more reticence, to put up directing-posts for my readers.　I am sure I was right.　After all, the ordinary man gets very much confused by new writers and is very likely to miss a good thing merely because he is put off by the title or the first few sentences.　Yet all the time, the essay or short story at which he shies is the very thing he would like to read if only it had been properly introduced to him. In Mr. De La Mare's case, however, there was no fear of being put off by reading the first few sentences. If you had once read these you were quite certain to finish. I never remember a better opening:

I awoke from a dream of a gruesome fight with a giant geranium. I surveyed, with drowsy satisfaction and complacency, the eccentric jogs and jerks of my aunt's head.

The performance is even better than this promise of strange things strangely told. In the end it is not "my aunt" but "my uncle" who sees visions, and visions whose subtlety and originality it would be hard to beat. I will tantalise my readers with a quotation:

My uncle stopped dead upon the gravel, with his face towards the garden. I seemed to *feel* the slow revolution of his eyes.

"I see a huge city of granite," he grunted; "I see lean spires of metal and hazardous towers, frowning upon the blackness of their shadows. White lights stare out of narrow window-slits; a black cloud breathes smoke in the streets. There is no wind, yet a wind sits still upon the city. The air smells like copper. Every sound rings as it were upon metal. There is a glow—a glow of outer darkness—a glow imagined by straining eyes. The city is a bubble with clamour and tumult rising thin and yellow in the lean streets like dust in a loam-pit. The city is walled as with a finger-ring. The sky is dumb with listeners. Far down, as the crow sees ears of wheat, I see that *mote* of a man, in his black clothes, now lit by flaming jets, now hid in thick darkness. Every street breeds creatures. They swarm gabbling, and walk like ants in the sun. Their faces are fierce and wary, with malevolent lips. Each mouths to each, and points and stares. On I walk, imperturbable and stark. But I know, oh, my boy, I know the alphabet of their vile whisperings and gapings and gesticulations. The air quivers with the flight of black winged shapes. Each foot-tap of that sure figure upon the granite is ticking his hour away." My uncle turned and took my hand. "And this, Edmond, this is the man of business who purchased his game in the City, and vied with all in the excellence of his claret. The man who courted your aunt, begot hale and whole children, who sits in his pew and is respected. That beneath my skull should lurk such monstrous things! You are my godchild, Edmond. Actions are mere sediment, and words—froth, froth. Let the thoughts be clean, my boy; the thoughts must be clean; thoughts make the man. You may never at any time be of ill repute, and yet be a blackguard. Every thought, black or white, lives for ever, and to life there is no end."

"Look here, Uncle," said I, "it's serious, you know; you must come to town and see Jenkinson, the brain man. A change of air, sir." "Do you smell sulphur?" said my uncle. I tittered and was alarmed.

Anyone who reads this and knows anything of literature will understand the feelings of a young editor in publishing such matter, especially in publishing it in 1896. At the present time the refrain that "All can raise the flower now, for all have got the seed" is a reality. In the 'nineties work like "The Mote" was rare. Connoisseurs of style will recognise what I mean when I say that what endeared "Walter Ramal" to me was that, in spite of the fact that Stevenson at that very time was at his best, and so was Kipling, there was not a trace of either author's influence in Mr. De La Mare's prose. The very occasional appearances of Stevensonianism were in truth only examples of common origin. He at once made me feel that he was destined for great things. When there are two such influences at work, happy is the man who can resist them, and resist them in the proper way, by an alternative of his own, and not by a mere bald and hungry reticence.

Mr. Walter De La Mare's second article was called "The Village of Old Age." It was a charming piece of what I simply cannot and will not call "elfish" writing. The word in me, foolishly, no doubt, produces physical nausea. If, however, someone with a stronger stomach in regard to words called it elfish I should understand what he meant, and agree. But, good as were these two essays, they were nothing compared to De La Mare's marvellous story, "The Moon's Miracle." That was a piece of glorious fantasy in which the writer excelled himself, not only as regards the mechanism of his essay-story, but as to its substance, and, most of all, its style. He prefaced it by this quotation from *Paradise Lost*:

> As when, to warn proud cities, war appears
> Waged in the troubled sky, and armies rush
> To battle in the clouds; before each van
> Prick forth the faery knights, and couch their spears,
> Till thickest legions close; with feats of arms
> From either end of heaven the welkin burns.

The following was his short synopsis of the story:

How the Count saw a city in the sky and men in harness issuing thereout—Of the encampment of the host of the moonsmen—Of how the battle was joined—The Count's great joy thereat and of how the fight sped.

The first sentences were these:

The housekeeper's matronly skirts had sounded upon the staircase. The maids had simpered their timid "Good-night, sir," and were to bed. Nevertheless, the Count still sat imperturbable and silent. A silence of frowns, of eloquence on the simmer; a silence that was almost a menace.

This enough for any man of adventure to know that he is in for a good time—in for something big. What he was in for in this case was a great aerial battle seen from Wimbledon Common—an admirable *locale* for such an event, as I have always thought. I can best prove the depth of the impression made upon me by the fact that twenty years afterwards, when on some summer evening one knew that an air raid had begun, I never failed, when I watched the skies, to think of the little group on Wimbledon Common. It had actually come true. They were scouring the fields of air in the story of fight. No doubt what one saw there was not as exquisite a spectacle as that seen by the Count. Still, there was always something thrilling and so delightful in scanning the vast battle-field of Heaven in order to find a Zeppelin, or, later, an aeroplane squadron. Here is the passage describing what the Count and his friends saw, when they discerned a city in the sky, and round it the tents of the moonsmen:

The tents were of divers pale colours, some dove-grey, others saffron and moth-green, and those on the farther side, of the colour of pale violets, and all pitched in a vast circle whose centre was the moon. I handed the mackintosh to the Count and insisted upon his donning of it. "The dew hangs in the air," said I, "and unless the world spin on too quick, we shall pass some hours in watching." "Ay," said he in a muse, "but it seems to me the moon-army keeps infamous bad watch. I see not one sentinel. Those wings travel sure as a homing bird; and to be driven back upon their centre would be defeat for the—lunatics. Give *me* but a handful of such cavalry, I would capture the Southern Cross. Magnificent! magnificent! I remember, when I was in it—" For, while he was yet deriding, from points a little distant apart, single, winged horsemen dropped from the far sky, whither, I suppose, they had soared to keep more efficient watch; and though we heard no whisper of sound, by some means (inaudible bugle-call, positively maintains the Count) the camp was instantly roused and soon astir like seething broth. Tents were struck and withdrawn to the rear. Arms and harness, bucklers and gemmy helms sparkled and glared. All was orderly confusion.

I could go on for many more pages than I am afraid my readers would approve to chronicle the joys of my editorship, and especially the joys of discovery. I will only, however, mention two or three more names. One is that of the late Mr. Bernard Capes. I think I am right in saying that my story of "The Moon-stricken," which was published in the *Cornhill*, was one of his first appearances before the English public. Another author whom, I am glad to say, I and those who helped me "spotted" as having special qualities of readability was Mr. Hesketh Prichard. In this case my wife did what Mr. Graves had done in the case of Mr. Bullen. After I had charged her, as she valued the peace of the family, to accept nothing, but to return all the MSS. which I gave her, she insisted upon my reading Hesketh Prichard's story. My judgment confirmed hers, and in spite of the difficulties of congestion, which was becoming greater and greater but which, of course, was my proof of success, I accepted the story. There was, of course, nothing novel in this experience. It is what always happens, and must happen, in journalism. An editor is like a great fat trout, who is habitually thoroughly well gorged with flies. It is the business of the young writer who wants to make his way, to put so inviting a fly upon his line and to fling it so deftly in front of the said trout's nose that, though the trout has sworn by all the Gods, Nymphs, and Spirits of River and Stream that he won't eat any more that day, he cannot resist the temptation to rise and bite. You must take the City of Letters by Storm. It will never yield to a mere summons to surrender.

The *Cornhill*, though so agreeable an experience, did not last long. *The Spectator* soon claimed me for its own. I had to resign the *Cornhill* in order, first, to find more time for *The Spectator*, and then, to carry the full weight of editorship which came to me with Mr. Hutton's death. Mr. Hutton's death was quickly followed by Mr. Townsend's retirement. This made me, not only sole Editor, but sole Proprietor, of the paper.

Before I proceed to describe the task I set myself in *The Spectator* when I obtained a free hand, and to record my journalistic aims and aspirations, I desire to describe Mr. Townsend—a man whose instinctive genius for journalism has, to my mind, never been surpassed.

CHAPTER XVI

MEREDITH TOWNSEND

TAKING *The Spectator* as the pivot of my life, I began this book by a plunge *in medias res*. This done, I had to go back and tell of my rearing and of my life in something approaching chronological sequence. In so doing, however, I have striven to remain true to Sir Thomas Browne's instructions and to keep the alabaster tomb in the barber's shop always before my eyes. Now, however, that I have reached the time when I became Proprietor and Editor of *The Spectator*, I may fitly return to my chiefs and predecessors.

Unfortunately I can do this only in the case of Mr. Townsend. In regard to any character-drawing or description of Mr. Hutton my pen must refuse to write. Just before he died Mr. Hutton made me promise not to write anything whatever about him in *The Spectator*, and though I am not sure that he meant that promise to extend to what I might wish to write elsewhere, I have always felt myself to be under a general and not merely a particular obligation of silence. Mr. Hutton and I were always the best of friends, and I regarded him with admiration as well as affection. On some points we differed strongly, but on more we were in full agreement.

Though I did not go nearly as far as he did in the matter of spiritualism I had deep sympathy with his main attitude in regard to things psychological. It was this fact, perhaps, which made him say to me, half humorously but half in earnest, when he knew that he was leaving the office to die, as I also knew it, "Remember, Strachey, if you ever write anything about me in *The Spectator*, I will haunt you!"

I obeyed his wish and clearly must alway do so, though not merely for this warning. Indeed, I remember well hoping that perhaps his spirit might still be anxious, and might find it possible to revisit his room, of which I had become the occupant. In this instance, at least, "the harsh heir" would not have resented the return. As I sat at his table late in the evening and heard, as we so often did in our river-side office, wild gusts of wind blowing up the Thames, rattling my windows, sweeping up the stairway, and shaking the door, I often caught myself trying to believe that it was Hutton's half-lame step on the threshold, and that at any moment he might fling open the door, put his hand in mine, and ask a hundred things of the paper and the staff. But, alas! he never came. As on many other occasions in my life, the desire to be haunted, the longing to see the dead was not potent, efficient, authoritative. But I must write no more of Hutton. If we cannot see the dead, at least we must keep troth with them.

Of Mr. Townsend I am happy in being able to speak quite freely. I am not trammelled by any promise. Before doing so, however, I would most strongly insist that no one shall suppose that because I say so much more of him than of his brother Editor, it is because my heart felt warmer towards him. I had, indeed, the warmest of feelings towards both, then. If anyone were to ask me which I liked the better, I should find it impossible to answer. They were both true friends. They made a

Meredith Townsend, Editor of the *Friend of India*, and his Moonshee, the Pundit Oomacanto Mukaji, Doctor of Logic in the Muddeh University.

(Taken at Serampore, Bengal, in 1849.)

great intellectual partnership. They were complementary to each other in an extraordinary degree. It was quite remarkable how little either intruded upon the intellectual ground of the other. This could never have been said of me, however, who for some years made a sort of triumvirate with them. I had a great deal of common ground with both. That was all very well for a subordinate and a younger man, but it would not have been half so satisfactory in the case of an equal partnership. Hutton was occupied with pure literature—especially poetry—and with theology and with home politics. Townsend, on the other hand, though he was a great reader and lover of books, and a man of real religious feeling, was specially interested in Asia and the Asiatic spirit and foreign affairs. To these subjects Hutton's mind, though he would not have admitted it, was in the main closed. Townsend knew a great deal about diplomatic history and about war by land and sea, as must every man who has lived long in India; Hutton's mind was little occupied with such things. Home politics, as I have said, were his field and had his deepest concern, while Townsend took in these no more than an ordinary interest. Again, Hutton was deeply interested in psychology and the study of the mind, whereas what interested Townsend most was what might be called the scenery of life and politics. Townsend looked upon life as a drama played in a great theatre and seen from the stalls. To Hutton, I think, life was more like some High Conference at which he himself was one of the delegates, and not merely a spectator.

And now for Townsend the man and the friend. What always seemed to me the essential thing about him was his great kindliness and generosity of nature, a kindliness and generosity which, when you knew him, were not the least affected by his delight in saying sharp and even biting things. He barked, but he never bit. You very soon came to find, also, that the barking, though often loud, was not even meant to terrify, much less to injure. Quite as essential, perhaps, as this kindliness, and of course far more important, was a fact of which I ultimately came to have striking proof, namely that he was the most honourable and high-minded of men. It is easy enough for any man of ordinary good character to keep a bargain when he has made it. It is by no means an easy thing for a man who has, or seems to have, cause to regret the consequences of a particular course he has taken, entirely to overcome and forget his dissatisfaction.

I can easily illustrate what I mean when I describe how, later on, I became first half-partner in *The Spectator* with Townsend and then sole Proprietor and Editor-in-Chief. Within eight or nine months of Hutton's retirement, Townsend, for a variety of reasons yet to be described, but also largely on account of the fact that his health was beginning to give way, determined that he would end his days in the country. He proposed, therefore, that I should buy him out of *The Spectator* altogether and become sole Proprietor and Editor. As I was some thirty years younger than he was, and on his death would become sole Proprietor, subject to a fixed payment to the executors of his Will, this was in fact only anticipating what would happen at his death. He promised, meantime, to write two articles for me every week as long as his health would allow, and to take charge during my holidays. The arrangement appeared favourable to him from the financial point of view, when it was made, and involved a good deal better terms than those contained in our Deed of Partnership. At any rate, the plan originated entirely with him. All I did was to say "Yes."

But to make an arrangement of that kind and to keep to it in such a way that I never had the very slightest ground for even the shadow of a "private grievance" was wonderful. Think of it for a moment. The position of chief and subordinate was suddenly and absolutely reversed. I became the editor and he the contributor. Like the shepherd in Virgil, he tilled as a tenant the land which he had once owned as a freehold. Yet he never even went to the length of shrugging his shoulders and saying, "Well, of course it's your paper now, and you can do what you like with it, but you're making a great mistake." His loyalty to his contract, and to me and to the paper, was never dimmed by a moment of hesitation, much less of grumbling or regret. He was kindness and consideration personified. I shall never forget how perfectly easy he made my position.

There was another factor in the situation which would have made it even more trying for anyone but Townsend. Directly I became sole Proprietor, I threw myself with all the energy at my command into the business side of the paper, and within a couple of years had doubled the circulation and greatly increased the profits. This did not, of course, take anything away from Townsend's share in the paper, but it might very well have made him feel, had he been of a grudging spirit, that he had made a mistake in selling out when he did. As a matter of fact, the paper would not have done so well under the partnership. I should have hesitated to risk his property by launching out, and he would probably have thought it his duty to restrain me. He disliked anything speculative in business, did not believe in the possibilities of expansion, and preferred the atmosphere of the Three per Cents. That being so, I could not have appealed to him to put more capital into *The Spectator*.

In effect, we should each have waited on the other and done nothing. However, the fact remains that there never was a trace of jealousy on his part. I have no doubt that he occasionally wished he had retained a share in the paper. He would hardly have been human if he had not done so; but he never showed any regret of a kind which would have been painful or embarrassing to me. Under conditions which might have been most trying we continued and maintained a close and unclouded friendship. It was unaffected by the slightest touch of friction. Take a small point: he even insisted on changing his room at the office for mine. His room, the room he had occupied for over thirty years, was on the first floor, and this, he insisted, was the place for the Editor-in-Chief, and so must be mine. I yielded only to his peremptory request.

Of Townsend's intellectual gifts I cannot speak without expressing a keen admiration. It is my honest belief that he was, in the matter of style, the greatest leader-writer who has ever appeared in the English Press. He developed the exact compromise between a literary dignity and a colloquial easiness of exposition which completely fills the requirements of journalism. He was never pompous, never dull, or common, and never trivial. When I say that he was the greatest of leader-writers I am not forgetting that at this moment we have in Mr. Ian Colvin of *The Morning Post* a superb artist in the three-paragraph style of matutinal exhortation. Bagehot, again, was a great leader-writer; so were Robert Low and Sir Henry Mayne; and so also was Hutton. But these men, great publicists as they were, never attained to quite Townsend's verbal accomplishment. I fully admit that many of them could, on occasion, write with far greater political judgment, and with greater learning, and with greater force and eloquence. But where Townsend excelled them and was easily first was in his power of dramatic expression and what can only be described as verbal fascination. No one could excite the mind and exalt the imagination as he did. And the miracle was that he did it all the time in language which appeared to be nothing more than that of a clever, competent man talking at his club. He used no literary artifice, no rhetorical emphasis, no elaboration of language, no *finesse* of phrase. His style was easy but never elegant or precious or ornamented. It was familiar without being commonplace, free without discursiveness, and it always had in it the note of distinction. What was as important, he contrived, even in his most paradoxical moments, to give a sense of reserve power, of a heavy balance at the Bank of Intellect.

He never appeared to preach or to explain to his readers. But though he had all the air of assuming that they were perfectly well-read and highly experienced in great affairs, he yet managed to tell them very clearly what they did not and could not know. He could give instruction without the slightest assumption of the schoolmaster. In truth, his writing at its best was in form perfect journalism.

But, all the same, Townsend both in matter and in style had his faults as a leader-writer. Though he was never carried away by language, was never blatant and never hectoring, he was often much too sensational in his thoughts and so necessarily in the phrases in which he clothed them. He let his ideas run away with him, and would sometimes say very dangerous and even very absurd things—things which became all the more dangerous and all the more absurd because they were, as a rule, conveyed in what were apparently carefully-balanced and carefully-selected words. His wildest words were prefaced with declarations of reticence and repression.

It was said of a daily newspaper in the 'sixties that its proprietor's instructions to his leader-writers were framed in these words:

"What we want from you is common sense conveyed in turgid language."

What the world sometimes got from Townsend was turgid thought conveyed, I will not say in commonplace language, for his style could never be that, but in the language of sobriety, good sense, and good taste.

Let no one think that in saying this I am being false to my friend. Townsend's faults of judgment were all upon the surface. At heart he had a great and sound mind, though sometimes he could not resist the temptation to drop the reins on his horse's neck and let it carry him where it would, and at a pace unbecoming a responsible publicist. Sometimes, too, the horse was actually pressed and encouraged to kick up its heels and go snorting down the flowery meads of sensationalism!

People generally went through three phases in the process of getting to know Townsend. To begin with, they thought he was a man inspired with the highest political wisdom and knowledge. His gifts of dialectical vaticination made them look upon him as the lively oracle of the special Providence which he himself was accustomed to say presided over the British Empire. After a time, however, they began to think that he was what they called too "viewy," too much inclined to paradox, too wild. Often, alas! the feeling in regard to him ended here, and he was written down as impracticable if amusing. That view, though probable, was certainly false. Those who had the good fortune and the good sense to persist, and were not put off by this discovery of a superficial flightiness of thought, but dug deeper in his mind, ended, as I ended, in something like veneration for his essential wisdom. They found again, as I did, that he was very apt to be in the right when he seemed most fallacious. After all, a house may be cool and comfortable, even if the front door is painted in flame-colour and has a knocker of rock crystal set in gold.

I may here appropriately point out how great an effect his book of collected *Spectator* articles dealing with Asia, and especially India, has had upon public opinion. *Asia and Europe* (Constable, London, Putnam, New York) remains the essential book on the subject handled, and every year its influence is widening. No one can understand Asia or Islam without reference to its inspiring and also prophetic pages. For example, I notice that Mr. Stoddard, in his recent book on *The Revival of Islam* (Scribner), constantly quotes Mr. Townsend on the subject. And this, remember, is not due to any fascination of style, but rather to the fact that many of Townsend's prophecies, which at the time seemed wild and unsubstantial enough, have come true.

Though I have said that Mr. Townsend's style as a journalist was perfect, and I firmly believe this, it must be confessed that occasionally he indulged in paradoxes which cannot be defended. I will not conceal the fact that these occasional kickings over the traces personally delighted me as a young man, and still delight me, but, all the same, they are indefensible from the point of view of the serious man—that dreadful person, the *vir pietate gravis*. For instance, it was always said by some of his friends, and I think with truth, for I have not dared to verify the point, that he began his leader recording the Austrian defeat and the Battle of Sadowa with these words: "*So God not only reigns but governs.*"

Another example of his trenchant style occurred in a "sub-leader" on a story from America, which related how the inhabitants of the "coast towns," *i. e.*, villages in one of the Eastern States, had refused to allow a ship that was supposed to contain cholera or fever patients from New York to land at a local port. The farmers went down with their rifles and shot-guns, so the story went, fired upon the sailors and even the invalids, while they were attempting to land, and drove them back to their ship. Townsend's leader on this legend, no doubt purely apocryphal, was full of wise things, but ended up with the general reflection that people are apt to forget that "mankind in general are tigers in trousers" and that the majority of them "would cheerfully shoot their own fathers to prevent the spread of infection."

No doubt, if you had asked Townsend to justify his statement, he would at once have admitted that the language was a little strong, and would have been quite willing to introduce some modification, such as "men occasionally behave as if they were tigers in trousers," and to add that "in certain instances some men might even go so far as to hold that it might be a public duty to shoot their own fathers to prevent the spread of infection." He was always rather sad, however, if one suggested a little hedging of this kind when one was reading over the final proofs of the paper. What he liked, and as a journalist was quite right to like, was definiteness. Qualifying words were an abomination to his strong imagination. No man ever loved the dramatic side of life more than he did. He even carried this love of drama to the lengths of honestly being inclined to believe things simply and solely because they were sensational. The ordinary man when he hears an extraordinary tale is inclined to say, "What rubbish! That can't be true. I never heard anything like that before," and so on. Townsend, on the other hand, was like the Father of the Church who said, "*Credo quia impossibile.*" If you told Townsend a strange story, and suggested that it could not possibly be true because of some marvellous or absurd incident which was supposed to have occurred, his natural and immediate impulse was to look upon that special circumstance as conclusive proof of its credibility and truth. His extraordinarily wide, if inaccurate, recollections of historical facts and fictions would supply him with a hundred illustrations to show that what seemed to you ridiculous, or, at any rate, inexplicable, was the simplest and most reasonable thing in the world. This leaning toward the sensational, which belongs to so many journalists and is probably a beneficial part of their equipment, should not be forgotten by those who are tempted to judge the Press harshly in the matter of scare headlines and scare news. When something has been inserted in the Press that turns out later to be a cock-and-bull story, the plain man is apt to think that it must have been "put in" because the editor, though he knew it was false, thought it good copy and likely to sell his paper. In my experience that is not in the least how the thing works. A great many editors, however, greatly like and are naturally inclined to believe in "good copy." And, after all, they have got many more excuses for doing so than the ordinary man realises. Nobody can have anything to do with a newspaper without being amazed at the strangeness, the oddity, the topsy-turvy sensationalism of life, when once it is laid bare by the newspaper reporters.

For example, they write an article to show how astrology has absolutely died out in England. A day afterwards you get a letter from some old gentleman in Saffron Walden or Peckham Rye or Romford, informing you that

in his small town, or suburban district, "there are ten
practising astrologers, not to mention various magicians
who do a little astrology in their odd moments." And all
this is written with an air of perfect simplicity, as if the
information conveyed were the most natural thing in the
world and would be no surprise to any ordinary well-
informed person.

But it was not only in outside affairs and in his view of
the world that lay outside the windows of his mind that
Townsend found life a thing of odd discoveries, strange
secrets, and thrilling hazards. His own existence, though
in reality an exceedingly quiet one, indeed almost that of a
recluse, was still to him a great adventure. There was
always for him the possibility of the sudden appearance of
the man in the black cloak with hat drawn over his brows,
either looking, or saying "Beware!" I remember well
his pointing out to a member of the staff who is still, I am
glad to say, a colleague of mine, a delightful reason for the
arrangement of the furniture in his, Townsend's, room at
1 Wellington Street, Strand. Townsend complained that
his writing-table was in a very cold corner, and that from
it he could not feel the warmth of the fire. It was suggested to him that the best plan would be to bring the
table nearer to the fire and to sit with his back to the
door. "But don't you see," said Townsend, "that would
be impossible? I couldn't see who was entering the
room." As he spoke there rose up visions of Eastern
figures in white turbans gliding in stealthily and with
silent tread, and standing behind the editorial chair, unseen but all-seeing. Alas! we did not often have such
adventures in Wellington Street, but no doubt it stimulated Townsend's mind in what might otherwise have
been insupportably dull surroundings to think of such
possibilities. This idea, indeed, of watching the entry

was a favourite topic of his. I remember his telling me
when I first came regularly to the office, that Mr. ——, the
then manager, who sat in the inner room downstairs, had
a mirror so placed that he could see all who came through
the main door, without himself being seen, and so appear-
ing to place callers under observation. At my expressing
some surprise that this was necessary, I was met with the
oracular reply that though it wasn't talked about, such an
arrangement would be found "in every office in London."
Of a piece with this half-reality, half make-believe, with
which, as I say, Townsend transformed his quiet life into
one long and thrilling adventure, was a remark which
I remember his making in the course of a most innocent
country walk: "If the country people knew the secret of
the foxglove root it would be impossible to live in the
country." Apropos of this remark, my painter brother,
who had always lived in the country and had plenty of
cottage friends in Somersetshire, pointed out that as a
matter of fact the country people knew the effects of digi-
talis as a poison exceedingly well, even though they were not
inclined so to use it as to make life in the country impossible.
He went on to tell, if I may be discursive for a moment,
how, one day he was painting quietly behind a hedge, he
caught a scrap of conversation between two hedge-makers
who were unaware of his presence. It ran as follows:
"And so they did boil down the hemlock and gave it to
the woman, and she died." That was the statement:
whether ancient or modern, who knows? For myself, I
have always wondered what the hedgers would have said
if they had suddenly had their rustic *on dit* capped with
the tale of how the hemlock was used in Athens 2,400
years ago. Did the "woman" of Somersetshire stave off
the effects of the poison by walking about? Did her
limbs grow cold and numb and dead while the brain still

worked? But such questions are destined to remain for ever unanswered. Country people do not like to be cross-questioned upon stray remarks of this character, and if you attempt to fathom mysteries will regard you with suspicion almost deadly in its intensity till the end of your days. "What business had he to be asking questions like that?" is the verdict which kills in the country.

CHAPTER XVII

MEREDITH TOWNSEND (*Continued*)

THOUGH I cannot resist writing upon the picturesque side of Townsend's character, I must take care not to give a wrong impression. Nobody must think, because of Townsend's emphasis and vividness of language, and that touch of imagination he introduced into every thought and every sentence, that he was an oddity or an eccentric. In spite of the fact that he would never take life plain when he could get it coloured, he was a perfectly sane person. As I have said, the more you knew him the more you felt that, though you might be shocked by the first rashness of his thought, it would very likely turn out to be a perfectly sane judgment—proper discount being allowed for his brilliance of vision. I used sometimes to put some of his most wonderful and hair-raising statements into dull English, and then ask him whether that wasn't what he meant. I generally received the instant assurance that my sober version exactly represented his view.

His attitude of mind might, indeed, be summed up by a thing that he once said to me in a period of political calm in the middle of August in the 'nineties. "*Strachey, I wish something dramatic would happen.*" He went on to explain how he was fretted almost beyond endurance by the dulness of the world. And yet I often wonder whether even he might not have found the last six years almost too

237

highly "accidented" even for him.   But I know one thing.
If he had the anxious mind developed to the highest point,
he was essentially a brave man and a true lover of his
country.   If he had been destined to live through the war
there would have been no stouter heart than his, and none
would have given a more stimulating expression to the
spirit of the nation than he.

I wish profoundly that I had made during his life, as
I ought to have done, a proper collection of Townsend's
aphoristic and sensational sayings.   They would have
been not only a source of delight and entertainment, but
also a storehouse of what might be called the practical
wisdom of an imaginative mind.   A good example of what
I mean is the following.   Townsend was once having an
exciting and not to say violent argument with a younger
man.   In the course of the combat Townsend, we may
presume, used a generous freedom of language, and it was
returned in kind by his opponent.   The clash of mind was
fierce.   Then the younger man pulled himself together.
He felt he had gone too far in some of the things he had
said, and apologised to Townsend.   If he had been rude
or over-vehement in the way in which he had maintained
and insisted upon his view—he hoped he should be forgiven.   "Not at all," was the instant reply.   "*You have a
perfect right to be wrong!*"   There was here a great deal
more than a felicitous epigram.   This acknowledgment of
every man's right to be wrong underlay Townsend's
philosophy of life and his religious attitude.   Though,
curiously enough, he had borrowed a certain touch of
fatalism from his intercourse as a young man with the
philosophies of the East, he felt very strongly the essential
freedom of the will.   But that freedom he saw could not
exist, could not be worthily exercised, could not, as it
were, have its full reward in a man's own soul, unless it

were a true freedom. Unless a man had the freedom to do
wrong as well as the freedom to do right he was not really
free. It was idle to pretend that you were giving people a
choice of freedom if you put restrictions upon them which
would effectually prevent their doing anything but that
which the inventor of the restrictions considered to be
right; if the doing of the right resulted not from their own
impulse but from the application of exterior force over
which they had no control, no virtue, no moral force.
"There is no compulsion, only you must," meant to him,
as it must to every man who knows what truth and justice
are, the utmost derogation of freedom.

I have spoken of the influence of the East upon Townsend's mind in matters of religion. Though he never became a mystic, and had not naturally the mystic's attitude
or even any true understanding of what mysticism is, as a
young man he had looked through the half-open door of the
Eastern world not merely with wonder and delight but
with a great deal of sympathy. He went to Calcutta, or,
rather, to one of its suburbs, when he was a boy of eighteen,
and remained there without coming home for over ten
years. In that time he acquired a fair acquaintance with
several Indian languages, and an intimate knowledge of
Bengali, which he always regarded as the Italian of the
East. In Bengali he was so accomplished that he was
given the post of Government Translator.

In the old daguerreotype here reproduced he is seen
sitting, by his moonshee, a Brahmin of the highest caste,—
see the mystic Brahmin thread which the Jesuits were
accused of wearing,—from whom he learned Hindustani
and, I think, a certain amount of Sanskrit. With the
moonshee he had many long talks upon those subjects on
which the intellectual Brahmins have discoursed and
delighted to discourse ever since the day when Alexander

took his bevy of Hellenic Sophists across the Indus. Greeks bursting with the new lore of Aristotle—Alexander's own tutor—at once got to work on the Brahmins and began to discuss Fate, Free-will, the Transmigration of Souls, the nature of thought, the power of words, and the mystery of the soul. The Brahmins met them half-way, as today they meet any wandering European metaphysicians. Townsend had an active, eager spirit, and he and the moonshee tired the sun with talk. But there was more than eternal talk between them. They grew to be real friends, in spite of an interval of some forty years. Townsend used to say of the moonshee, "If there is a heaven, that old man is there." Though belonging to the caste of the High Priests of the Hindu faith, he was poor in worldly possessions. But though holy and learned he had no touch in him of sacerdotal arrogance—difficult achievement, considering the sort of veneration with which Brahmins of his exalted spiritual rank were treated in Bengal.

To illustrate the depth of this veneration, Townsend was fond of telling a story of how he had in his employment in the printing office of his paper, *The Friend of India*, a high-class Brahmin engaged, I think, as a proof-reader, at low wages. It chanced that on some occasion Townsend was interviewing a very rich Bengal magnate, a mediatised Prince, so far as I remember, though of comparatively humble caste. When the Brahmin entered to bring Townsend a proof, or upon some other business of the paper, the rich noble rose, and, as Townsend picturesquely put it, "swept the dust off the Brahmin's feet with his forehead." The Brahmin received the obeisance without the slightest embarrassment, as a right entirely his due. "There," said Townsend, "is the whole of the East." Fanciful shapes of the plastic earth, the wealth and the power of the rich man, and the man of semi-royal rank, are perfectly real and fully recognised, but they make no difference to the essential fact of religion. Caste in its religious aspects is something of which we English people have no conception.

I remember pleasing Townsend with an illustration of the truth of how English people cannot conceive of great rank without a considerable amount of riches. When reading for the Bar, I came across a short Act of Parliament, in the reign of Henry VI, which was passed to deprive the existing Duke of Buckingham of all his rank and titles "because he was so poor." The two Houses of Parliament were sorry, no doubt, to have to act, but they felt it was no more respectable for a Duke to go about without money than for an ordinary man to go about without clothes. They were doing the right thing by him in reducing him to the ranks of the proletariat in name as well as in fact. English people, insisted Townsend, never seem to realise that the distinction of birth is so valuable because it is incommunicable. That, of course, is quite true. English people, happily, as I think, never have, and never will, regard mere birth with any veneration or even interest. What affects them is that potent, if rather indefinite, thing, position—the aura of distinction which surrounds great office, great wealth, and even great learning; and, oddly enough, most of all by the acclamation of fashion. The Committee of Almack's put the thing exactly, when a certain Duchess, to whom they had refused invitations for a ball, writing in expostulation reminded them of her rank. They simply replied that "the Duchess of Newcastle, though undoubtedly a woman of rank, was not a woman of fashion." It was only to "persons of fashion" that the doors of Almack's stood always open.

Townsend's conversation was a curious contradiction.

16

Half of it consisted of tremendous generalities, which made the hearer gasp with a kind of mental deflation. The other side consisted of specific statements of the most meticulous kind. And these contradictory forms of attack upon the intelligence with whom he was in conversation were mixed together in the most admired disorder. I remember well a lady who met Mr. Townsend for the first time at a luncheon-party in London, telling me that at a pause in the conversation she heard him say of a Polish actress, Madame Modjeska, then performing in town, "She has the most mobile face in South-western Europe." On another occasion the oracle gave forth this tremendous sentence: "*Musicians have no morals*," but then, remembering a musician who was a close friend of his and mine, Townsend added, "Except G——."

This is a beautiful example of the extreme generalisation followed by a headlong descent to the minutely specific. If you had suggested to Townsend that this was rather a large order, he would have replied, without turning a hair, that you were no doubt perfectly right, and would probably have limited himself in a lightning flash—"Statisticians would probably put the figure at $27\frac{1}{2}$ per cent, or some such figure."

If he had been made to choose in his writings between the specific and the general, he would, however, I am convinced, have chosen the specific, for the specific statement was his leading rule in journalism, as no doubt it was one of the sources of the charm of his style. You should always be specific even if you could not be accurate, might be given as an accurate parody of his principle.

This predilection sometimes led him into strange difficulties, especially in medicine, where he loved to use all the "terms of art." Technical expression had a fatal fascination for him, especially when he did not understand them. I remember his saying, with a naïveté which was quite delightful, apropos of a common friend in illness, "I have discovered the nature of H's ailment. There is no doubt now that he is suffering from the true Blankitis. By the way, Strachey, what is Blankitis?" I am afraid in the case in question I did not know, and he did not know, and in fact none of us but didn't know what the word meant. (I have adopted the phraseology of the little boy when the magistrate asked him if he knew where he would go to if he gave false evidence.) But Townsend had no sympathy with agnosticism of this kind. In spite of the vastness of his view, he loved placing things neatly, correctly, and in order.

He used to tell an excellent story about himself and of the kind of answer you are apt to get if you try to catalogue English people too exactly, especially in regard to their religious opinions.

Twenty-five years ago [said Townsend], when I first came here on leaving the East, I did not realise this peculiarity. I was very much interested in finding out the religious views of all sorts of people, and especially of uneducated people; and so I asked Mrs. Black (the then reigning housekeeper at the *Spectator* office) what her religious views were. I expected to be told that she was either Church of England, or Chapel, or Presbyterian, or something of the kind. To my surprise this is how she met my inquiry. She looked me straight in the face, and said, "I am a moderate Atheist."

By that name she always went in the secret councils of the office. After all, only an English person could have invented that particular form of religion. I always felt that answer would have delighted Voltaire and given him another ground for quizzing English moderation even in negation. I thought then, and have often thought since, how far the principle of moderation might be extended, and whether you could be a moderate agnostic or a moderate fatalist or a moderate logician.

Townsend had a capacity for wit, but, as he was fond of saying himself, no sympathy with farce or mere high spirits. I doubt even if he had a sense of humour in the ordinary meaning of that term, or in the Frenchman's definition: "la mélancholie gaie que les Anglais nomment 'humour.'" To say this is not to say that he did not enjoy a humorous, an ironic, a witty, or an epigrammatic story or saying. He enjoyed such things immensely and would laugh heartily at them. But he had no use for a "droll," as I must fully admit I have. I can thoroughly enjoy the long-toed comedian, and feel quite sure that if time and opportunity could combine to let me see once a week a film figuring Charlie Chaplin I should be transported with delight. Good clowning, or even bad clowning, or what people call the appalling, or melancholy, or "cut-throat," jokes in a comic paper I always find captivating.

Of good stories and laughable stories Townsend was in many ways an admirable *raconteur*. Many people would say that cannot be true. On your own confession he was too much of an exaggerator. I don't agree. Exaggeration is not a fair word for what he did to his stories. He had in him a kind of mental accelerator, and upon this he depended, no doubt, too much on occasion, as do so many motor-drivers. All the same, his stories always got home, and, strangely enough, this perpetual speeding-up of his mind never seemed to injure it or to wear it out. On the whole, his stories and his quotations were splendid, though I confess one dared not verify his dates and facts and quoted words, for fear of spoiling a real work of art. Strangely enough, he was nearly always accurate in the spirit if not in the letter. Some day I should like to tell

some of the stories that he told me of Lord Dalhousie, or
Lord Canning and the White Mutiny, and of Lady Canning as a hostess.

That Townsend was a masterly letter-writer this account of him will, I feel, have already suggested. He was
vivid, picturesque, and attractive to a high degree. The
place he lived in when he was taking a country holiday
was always the most wonderful place in the world and the
people he met there marvellous and mysterious beyond
words. Even if they were bores, they were bores raised to
such a high power as to become intensely attractive.

A curious example of the impact made upon his mind
by the Eastern religions was shown in his belief that there
was a great deal to be said for the Eastern view that Almighty Providence had entrusted the world and its government to a "demi-ergon" or angelic Vizier, who was given
the governance of the world under certain conditions of
rule which he had to observe. I remember well Townsend
once saying to me: "Some day I will write a book upon the
neglected religion—the religion which holds God to have
'devolved' the government of the world on a great Spirit
or Angel. It was his belief, or an assumed belief (for the
thing to him was really a day-dream), that in this way the
great antinomy between free-will and that predestination
which is implicit in omnipotence, could be got rid of.
Townsend thought that this matter had never been discussed as fully as it ought to have been. I am not theolo-
gian enough to know how far this is true, but I suspect
that this is just the sort of point upon which Townsend
would have been misinformed. It seems almost certain
that every conceivable abstract point of view, in pure
theology not depending upon examination and observation,
must long ago have been discussed exhaustively. Not
only did the Schoolmen and the Jesuits sound every space

of water, but the Byzantine Greeks in the early days of the Christian Faith produced "heresies" of every imaginable kind. The union of Semitic revelation and neoplatonic mysticism, first at Alexandria and later in the City of the Christian Emperor Constantine, constituted a forcing-house of theological systems.

Before I leave my recollections of Mr. Townsend, I want to say something of a curious incident in his last illness; and I must also attempt to describe his personal appearance. During the last six or nine months of his life—he was nearly eighty and his health had been undermined by his hard work in the Delta of the Ganges—his brain and memory failed him almost completely. His intellectual life sank, indeed, to what was practically a perpetual delirium. Occasionally, however, there would be a lucid interval, in which he became for a short time truly conscious and could make sensible and rational remarks. For example, on one occasion when he was in the middle of a paroxysm of loud, violent, and incoherent talk, almost approaching raving, he suddenly turned to his wife or daughter with an apology of bewildering poignancy. "I do wish that man on the sofa would keep quiet. I am afraid his noise worries you. It worries me quite as much." Even stranger, more curious, and more suggestive of the double personality is the following circumstance. Though I remember his telling me only some six or seven years before his death that he had entirely forgotten his Bengali and did not suppose he could now speak a word of it, he talked when his memory went a very great deal in the Indian vernacular and apparently with great fluency. And here I may note that he was always very fond of correcting people who talked as if the inhabitants of Bengal talked Hindustani, saying that it was Bengali that they talked, that the language was entirely different from Hindustani, and was

also the language of some fifty or sixty million people and
not by any means a patois. On the first occasion, when
the doctor was present, when Mr. Townsend reverted to
the language of the East, Mrs. Townsend in explaining
what was happening, made a very natural slip, and said:
"You hear, he is talking in Hindustani."

Immediately there came from the bed a voice in Townsend's old tone and manner, and making a correction
quite in his old style: "No, not Hindustani, Bengali."
But though the true consciousness was, as it were, on the
watch and quite able to make a correction, its force was
spent, at any rate for the time. Nothing more was said
for a long interval by the consciousness.

Here I should like to put in a plea for a much closer
psychological study of the sayings of the delirious, the
insane, and of persons in the hour of death. Such words
are not, as a rule, recorded and are often passed over in fear
or pity. This seems to me a great mistake. No harm could
be done, but, rather, a great deal of good, if nurses were
taught to record such expressions. This would result, I
feel sure, in a greater kindness to delirious persons and to
those who are insane or on the verge of insanity, quite
apart from the benefit which would accrue to scientific
investigation. If people understood something of the
double or multiplex personality there would be less terror
and surprise at some of the phenomena of the emergence
of the uncontrolled subconsciousness. It might at first
be thought that the doctor was the proper person to make a
record of the kind I am suggesting. But the doctor is, as
a rule, too busy to do this sort of work, and, what is more,
it is not he who generally has the opportunity to note the
real expressions of the subconsciousness or to witness the
struggle between the two personalities. Even in the case
of delirious or semiconscious persons, the patient, when the

doctor is there, makes an effort and pulls himself together and so reconstructs the normal personality. It is the nurse who sees the patient mentally off his or her guard, and who is, as it were, in a position to note the things of most value to the psychologist.

Townsend's personal appearance is difficult to describe. He had, from the time I first saw him in '85, grey hair and a grey moustache. He was a small man, wiry and full of energy, and in the first ten years of our friendship quite capable of taking long country walks. He always wore, even in the country, black or dark-grey clothes, which indeed constituted for him a kind of uniform. His eyes were grey and glittered brightly and keenly behind his gold-rimmed spectacles. These he never removed, except for a moment of polishing on a large silk bandana handkerchief. He smoked comparatively little, but was a perpetual snuff-taker. Nothing was more amusing than to hear him discourse on snuff-taking and describe his adventures with snuff merchants. In fact, snuff-taking in his mind had become endowed with a kind of freemasonry. All snuff-takers, he declared, knew each other. They were so few in number. He was also very interesting about snuff-boxes, and the lost art of making hinges through which the almost impalpable dust of well-ground snuff would be unable to penetrate.

I might indeed have exampled his snuff-taking as a proof of his power of endowing everything with a sense of adventure and pregnant interest.

His step was light and very quick, his voice pleasant and refined, and his manner of talking, as may be imagined, what I must—in spite of the associations—call arresting. The saying that if you had taken refuge under an arch during a rainstorm and found yourself next to Dr. Johnson you would have realised in his first ten words that you were face to face with a man of true distinction might well have been applied to Townsend himself.

But, after all, Townsend is not a man who can be described. You may describe a Mrs. Siddons with a faultless profile, a great statesman or writer with what an old family servant of ours called "an iron countenance"; but it is impossible to describe the intelligence, the nervous energy, the versatility of expression which quick-coming, eager thoughts throw upon the human face. Who can paint a thought, or number the flashes of wit? Townsend was to be appreciated, not to be described. Moreover, he was a man who impressed you more the hundredth time you saw him than on the first. It is the old mystery, the old paradox set forth by Wordsworth:

> You must love him ere to you
> He will seem worthy of your love.

It was only when you had learned to love his wit and the gallant cataract of his mind that you could fully understand and value its fascination.

As a postscript to Townsend's oracular sayings I must add one of his dicta on women. Here his generalisations were enormous and almost always included a wild nose-dive from the empyrean of generalities to that purely specific element, the hard earth. For example, he was never tired of saying—in various forms, for he never really repeated himself—that women were far more trustworthy in money matters than men. He used to say that he had never in any single instance in his whole career been repaid a loan of money made to a man. On the other hand, he had never been cheated by a woman.

It may perhaps be said that, considering I am writing a biography of myself and not of Townsend, I have dwelt too long on my predecessor in title. But, in truth, I have hardly dwelt long enough, for I am describing the making of my mind. I could hardly be too detailed or too particular in my description of Townsend, for his influence upon my journalistic career was of enormous importance. Though I very soon realised Townsend's defects as an editor, as a critic of public affairs, as a man of letters, and as a user of words, my admiration for him as a great journalist did not diminish but grew year by year.

I learned as time went on to disregard the faults and exaggerations which so often greatly displeased the statesmen or men of letters who had not the time or the patience really to understand and so to be tolerant. Townsend had to some extent done what is very rarely done in England, though it is so much done in America; that is, he had thought out a good many of the problems of publicity and arrived at very sound conclusions. If he had lived in America, I have no doubt that, with the encouragement of a public that understands publicity, he would have carried his ideas much further than he was able to carry them here, and would have been hailed as a master in his art. As it was, he never wrote anything on the function of the newspaper editor, and it was only in the shape of sparkles from the wheel that one saw the tendency of his mind to do what the Americans have done. They have succeeded in isolating publicity and making it a special art, so that it has now become with them a special art with special conditions of its own.

Townsend, as far as I remember, never talked about the ethics of journalism or the duties of the journalist. It must not be supposed for a moment that this was because he did not realise or respect those duties, or was indifferent. It was rather due to the fact that he had a kind of innocence, a *sancta simplicitas*, on this as, indeed,

on many moral and social questions. He took sound and
honourable behaviour as a matter of course, and he would
no more have thought of praising other people or himself
for having a strict sense of honour in their conduct of a
newspaper than he would of praising them or himself for
not committing petty larceny, perjury, or fraud. He took,
indeed, a very hopeful view of mankind and did not the
least believe they were really bad, even if they did show
themselves to be tigers on occasion. For instance, I
remember his saying to me once, with that naïve gaiety
which was peculiar to him, that though he and Hutton
differed a great deal in matters of theology they never had
any differences as to the line the paper should take.
Though Hutton inclined to an extremely "high" section of
the Church, to what, indeed, might be described as a kind
of sublimated sacerdotalism, and Townsend to a Broad
Church Presbyterianism, buttressed by an intense opposition to every form of priestly function, he went on to point
out that everything was made easy "because both Hutton
and I are at heart on the side of the angels."

Apropos of angels, I remember with intense delight one
of Townsend's most characteristic sayings. In the course
of a conversation which began on some mundane theme
and drifted on to spiritual lines, I remember his suddenly
throwing the noble horse of dialectic on to his haunches
with the catastrophic remark: "Strachey, remember this.
If there are angels, they have edges." Here was the whole
man. The idler or the fool will think, or pretend to think,
that this was simply ridiculous nonsense, and will pass on
with the comment, "We are not amused." As a matter of
fact, there was a great deal of good sense packed under a
kind of semi-humorous hydraulic pressure in this amazing
dictum. What he meant was that if there were angels,
they were not vague, fluid, evanescent creatures, some-

times part of a general angelic reservoir and sometimes in single samples, but definite personalities. His was only a fierce and violent way of saying what Tennyson said so exquisitely in the immortal lines:

> Eternal form shall still divide
> The eternal soul from all beside,
>   And I shall know him when we meet.

There can be no eternal form without an edge. The edge, the dividing-line, is the essential thing in individuals, and Townsend's mind had pounced upon this as a cat will fall like a thunderbolt upon a mouse. It was in this vivid, practical way that his mind worked. He jumped all the intermediate things and came out with the essential in his mouth. But those who had slow or atrophied minds and did not see the process often failed to recognise what he was after, or what a clever kill he had made.

CHAPTER XVIII

MY LIFE IN LONDON IN THE 'NINETIES

I HAVE described how I came to London, how I became established at *The Spectator* Office, and what, before I succeeded to the Editorship of *The Spectator*, were my various *extra* activities in journalism and literature. I must now say something of my personal life. In 1887 I married. The year or so spent in my father-in-law's house, 14 Cornwall Gardens, where my first child was born, was very happy and delightful. As my people lived either in Somersetshire or on the Riviera, I knew "on my own" comparatively few people in London, though those I did know were for the most part people to whom special interest was attached.

It happened that my mother-in-law, Mrs. Simpson, was not only a very charming person in herself, but, partly owing to a natural gift for, and love of, Society, and partly owing to the fact that her father, Mr. Nassau-Senior, the conversationalist, had been one of the best-known men in the political-literary world of London and of Paris, from 1820 to 1860, she knew a very large number of distinguished men and women of the middle Victorian epoch. By this I mean such men as Thackeray, Matthew Arnold, Robert Browning, Leslie Stephen, Mr. Justice Stephen, Sir Mountstuart Grant-Duff, Sir Louis Mallet, Mr. Lecky, Lord Arthur Russell and his brothers—to choose a few names almost at random. The last-named, Lord Arthur Russell, was the most kindly and friendly of men. Probably without being conscious of it themselves, he and his distinguished wife formed what a pedantic social analyst might call the centre of a social group.

I shall, for this reason, choose the Arthur Russells for description in detail. They were very old friends of the Nassau-Seniors and so of Mrs. Simpson, and friends with a double liaison. Mr. Nassau-Senior and his family had been throughout his life on very friendly terms with Lady William Russell, one of the most remarkable women of Regency and Victorian London as regards her beauty, her intellectual ability, and her social qualities. When Byron wrote the graceful and lively stanza which so audaciously recommends the gilded youth, who want to know whether their partners' complexions are real or synthetic, to wait till the light of dawn comes through the ballroom windows and then note what it discloses, he breaks off to say that, at any rate, there is one lady who will always stand the test, and adds:

> At the next London or Parisian ball
> You're sure to see her cheek outblooming all.

That lady was Lady William Russell—sister, by the way, of the unhappy Lady Flora Hastings so cruelly caught in the meshes of an angry Court intrigue based on the natural, nay, inevitable, ignorance and want of worldly knowledge of a girl-Queen, the stupidity and lack of worldly wisdom of the Court Physicians, and the blundering bitterness of a group of Great Ladies—the whole assisted and inflamed by the baser type of party-politician.

Lady William Russell had three sons, each destined to play, if not great, yet important parts in the world. The eldest became the Duke of Bedford. Though he lived in many ways a sequestered, almost hermit-like, life, he was a man of singular ability. Of him Jowett was wont to record a curious piece of private history. The Duke had said to him, that in the course of his life he had lived upon all incomes from £300 to £300,000 a year and in each category had been happy and contented. Perhaps the best way to describe Hastings, Duke of Bedford, is to say that he was a typical Russell, though a man with a Melbourne-like mind would perhaps add that his untypicalness was the most typical thing about him. The next brother was Lord Odo Russell, who played a very distinguished, brilliant, and useful part in the diplomacy of the period marked by the rise first of Prussian and then of German power. His son is the present Lord Ampthill. The third son was Lord Arthur Russell. All three boys were brought up in what might be called a nursery or schoolroom friendship with the children of the Nassau-Senior family. My mother-in-law remained in touch with all three Russells throughout her life; but her special friend, partly because he always lived in England, and partly because he married a friend of the Seniors, was Lord Arthur.

Among Mr. Nassau-Senior's Parisian friends was the brilliant and distinguished Mme. de Peyronnet, an Englishwoman by birth, married to a man of distinguished French family, who occupied an official post in the post-Restoration Administration. Mme. de Peyronnet formed part of the memorable group of Liberals of which Tocqueville was one of the most distinguished members;—a group which from the latter part of Louis-Philippe's reign to the break-up of the Third Empire comprised as notable a body of intellectuals as were ever brought together even in the city of Paris—the natural home of Social intellectualism. This, too, was the group of which M. and Mme. Mohl

were shining ornaments. M. de Peyronnet was, I believe, a very charming man, but somewhat eclipsed by
his brilliant wife, whom I am glad to say I knew, and
whose talk was to my mind one of the most delightful of
mental experiences. Poignant, free, brilliant, and yet
never pedantic or laboured, and, above all, never trivial,
Mme. de Peyronnet's conversation was a perpetual source
of joy to all who had the good fortune to know her and
the ability to understand her. She had three daughters,
who all inherited their mother's brilliancy and good looks.

Of these three daughters one, as I have said, married
Lord Arthur Russell, the next, and she, I am glad to say,
lives in full intellectual vigour, married Lord Sligo, a
typical "great gentleman" of the middle Victorian period.
Except for his perfect manners and absence of any traces
of grandiloquence or pomposity, he might have stepped
out of Disraeli's novels, or let us say an expurgated edition from which all the vulgarity and false-taste had been
eliminated and only the picturesqueness and cleverness
retained. The third sister, Mlle. de Peyronnet, never
married, but remained the devoted companion of her
mother.

I am not going to imitate the pomposity of Lord
Beaconsfield, which I have just denounced, by talking
nonsense about *Salons*, the Eighteenth Century, or of the
spirt of Mme. du Deffand or of Mlle. de Lespinasse living
again in these fascinating women. I am content to take
them as they were and quite prepared to believe that they
were not only very much nicer women, but also quite as
able and quite as brilliant as those whom the spirit of
Convention would be sure to name as their prototypes.
I am quite certain that, though they took a natural and
proper interest in history, it never for a moment crossed
the minds of any of them to talk like the ladies of the

ancien régime or to imitate them in any sort or way.
They were as natural and unsophisticated as they were in-
cisive, intrepid, and amusing in their conversation.

Never has it been my good fortune to hear better talk
than that which flowed so easily from them, and happily,
in the case of Lady Sligo, still flows. What struck me
most was the way in which anecdote, recollection, and
quotation, though not frigidly or formally dismissed, kept
a subordinate place in the talk and had to make way for
comments which were actual, original, personal, and
therefore in a high degree stimulating. Their talk had
nothing of the flavour of the second-hand or of hearsay,
however good.

I had been accustomed as a boy to hear the best type of
what I may call old-fashioned after-dinner English conversation, from the mouth of a master, Abraham Hayward. Hayward was an excellent example of the special
type of *raconteur* who first became famous in the Regency
period. These men, who were chiefly anecdotal in their
talk, are well described by Byron in the immortal account
of the House-party, *Don Juan*—"Long-bow from Scotland, Strong-bow from the Tweed." Hayward was a man
of real ability, though in a narrow sphere, and with a remarkable power of style. With him talk meant telling
stories of Byron, Melbourne, Castlereagh, Cobden,
Bright, Peel, and later Gladstone, Palmerston, and Lord
John and other eminent Victorians. He told these with
great intensive force and was vivacious as well as concise.
All the same, the talk was anecdotal, and that can never
be as stimulating as when it is spontaneous. It was the
difference between fresh meat and tinned meat—the difference between a vintage claret on the day it is uncorked
and the day after.

Do not let it be supposed that by this comparison I

17

am suggesting that the talk of Mme. de Peyronnet and her daughters was naturalistic and so artless. It was nothing of the kind. Though original and spontaneous, it was the result, consciously or unconsciously, of a distinct artistic intention. When they talked, they talked their best, as does the writer of good familiar letters. Lady Arthur Russell was the most pungent talker of the three, Lady Sligo the most reminiscent and, in the proper, not the derived sense, the most woman-of-the-worldly. I mean by this that she dealt most with the figures of the great world, but by no means in a grandiloquent, consequential, or Beaconsfieldian sense. She had travelled a great deal and seen an enormous number of people in every country of Europe as well as in England, and, therefore, she was and is more cosmopolitan in her talk than were her sisters.

Mlle. de Peyronnet was the most epigrammatic. She had the happy gift of improvising in a lightning-flash epigrams and *jeux de mots* which would not have discredited the best wits even of France. I think her repartee, or rather *jeu de mot*, at the dentist's, which went the round of London, the best example I can take by way of illustration. Most people are dreary and depressed in a dentist's chair. Not so Mlle. de Peyronnet. Even here she kept not only her good-temper, but also her brilliant imagination and, above all, her verbal felicity.

The scene passes in a Dental *Atelier* in Paris. Mlle. de Peyronnet must be imagined seated in the fateful chair, dreading the pain but hoping for the relief of an extraction. But, as Tacitus said, that morning she saw all things cross and terrible. The dentist, instead of doing his work deftly, bungled it, or else it was the fault of the patient's jaw. At any rate, the tooth broke off in the forceps, and the dentist had to confess to his patient that all the pain he had given her was useless. He had left in the root! *"Ah, mademoiselle,"* he exclaimed, *"quelle Tragédie!"* But the patient, though suffering acute agony, was worthy of the occasion. She did not pause for an instant in her comment—*"Une Tragédie de Racine!"*

There have been, no doubt, greater and deeper witticisms than that, but could anything have been happier, neater, more good-tempered, more exactly appropriate?

I sometimes feel I would rather have said that than have written Racine's *Mithridates*.

I have summarised the characteristics of each of the sisters' talk. Of Mme. de Peyronnet, who in many ways was more brilliant than her daughters, I will say only that she combined their several qualities. When I add that her talk, like that of her daughters, was original, it must not be supposed that she had not a proper appreciation of great events or of great people. Her memories naturally stretched a great deal further than those of her daughters. I remember well asking her whether she had seen any of the human *remanets* of the Revolution, some of whom, at any rate, must have been alive during her early married life in Paris. She told me that, though there were no reprisals after the Restoration, it was curious how few of the Terrorists were visible in the Paris of her youth. Some, of course, had gone to earth under aliases, but most of them were dead. The Terror which the Terrorists felt as much as inspired, the excitement, and probably also the debauchery of the time when everyone felt, "Let us eat and drink, for tomorrow we die," did not create an atmosphere in which people cultivated hygienic habits or studied rules of "how to live till eighty."

And then, I remember well, she corrected her denial. "Yes, but I did see one of the Terrorists," and then she told me how she actually saw in the flesh the man who was perhaps the worst of them all, the implacable, irresistible Fouché, the man who had been an incendiary, an extremist, and yet who was never in reality a fanatic or a profligate. Fouché always dressed in black, and in a fashion which seems to have resembled Cruikshank's caricatures of the Chadbands of the Regency period. He was a loyal, hard-working servant of any Government which employed him. If the policy of those he was working with was killing, he would kill in battalions, as indeed he did at Lyons. Yet all the time he felt no touch of the blood-lust which inspired men like Carrier. He would never have thought of killing for the sake of killing, or of committing acts of unnecessary cruelty. He was, indeed, a man of spotless private character. He was guilty of no excess except the awful excess of knowing no difference between right and wrong.

"What," I asked Mme. de Peyronnet, "did he look like, and how did you come to see him?" Here is her reply.

When quite a young woman I was in the theatre one night and suddenly saw a great deal of commotion. People were standing up and looking about them and talking eagerly. This commotion, I soon saw, was caused by a very old man with white hair who was making his way through the crowd to his stall. As he moved, there ran through the house the excited whisper, "*C'est le Duc d'Otranto.*"

That was the melodramatic title which Napoleon had conferred upon the man he could not trust, but dare not openly distrust or dismiss, any more than could Louis XVIII. Even in the calmest and most peaceful times the Duke of Otranto remained menacing and terrible. The background which I see when I think of Fouché is not the

Convention or the Committee of Public Safety. I see him as he is described to us by the youth who went to Lyons, to plead with him for the right to cross into Switzerland. He found Fouché busy. He was doing his best to execute the command of the Convention to lay Lyons low, and to kill the greater part of her principal inhabitants. Fouché, always loyal and always punctiliously exact in his work, saw what a difficult job was the killing of seven or eight hundred men at once unless by a well thought-out plan. The mere collecting and dragging away the corpses for burial would be an immense task. The plan he ultimately devised was admirably simple. He first made the prisoners dig a long, wide, and deep trench—I understand that the Bolsheviks use the same method. He then lined them up at the very edge of the ditch. When the firing-party got to work their victims fell neatly backwards into their long grave. All that was needed was to shovel in the earth, which had been piled on the opposite side of the trench.

The young man of whose account I am thinking uses language in describing Fouché superintending the preparation of the trench which reads like a paraphrase of Tacitus' account of Tiberius at the trial of Piso and Placentia. "Nothing so much daunted Piso as to behold Tiberius, without mercy, without wrath, close, dark, unmovable, and bent against every access of tenderness." So stood Fouché.

When Mme. de Peyronnet saw him, the Terrorist had been entirely replaced by the "civilised Statesman." What passed before her eyes was a very old, white-haired man, with a regard deep and impenetrable. She added, however, "I remember noting that everyone seemed to treat him with the greatest awe." By that time, strange to say, he was one of the richest and most respected men in France. Further, he had by his second marriage entered one of the greatest families of the *ancien régime*, and had actually been accepted as "one of us" by the inner hierarchy of the French noblesse! He had even made his peace with the Church and become, at any rate in all outward forms, perhaps *ex animo*, a devout Catholic. What is even more astounding is that his second wife was as devoted to him as was his first, and so, apparently, was he to her. Fouché, indeed, may be said to have been an expert in domestic felicity. The man is as inexplicable as the Emperor to whom I have dared to compare him. Only, unfortunately for us, Fouché had no Tacitus to chronicle his deeds of horror and his ineffable treacheries and his complacent moderation in infamy. Would that the author of the Annals re-incarnated could have given us pictures not only of Fouché but of Robespierre, Marat, Saint-Just, Camille Desmoulins, Fouquier Tinville, and the rest!

Nothing was more fascinating than to hear Mme. de Peyronnet talk of the street-fighting in '48 and of how life went on, I had almost said, as usual, in the intervals of the fusillades. She told me, I remember, that when you were walking in a side-street and heard firing in the boulevard or main street at the end of it, it was almost impossible not to creep up what you thought or hoped was the safest side, and put your head round the corner and see what was happening. Who is getting the best of it in a fight is a question that will not be denied, though it may easily mean a stray bullet in your head.

Speaking of '48, though it breaks my rule, I must recall an account which I induced Lady Sligo to give last year to me and my son, of her recollections of Lamartine during this very period. I happened, if I remember rightly, to be comparing Lamartine's ceaseless flow of admirable ora-

tory with that of Mr. Lloyd George. Both men seemed to
find it possible to speak all day and manage affairs all
night, without apparently exhausting themselves. In-
exhaustibility in the matter of vital energy seemed to be
the gift of each. Most men are soon pumped dry by
skipping from China to Peru, from Upper Silesia to the
Lower Congo, from Vladivostok to Washington. Not so
Mr. Lloyd George, and certainly not so Lamartine.
During his amazing tenure of the office of President of
the Second Republic, he would make a perfectly correct
and yet perfectly sympathetic speech to a deputation
from Ireland in the early part of the morning, and to one
from Chili in the afternoon. He always contrived to
soothe men's minds, without really saying anything.

Full of my readings of the Poet-President's orations and
Despatches, I asked Lady Sligo whether she had ever
seen or heard the great man. She told us how, when a
girl of fourteen or fifteen, M. Lamartine, either President
or ex-President, I am not sure which, and his pleasant
wife, took a great fancy to her and how on several occasions she drove out with them in their capacious landau.
Lamartine's dress was marvellous. Apparently it chiefly
consisted of white duck trousers, which were folded round
his portly form in some extraordinary manner. There
was also a white waistcoat, and, as far as I remember,
something in the nature of a tight-waisted frock-coat.
But what seems to have stuck most in her memory is that
the pockets of the white pantaloons were stuffed with
gold coins, and that these gold coins, whether in the carriage, in the armchairs, or on the sofas on which the great
man was apt to fling himself, would tumble out on the
floor. It was the duty of the younger portion of the
family and friends to collect the product of these golden
showers.

"Why," I asked, "did M. Lamartine make himself into a kind of walking gold-reserve?" The answer was as curious as it was simple. Lamartine, it may be remembered, was not only President of the Provisional Government, but also the most popular man of letters of his day in France—a kind of Walter Scott, Charles Dickens, and Carlyle rolled into one exuberant whole. But Lamartine, though he made enormous sums by his books, also spent enormously, and in the middle part of his life, in order to augment his always insufficient income, he founded a kind of personal magazine, half newspaper and half institute, to which apparently people from all over France subscribed. There was, however, no actual office, except Lamartine's house, and the subscriptions, which were paid in advance in gold, poured literally into his pockets, and were either spent at once or put into some sort of receptacle which represented the immortal and inexhaustible French family stocking.

Lady Sligo had the good luck to hear one of the daily orations by which Lamartine governed France under ideal conditions. It will be remembered that in the worst part of '48, Lamartine literally kept France quiet by day and by night by speaking whenever and wherever an audience of fighters or revolters or simple citizens were gathered together. Often before have men incited mobs to violence by their subtle and deceiving tongues. Lamartine is probably the only man who spoke *en permanence* not to inflame, but to pacify, not to intoxicate with furious words, but to hypnotise into sobriety.

On one occasion when Monsieur and Madame were starting on an afternoon excursion in the great landau, with Mlle. de Peyronnet wedged between the white pantaloons and Mme. Lamartine's skirts (I presume I might at that date have said crinoline), a deputation of *ouvriers* suddenly appeared. Lady Sligo described them exactly as they are to be seen in Gavarni's wonderful drawings in *The Illustrated London News* of 1848—strange beings with long beards and rakish caps, sometimes of liberty and sometimes of less pronounced cut, with belts round their trousers through which their shirts were pulled, and heavy, strange-looking muskets in their hands. The queer crowd who surged round the carriage were a deputation who wished to put some of their special woes and difficulties before Lamartine, and to get his help and advice. Doubtless they also longed to see their leader face to face and to be soothed by the golden voice and fervent words. They greeted him with respect and enthusiasm but immediately the cry went up, "*Un discours! Un discours!*" Lamartine, who was always more ready to speak than even the Parisian mob to hear, at once stood up in the carriage and addressed the crowd. No doubt he harangued in that magnificently platitudinous manner of which he was the master. Lady Sligo could only remember the general impression made on her, which was that the great Lamartine spoke with deep feeling as well as with conspicuous charm. Very soon he had satisfied the wishes of the deputation and reduced them to that peculiar condition which newspapers of the day described as "fraternisation."

I have often wondered exactly what happened when it is recorded that "fraternisation" became general. Apparently it was not very much more than everybody shaking everybody else's hands and talking at once. You felt happy and full of brotherly affection, and exchanged the compliments of the Revolution with everyone you encountered. Even our own forefathers did this on occasion, and not merely when they were politically moved, but also at any emotional moment. Amazing as it sounds,

I remember my mother-in-law, Mrs. Simpson, telling me that when she was a girl in the 'forties and 'fifties, she had seen people in the Covent Garden Opera House so moved by the singing and acting of Mario and Grisi as to rise in their places not merely to cheer, but to do something which I suppose would have been called "fraternisation." In a sudden burst of emotion they all shook hands with each other and, as it were, congratulated themselves on hearing the Diva's glorious song or Mario "soothing with the tenor note the souls in purgatory." And then we talk as if these same people of the 'forties and 'fifties were unendurably stuffy and stodgy! In truth, they were nothing of the kind.

Have I not myself heard the old Lady Stanley of Alderley describe how when she and her people were having their luggage examined at the Genoa Custom House, someone rushed in with the news that Byron was dead? Upon this, everybody present burst into tears— not merely the matron and the maid, but the men old and young. We all admire "le Byron de nos jours" very greatly (I shall not name him for fear of the consequences) but honestly I don't think you could now get the tiniest trickle of tears down the cheek of anyone at a *Douane*, or anywhere else, by announcing his demise. "Other times, other emotions."

But I have wandered far from the family of Arthur Russell and the double ties, French and English, which bound them to my wife's family. Quite apart from my marriage connection, I came in touch with the Arthur Russells. Lord Arthur was a close friend of Sir Louis Mallet, and I have already described my friendship with Sir Louis, first through his son, and then through my own admiration for that able and delightful man—a great charmer as well as a great thinker in the region of Political

Economy, "a social creature," as Burke might have called him, as well as a wise man—a man who could be an earnest devotee of Cobden on the one side of his nature, and on the other fastidious in a high degree in his social outlook. But if I go on to express my admiration of Sir Louis Mallet this will cease to be an autobiography and become something in the nature of Bossuet's eulogies, so ardent was my cult for Cobden's friend.

The Russells were also on intimate terms with the Grant-Duffs, with whom I had become acquainted through the Mallets, and also through Sir Mountstuart's eldest son, the present Arthur Grant-Duff, who was at Balliol with me. He soon entered the Diplomatic Service, in which, like his brother Evelyn, he has had an honourable and useful career. I had, therefore, every sort of reason for liking the Arthur Russell family. They were friends of my friends as well as friends of my relations. But Lord Arthur Russell and his family were destined to be to me much more than "friends-in-law." I had not been more than two or three times in the company of Lord Arthur without feeling that attraction towards him which a young man sometimes experiences, and if he does, always with high satisfaction, in the case of a man or woman belonging to an older generation. I am proud to think that he liked me almost at first sight, I am not vain enough to say, as much as I liked him, but, at any rate, quite enough to create a sense of social relationship exceedingly flattering as well as exceedingly delightful. I was just entering the intellectual world of London, and knew that it was no small thing to get at once on the best of terms with a man like Arthur Russell. He had known and knew almost everybody worth knowing in London, in Paris, and in most of the European capitals from Berlin to Rome. By this I do not mean social grandees, but the true men of light and leading, in science, literature, the Arts, philosophy, and politics.

Though Lord Arthur never held office, he had been for many years a Liberal Member of Parliament, and had also been a member of almost every literary and political club in London, such as "The Club," "Grignon's," "The Breakfast Club," and so on. Besides his literary and historical sympathies and interests, he was a man devoted to natural history, and had a great many friends on this side of knowledge. He was also a friend both of Hutton and of Townsend, always a diligent reader and a fairly frequent contributor to the columns of *The Spectator*, which made yet another tie between us. Finally, Lord Arthur, hitherto a very loyal, if sometimes critical, supporter of Mr. Gladstone, became, as I had become, a Liberal Unionist. He followed, that is, Lord Hartington into opposition on the Home Rule question. But I, as a member of the Liberal Unionist Committee and Editor of *The Liberal Unionist*,—the organ of our new Party,— had a position amongst Liberal Unionists rather above what might have been expected at my age—I was then about twenty-seven—a position which brought me into touch with Lord Hartington, Mr. Bright, the Duke of Argyll, Mr. Chamberlain, and, in fact, all the Liberal and Radical Unionists of the day. Finally and, as it were, to cement my wife's old and my new friendship with the Arthur Russells, I bought a piece of land on which to build a Saturday-to-Monday cottage, which, though I did not fully realise it at the moment, was close to the Arthur Russells' Surrey house, The Ridgeway.

No sooner had we pitched our tent in what was then the fascinating wilderness of Newlands Corner, than we discovered that we were only an easy Sunday afternoon walk from our friends. Soon it became a fixed habit with us,

from which I think we never varied, to descend from our
Downs every Sunday and walk by a series of delightful
bridle-paths to The Ridgeway for tea—a serious institution in a family where there were two girls and four boys.

At the Arthur Russells, when re-enforced by Mme. and
Mlle. de Peyronnet, Lady Sligo, who had also settled in
Surrey, one heard talk such as I have never known bettered and very seldom equalled. Nothing could have
been easier or more stimulating. Those were gatherings
at which no one assumed the attitude described in *The
Rejected Addresses:*

> I am a blessed Glendoveer.
> 'Tis mine to speak and yours to hear.

I was, except for the Russell boys and girls and my own
wife, the youngest member of the party, but I was always made to feel at The Ridgeway that they were as willing to hear as even I was willing to talk, which, as my
friends will vouch, was saying a good deal. I was, in
truth, bursting to give my view, as a young man should be,
on a hundred subjects. The intellectual world lay all before me. But though Providence was my guide, I was
not yet confined to any fixed course, but with joyous in-
consequence raced up and down the paths of the Dialectical
Paradise as unconscious and as unashamed as a colt in a
green meadow.

Lord Arthur Russell, though a man of a gentle, tran-
quil spirit, had a great sympathy with youth. He was,
like all his race, a Whig, and a Moderate, in every human
function and aspiration. He did not, however, allow that
liberal spirit to be dimmed by fear or by selfishness. He
was one of those fortunate men who are not awed by
rumour or carried away by prejudice. Still less was
there any touch of pride or vulgarity in his nature.

Meanness and commonness of mind were as far from
him as from any man I have ever known. Yet there was
nothing either of the recluse or of the saint about him.
He was not afraid to look on life, and its realities, and he
took the very greatest interest, not only in what concerned
homo sapiens, but also *homo naturalis*. He loved good
stories and told good stories, and loved also to analyse
and comment upon the actions of the great men of his own
day and of past days, for it need hardly be said that as the
nephew of Lord John Russell, the son of Lady William
Russell, and the cousin of half the politicians of his day,
he was the repository of every sort of social and political
tradition. He was an extraordinarily accurate man, and
by no means willing to pick up, or record, or pass on stray
pieces of gossip about historical people, without verifi-
cation.

Lord Arthur's first-hand and personal recollections,
though never of the tiresome kind, had often great poignancy and actuality. I remember being thrilled by an
account which he had had direct from his uncle, Lord John
Russell, of the latter's visit to Napoleon at Elba in the
early part of 1815. The interview, of course, made a great
impression upon him and the account he gave was vivid
and picturesque. I must omit a detail which shows what
a dirty savage Napoleon was, and how he maintained
even in his little palazzo at Elba the manners not only of
the camp, but of the rudest soldier. In describing this
episode, which would have been too trivial for narration
if not so nasty, Lord John was wont to say, "I was very
much surprised." It must be remembered here that not
only in 1815, but even fifty years before (witness the
testimony both of Dr. Johnson and Horace Walpole),
Englishmen were apt to be shocked by continental habits
in the matter of personal cleanliness.

Another detail, however, is quite fit to tell. Napoleon knew quite well that the brother of the Duke of Bedford and a Member of the House of Commons was an important person, and was accordingly exceedingly civil to the young man. But Lord John told his nephew that very early in the conversation Napoleon seized him by the ear and held it almost all the time he was talking, or rather, pouring forth one of his streams of familiar eloquence as to the harshness and cruelty of the Allies. Napoleon, when he was cross, would sometimes wring people's ears till they screamed for pain. Talleyrand, for example, was on one occasion, when held by the ear, so much hurt as to be deprived of his habitual insensibility to Napoleon's insults, and gave vent to the famous aside, "What a pity that so great a man should have been so badly brought up!"

In any case, Lord John's ear, though held for ten or twelve minutes, was not screwed up. I remember when I heard the story, thirty years ago, at once asking the question, "Which ear was it he held?" That sounded almost to myself as I asked it a silly question, but, as the reply showed, it was not. Lord Arthur replied, "That is curious. It is exactly the question I asked my uncle, and he, instead of treating it as trivial, answered as if it was a matter of the first importance, 'My left ear.'" Certainly it seems to me a strong link with the past. Here was Lord Arthur, who would not have been much over eighty if he had lived till today, who had seen a piece of human flesh which had actually been held by the Corsican Tamerlane.

Lord Arthur once showed his belief in my discretion and also his divination that I was not one of the supercilious intellectuals who think details of family history are tiresome and unimportant, in a way which greatly pleased me.

He confided to me the true story, which he had had from
various people of the older generation who knew the facts,
as to the relations between the two Duchesses of Devonshire.   The elder Duchess, Georgiana, was the Juno of the
Whigs.   It would be folly to call her the Madonna of the
Whigs.   It was at her eyes that the coal porter at the
Westminster Election wanted to light his pipe.   Sir
Joshua immortalised her in his picture of the young
mother and her child.   To her the mystic poet and
philosopher bent the knee of admiration, in the enchanting couplet:

> Oh, lady, nursed in pomp and pleasure,
> Where got you that heroic measure?

The other Duchess was born Elizabeth Harvey—the
woman whose eyes still scintillate also from Sir Joshua's
canvas, with an energy so overwhelming as to be uncanny
—the woman who fascinated without actual beauty, but
whose smile might have embroiled the world—the woman
who stirred even the sluggish Gibbon and made him say,
with a personal vivacity and poignancy which is unique
in his writings, that if she had entered the House of Lords
and beckoned the Lord Chancellor to leave the Woolsack
and follow her, he must have obeyed.   Gibbon had evidently racked his brains to think of the most audacious act
of which a woman could be capable, and that quaintly
proved in his case to be the enchantment of a Lord Chancellor!   If, at the present moment, there is a lady possessed of charms equal to those of Elizabeth Duchess of
Devonshire, let us hope that the precincts of both the
Lords and the Commons Houses are well guarded!

I shall not on the present occasion say more than that
Lord Arthur gave me a note of the true facts of the story,
to which many allusions, generally incorrect, have ap-

peared in various memoirs—a story of incidents which, strangely enough, quite possibly affected the history of the world. These incidents had as their sequel the appointment of the son of a well-known Scottish doctor, Dr. Moore, to an Infantry regiment. That Infantry subaltern became Sir Thomas Moore—the man who lost his life in saving the British Empire, and first taught the people of these islands and then, what is more important, the whole of Europe, that there was nothing invincible about the troops of Napoleon, when they were faced by British regiments properly trained, as Moore trained them at Shorncliff. Just as the destruction of the Spartan Hoplites in the Island of Sphacteria broke the military spell cast by the armies of Sparta, so Moore's victorious retreat to, and action at, Corunna broke the spell of the Napoleonic Legions.

Though I have Lord Arthur's notes, and though he in no way bound me to secrecy, they want an interval longer than a hundred and ten years "prior to publication." Therefore they will rest in my safe, or wherever else they may have been affectionately mislaid, and where it would probably take a day's hard work to find them. There is no such secrecy and security as "filing for future reference." When the notes are found by my literary executors, they will please remember that they should not be given to the public until they have ample assurance that the head of the Devonshire family sees no objection. It is not a family skeleton in any sense, but till family facts become historic, the utmost discretion is demanded alike by courtesy and good feeling.

I had, alas! no sooner fully realised that I had made a friend in Lord Arthur and that I might look forward to many years of intimate intercourse with a man of knowledge and sympathy, from whom I could learn much and

in the most fascinating and delightful way, than the end
came. A short illness, followed by a rapid operation—
hopeless, or almost hopeless—cut short this honourable
and gracious life.   I was one of the very few people whom
Lord Arthur asked to see in the few days allowed him
between life and death. He wanted to see me out of
pure friendliness, to talk about his children and to show
me, as only such an act could, that he, like me, had hoped
much from our friendship.   He was the kind of man who
would be sure to prefer saying this by deed rather than by
word.

But for the simplicity and essential nobility of character which he possessed, he might well have sent for me to
see how a good man could die.   There was everything to
strengthen and so to quiet one in the way in which he
faced the message which comes to all—a message so
deeply dreaded by most of us, yet which, when it does
come, proves to be not a sentence, but a reprieve—the
mandatory word that does not imprison us, but sets us
free, which flings the gates and lets us see the open heaven,
instead of the walls and vaulted ceiling of the cells of
which we have been the inhabitants.

But though the very last thing that Lord Arthur was
thinking about was the impression upon my mind, that
impression was intense both in kind and in degree.   That
short last talk at his bedside, in which so little was said,
so much felt by both of us, has never left my memory.   If
for no other reason, it must be recorded here for it had, I
feel, an essential if undefinable influence upon my life.

CHAPTER XIX

MY LIFE IN LONDON IN THE 'NINETIES (*Continued*)

I AM afraid that throughout these memoirs I have
talked too much about the volumes which I might fill,
but am not filling. Yet I must do so once more in this
chapter. My mother-in-law, Mrs. Simpson, was an admirable talker and full of clear and interesting memories.
I had no sooner entered the Simpson house and family
than I found that there were a hundred points of sympathy between us. She had known everybody in London,
who was worth knowing, through her father, Mr. Nassau-
Senior, and had visited with him—she acted for some
twenty years as his social companion owing to her mother's
ill-health—most of the political country-houses in England, and had known in London everyone worth knowing
on the Whig side, and most of the neutrals. Macaulay
was one of her father's closest friends; so was the third
Lord Lansdowne, the Lord Henry Petty of the Cabinets
of the 'thirties and 'forties—Lord Aberdeen, Lord John
Russell, and Lord Palmerston, and, earlier, Lord Melbourne, Lord St. Leonards, Lord Denman, and Lord
Campbell, to mention only a few names and at random.
It was her father's habit to ride every day in the Park for
reasons hygienic and social, and she rode with him. There
they were sure to be joined by the Whig statesmen who
sought Senior's advice on economic points. She saw

little of the Tories,—except perhaps Mr. Gladstone, soon
to become a Liberal, and Sir Robert Peel. Disraeli was
of course, in those days, considered by the strict Whigs
as "impossible"—a "charlatan," and "adventurer,"
almost "impostor."

In the world of letters she saw much of Sydney Smith,
who was early a friend of her father's. She actually had
the good fortune, while Miss Minnie Senior, to stop at the
Combe Florey Rectory, and to discover that the eminent
wit took as much trouble to amuse his own family when
alone as to set the tables of Mayfair upon a roar. He
liked to tease his girl guest by telling her that her father,
then a Master in Chancery, did not care a straw for his
daughter "*Minnie.*" "*De Minimis non curat Lex*"—"the
Master does not care for Minnie"—was a favourite
travesty of the well-known maxim.

Rogers was also a friend, and as a girl she remembered
going to his "very small" breakfast-parties, in the celebrated dining-room in which hung his famous pictures.

They were hung high, so as to get the light which was at
the top of the room. It was this arrangement, by the
way, that made Sydney Smith say that Rogers' dining-
room was like Heaven and its opposite. There were
gods and angels in the upper part, but below was "gnash-
ing of teeth." While Rogers talked about his pictures,
he would have them taken down by his man-servant,
Edmond, and placed upon a chair at his side, or almost
upon the lap of his guest, so that he might lecture about
them at his ease. Mrs. Simpson often told me of the
horror she felt as a girl lest she should throw a spoonful
of soup over a Raphael or by an accident run a knife or a
fork into the immortal canvas! She had not learnt that
pictures are about the most indestructible things in the
world.

J. St. Loe Strachey.   Ætat. 32.

Through her father Mrs. Simpson also knew the great French statesmen of her day, *i. e.*, the middle period of the century, 1840 to 1870. He was the friend of Alexis de Tocqueville, and of Thiers and Guizot, and of most of the statesmen and men of letters who were their contemporaries. The leading Italian statesmen, such as Cavour, were also his friends. In fact, there were few people in Europe worth knowing whom he did not know. What was more, he had a most astonishing personal gift—the gift for photographing in words the talk of the statesmen whom he encountered, not, remember, as a mere recorder but on terms of mutual benefit. Though he liked to draw their opinions, in both senses, they sought his wisdom and advice with equal assiduity. He was quite as much Johnson as he was Boswell, or rather, almost as much Socrates as he was Plato, for that is the best analogy.

Conversations with the Statesmen of the Third Empire, in two volumes, crown octavo, sounds a pretty dull title, and yet anyone who takes the trouble to read these conversations will find that they are some of the most vivacious dialogues in all literature. Senior's system of recording conversations throws a curious light, by the way, upon the mechanism of the Platonic Dialogues. For some twenty-four centuries the world has wondered how much of these Dramas of the Soul is to be attributed to Socrates and how much to Plato, and the general verdict has been that in most of them there is very much more Plato than Socrates. In a word, they have been judged to be works of art in which certain very general ideas and principles derived from Socrates are expanded, put into shape, and often greatly altered by the alleged recorder, or rather dramatic recounter.

Mrs. Simpson told me something of her father's method of putting down his conversations which bears closely upon the value of this theory of the Dialogues.   But first I must note that Senior's reports of conversations were famous for their extraordinary accuracy.   Mrs. Simpson well remembered an incident in proof of this statement. Her father had written out a very important talk with Thiers in which by far the greater part of the talk was sustained as usual by the great Frenchman.   When Senior had written it out, that is about a couple of days after the conversation, he sent it, as was his habit, to Thiers for correction.   Thiers sent it back, saying that he could not find a word to alter, adding that he was astonished to find that Senior had not only put down his views and ideas, but had given his actual words.   Yet, as a matter of fact, Senior had done nothing of the kind.   He had not even tried to do so.   What he had aimed at was something very different.   His aim was to give the spirit of the conversation, to produce the extreme characteristic impression made on his mind by the talk of his interlocutor, not the words themselves.

To show in a still more convincing way that I am making no exaggerated deduction from my premises, I may call the further testimony given me directly by Senior's daughter.   It is this testimony which convinces me that in the Platonic dialogues there is less Plato and more Socrates than is generally imagined.   Mrs. Simpson, or Miss Senior, as she then was, once said to her father that she would like to listen to one of his conversations and try to see whether she could not write it down as he did. Her father, delighted that she should make the experiment, explained to her the art as he practised it and gave her the following directions.

To begin with, you must never try to remember the actual words that you hear Thiers, or Guizot, or Lord Aberdeen, or

Mr. Bright, or whoever else it may be, use. If you begin to rack your brains and your memory you will spoil the whole thing. You must simply sit down and write the conversation out as you, knowing their views, think they must have spoken or ought to have spoken. Then you will get the right result. If you consciously rely on your memory, your report will lose all life and interest.

While the conversation was going on Senior attended very accurately to the ideas expressed and got a thorough understanding of them. When he took up his pen he put himself in the position of a dramatist and wrote what he felt sure his interlocutor would have said on the particular theme. He put himself, that is, in his interlocutor's place. The thoughts got clothed with the right words, though, no doubt, under great compression.

That is interesting and curious, not solely from the point of view of Plato, but of a great many of the speeches in classical history. People have often wondered whether the men who speak so wisely and so well in Thucydides or Tacitus really talked like that. Judging from Senior's case, they very probably did. Thucydides, indeed, when describing his method, uses expressions by no means at variance with the Senior system of reporting, the system which, though aiming only at the spirit, often, if we are to believe Thiers, hits the words also. It is quite possible then that the British chieftain really made the speech recorded as his in Tacitus, the speech which contains what is perhaps the greatest of all political epigrams, "I know these Romans. They are the people who make a desert and call it Peace."

There is another point in regard to the secret of Senior's power of recording conversations which is worth noting by modern psychologists. I cannot help thinking that what Senior did, unconsciously of course, was to trust to his subconsciousness. That amiable and highly impressionable, if dumb, spirit which sits within us all, got busy when Thiers or Guizot was talking. The difficulty was to get out of him what he had heard, and had at once transferred to the files in the Memory cupboard. Senior, without knowing it, had, I doubt not, some little trick which enabled him to get easily *en rapport* with his subconsciousness, and so tap the rich and recently stored vintage. His writing was probably half automatic. It certainly was vivid and dramatic in a high degree.

If anyone wants proof of my eulogy of Nassau-Senior's powers as a conversationalist, let him go to the London Library and get down Senior's works. Perhaps the best volume to begin with is *Conversations and Journals in Egypt*—a book which Lord Cromer used to declare was the best thing ever written about Egypt. I remember also Sir Mountstuart Grant-Duff saying that one of the conversations with Hekekyan Bey, describing how he—the Bey—on a certain occasion saw Mehemet sitting alone in his Palace by the Sea, deserted by all his followers, was as poignant as anything in Tacitus. It will be remembered that in 1840 we sent a fleet to Egypt under Sir Charles Napier, to enforce our Syrian policy. The private instructions given by Lord Palmerston to his admiral were as pointed as they were concise: "Tell Mehemet Ali that if he does not change his policy and do what I wish, I will chuck him into the Nile." In due course our fleet appeared at Alexandria. The Pasha was at first recalcitrant, but when our ships took up position opposite the town and palace and cleared for action he gave way and agreed to the British terms. During the crisis and when it looked as if the old tyrant was either bent upon political and personal suicide, or else had lost all sense of proportion, the courtiers and the people of Alexandria generally fled from their doomed Lord and Master. As if by magic his palace was utterly deserted. No Monarch falls so utterly as an Oriental Despot. Hekekyan Bey described the scene of which he was a witness in words which could hardly be bettered:

I was then the engineer charged with the defences of the coast. We were expecting an attack from Sir Charles Napier, and I had been to Rosetta to inspect the batteries. It was on a tempestuous night that I returned to Alexandria, and went to the palace on the shore of the former Island of Pharos, to make my report to Mehemet Ali.

The halls and passages, which I used to find full of Mamelukes and officers strutting about in the fullness of their contempt for a Christian, were empty. Without encountering a single attendant, I reached his room overlooking the sea; it was dimly lighted by a few candles of bad Egyptian wax, with enormous untrimmed wicks. Here, at the end of his divan, I found him rolled up in a sort of ball,—solitary, motionless, apparently absorbed in thought. The waves were breaking heavily on the mole, and I expected every instant the casements to be blown in. The roar of wind and sea was almost awful, but he did not seem conscious of it.

I stood before him silent. Suddenly he said, as if speaking to himself, "I think I can trust Ibrahim." Again he was silent for some time, and then desired me to fetch Motus Bey, his admiral. I found him, and brought him to the Viceroy. Neither of them spoke, until the Viceroy, after looking at him steadily for some minutes, said to me, "He is drunk; take him away." I did so, and so ended my visit without making any report.

That heart-cry of the deserted tyrant, "*I think I can trust Ibrahim*"—his own son, in all probability, though called his stepson (Ibrahim's mother was a widow)—is comparable to the cry of Augustus: "*Varus, Varus, give me back my legions!*"

Wonderfully Tacitean is a later comment of the Pasha —an Armenian by birth. He told Senior that the Pasha could never forget or forgive that he had seen his master in the day of his humiliation. So intolerable was the thought that Mehemet Ali made two secret attempts to kill his faithful servant. "He wished me to die, but he did not wish to be suspected of having killed me." In my recollections of Lord Cromer, in an earlier chapter, I have told a story of one of Mehemet Ali's removals of inconvenient servants which is well worth recalling in this context.

If I say much more about Mr. Nassau-Senior I shall fill a book. I admit that it would be a very curious and attractive work, for he was in the truest sense a man of note, but I cannot put a book inside a book. Therefore this must be, not merely one of my unwritten chapters, but one of my unwritten books.

In the same way, I cannot dwell upon dozens of delightful men and women with whom I became acquainted through my wife and her people, and who remained fast and good friends, though, alas! many of them have long since joined the majority,—for example, Lecky, Leslie Stephen, and Mr. Justice Stephen, and Mr. Henry Reeve of the *Edinburgh*. The last-named, very soon after our acquaintanceship, invited me to write for him, and thus I was able to add the *Edinburgh* as well as the *Quarterly* to the trophies of my pen. My wife and I used often to dine at his house—always a place of good company even if the aura was markedly Victorian. Reeve was full of stories of how Wordsworth used to stop with him when he came up to London in his later years. He lent his Court suit to Wordsworth in order that the Poet-Laureate should present himself at a Levee in proper form. But again these remembrances must be repressed for reasons of space.

Just as I have taken the Arthur Russell group as a type

of the people with whom my marriage made me friends, so I shall take as typical two men of high distinction who were friends of my mother-in-law, and whom I saw either at her house or at houses of friends to whom we were bidden through the kindly, old-fashioned institution of wedding-parties. These were Matthew Arnold and Robert Browning. I met Matthew Arnold at a dinner at Mrs. Simpson's, given largely, I think, because I expressed my desire to see a man for whose poetry and prose I had come to have an intense admiration. When quite young I was a little inclined to turn up my nose at Matthew Arnold's verse, though I admit I had a good deal of it by heart. By the time, however, that I had got to my twenty-seventh year, I bent my knee in reverent adoration at the shrine, and realised what the two *Obermann* poems and *The Grande Chartreuse* stanzas meant, not only to the world but to me.

I was captivated in advance by Matthew Arnold's literary charm. I delighted also in the stories about him of which London and Oxford were full. I had only to watch him and listen to his talk across the dinner-table to realise the truth of his own witty self-criticism. When he married, he is said to have described his wife thus: "Ah! you must see my Fanny. You are sure to like her. She has all my graces and none of my airs." The said airs and graces were, of course, only a gentle and pleasant pose. They winged with humour Matthew Arnold's essential, I had almost said sublime, seriousness. Truly he was like one of the men for whom he longed:

> Who without sadness shall be sage,
> And gay without frivolity.

Though, of course, Socrates had more fire, more of the demon in him, one can well believe that at times, and when his circumambient irony was at its gentlest, it must have been like that of Matthew Arnold. Matthew Arnold has been called over-fastidious, but I do not think that is fair. Fastidious he no doubt was. Also he thought it his duty to rub in our national want of fastidiousness, and our proneness to mistake nickel for silver. It must not be supposed, however, that Matthew Arnold could not endure to look upon the world as it is because of the high standard he had set up in Literature and in the Arts. In reality his was a wise and comprehensive view. He could enjoy men and things in practice even when he disapproved of them in theory. His inimitably delicate distinctions were drawn quite as much in favour of the weak as in support of the strong. Take, for example, his famous *mot*, "I would not say he was not a gentleman, but if you said so, I should understand what you meant." For example, Matthew Arnold would not have said that Shelley was not a poet. If, however, you had said so, he would have *very nearly* agreed with you, and would have given all sorts of reasons to support your view. Yet, in all probability, he would at the same time have urged you not to forget that all the same he had a claim to a good place, if not a front place, in the glorious choir of Apollo.

I cannot remember any particular thing said on that occasion by Matthew Arnold, but I do remember very well how pleased and touched I was when after dinner he crossed over from his side of the table, and sitting down by me, began talking about the members of his family, whom he seemed to know that I knew. I knew Mrs. Ward; I knew his niece, Miss Arnold, Mrs. Ward's sister, soon to become Mrs. Leonard Huxley, and, last but not least, I was on the closest terms of intimacy with that most admirable of journalists, Willie Arnold of the *Manchester Guardian*. Probably because I was acting as a sort of aide-de-camp and son of the house to my father-in-law, Mr. Simpson, I did not get a connected literary talk. Besides, I felt sure that from his friendliness I should later have plenty of opportunities to ask a hundred things of his spiritual home. Little did I know how soon he was to be cut off. These were the years which saw the deaths of Barnes, Browning, Tennyson, and Matthew Arnold—years of which one was tempted to say with Wordsworth:

> Like clouds that rake the mountain-summits,
> Or waves that own no curbing hand,
> How fast has brother followed brother
> From sunshine to the sunless land.

Browning was the other poet for whom I felt a very strong admiration and whom I had often wanted to meet. Though a friend of the Simpsons, and a visitor and diner at their house, I met him not at 14 Cornwall Gardens but at a very small dinner-party in the house of a common friend. After dinner Browning, Sir Sidney Colvin, another man, and I were left drinking our coffee and our port and smoking our cigarettes. Browning was, I believe, often inclined to talk like a man of the world about people or stocks and shares rather than about literature. But I was determined to do what I could to prevent him pushing that foible too far. Therefore I did my very best to lead the conversation on to better pastures. I had always loved Landor, and something or other gave me an opportunity to ask a question about him. Mr. Browning, I felt sure, must have known him in his last years at Florence.

I was happy in my venture and struck a vein of reminiscence of a very poignant kind. Browning told us that he did not know Landor very well, but that he saw him in the last years of his life under circumstances of a terribly pathetic kind. Landor played almost exactly the part of King Lear—though from a different reason—and got almost exactly King Lear's reward. Landor, it will be remembered, was originally a rich man. It will also be remembered that he was possessed of a very arbitrary and turbulent nature and quarrelled with many members of his family, and especially with his own children. However, they lived in a villa at Fiesole for some time, in a kind of turbulent domesticity. Landor, on leaving England, had unwisely given away his property to his children, thinking that he could rely upon them to be kind to him. But he had not trained them in the ways of kindness. He had been hot, brutal, and tyrannical to them when he had the power. When they got it they were equally brutal to him. At last his daughter determined to bear the old man's ill-temper—ill-temper, apparently, approaching to madness—no longer. He was told by Miss Landor that if he could not control himself better she would not tolerate him any longer in the villa, and would, in fact, turn him out of doors. He disobeyed her injunctions, or, as she probably put it, failed to keep his promise of better behaviour, and then, incredible as it sounds from anyone who had ever read *Lear*, she actually barred the doors of what had once been his home against the unhappy old man and drove him out to wander whither he could. If she did not physically put him out of doors, she put humiliations so unendurable upon him that, like Lear, he left the house in an agony of broken-heartedness and despair. The once-proud poet had very few friends in Florence, little or no money, and literally nowhere to go. The result was that he wandered, half-distracted, like Lear, bewailing the wound at his heart which a daughter's hand had given. Somehow, like an old, stray, and starving dog, he wandered to the Brownings' house. There, need-less to say, he found rest for the body and comfort for the soul. Mrs. Browning did everything she could for Landor —took him in, fed him, put him to bed, and strove to quiet and soften his fierce and pitiful and outraged heart.

Browning went on to tell how as soon as the old man was a little composed, he drove up to Fiesole to see Miss Landor—thinking that perhaps, after all, it was only a family quarrel which could be tactfully adjusted. That supposition proved entirely mistaken.

I found [said Browning] an almost exact reincarnation of the daughters of Lear in Miss Landor. She was perfectly hard and perfectly cold. She told me of her father's troublesome ways, nay, misdeeds, of how she had borne them for a long time, of how he had promised better behaviour, and of how he had broken his word again and again. At last the limit had been passed. She could endure him in her house no longer. I argued with her [he went on] as well as I could, urged that she evidently did not realise her father's mental condition, and pointed out that whatever his past faults he was now lying in my house a dying man, and dying of a broken heart. I hoped and believed that my description of his anguish and his dis-traction would melt her.

Then came the most terrible part of the story. Miss Landor must, I suppose, have accompanied Browning through the garden to the gate of the villa, and there spoke her final words. Browning said something about the remorse which she would inevitably feel. Her father had, no doubt, given her great provocation, but if the end came before she had forgiven him and helped him, she would never be able to forgive herself. His words were of no avail. She had Goneril's heart. Pointing to a ditch at the side of the road, she answered, "I tell you, Mr.

Browning, that if my father lay dying in that ditch, I would not lift a finger to save him."

And so Browning went back to Casa Guido. He had looked into the awful depths which Shakespeare had explored—an agony of the mind beyond words, and beyond solution. The sense of pity and terror had been raised for which even the poet's art could find no purgation.

What he said to the unhappy old man when he returned to Florence he did not tell us. Mercifully, Landor's memory was failing, and so one may hope that the waters of the Lethe brought him like Lear their blessed relief.

Strangely enough, no poet ever sang their healing virtues more poignantly than did Landor. When Agamemnon, in Landor's poem, red from Clytemnestra's axe, reaches the Shades, the Hours bring him their golden goblet. He drinks and forgets. He is no more maddened by the thought that his daughter will learn his fate. Till then he had felt:

> the first woman coming from Mycenæ
> Will pine to pour the poison in her ear.

I have set down, I believe correctly, what I heard Browning tell, but I am bound to add that it does not quite correspond with the facts given in the *Dictionary of National Biography*. Leslie Stephen in the life of Landor mentions the quarrel and the kind intervention of the Brownings, but does not make the incident nearly so tragic. Very probably indignation made Browning emphasise the bad side of the story. Also he was telling of something which had taken place thirty years before. Finally, it is thirty-five years since I heard the conversation here recorded and indignation has also, no doubt, played its part in deepening the colours of my narration.

But, though for these reasons I do not suggest that the details I have given are of biographical importance, I feel absolutely certain on two essential points: (1) Browning unquestionably compared the scene he witnessed to *Lear* and compared it in the most striking and poignant way. (2) The words put into the mouth of Miss Landor are not any invention or addition of mine. They made a profound impression upon me and I am sure they are the actual words I heard Browning use. He spoke them with passion and dramatic intent, and they still ring in my ears. My memory for many things is as treacherous as that of most people, but when a certain degree of dramatic intensity is reached the record on the tablets of my mind is almost always correct and remains unchanged.

Before I leave the subject of my wife's family and friends and of the warm-hearted kindness with which they received me, I ought to say something about my father-in-law, Mr. Simpson. Though he had not his wife's charm of manner and delight in all the amenities of life and of social intercourse on its best side, he was to me a very attractive man, as well as one of very great ability. Through his shyness he made all but his intimates regard him as dull. There was in truth no dullness about him. His mind was one of great acuteness within its own very special limits. Either by nature or training, I can hardly tell which, he was exactly fitted to be what he was, that is, first a Second Wrangler at Cambridge, then a Conveyancer, and Standing Counsel to the Post Office. Though he never took silk, he was in the most exact sense a counsel learned in the law, and received the singular honour of being made a Bencher of Lincoln's Inn, although he was not a Queen's Counsel. His special gift in the study and practice of the law was his skilful draftsmanship whether in wills, conveyances, or clauses in Acts

19

of Parliament. His vast knowledge and his judgment as to what was the proper interpretation of the Statutes, of the rules of Equity, of the principles of the Common Law, and of the practice of the Courts, was unrivalled.

Mr. Simpson was, in private life, one of the most honourable and high-minded men that I have ever known. Most honourable men are content to be careful of other people's rights and conscious of their own duties in big things, but do not bother themselves to ask whether they have done exactly right in little things. Mr. Simpson was as particular in the minutiæ of conduct as he was in great affairs. Take, for example, the way in which he regarded the duty of silence in regard to any knowledge of clients' private affairs which he had derived in the course of his professional work. He never yielded to the temptation to gossip, even about cases which were thirty or forty years old, cases which it might have been argued had become historical. This care extended not only to his own cases, but to matters which he had heard discussed in his chambers in Lincoln's Inn or in those of his brother barristers.

You could not move him by saying that everybody was dead in the case concerned, or that it would be to the credit of particular people to tell what really happened and what were the true causes and motives of the action. Nothing of this kind would affect him. He gave for his silence reasons similar to those which Dr. Lushington gave when, on his death-bed as a very old man, his family asked him to leave for historical purposes a record of the truth about Byron's quarrel with his wife. Dr. Lushington replied that even if he could do so without a breach of faith with any living person, he would not. He had a higher duty, and that was to help men and women to feel that they could unburden themselves fully to their professional advisers, and that there was no risk of those advisers in the future constituting themselves the judges of whether this or that thing should become known to the world at large.

What the client wants is the seal of the confessional. If he cannot have that, he will often refuse to speak the whole truth. But this may mean not only personal injury to those who would speak out if they could feel sure of secrecy, but might inflict injury on others, and indeed on the community as a whole. There is, I feel, no rational denial of this point of view. At any rate, this was the principle which Mr. Simpson carried out in the most meticulous way. He would only talk about the law in the abstract or upon points made in open court. He would not even go so far as to say, "I drew up that marriage settlement, or made that will, or advised this or that man to take action."

He carried his reticence beyond even professional knowledge. For example, he regarded what was said in a club smoking-room as said under the seal of secrecy, and nothing would induce him to repeat what he had heard. Strangely enough, he was a member of the Garrick Club, and I remember him once mentioning that Thackeray used to hold forth in the smoking-room to all present. Naturally I thought that he would be willing to describe some of these talks, for they had obviously made a great impression on him. He, however, was adamant in this matter. When people talked in club-rooms, he argued, they ought to have the feeling that it was like talking in their own house and to their own family. For him Clubs were "tiled" houses.

I think, myself, that he went too far here; but certainly he was erring on the right side. At the present moment the habit of certain lawyers, doctors, and business men, to discuss the private affairs of their clients and customers in public is much too common. No doubt most of them are careful to use a good deal of camouflage and to tell their stories as "A" "B" cases, without mentioning names. But that is not always successful. Chance and the impishness of coincidence will very often enable one to discover the most carefully camouflaged secret. I remember, as a young man, coming across an instance of this kind which very much struck me. It happened that the barrister in whose chambers I was a pupil said, very properly, to me on the first day that he supposed I understood that whatever I saw in papers in chambers must be regarded as strictly confidential. It might, he said, happen that I should see things of a highly confidential nature about someone whom I knew in Society; and he went on to tell a story of how, when he was young, two young barristers or students came across a set of papers in which two young ladies, sisters, who happened to be acquaintances of these young men, were mentioned as having a reversionary interest in a very large sum of money with only one old life between it and them. Though apparently only daughters of a struggling professional man, they would soon, it appeared, be great heiresses. The result was two proposals and two marriages! Whether they lived happily ever afterwards is not stated, but they lived, at any rate, "wealthily."

I did not condemn the principle as unsportsmanlike but I remember thinking that there must be a million chances against a barrister ever seeing papers relating to someone he knows. Yet, within two or three days, I was told to help in drafting a marriage settlement which dealt with people at whose house I was going to dance on the very night in question. To my surprise I found that my host and hostess were very rich people.

Though I lived for nearly two years in Mr. Simpson's house, and for the next fourteen years, that is, till his death, I saw him constantly, I neither exchanged a bitter word with him, nor felt the slightest indignation or annoyance at anything he did or said. He was at heart one of the kindliest as well as one of the shyest and apparently most austere of men. Mathematics and law may have dried up his intellect, but they never dried up his heart.

Though he was a man of fine intellect, and had a great and deep knowledge of many subjects, I think I never saw a man who was so absolutely devoid of any interest in poetry or *Belles-Lettres*. I believe indeed that he was quite without any understanding of what poetry meant. If I had been told that he was the Wrangler who said that he could not see "what *Paradise Lost* proved," I should not have been the least surprised. And yet the style of his writing was often remarkable for its perfect clarity and perfect avoidance of anything in the shape of ambiguity. He could say what he wanted to say in the fewest number of words and in a way in which the most ingenious person could not twist into meaning something which they were not intended to mean. He was indeed a super-draftsman. But that is a gift which every man of letters who is worthy of his salt ought to salute with reverence.

My treatment of many things in this book has been inadequate owing to want of space, but in no case has it been so inadequate as that of London of the 'nineties. But my complaint here is, of course, a complaint common to every biography.

Biographers, I am told, always write in this strain. They begin by declaring that they have nothing to say and end by wailing over the insufficiency of the space allowed them

CHAPTER XX

THE ETHICS OF JOURNALISM

WHEN I became not only sole Proprietor of *The Spectator* but also Editor-in-Chief, Chief Leader-writer, and Chief Reviewer, it was natural that I should confront myself with the problem of the position and use of the journalist—in a word, that I should ask myself what I was doing. Should I accept and be content with the ordinary outlook of the journalist on his profession, or should I in any particular strike out a new line, or an extension of an old one for myself?

At that time, i.e. in 1898, the air was full of talk as to the functions and duties of the journalist, for journalism was emerging from its period of veiled power and was beginning to fill a much larger space in the public mind. But in my case this was not the whole of the opportunity. By a singular set of circumstances I found myself in the unique position just described. Townsend and Hutton, it is true, were joint Editors and joint Proprietors; but the sense of responsibility of each to the other was a strong check. I, however, as sole Proprietor and sole Editor, could do exactly what I liked. I could decide, without reference to anyone else, the policy to be adopted. Further, as Chief Leader-writer, I was the man who had to carry out the policy adopted. I had, that is, the function of making the decisions immediately operative. This is

more important in fact than it is in theory. In theory an
Editor's word—subject to the Proprietor's veto—is final.
He gives his instructions to the leader-writer, and the
leader-writer, presuming that he is not a fool or a head-
strong egoist or a man determined to flout his Editor's
wishes, obeys them. That is the theory. But there are
several mitigating circumstances. In the first place, it is
often difficult for an Editor to make his policy quite clear to
his staff. Next, the leader-writer, no matter how strong his
intention to obey his instructions and to enter into the
spirit of his chief, may fail to do so, from want of that
complete clarity of mind that comes only with personal
conviction. If not his own view, his own understanding of
the facts is apt to get in the way and prevent him carrying
out his duties exactly as his chief meant him to perform
them, and exactly as he himself wishes to perform them.

Again, by a sort of law of reversed effort, the leader-
writer may be too anxious to carry out his chief's wishes
and so may distort the Editor's view. There is yet another way in which a loss of power may occur. If the
Editor had himself been writing, he would have seen as he
wrote that this or that particular line of policy that he
had adopted was not tenable, and therefore he would have
altered that line. The conscientious leader-writer may,
however, resist this conversion by circumstantial argument.
He may feel:

This seems to me to be all wrong, but I have got to make the
best of it. Otherwise I shall be taking the responsibility,
which I do not want to take, of altering my Chief's instructions. He said, "Defend the Government's action," so
defend it I must.

But the Editor himself may be in a similar position. If
he has an active Proprietor who gives regular and specific

instructions, he is not really the Editor but only the Proprietor's mouthpiece. In that case, he, too, can, as it were, avoid a great deal of the feeling of personal responsibility. He may say,

I do not like this view. But, after all, it is the matter for the Proprietor, and he may have good reasons for his decision. Anyway, I cannot in a matter of this kind attempt to dictate to him, because if a mistake is made, he will have to stand the racket. After all, I may be wrong as to the policy we should pursue, and if I am, then I shall be doing what I do not want to do, that is, gravely injuring somebody else's property and position. A man may make great sacrifices and run great risks with his own property, but I don't want to be told later that I was the man who insisted on taking his own line against the opinion of his chief with the result that a fatal blow was given to the position of the paper. I don't feel justified in risking another man's property.

The Editor, in fact, is very much in the position of the leader-writer.

These things being so, I realised that the responsibility for whatever was done in *The Spectator* was going to be my responsibility in a very special degree. I could not plead consideration for anyone else's need if I had to defend *The Spectator's* position. Therefore, I must be not only specially careful as to what I did from day to day, but I must think out for myself an answer to the journalistic interrogatory "*Quo vadis?*" What is the journalist's function in the State, and how am I to carry it out? The formula for the discharge of the journalist's functions, which I ultimately came to consider to be true in the abstract and capable of being translated into action, was, curiously enough, the formula of a man whose judgment I profoundly distrusted, whose work as a journalist I disliked, and who as a man was to me exceedingly unsympathetic. It was that of Mr. Stead, the erratic Editor first of the *Pall Mall* and then of the *Review of Reviews*. The journalist, he declared, was "the watch-dog of society." Stead, though a man of honest intent and very great ability, was also a man of many failings, many ineptitudes, many prejudices, and many injustices—witness the attitude he adopted in his last years towards Lord Cromer. Further, there was an element of commonness in his mental attitude as in his style. But with all this, he had a very considerable *flair*, not only in the matter of words, but in ideas. Though the phrase was not used in his time, he was a pastmaster in the art of making "slogans." This, of the watch-dogs in the case of the Press, was one of his best. It exactly fitted the views which I was gradually developing in regard to the journalist's functions. In the course of my twelve years' apprenticeship at *The Spectator*, *The Economist*, *The Standard*, and the other journals for which I wrote, I made it my business to study the work of my colleagues. I soon saw that the men who did the best and most useful work were the watch-dogs; the men who gave warnings. But I also very soon found out that in practice the part is one which cannot be played if the performer wants to have a pleasant time in the world, or to make himself generally liked by his fellow-men. A watch-dog is never popular. How could he be? People do not like to be disturbed, and to be warned generally means a loud noise and often a shock to delicate nerves. Besides, it generally ends in asking people not to do something they are strongly tempted to do. The bark of the watch-dog is, in a rough-and-ready way, much too much like the voice of conscience to be agreeable to the natural man. Though sometime after he may be very grateful to the watch-dog for his bark, when he first hears it he is inclined to say:

Oh! drat that dog.   I wish he'd shut up.   There he is barking away, and it is probably only the moon, or some harmless
tramp, or a footstep a mile away down the road, for the brute's
power of hearing is phenomenal.   Yet if he goes on like that I
must pay some attention, or else there'll be an awful row with
the Boss to-morrow morning if anything was stolen or any
damage done.   The creature's spoilt my night, anyway; I must
get up and see what's going on.

The result is that the tired householder paddles about
the house in carpet slippers, grumbling about this folly of
thinking that anyone could be so unjust or unfair as to
attack a well-meaning man like him.   It would be an
infamy to think of any such scheme.   "I want my neighbours to trust me, and they will never do that unless I trust
them.   So I will have another glass of port and get to bed,
and, if that infernal dog will allow me, go to sleep."

"All's Well" is always a more popular motto for life
than "Beware!"   It is not only the householder who dislikes the watch-dog.   There are people who have more
sinister motives than a love of peace for disliking the
watch-dog.   Those who like to have a night out occasionally without comment from the Master; and those who
think it only fair that certain perquisites should be smug-
gled out of the house by the charwoman and others without any fuss, "cannot abide" the dog and its horrid way of
barking at a shawl thrown over a large plaited basket.

Nobody [they argue] wants to see the master robbed, but
there is a great difference between robbery and having things
a little easy now and then, and no tiresome questions asked.
If we are all to be deprived of our night's rest by that dog,
there will be no end of trouble, and if it goes on much further
we shall have to see about getting rid of him, or else changing
him for a dog that is more reasonable.

But that is not the whole of the trouble. Not only is the watch-dog generally disliked, but he is in danger of being turned from what he ought to be, into a gruff old grumbler. You cannot go on perpetually barking out warnings without getting a hoarse note into your voice, and that makes you compare very ill with the parlour dog and his charming manners, or with the sporting dogs who go out and attend their masters at their pleasures. The working dogs, too, such as those of the shepherd, are far more popular and far more picturesque.

Finally, the watch-dog is often misunderstood because he has got a very narrow gamut of notes. His bark is taken as an angry warning, when all he means to say is: "This is a new man and a new policy, and you had better look into it and see whether it is all right. I should not be doing my duty if I did not warn you to look out." Then if the new-comer turns out to be a harmless or useful person, the watch-dog is blamed because he did not recognise merit on the instant.

But if acting as watch-dog is a disagreeable job, as it most undoubtedly is, it has its compensations. Journalism of which the mainspring is the gaining of pleasure may easily degenerate into something akin to the comic actor's function. Stevenson in a famous passage compared the writers of *belles-lettres* to "*filles de joie.*" That was not, I think, appropriate to the artists in words, but at any rate it is a condition into which the journalist who knows nothing of the watch-dog's duties can easily descend. Our danger is to fall into a kind of intellectual prostitution, and from this the duty of barking keeps us free.

"But," it may be argued in reply, "why need you bark in such a loud and raucous way? Why need you be so bitter?" Here comes a close and interesting issue. How is it possible to give a warning in earnest without exposing one's self to the accusation of being bitter? I have again and again tried, as a journalist, to consider this question, for it has often been my lot to be accused of "intense personal bitterness." Yet in reality I have felt no such feeling. What people have called bitterness has to me seemed only barking sufficiently loud to force attention. I have often, indeed, had a great deal of admiration and sympathy for the men for whom I have been supposed to entertain angry feelings. I have longed to say nice things about them, but that, of course, is impossible when you are on a warning campaign. The journalist that does that is lost. At once the friends of the person against whom the warning is issued complain of your lack of character, of your want of stability, of your habit of turning round and facing the other way. You cannot be a watch-dog only at stated hours, and on off days purr like the family cat.

I will take a specific illustration of what I mean by the watch-dog function in journalism. Throughout my life I have been a strong democratic Imperialist. To me the alliance of free self-governing Dominions, which constitute the British Empire, has a sacred character. It has rendered great help to the cause of peace, civilisation, and security, and it will render still more. I feel, further, that throughout Africa, as throughout India, we have done an incomparable service to humanity by our maintenance of just and stable government. Our record on the hideous crime of slavery, even if it stood alone, would be a justification for the British Empire. But it does not stand alone; there are hundreds of other grounds for saying that, if the British Empire had not existed, it would have had to be invented in the interests of mankind. But though I was always so ardent a supporter of the British Empire and of the Imperial spirit, I was not one of those people who thought that the mere word "Imperialism" would cover a multitude of misdeeds.

To come to close quarters with my illustration, I thought that the watch-dog had to do a good deal of barking in the case of Mr. Rhodes's practical methods of expanding the British Empire. They seemed to me so dangerous and so little consistent with a high sense of national honour and good faith that I felt it was part of my job to protest against them with all my strength. We were told, for example, by his friends, that Mr. Rhodes believed in the policy of the open cheque-book. If you wanted a thing, you must pay for it, and he did. He went further than that: his favourite maxim was said to be, "I never yet saw an opposition that I could not buy or break." It appeared to me that here was an extremely dangerous man, and one against whom the public ought to be warned, and as loudly as possible.

What first set me on his track was Rhodes's gift of £10,000 to Mr. Parnell for the funds of the Irish Nationalists. The gift was made about the time when Mr. Rhodes wished to get his Charter through the House of Commons. Of course, I know that Mr. Rhodes was accustomed to say that the gift and the Charter had nothing to do with each other, and even that the dates would not fit. It was, he declared, an unworthy suspicion to suggest that it had ever crossed his mind that Parnellite criticism, then very loud in the House, could be lulled by a good subscription. Besides, he was and always had been a whole-hearted Home Ruler. Mr. Rhodes, who bought policies as other men buy pictures, made it a condition, of course, that the Nationalists should assure him that they had no intention of leaving the Empire!

My view of the facts was different, and I believe it was the true view.

Mr. Rhodes wanted the Charter badly, and he did not much mind how he got it. He did not, of course, want the Charter in order to make himself rich. He wanted to extend the Empire in South Africa on particular lines, and these included a Chartered Province under his personal guidance. To accomplish this he was perfectly willing to take the help of bitter enemies of the Empire and of England, like Mr. Parnell; men who wanted to give our Empire the blow at the heart. Worse than that, he was willing to give them the pecuniary help they needed in their effort to destroy England, and to risk the consequences. That was surely a case for the watch-dog. "Look at what the man in the fur-lined Imperial cloak has got under it."

To my mind what was even worse than the Parnellite subscription was the way in which the Chartered Company was run and the way in which its shares at par were showered on "useful" politicians at home and in South Africa. The Liberal party at Westminster professed to be anti-Imperialist and pro-Boer. Yet I noted to my disgust that Mr. Rhodes not only called himself a Liberal, but that quite a number of "earnest Liberals" were commercially interested in the Charter.

In this context I may recall a phrase used by a witness before a Parliamentary Committee at Capetown, which made inquiries as to the distribution of "shares at par" when the selling price of Chartered stock was very high. The witness was asked on what system certain authorised but unallotted shares were distributed at par. They were, he stated, given to journalists and other persons *"who had to be satisfied on this Charter."* I am not by nature a suspicious person, but, rightly or wrongly, that appeared to me to be a short cut to ruining the Empire. Though personally I knew nothing about Rhodes, and was inclined to like an adventurous, pushful spirit, it was clear to me that, holding the views I did as to the functions of the journalist, I had no choice but to bark my loudest. My Imperialist friends were for the most part horribly shocked at what they called my gross and unjust personal prejudices against a great man. Some of them, indeed, asked me how I could reconcile my alleged Unionist and anti-separatist views with opposition to the great Empire-builder. When I told them that it was just because I was an Imperialist, and did not want to see the Empire destroyed, that I opposed Rhodes, pointed out to them that he was an arch corrupter, and insisted that corruption destroyed, not made, Empires, I was told that I did not know what I was talking about. I was a foolish idealist who did not understand practical politics. Such self-righteous subtleties must be ignored in the conduct of great affairs.

This talk, instead of putting me off, made me feel it was absolutely necessary, however disagreeable, to pursue my policy. In this view I soon had the good fortune to obtain the support and encouragement of Lord Cromer. Here, by the admission of all men, was the greatest of living Imperialists. Yet I found that he was in full sympathy with my determination to let the British public know what was going on.

As I have said, I felt very deeply about the gift to the Nationalists. Later, I heard that Mr. Rhodes had not only bought off, or tried to buy off, Irish opposition, but that he had actually offered and given a considerable sum of money to the funds of the Liberal Party in order to get them to change their policy in regard to Egypt. The great part of the Liberal leaders and the party generally considered that we were pledged to leave Egypt. This did not suit Mr. Rhodes, with his curious shilling-Atlas and round-ruler point of view about a Cape to Cairo Railway. What would happen if, when the railway was completed to the Egyptian frontier, the platelayers found either a hostile Egypt or a foreign power in possession, and determined to prevent a junction of the rails? Mr. Rhodes regarded such a possibility as intolerable, and, after his manner, determined to buy out the opposition to his great hobby. Accordingly, he approached Mr. Schnadhorst, the Boss of the Liberal Party, and told him that he, Rhodes, was a good sound Liberal, and wanted to give £10,000 to the Liberal funds, which were then much depleted—owing to the secession several years previously of Lord Hartington and Mr. Chamberlain. But the gift was conditional. Mr. Rhodes did not see his way to present the money unless he could have an assurance from Mr. Gladstone himself that the Liberal party would not, if they came into power, evacuate Egypt. In a word, he proposed to buy a non-evacuation policy, and offered a good price for it. Mr. Schnadhorst wanted £10,000 for his party, and wanted it badly. Accordingly he wrote a letter to Mr. Rhodes, assuring him that the party would not evacuate Egypt. The letter would not do for Mr. Rhodes. He wanted a categorical pledge from Mr. Gladstone. This he only obtained indirectly, and ultimately I believe that only about £5,000 was paid.

But though for several years I heard rumours of a large subscription by Mr. Rhodes to the Liberal funds, they were vague. Chance, however, enabled me to prove what I felt was probably the truth. It happened that Mr. Boyd, one of Mr. Rhodes's private secretaries, sent a letter to *The Spectator* about Rhodesia, in which he made a clear allusion to the subscription to the Liberal funds. I at once noted this admission and insisted that the matter should now be cleared up. The Liberal leaders ought, I declared, to say frankly whether any subscription had ever been accepted from Mr. Rhodes.

Sir Henry Campbell-Bannerman, as leader of the Liberal Party, wrote an indignant letter to *The Spectator*, declaring that the statement was a lie. He added that he was authorised by Sir William Harcourt to say that he joined in the denial and so in the accusation of falsehood against Mr. Rhodes's secretary. I then called on Mr. Rhodes in justice to himself to make good, if he could, the allegations of his private secretary.

Then the whole strange story came out. Mr. Rhodes wrote to say that the correspondence with Mr. Schnadhorst was at the Cape, but that he had cabled for it, and that when it came he would send it to *The Spectator* and let the British people judge whether the story was or was not a lie. When the letters arrived they showed that Mr. Rhodes had actually proposed to buy the policy he wanted, as he might have bought a shirt or a suit-case, and that the famous Liberal Manager was quite willing to do business—especially as it was pretty obvious that the evacuation of Egypt was no longer popular with a considerable section of Liberals.

I was, naturally, well satisfied with the result of the warnings which I had given in regard to Mr. Rhodes. I had brought about an exposure of his methods, and had also exposed the carelessness and recklessness which allowed the agents of the Liberal Party to make a secret deal with a man like Mr. Rhodes, and a deal in which the consideration was a large sum of money. And all the time a number of the conventional Liberals were denouncing Mr. Rhodes for his shoddy Imperialism! The attitude of the public at large in regard to my action was curious. The politicians on my own side evidently thought that I had pushed things too far, and had been indiscreet. Some

20

of them naïvely asked, in effect, where should I be if something unpleasant were to come out about the past of my own leaders. When I suggested that I should have to do exactly what I had done in the case of the Liberals, they were very much shocked at my "disloyalty to my party."

The Liberals, on the other hand, though the vast majority of them, leaders and led, had known nothing whatever of the transaction, and were in truth greatly ashamed of it, instead of being angry with their chief Party Manager, were violently angry with me. They declared that I was showing a most vindictive spirit towards a great and good man like Mr. Gladstone. I had "entered into a conspiracy with Mr. Rhodes in regard to the publication of a private correspondence." When I pointed out that, as a matter of fact, I disliked Mr. Rhodes's methods quite as much as they did, and held that it was as bad to buy a policy as to sell one, they inconsequently murmured that I had dealt a deadly blow against the sanctity of public life by helping Rhodes to break faith, and that my conduct was unforgivable.

I may end my story by a description of an interview which I had in regard to this matter with Mr. Rhodes at his hotel in Mayfair. It was the only occasion on which I saw or spoke to him. His private secretary, Mr. Boyd, came to me and said that Mr. Rhodes was very anxious to hand over to me in person the letters between himself and the Liberal Manager. Would I therefore mind going to see Mr. Rhodes, and letting him tell me the whole story in his own words? I did not feel in a particularly kindly frame of mind towards Mr. Rhodes, and I knew and thoroughly disliked his ways with the Press. Further, I did not want to run any risk of Mr. Rhodes hinting later that I had tried to blackmail him, or that he had made a suggestion as to interesting me later in the Chartered Company which had been apparently welcomed by me, and so on and so on. I therefore expressed my opinion that there was no need whatever for a personal interview. Mr. Boyd thereupon made a strong plea *ad misericordiam*. Mr. Rhodes was, he said, exceedingly ill and was worrying himself greatly about the matter. He had not long to live, and I should be playing a very inhuman part if I did not gr nt the interview to a very sick man. Melted by Boyd's evident sincerity and anxiety I agreed, but only on the condition that if Mr. Rhodes had anyone present at the interview, I also must have a friend present. That I felt was rather an insulting condition, and I rather expected that Mr. Rhodes would have replied: "If Mr. Strachey cannot treat me like a gentleman, I don't want to see him." Instead, a most polite message came back from Mr. Rhodes, saying that he gladly agreed to my suggestion and that he would see me quite alone. Why Mr. Rhodes was so insistent as to an interview I cannot tell, unless it was that he had been rather worried about *The Spectator's* hostility to him, and he thought he might be able to mollify me in the course of a private talk. I remember Mr. Boyd told me how he had heard Rhodes often express great trouble and surprise at my attitude towards him. Why should a journalist whom he had never seen be so hostile? What could have induced him to take the line he took in *The Spectator?* "I have never been able to make him out," was how he summed up the position. That struck me as very characteristic. It had evidently never occurred to Rhodes that a journalist could act on the watch-dog principle. The way his mind appeared to work was something like this.

Strachey and *The Spectator* are avowedly Imperialists and strong anti-Little Englanders. Therefore they ought to be on my side. If they are not with me, it can only be that they are standing out for some reason or other. What is it?. It isn't money. If they had wanted to be "satisfied on this Charter" they would have made it clear to me. It can't be pride or prejudice. You can't wound or injure a man you have never seen. As far as I know, Strachey has not been got at by any of my personal enemies. He hates Kruger and his party even more than he does me. It's a most disagreeable and distracting puzzle.

That, I am told, was the way the great man argued till his *entourage* called the spectacle of the puzzled pro-consul deeply pathetic. Rhodes was, I believe, genuinely "haunted" by the problem which he could not solve. I and *The Spectator* got on his nerves. But perhaps if he saw me he could get the solution he desired. He had squared Boers and Governors and high British Officials, and Generals and Zulu Chiefs, and missionaries, and miners, and Jewish diamond-dealers by talk and nothing more. Why not this journalist? He would try. He would worry his secretaries to within an inch of their lives till they got the Editor to see him.

Touched, as I have said, by the appeal about the anguish of the dying lion, I yielded, went to his hotel, and was ushered in by Boyd. I did not feel the charm which was supposed to flow from Rhodes. To begin with, I thought him an ugly-looking fellow. The "late Roman Emperor" profile was a very flattering suggestion. Instead, his appearance explained a quaint and Early Victorian saying which had greatly tickled me when it fell from Lord Cromer's lips. "I saw him once in Cairo. I didn't like him. He seemed to me a great snob." Rhodes ought to have had the manners and mental habits of a gentleman, but apparently these had suffered a good deal of dilution in the diamond-fields. His address was distinctly oily, and I remember thinking what a mistake he had made in his conception of the stage directions for the short dialogue scene which he had insisted on his *entourage* producing.—"*Empire-Builder*, generous, human, alert, expansive, and full-blooded. *Publicist*, dry, thin-lipped, pedantic, opinionative, hard." That was what he, no doubt, expected of the cast. In a word, his attempt to fascinate lacked polish. It was clumsy, almost to the point of innocence, and opportunist to the point of weakness. He did not know how to take me, and was obviously "fishing."

I was determined to seize the opportunity of telling Mr. Rhodes fairly and squarely what I thought of him and his policy. I therefore received his elephantine flatteries and civilities with a grim silence, and then told him I should like him to know what had made me oppose him, and would continue to make me do so. I was an Imperialist, I pointed out, and I regarded him as an enemy to the cause of my country. He had given payments of money to the Irish enemies of Britain and the Empire, and that I could never forgive. "The Parnellites were engaged in a plot to ruin the British Empire. You knew it, and yet you helped them. You gave them the means to arm and fortify their conspirators and assassins." Mr. Rhodes appeared put out by this frontal attack—no doubt an unpleasant one, and so intended. He began by making elaborate explanations, and by declaring "the dates won't fit," but his arguments were muddled and incoherent. "I assure you you are doing me wrong about the Irish policy. I know it is not an intentional injustice, but indeed you are wrong. I am sure I could convince you of this if there was only time."

Though I was not mollified I felt there was no more to be said. Mr. Rhodes was not going to convince me nor I to convert him. Accordingly, I got up and moved to the door.   On this Mr. Rhodes said, very flatteringly, by way of goodbye, that he was greatly pleased that "these letters," as they were obliged to be published, should appear in *The Spectator*.   His device was pathetically obvious.   He knew, or believed he knew, that the journalist's passion was "copy," and he wanted to remind me that he had supplied me with one of the very best political "stories" ever put before an Editor.

I was comparatively a young man then, only a little over forty, and I was disgusted at what I felt was an impertinent attempt to "land" me.   I instantly pulled the papers out of my pocket and flung them on to the table, saying,

You are entirely mistaken if you think I want your letters for *The Spectator*.   As far as I am concerned, they may just as well appear in *The Times* or any other paper.   All I want is publicity.   I have been accused by Sir Henry Campbell-Bannerman of publishing lies, and that I do not mean to endure. I make no claim, however, on behalf of *The Spectator*.   Choose your own paper.

Here Mr. Rhodes showed an excellent command of himself.   He urged me strongly, nay, he implored me to take the papers.   No other course would be fair to his secretary, who had been called a liar.   "As poor Boyd was unjustly accused of lying, in *The Spectator*, I am sure you will agree that it is only fair that his good faith should be vindicated in the same place."   To this plea I could, of course, offer no opposition.   I therefore replaced the papers in my pocket, said "good morning," and walked away.

I suppose many people, certainly Mr. Rhodes's admirers, will say that I was brutal and unjust.   If they do, I think I have a good defence, but I am not going to set it forth here.   More interesting is the general opinion I formed of Rhodes after seeing him in the flesh, and experiencing what was supposed to be his special gift—that of talking a man round.

Rhodes, I had to acknowledge, was not the kind of magnificent man that I had sometimes envisaged him. I think he was a lucky man rather than a man of genius. The chief trouble with him was that he really believed that all men were buyable. He was a kind of throw-back to the eighteenth century, just as the eighteenth-century politicians were to the age of Juvenal and Tacitus. He took their records seriously and acted on their views of humanity. If he chose to use his money for buying policies as other people used theirs to buy places, why not? What else, granted that he was the kind of man described, could Rhodes do with his money?

But these excuses, though I admitted them, made me not less but more eager to oppose Mr. Rhodes and the influences he employed. My duty was to expose Mr. Rhodes, *i.e.* to get people to understand his methods. These almost entirely depended upon secrecy, and that made publicity my best weapon. When once the Rhodesian moral strategy was made public, the game was up.

I believe I did some good by my double warning. In the first place, I warned the British public that Rhodes, if not watched, would secretly buy policies behind their backs and that the party machine, when in want of money, would with equal secrecy sell them. And I proved my point, incredible as it may seem.

"But why rake up an old scandal?" asks Urbanus with an ironic smile. Because the warning ought to be a standing warning. I am by no means sure that when all the secrets are known, we, or rather our grandchildren, will not find that Mr. Rhodes has had imitators, in recent times.

I could, of course, mention other examples of the way in which this particular watch-dog gave trouble, and got himself heartily disliked, but the one I have given will serve.   Besides, the other examples touch living people, and with living people I want to have as little to do as possible in these memoirs.

CHAPTER XXI

THE PLACE OF THE JOURNALIST IN MODERN LIFE

THE watch-dog's function by no means exhausts the work of the journalist. There remains that strange function which is not yet quite realised or understood in a modern community, the function of publicity. Publicity is, in one sense, the method or instrument by which the watch-dog gives its warning: it is his bark. But there is something more in publicity than this. Publicity is an end as well as a means. There are positive and distinct virtues inherent in publicity quite apart from the fact that it is the medium through which the journalist works. This fact is beginning to be realised more and more in this country. In America, it has long been recognised. There, indeed, publicity may be said to have been crowned. It is considered one of the pillars of society, and so in truth it is.

I can best illustrate what I mean by this, by telling a story of Delane, the editor of *The Times* when *The Times* was at its greatest. It is one which should never be forgotten by the critics of journalism and journalists. Someone had been taking Delane to task over an incident connected with his newspaper, and Delane replied: "You appear to forget that my business is publicity." If the public would not forget this essential fact in regard to newspapers they would attain to a much clearer and juster understanding of the problems of the Press. We must

313

always remember that the journalist's business is publicity. At first the plain man may be inclined to say that Delane's words have nothing to do with the matter, or, rather, he may feel inclined to reply in the spirit of Talleyrand's answer to the man who said he had to live—"I do not see the necessity." A very little reflection, however, will show the necessity of publicity, will show, I mean, that publicity has a real and very important function in the State, and that it is literally true that the modern world could not live and progress without the newspaper. The newspaper is indispensable to progress, and to progress in the right direction. Unless we know, day by day, what people are doing, in our nation, in our country, in our town, in our village, we should be like men wandering about in the dark, and we should find it far more difficult than we do now to obtain the co-operation of others for good and worthy objects. We should fail also to get that encouragement, moral, intellectual, and social, which is obtained by knowing that others are thinking the same thoughts and entertaining the same aspirations that we are. It is good to know of the righteous work which is being done by others. It is even good to know, within reasonable limits, the evil that is being done under the sun, in order that we may lay our plans and bring up our forces to check that evil. Without that daily report on the world's doings, which is the modern newspaper, we should for the most part be blind and deaf, and if not dumb, at any rate hardly able to speak above a whisper.

This view may at first sight seem the presumptuous claim of a journalist for his trade. Let any of my hearers, however, try to imagine a newspaperless world and he will soon realise that I am not exaggerating. It is not merely a desire for amusement that makes the leaders of men in a besieged town, or even in so narrow a field as an Arctic expedition, encourage the foundation of a newspaper. They want it as a means of illumination quite as much as of entertainment.

People sometimes talk of men's instinctive desire for news, but, like many other instincts, this one is founded on convenience and the law of self-preservation. Readers of Stevenson's *Kidnapped* will remember how, after the Appin murder, the fugitives on the heather obeyed, even at very great risk to themselves, the sacred duty of the Highlands to "pass the news." In savage countries and in troubled times a man is looked upon as a wild beast rather than a human being if he does not pass the news. Asian travellers dwell upon the way in which the Bedouins observe the duty of passing the news, and described how, if a solitary Arab is encountered, the news is, as a matter of course, passed to him. The seclusion of women even yields to this imperative law of the desert, and an Arab man and an Arab woman may be seen with their horses, tail to tail, and so themselves back to back also, giving and receiving the news over their shoulders.

I am tempted to give a modern example of the advantage of news in the purest sense. Some years ago, in the course of one of those brave attempts which have been made to cleanse the Augean stable of municipal politics in San Francisco, the editor of the chief newspaper engaged in the campaign of purity was kidnapped in the streets of San Francisco. He was hurried off in a motor-car and placed under restraint in a train at a suburban station, from which he was to be carried to a place some 500 miles away. It happened, however, that a reporter caught sight of the editor's face in the reserved portion of the Pullman car where he was imprisoned, and telegraphed to a San Francisco evening paper that the well-known Mr. So-and-So was "on the —— train, going North."

The reporter had not the slightest notion of the romantic circumstances of the kidnapping and thought he was merely telegraphing an item of social news. One of the editor's colleagues in the campaign against corruption happened, however, to see this item in the evening paper and at once realised what it meant. He instantly telephoned to the proper authorities at a town halfway between San Francisco and the kidnappers' destination; the train was stopped, and the kidnapped man brought before a judge on a warrant of Habeas Corpus, and promptly released. No doubt mere publicity can occasionally serve the evildoers equally well, but here, at any rate, is an instance of its utility which may be regarded as proof of the advantage of collecting and transmitting news even of the most unimportant, or apparently unimportant, kind.

Though I hold that publicity is a function of very real utility to the State, it must not be supposed that I think it can be practised without limitations, or that I do not realise that it has dangers both great and many. It has been said that honesty is not as easy as Blind Man's Buff. The same thing may well be said of publicity. The first and most obvious limitation of publicity is that publicity should only be given to truth and not to error. Here, however, we must not forget that there are certain forms of error which can only be exposed and got rid of by publicity, and, again, that it is often only possible to find out what is truth and what error by submitting the alleged facts to the test of publicity. What at first seems an incredible rumour turns out to be literally true, and therefore a failure to report it would actually have been a suppression of the truth. The more one studies this question of publicity the more it appears that what is wanted in the public interest is a just and clear understanding of the way in which publicity is to be achieved. The journalist's business is publicity, but it is also his business to see that this duty of publicity, though carried out to the full, is carried out in a way which shall do not harm but good. If the methods of publicity are sound, fearless, and without guile, all is well. If they have not these qualities, then publicity may become the most dishonourable and degrading of all trades.

It must not be supposed, however, that by saying this I am trying to give a defence of the Yellow Press. I fully realise its evils, only I desire that the Yellow Press should be condemned for its faults, and not merely for its virtues when carried to excess. What the Yellow Press should be condemned for is its tendency to that supreme evil—indifference to veracity of statement. Another of its extreme evils, an evil made possible by publicity, is that of triviality. It debauches the public mind, in my opinion, much more by its triviality than by its vulgarity or grossness. Sensationalism and want of reticence will in the end cure themselves, but triviality is a defect which grows by what it feeds on. People get a habit of reading silly details about silly people, and the habit becomes an actual craze; they can no more do without it than they can rest without chewing gum. This triviality is indeed twice cursed. It degrades both him who reads and him who writes. As to the public, indeed, I sometimes feel inclined to say with Ben Jonson in his famous Ode:

> If they love lees and leave the lusty wine,
> Envy them not their palates with the swine.

But it is a pitiful sight to see unfortunate men who might do better work, condemned to filling the trough with insipid and unsavoury swill collected from the refuse-pails of the town.

Twenty years ago, I had a conversation in regard to this point with the reporters of two very Yellow newspapers, on an Atlantic liner outside the port of New York. The *Lucania* had run upon a sand-bank, and we had to wait all day in sight of that towered city, exposed to the full fury of the interviewer. When I ventured to ask the two reporters in question whether they did not think it was perfectly absurd and ridiculous to print the chronicles of small beer, or, rather, of small slops, such as appeared in their columns, they readily, and I believe perfectly honestly, agreed, but said in defence that they had to obey their editor's orders. To me, at any rate, they acted most honourably and gave no report of our conversation, for I had reminded them that dog did not eat dog. A third reporter, however, to whom I had not thought it necessary to indicate as "private and confidential" an enthusiastic remark drawn by the beauty of New York harbour in an autumn sunset, was not so sensitive. "This is more splendid," I said, "than even the approach to Venice. There is nothing in the whole world like the sea-front of New York seen from the sea." This reporter honoured me next day with a headline of such magnificent triviality that I cannot refrain from quoting it: *"Editor Strachey says New York skins Venice!"*—a contribution to the illimitable inane worthy to stand by a headline in an English provincial paper: *"Vestryman choked by a whelk!"*

Publicity, when it is honest publicity, is as important a thing as the collection and presentation of evidence at a trial. Without the evidence, of what avail would be advocacy or judgment? I have dealt with the problem of publicity, but publicity of course is not the whole of journalism. Besides news there is comment, and comment, at any rate among serious-minded people like the British, is quite as well thought of as news. It is with that part of journalism, indeed, that the editor of a weekly newspaper has most to do. The journalism of comment may be divided into parts, both perfectly legitimate. There is what I may term judicial journalism, and the journalism of advocacy. In judicial journalism the writer attempts to approach the jury of the public rather as a judge than as a barrister, to sum up rather than make a speech for the prosecution or the defence. This does not, of course, mean that he does not in the end take a side or give a decision. He forms a view and states it, but in stating it he admits the existence of the other side and does not try to carry the jury away with him by the arts of rhetoric. Such journalism is not necessarily cold-blooded. Just as a judge may denounce baseness or misconduct in burning words, so the journalist who endeavours to maintain the judicial attitude may, when the necessity arises, be strong in his denunciation of what he holds to be weak, dangerous, or evil. He, however, who is bold enough to essay this form of journalism must never forget that a judge who professes to be judicial in tone, but who ends in being partial, is a worse man than an honest advocate, because he is, in fact, cloaking partisanship by hypocrisy.

Little need be said in defence of the advocate journalist. He makes no pretence to be doing anything but pleading the cause of his party, and placing it in the best possible light. It is not his business, but that of the opposition writer, to put the case for the other side, and if he occasionally pretends to an enthusiasm which does not really belong to him, he is only practising the innocent artifice of the counsel who tells the jury that he will be an unhappy man should he have failed in the task of persuading them to restore his long-suffering, if burglarious, bibulous, or bigamous, client to his best wife and family.

It must not be supposed, however, that the advocate

journalist is a cynic who realises that his own cause is a
poor one, but calls it the best of causes because he is paid
so to do.   That, as all men of experience know, is a fallacy
as regards the barrister, and it is still more a fallacy as
regards the journalist.   We should remember the story of
the barrister who, at the end of a long career, declared that
he had been ,singularly fortunate.   He had never been
called upon to defend a guilty person or to argue a case
where the merits and the law were not strongly on his side.
If this feeling grows up in the case of a man who, changing
from prosecution to defence and from plaintiff to defend-
ant, may often have to alter his point of view completely,
how much more is it likely to grow up in that of the advocate journalist who is always on the same side?   Believe
me, the notion of the political journalist perpetually writing leaders against his own convictions is a pure figment of
the popular imagination.   No doubt an editor will sometimes ask a leader-writer not to put a particular view so
strongly as he, the leader-writer, is known to feel it, but
such reticence cannot surely be regarded as insincerity on
the ethics of anonymity in journalism.   The public are
apt to suppose that anonymity is the cloak of all sorts of
misdoings, and I have often heard people declare that in
their opinion every leader-writer should be forced to sign
his name.   As I once heard it picturesquely expressed,
"The mask should be torn from the villain's face.   Why
should a man be allowed to stab his neighbour in the
dark!"   As a matter of fact, I am convinced that anonymity makes, not for irresponsibility but for responsibility,
and that there are many men who, though truculent, offensive, and personal when they write with the "I," will show
a true sense of moderation and responsibility when they
use the editorial "we."   The man who writes for a newspaper very soon gets a strong sense of what is right and

proper to be said in that particular organ, and he instinctively refuses to give way to personal feeling and personal animosity when he is writing, not in his own name, but in that of his newspaper.

I have hated and distrusted So-and-So ever since I was at Cambridge with him. I know what a false-hearted creature he was then, and how vain and supercilious, and I should like to get my knife into him some day. I feel, however, that the *Daily Comet* could not possibly attack him in this way. Even though my editor has told me that I may say what I like about him it would not be fair to go for him unless I signed my name.

That is an imaginary soliloquy which, I am sure, represents the feelings of plenty of leader-writers when confronted with a personal issue.

Again, men who write anonymously, and in the name of their paper and not of themselves, are much less likely to yield to the foolish vanity of self-assertion. When Zola visited England, I remember a very striking passage in which he expressed to an interviewer his astonishment at the anonymity of the British Press. He wondered how it was that our writers refused themselves the "delicious notoriety" which they might obtain through signed articles. Thank heaven, our writers prefer the dignity which can be maintained through the honourable tradition of a great journal to such "delicious notoriety." The delicious notoriety of the individual is the ruin of the better journalism.

Again, we must never forget that the signed article, however true and sound it may be, is always to some extent discounted through the personality of the writer. "A" may have written in perfect sincerity of a particular statesman, but if he signs his name the gossip-mongers are sure to say that the article in question is to be accounted for by the fact that a fortnight before the writer was stopping with the Cabinet Minister who has been well spoken of, or because the writer's wife is well known to be a friend of the statesman, or for some equally trivial reason. Just as a good chairman of a committee should sink his individuality and speak for the committee as a whole, so a good leader-writer can with perfect honesty and sincerity sink his individuality and speak for his newspaper rather than himself.

But, though I incline to anonymity as the rule of political journalism, I quite admit that in pure literature and in the arts the signed article is often to be preferred. For the object with which the reader approaches a literary article is the desire for pleasure, and that pleasure is naturally heightened by knowing the name of the actor who is on the stage. Though it might be an amusing trick it would be on the whole very disappointing to the public if the play-bill on which the names of the characters appear had instead of the actors' names arbitrary letters, like X, Y, and Z. They would probably not appreciate the task of guessing who was concealed under the wig or the shadows painted on the face which converted Miss Jones' somewhat aquiline features into a *nez retroussé*. No one can doubt that the Parisian public liked to know that the *Causeries de Lundi* were by Sainte-Beuve, just as they now like to see the signature of Mr. J. C. Squire at the end of an article. To push the point to extremes, who would care to grope through a nameless Georgian Anthology in which each poem had to be taken on its intrinsic merits? Even if the public could stand the test, I feel certain that the critics could not. I have always had a good deal of sympathy for the dramatic critic in Mr. Shaw's play when he declares that he can place a play with perfect certainty if he knows whom it was written by, but not unless. Fancy the poor critic going through a volume and saying to himself: "Now is this Shanks or is it Graves trying to score off him by a parody? Again, is this one of the Sitwells writing like Sassoon in order to drive the grocers to delirium?" But, harrowing thought, perhaps it is neither, but only some admirer of the Georgian Mind at Capetown or Melbourne, who has produced for his own use an amalgam of several styles. The mere writing about it is making me so uncomfortable that I must hastily desist!

There is another point upon which I must touch, though very shortly. That is the ethics of newspaper proprietorship. People sometimes talk as if it were a great misfortune that the newspapers of England are, as a rule, owned by rich men. I cannot agree, though I do think it is a great misfortune that a newspaper cannot be started by a poor man. My reason for desiring that as a rule a newspaper proprietor should be rich is the danger of newspapers being bought, or, at any rate, of their articles being bought, as too often happens in countries where newspapers are not great properties. It is often said, for example, that a hundred pounds or so will procure the insertion of an article in most continental newspapers. This is no doubt a gross libel on the best foreign newspapers, but it indicates a danger when newspapers are owned by men of small means and make small profits. When a newspaper is bringing in £50,000 or £60,000 a year it is obvious that even if we assume the newspaper proprietor to have no sense of public duty, it will not be worth his while to sell the influence of his paper. He is not going to risk the destruction of a great property— destruction would surely ensue from his corrupt act becoming known—for a few hundred pounds. To put it brutally, "his figure" would be too high for any to pay—a quarter of a million at least.

But though it makes for soundness that newspaper proprietors should be personally independent, it is also most important that they should be men whose wealth is derived from their newspapers and not from other sources. A great newspaper in the hands of a man who does not look to make a profit but owns it for external reasons is a source of danger. Strange as it may seem at first sight, the desire for direct and legitimate profit in a newspaper is an antiseptic and prevents corruption. One does not want to see a newspaper proprietor, with his ear to the ground, always thinking of his audience, but the desire to stand well with his readers is often a power in the direction of good. The proprietor who endeavours to be the honest servant of his readers will not go very far wrong. When I say honest servant I mean the man who plays the part of the servant who, though he will do his master's bidding when that bidding is not positively immoral, at the same time is prepared to warn that master, courteously but firmly, against rash or base actions. There is nothing corrupt in such honest service, when rendered either to a man or a nation, or even to a Party.

To put it in another way, there are worse things than studying public opinion and endeavouring partly to interpret it honestly and partly to guide it in the right direction.

I will end this chapter by asking the readers of a Journalist's Memoirs to do two things. Firstly, to think better of journalists and their morals than they are at first sight inclined to do. Secondly, not to exaggerate the influence and power of the Press. No doubt it has some great powers, but those powers are much more limited than is popularly supposed. Remember that by using exaggerated language in regard to the power of the Press, people increase the evil which they desire to diminish. Dr. Johnson said very truly that no man was ever written down except by himself. Believe me, this is as true now as when Dr. Johnson said it. I do not believe in the power of the Press either to crush a good man and a great man, or to exalt a weak man or a base man. No doubt a conspiracy of journalists might conceivably keep back a wise statesman or public man for a year or two, and, again, might for a time advertise into undue prominence an inferior man. In the end, however, matters right themselves. The public have a very sound instinct in persons as well as in things, and when they recognise real worth in a man they will know how to prevent the newspaper from doing him wrong, supposing him for some reason to have incurred the enmity of the whole Press—not an easy thing to accomplish. If the *Dictator* makes a dead set against Smith, the *Detractor* is pretty sure to find good in him, and may even run him as a whole-souled patriot! We are a contradictious trade.

Don't be afraid of the Press, but do it justice and keep it in its place, that is, the place of a useful servant, but not of a master.

This is the last word on the Press of a working journalist, one who, though he holds no high-falutin' illusions as to his profession, is at the same time intensely proud of that profession, and who believes that, taken as a whole, there is no calling more worthy of being practised by an honourable man, and one who wishes to serve his country.

CHAPTER XXII

A WAR EPISODE—MY AMERICAN TEA-PARTIES

THE war is too near, too great, and also too much an object from which people turn in weariness and impatience to be dealt with by me, except very lightly. In spite then of the transcendent effect which the war had upon my life I shall only touch upon one or two salient points. The first that I select is as curious as it was interesting. It is also appropriate, for it marked a step, and a distinct step, if one which covered only a small space, towards the goal that I have always put before me. That goal is a good understanding between both branches of the English-speaking race. It involves above all things that Americans shall never be treated, either in thought, in deed, or in word, as foreigners. When the war had been going a week or two, I and a number of other editors were summoned to a solemn conclave presided over by a Minister of the Crown. We were asked to give advice as to how the Government should deal with the American correspondents. Owing to the increasing severity of the censorship they were unable to get any news through to their newspapers. Though they were quite friendly and reasonable in one sense about this, they were in a state of agitation because their editors and proprietors on the other side, unable as yet to understand what modern war meant, and to envisage its conditions, were cabling them imperative messages to send something, and something of interest, to the American public which was suffering from a news-hunger such as had never before existed in the world's history. If the correspondents could not get anything to send they must make room for those who could. The notion that the order for news could not be obeyed was regarded as "impossible."

But the Government, though anxious to do everything they could for the American correspondents, was itself in the grip of the censorship. The Prime Minister's speeches, even, were censored lest they should afford information to the enemy. This policy of intensive suppression was enforced by all sorts of gloomy prophecies from Naval and Military chiefs.

If you allow things to be sent out before they have been carefully considered, and that means long considered, we cannot be responsible for the consequences. Things which look perfectly innocent to you or to the people who send them, when read by the keen-eyed men in the German Intelligence Office may give them all sorts of hints as to what are our doings and intentions. By pleasing one American newspaper you may send thousands of men to their doom by sea or land.

That being the tone of the Censor's Office, the Government was naturally in a state of perplexity. At the same time they felt, and rightly felt, that it was most undesirable to confront our American friends of the Press (for they were all friendly) with a pure *non possumus*. What made it worse was the fact that the correspondents had told Ministers in plain terms that if they could get no news here they must pack their portmanteaus and go to Holland and thence to Berlin, where correspondents were made much of and allowed to send any amount of wireless.

Many plans were suggested at the meeting, but those

which found favour with the Press made the representatives of the Government shiver with horror, while the official suggestions, on the other hand, were, I am afraid, greeted with polite derision by the journalists. Greatly daring, I proposed that we should do for the American correspondents what was done for them in their own country by the President. President Wilson met the correspondents at Washington every Monday for a confidential talk of twenty minutes or so. What he said and they said was not to be reported, but they were "put wise" as to the general situation. I suggested that in a similar way Mr. Asquith might give a quarter of an hour once a week to the American correspondents. He would not, of course, be able to give them anything to publish, but at any rate if they saw him they would not feel so utterly out of it as they were at the moment. To see no one but a Censor who always said No, was like living on an iceberg on a diet of toast-and-water. They would be able at least to cable to their chiefs saying that they had seen the Prime Minister and had heard from him the general outline of the situation, though they could not at present publish any of the confidences which had been entrusted to them. Anyone who knows anything about the relations between the Government and the Press at the beginning of the war will be amazed at my daring, or shall I say "impudence"?—though by no means astonished to hear of the response with which it met. The spokesmen of the Government said in effect: "Mr. Strachey, you must be mad to make any such suggestion. It cannot be entertained for a moment. You must think of something better than that." Unfortunately I could think of nothing better, the other journalists could think of nothing better, the officials could think of nothing better, and so the meeting, as the reporters say, broke up, if not in confusion, at any rate in depression.

I was so much alarmed by the notion of the correspondents leaving the country, and also sympathised so strongly with my American colleagues that I felt that I must do something on my own. I therefore went straight back to Brooks' and wrote to Mr. Asquith, telling him what the situation was, what I had proposed, and how I was regarded as quite crazy. I went on to say that I knew this would not affect his mind, but that I was afraid that he would probably not be able to spare the time for a weekly interview, and that I therefore suggested a compromise.

Will you [I said] come and lunch with me next Wednesday at my house at 14 Queen Anne's Gate to meet all the American correspondents, and so at any rate give them one talk? As it happens I don't know any of the American correspondents, even by name. All the same, I am quite certain that if you show them this mark of your confidence you will never regret it. There is not the slightest fear of any betrayal. I am, indeed, perfectly willing to guarantee, from my knowledge of the honour of my own profession, that not a single word that you say but do not want published will ever be published.

In a word, I guaranteed not merely the honour but the discretion of my colleagues from across the water. I am not a political admirer of Mr. Asquith, and have had, perhaps, to pummel him with words as much as any man in the country. I was not, however, the least surprised to find that he would not allow himself to be overborne by the suggestion of his subordinates that the scheme was mad and so forth. Very characteristically he wrote me a short note with his own hand, simply saying that he would be delighted to meet my friends at lunch on Wednesday next as proposed. This acquiescence relieved me greatly, for I was convinced that the situation was exceedingly dangerous and disagreeable.

My next step, and one that I had to take immediately, was to get my guests together. As I have said, I knew nothing of them and for a moment thought it not improbable that even if I did manage to get hold of their names and addresses they might when they received the letter think it was a hoax. However, the thing had to be done, so it was no use to waste time by foreseeing difficulties. My first step was to get the help of my friend, Sir Harry Brittain (then Mr. Brittain). I wrote to him, asking for the names and addresses of all the correspondents of American newspapers in London, for I had reason —I forget exactly why—to believe that he possessed the information I so greatly needed. The messenger whom I had despatched with my note brought back a prompt answer conveying the information I required. I immediately sat down, dictated my notes, about twenty I think, and had them posted. In these I described the situation quite frankly. I said that as a journalist I had been very much struck and also very much worried by the thought of the situation in which the correspondents had been placed. They were, I said, like men in a house in which all the lights had gone out, and that house not their own. In such circumstances, who could wonder if they knocked over half the furniture in trying to find their way about or to get hold of a light somewhere. I ventured further to propose, though not known to them, that they should give me the pleasure of their company at luncheon on the following Wednesday, at 14 Queen Anne's Gate, to meet the Prime Minister, in order that they might, by means of a talk with him, get a general outline of the situation.

I knew, of course, that it was not necessary to put my colleagues formally on their honour not to publish anything without definite leave so to do. The first principle upon which an American correspondent acts is that, though he expects frankness from the people he talks to, nothing will ever induce him to reveal what he has been told is confidential and not for publication. You can no more get stuff not meant for publication from an American correspondent than you can get the secrets of the confessional from a priest. Reticence is a point of honour. I have no doubt that some of my American journalistic friends will say that there is no great merit in this, because the correspondents know quite well that if they were once to betray a public man they would never have a chance to do it again. Their professional careers would be utterly ruined. Though I should not agree that self-preservation was the motive, I knew at any rate that every consideration of sound business and professional pride as well as of honour made it quite certain that there would be no betrayal.

I was, therefore, most anxious not to appear ignorant of this fact or to seem to doubt my guests. Accordingly I merely added that whatever was said was not for publication and also that I was anxious that the fact of this luncheon taking place should not be disclosed. I gave my reason. If the luncheon, and if any other meetings which I hoped to arrange, became known about by the representatives of Foreign newspapers, I felt that pressure might be put upon me to include them in my invitations. The result would be a small public meeting, and not an intimate social function such as I desired. My wishes were respected in every way. No word said at the luncheon, or at any of the weekly gatherings that followed it for nearly three years, was ever made public. Further, their existence was never alluded to, though the meetings would have made excellent copy, quite apart from anything that was said at them. The secret was religiously kept.

I was deeply touched by the letters which I received in reply to my invitation. They were all from men then unknown to me, though I am glad and proud to say that many of them were from men who have since become intimate friends. They were written with that frankness, genuineness, and warmth of feeling which are characteristics of the American, and contrast so strongly with the stuttering efforts of the Briton to be genial and forthcoming.

Owing to the fact that we had moved to our house in the country in the last days of July, 1914, my London house was shut up except for a caretaker, and my wife could not bring up servants for the occasion or give me her help, which would have been invaluable, because she was tremendously busy with Red Cross organisation and getting our house ready for what it was so soon to become, *i.e.* a hospital with forty beds. I had, therefore, to do the necessary catering myself. I felt that, considering the need for discretion, my best plan would be to go to so old-fashioned an English house as Gunter's. The very name seemed stable and untouched by the possibility of spies.

Accordingly I told Gunter's representative to make arrangements for a luncheon for twenty people and to be sure that all the waiters were Englishmen and, if possible, old service men. That accomplished, I awaited the hour. I do not think I was anxious as to how my party would go off. I was much too busy for that. I was at the time deep in work that I considered appropriate to the Sheriff of the County of Surrey, which office I then held. On the Tuesday before the luncheon I was sleeping at Queen Anne's Gate, but went as usual to *The Spectator* office in the morning, transacted my business, and got back half-an-hour before "zero," which was 1.30, so that I might arrange the places of my guests, a task in which I was helped by Sir Eric Drummond, then Mr. Asquith's Private Secretary. Unfortunately I have not a record of all the people who were there, but I know that among them was Mr. Edward Price Bell of the *Chicago Daily News*, known throughout the newspaper world of London as the doyen of American correspondents. He is a man for whom respect is felt in this country in proportion to the great number of years which he has devoted not only to the service of his newspaper but to improving the relations between this country and his own. Mr. Price Bell is the most patriotic of Americans, but he has never hesitated to make it clear that the word "foreign" does not apply to the relations between Great Britain and America.

Mr. Roy Martin, now the General Manager of that wonderful institution, The Associated Press of America, and his colleague and successor now head of the London office, Mr. Collins; Mr. Keen of The United Press and Mr. Edward Marshall of *The New York Times* were certainly there. Another of the men present with whom I was in the future to become intimate was Mr. Curtis Brown, the well-known and very able Literary Agent and the representative of the New York Press. It was, indeed, at his suggestion that these Memoirs, which have proved the pleasantest literary task ever undertaken by me, were begun and were placed in the hands of Messrs. Hodder & Stoughton in England and of Major Putnam in the United States. Mr. Fred Grundy, Mr. Patchin, Mr. Tewson, and Mr. Tuohy were also among my "first-nighters."

These men became the stalwarts of my regular parties, but there were also a number of other good friends and men of interest and ability, such as Mr. Palmer, who occupied journalistic posts here for a short time only, and then were moved either to the front or to some other part of Europe or back to their own country.

The luncheon proved a great success. From the first moment I realised that there was to be no coldness or official reticence or shyness, but a perfectly easy atmosphere. Mr. Asquith made himself exceedingly agreeable to my guests, and they did the same, not only to him, but to each other, to Mr. Asquith's staff, and to me, their host. Needless to say that as my object was to introduce the journalists to Mr. Asquith and get him to talk to them and they to him, I placed myself as far away from him as I could, though I was still able, if the conversation flagged (which, by the way, it never did) to put in a question or to raise some point about which I knew there was a general desire to get information. Wisely, as I think, I would have no speechmaking. After luncheon we retired into my library for our coffee and cigars, and I was then able to take each one of my guests up to Mr. Asquith for a few minutes' talk. The result was excellent. Mr. Asquith was very frank, but, though light in hand, he was as serious as the occasion demanded. I felt that the general result was that my guests felt that they were receiving the consideration they ought to receive, which I knew the Government desired that they should receive, but which they had very nearly missed, thanks to the fact that Governments so often find it impossible to do what they ought to do, and, indeed, want to do. Official efforts at politeness, instead of being the soft answers which turn away wrath, too often prove violent irritants.

So great was the success of the luncheon that when it was over and Mr. Asquith had to leave for a Cabinet Committee (he remained for over two hours in the house— not a bad compliment to the correspondents in itself, when one remembers that the date was early September,

1914), I made the following proposal to my guests. I told them what a pleasure it would be to me if we made an arrangement to meet at 14 Queen Anne's Gate every Wednesday afternoon till further notice, for tea and cigarettes. We were all busy, but we must all have tea somewhere, and why not in a place close to the Houses of Parliament, the Foreign Office, Downing Street, and the War Office? I went on to say that though I could not promise a Prime Minister once a week, I would undertake to get one of his colleagues or else some distinguished general or admiral whose conversation about the war would be worth hearing, to ornament my Conversazione. The proposal was met with the charming ease and good sense with which every suggestion that I made to my guests was received, and it was arranged that we should begin in the following week.

Oddly enough, I cannot now remember who was my next guest of honour, but I do remember that in the course of that year I twice got Sir Edward Grey, and that on one occasion he spent over two hours, from 4.30, that is, until nearly 6.30, over my tea-cups. Other Cabinet Ministers were equally obliging, and if I remember rightly, among the number were included two Lord Chancellors, Lord Haldane, and Lord Buckmaster. Mr. Balfour and Mr. McKenna were also visitors, as was Earl Grey—the cousin of Sir Edward Grey. Lord Roberts was to have come, but Death intervened to prevent his visit.

Lest the diet should be monotonous, I also got distinguished people like the Archbishop of Canterbury, the Bishop of London, Admiral Sir Cyprian Bridge, Admiral Sir Reginald Custance, General Ian Hamilton, and Admiral Sir Reginald Hall, at that time the head of the Intelligence Department at the Admiralty. There was also Sir Maurice Hankey, the Belgian Minister, the American

Ambassador, Mr. Page, and Colonel House, whom I was lucky enough to catch on one of his flying visits. Last, but not least, I had the two Censors, Sir Edward Cook and Sir Frank Swettenham. It was as if The Thunderer and Mercury had descended to play with mere mortals. My two naval experts, Admiral Cyprian Bridge and Admiral Custance, were among the most constant supporters of my Conversaziones. They proved very popular with the correspondents.

I know that the lions I provided for my arena in Queen Anne's Gate were quite genuine when they told me how much they had liked meeting the able and keenly-interested young men who formed the bulk of the correspondents.

I suppose I ought not to flatter my own tea-parties, but I am bound to say that I don't think I ever listened to better talk than the talk I heard on those occasions. I specially remember a conversation which took place when Lord Buckmaster became Chief Censor, shortly before he was made Chancellor. Naturally enough, the correspondents were inclined to be critical, though friendly, and he, though equally friendly, was sternly determined to defend the policy which his office was pursuing. Curiously enough, our dialectic on that occasion seemed to have made as strong an impression upon others as upon myself. I found, later, one of the most distinguished of news experts of his own or any other country, Mr. Roy Martin, of the Associated Press of America, in a little tract which he wrote about the censorship when America entered the war, spoke of my parties and the talk with Lord Buckmaster in terms which showed that he had been impressed. The tract in question was entitled "Newspaper Men should direct the Censorship." The following is the passage to which I am referring:

On the day when Lord Buckmaster became Lord High Chancellor I met him at the hospitable home of St. Loe Strachey, of *The Spectator*, the best friend American newspaper men have had during this war, in London, and told him that newspaper men had probably been a more constant nuisance to him than to any man in Great Britain. With characteristic suavity he assured me that he had only the pleasantest recollection of all his relations with the press. An American probably would have admitted a part of the indictment. We do not produce that type of urbanity in this country; like the colour on the walls of St. Paul's and the Abbey, it comes only with centuries.

But all the dreadful lapses of the British censorship and all its inequalities can be avoided by the United States. The mistakes which required months to correct are signposts for us. Its printed rules reveal its slow growth. Our censorship can develop equal efficiency in a month, if it notes the charted pitfalls in Whitehall.

I think my tea-parties would have run to the end of the war if it had not been that my health temporarily gave way. Owing to my illness I had to be a great deal away from London, and in any case was not equal to the extra strain they imposed. If I remember rightly, the last meeting was held at *The Spectator* office, for 14 Queen Anne's Gate was let at the time, *i.e.* in April or May, 1917.

I hope I shall not be thought indiscreet if I take note of an incident which occurred in the last six months of the Strachey teas, for it marked the extreme kindness, consideration, and true-hearted friendship shown me by my guests. For some reason, I daresay a good one, though I have forgotten it, the Foreign Office suddenly took it into their heads that they might improve upon my tea-parties by making them more official. Accordingly they asked me whether I should mind handing over the conduct of

23

them to a gentleman whom they named.   He had lived, they pointed out, for over twenty years in the United States and was therefore likely to be a better host than I was.   Indeed, it was suggested, of course most politely and considerately, that on general grounds he would be more acceptable to the correspondents than I should be and would understand them better.

We were at war, and we did not in those days waste time upon compliments, but spoke our minds freely—and quite rightly.   I was not in the least hurt..   Though I loved the parties, which had given me such good friends and such good talk, I was very busy, and indeed very much overworked, and was in a sense relieved at the idea of getting a couple of hours of much needed leisure in the week.   Accordingly, it was arranged that I should retire gracefully and recommend my official successor to my American friends in a short speech. This I did with perfect good-will.   But the Foreign Office, though they did not reckon without their host, had reckoned without his guests.   When the concrete proposal (well-meant, I am sure) was made in all its glorious naïveté in a little speech by the new host, it was received with something like annoyance—a fact which worried me not a little, for I had, rather unwisely perhaps, assured my official mentors that there would be no objection.

Things, however, went further than the grim silence with which the initial proposal was met at what was designed to be "the positively last appearance of Mr. Strachey."   After a few days I heard that three or four of the correspondents, representing the whole body (with their usual tact they had kept this from me), had gone to one of the officials at the Foreign Office and told him plainly that if the scheme was not abandoned and I was not continued as host, they would none of them put in an appearance at the weekly gatherings. The result was that the official scheme was abandoned and that my Conversaziones continued as before.

Many people may think this action somewhat strange. I do not think so. Noting that I had only spent three weeks in America, it was most natural that the officials concerned should consider that I must be ignorant of American minds and ways and that my ignorance might be liable to become offensive. But this view, to borrow Gibbon's immortal phrase, "though probable is certainly false." It is logical, no doubt, but it is not consistent with the inconsistency of human nature.

I ought, perhaps, at the same time to record that earlier in the war, when, owing to the amount of work I had on hand, I offered to retire from the office of host and let it be carried on by others, I was sternly rebuked by the Prime Minister's Private Secretary, and told peremptorily that it was my duty to go on exactly as before—a mandate which I naturally regarded as a compliment as well as an order.

The incident was indeed a pleasant one, and I have reason to believe that what I did was regarded with satisfaction and with gratitude by the Prime Minister and his colleagues in the Cabinet. In any case, the whole episode was characteristically English. I suggested it myself, I carried it out myself, and though my little organisation had no regular official sanction or recognition, it was regarded as I have just recorded as war-work from which I could not retire, without leave. It was valued as a useful method of keeping touch between the men who were directing the war and the journalists of America. Without frightening anyone by making official inquiries, it was easy to find out the temper of the men who kept America informed. Those concerned had only to drop in at the next Strachey tea and sound the correspondents.

Is it to be wondered at, then, that I am intensely proud of what I was able to do? and proud in three capacities: as a man who wanted to help his country during the war, as a working journalist who wanted to help his colleagues, and last, but not least, as one whose life's object has been to improve the relations between this country and America.

To this account of my tea-parties I will further add as a postscript some proofs of what was the opinion of the correspondents as to these gatherings.

I had plenty of kind words from my American journalist friends, but as, I am thankful to say, they are almost all living, I shall obey my rule and not quote their letters or my recollections of their words. One of them, Mr. Needham, who, alas! died in an aeroplane accident in the spring of 1915, wrote me a letter not long before he died, from which I may quote the following. The letter was written from Paris, and is dated 11th April, 1915.

The thing I miss most, now that I am away from England, is your charming tea every Wednesday afternoon. I know of nothing to compare with it, and I find myself wishing that I could drop in, have a good time, and incidentally pick up some really useful knowledge, which one can't so easily do, you know.

Having said so much, I think I must quote the next sentence, because it involved a question which was often discussed in the spring of 1915 at the tea-parties. That was a rather plain-spoken article which I had written in *The Spectator* in regard to President Wilson's policy of neutrality on a moral issue. I spoke frankly, and my words were not unnaturally resented by those of Mr. Wilson's friends who were personal admirers and supporters of the President.

I want to tell you, also, that privately speaking with my finger to my lips, I quite approve of your article on Wilson. You will find it hard, at least over here, to find anyone to disagree with you, except, of course, on American top-soil, namely, an American Embassy or Legation.

I may add another proof that the correspondents met my efforts to help them and also do them the honour they deserved for the magnificent work they did individually and collectively in preventing the growth of ill-feeling, or, at any rate, misunderstanding, between what I may call their and our two nations.

On November 4th, 1914, my friends gave me a dinner at Claridge's Hotel, which was, I can say without flattery, the easiest, the most pleasant, the most natural, the least strained function of the kind in which I have ever taken part. Here is the list of my hosts—as representative a body both for men and newspapers as any journalist could desire to entertain him ·

Edward Bell	*Chicago Daily News*
Sam Blythe	*Saturday Evening Post*
Curtis Brown	*New York Press*
John T. Burke	*New York Herald*
R. M. Collins	*Associated Press*
Herbert Corey	*Associated Newspapers*
Fred Grundy	*New York Sun*
Edward Keen	*United Press*
Ernest Marshall	*New York Times*
Roy Martin	*Associated Press*
H. B. Needham	*Collier's Weekly*
Frederick Palmer	*Everybody's*
Philip Patchin	*New York Tribune*
Fred Pitney	*New York Tribune*
J. Spurgeon	*New York World*
W. Orton Tewson	*New York American*
J. M. Tuohy	*New York World*

The dinner was as good as the company, and that is saying a great deal. I shall record the Menu, to show that in 1914 the cooks of London were still bravely ignoring the ugly fact that we were at war.

MENU

Oyster Cocktail à la Strachey

Lobster—Newburg
Chicken à la Maryland

Selle d'Agneau

Haricots Verts
Pommes Anna

Bécassine Fine Champagne

Aubergine

Bombe à la Censor

Friandises

Cheese Savoury à la "Spectator"

Corbeilles de Fruits

Café—Liqueurs

The speeches I remember well. Those about me were much too flattering, but I liked them none the less for that. I am sure they were sincere. Certainly mine was. I had started out on the hard track of duty to my profession and my country, and behold, it had turned into the Primrose Path of pleasure! I expected to deal with a body of severe strangers and I found myself with a band of brothers— men to whom you could entrust your secrets in the spirit in which you entrust a bank with your money.

CHAPTER XXIII

IDYLLS OF THE WAR

PEOPLE are getting tired of military controversies, and if they were not, I should be precluded from dealing with them by the fact that I intend to avoid as far as possible matters which concern living men, unless these are non-contentious. *Horas non numero nisi serenas.* Again, and even if it were desirable to add fresh fuel to the controversial fire, I could not, speaking generally, add to knowledge without violating confidence.

Nevertheless I cannot treat the war as if it had never existed, or as if it had no influence on my life. It had, of course, a profound influence, and that I am bound to display in an autobiography of the kind I am writing.

This influence, however, must be gathered indirectly rather than directly. All I propose to do at present is to touch the war on two points. First, I want to give one or two examples of what I may call "War Idylls"—recollections which were of so picturesque and poignant a character that they made a fast impression on my mind. Later, I must say something of the adventure of living continuously for four and a half years in a hospital. There I learnt great and useful lessons about my countrymen and countrywomen and confirmed from direct knowledge what had been but guesses or intuitive visions.

My Idylls of the conflict are partly objective and partly

343

subjective. In my visits to the front and in such war-work as I did at home, I witnessed many striking and even entertaining things, and I saw them at moments of mental concentration and exaltation which no doubt heightened them and sometimes made them assume an interest and importance not altogether their own.

The first visit to the front undertaken by me began on the 8th of May, 1915, that memorable day on which was received the news of the sinking of the *Lusitania*.

I shall not give any account of my feelings when hearing for the first time a great cannonade, or seeing shells burst, or catching a glimpse of the German line. Of all such things none were or could afford an experience so terrible as the sight I saw at Bailleul. A number of men still in the agonies of gas-poisoning, men hovering between life and death, lay on their stretchers in rows in the vestibule of the Hospital, awaiting removal. They spoke in strange, lifeless voices, like men recalled from death by some potent spell. But on this unnecessary horror of war I do not mean to dwell. I shall, however, quote from my War Diary an account of a visit to the Scherpenberg, because it gives a glimpse of a side of war too often neglected or ignored.

May 10th, 1915:—From the hospital we went to one of the most wonderful places in the theatre of war, a place of which I had heard a great deal, but not a word too much, from my guide. This was the Scherpenberg. Directly overlooking the plain in which Ypres stands are two hills, Scherpenberg and Kemmel. Kemmel is constantly being pounded by artillery fire of all sorts, but Scherpenberg, for some strange or at any rate unknown reason, is never shelled, and the windmill on the top of it is still going merrily. As I sat on the grass of the hill-top, with the men working at the mill behind us and a nightingale singing in the little hazel brake on our left, it was very difficult to believe that one was looking not only at the scene of recent battle, but at the scene of a battle proceeding at that very moment. The Germans were engaged in a fierce counter-stroke on the North-Eastern front of the Ypres salient. The only indication was the bursting of a good deal of shrapnel at this point. It was here that I first saw shrapnel shells and noticed the little white puffs of smoke, which for all the world looked like the steam let off by an ordinary locomotive. Behind us, or rather, on the right of Scherpenberg hill, there was a big British gun which was firing steadily on the German trenches. The rush of the shell made a distinctly cheerful sound. My companion told me that the sound was anything but cheerful when the direction was reversed and the shell, instead of going from you, was coming towards you. Then the noise was converted into a melancholy moan. While the German and British shrapnel was bursting on the trenches to the North-East of us, there was noticeable a good deal of dark cloud round Ypres, due, as we learnt afterwards, to some buildings having been set on fire during the German attack that morning. With glasses one could see quite clearly the tower of the Cloth Hall, which had not apparently been at all injured. The towers of the Cathedral were also quite plain, but owing to the roof having been blown off, it was very difficult to realise that they belonged to the same building and were not independent towers. The wood to the South-East of Ypres was very clearly seen. This is the wood, as far as I can make out, which R—— had on several occasions told me was a dreadful place, filled with unburied bodies, pitted with shell-holes and with half the trees broken by explosions and ready to fall. None of this, however, could be seen from a distance. As one looked from the windmill, Poperinghe with its prominent church spire was to the left and it was quite impossible to discern anything abnormal in its appearance. It looked even then like an ordinary prosperous Flemish town. In the foreground, that is between the Scherpenberg and Ypres, lay what everyone calls "Dickybush" and Voormezeele, or as the soldiers would say, Vermicelli. There were plenty of people moving up and down the road, which ran straight from the base of the Scherpenberg into Ypres, passing through "Dickybush." The ground all round was being tilled quite as assiduously as if there had been no war. In fact, close to us the only difference the war made was that there were a great many Tommies, either alone or in small parties, going backwards and forwards on the road, just as one sees them at manœuvres. They appeared to be perfectly at home, quite cheerful, and on the best of good terms with the inhabitants.

Just below the hill, or, rather, half-way down, is a very pleasant-looking small farm, or big peasant's house. As I had not yet talked to a Belgian peasant I felt I must make the picture complete by doing so. We therefore went to the house and made an excuse for talking to the people. Several women came out and all more or less talked volubly—but unfortunately in Flemish. Soon, however, a typical farmer's daughter of about sixteen or seventeen came out and fired off a great deal of very bad French and English intermixed with Flemish. She was a pleasant-looking, fat girl, with beady black eyes. She told us that she had been living in Ypres up till a fortnight before. I suppose as a servant or possibly in a shop. It seems that at first she found nothing disagreeable in the bombardment, but of late things had got so hot that she determined to leave. Indeed, although she looked the picture of health and good spirits, she told us that towards the end she had felt rather nervous. She had been near too many bursting shells and burning houses and seen too many people killed. In fact, as the Tommies would say, she could not stick it any longer. I asked her how she had got away. The answer was simple. She had merely walked down the road to Poperinghe and then, "fetching a compass" like St. Paul, had got into "Dickybush" and so home. "A very long walk?" I queried. At this she giggled, and added that "les soldats Anglais sont si gentils." She had had a good many lifts in motor-cars on the road. I did not doubt it. She was just the kind of girl, perfectly straight and of good intent I am sure, who, whether in peace or war, would get lifts from any British soldier engaged in driving anything, from a motor-car to a gun.

As we finished our conversation with the group of women I looked in at the window with the innocent idea of seeing what the furnishings of a Flemish farmhouse were like. There, to my amazement, I saw two prim and perfectly well-behaved Tommies sitting at a table and just beginning to have tea, or, rather, coffee. It was the modern version of those seventeenth century Flemish pictures which one sees in most Museums, where a brutal and licentious soldiery are in possession of some wretched Belgian yeoman's house. The Tommies were, of course, going to pay liberally for their coffee and were evidently behaving with the pink of propriety.

From the farm we walked down the road half-way into "Dickybush" and then, turning to the right, took a field-path up a little hill to get one last view of Ypres under its canopy of mist and smoke, pierced by the towers of the Cloth Hall and the Cathedral. The little field-path was of the kind which one sees everywhere on the Continent, a path somehow quite different from the English field-path. At the end of it stood a typical Belgian peasant, for we were over the border. I asked him a question, but he shook his head, for he could only talk Flemish, and muttered something about "les Allemands," making the usual sign for throat cutting. It was curious to see that this was not done in the conventional, theatrical way, but with a grim stoicism which was not unimpressive. He was not in any kind of panic and was working hard in his fields. He meant merely to convey in gesture some expression like "those damned cutthroats of Germans." I left the Scherpenberg Hill with great regret. It was a wonderful "specular mount." As one stood by the side of the windmill and gazed over the battle-ground, one seemed to get war in its true perspective, something not quite as horrible or sensational as one gathers from special correspondents at the front, and yet something full of a deadly earnestness, intensity, and most impressive fatefulness. Though one forgot it at moments, there was always present to one's mind "the rough edge of battle" of which Milton spoke, out yonder in the trenches. The battle-field seen from a distance and in a position of complete safety is like going over a hospital and seeing the flowers in the wards, the perfect sanitary arrangements and the general air of orderly comfort, and ignoring the operating-theatre with all its grim tragedies. In a battle of this kind the first-line trench is the operating theatre, hidden away from the people who have no business in it.

As a pendant to what I saw from the Scherpenberg while heavy fighting was going on in the salient, I may set forth how, a year later (that is, in August, 1916), I and a friend climbed the steep path of yellow sand which leads to the top of "Le Mont des Cats," a sister summit. From this isolated sandhill, one sees the whole plain of Flanders laid out like a green map at one's feet. But on this occasion, instead of seeing, as I had seen from the Scherpenberg, the pomp and circumstance of war, the view on that particular August afternoon from the Mont des Cats was apparently one of perfect peace.

The opposing armies lay quiet in their trenches. Only the boom of an occasional gun which the foe or the British were firing (cheerfully rather than sullenly) and now and then the noise of an "Archie" warning a Taube to "keep off the grass" in the vault of Heaven, destroyed the illusion of profound rest and reminded one that the wide world was at war. Otherwise the pacific fallacy was for the moment complete. In the sober sunlight of the late summer afternoon the whole earth seemed lapped in happy slumber.

Yet two hours after, and at the actual sunset, so quick are the changes at the front, the present writer, by that time off the hill and in the plain below, saw the heavens gloriously alive with the pageantry of conflict. The vault was pitted with woolly tufts of shrapnel and beautiful dead-white smoke-wreaths from the phosphorescent bombs.

These spread their sinuous toils high and low and seemed
to fill the skies. On both sides the aerial combatants were
going home to roost, exchanging challenges by the way.
And all the time, hidden in a hundred woods and brakes,
the Archies sang in chorus. These evening voluntaries,
including the winding-up of a good many aerial sausages,
were competing with the last rays of the glorious indolent,
setting sun, and were made complete and appropriate by
a good deal of "field music" from the big guns. But even
this, though it was a reminder of war, seemed to those who
watched rather part of the setting of a dramatic fantasia
of the sky than a real cannonade. It was one of the most
wonderful pageants of the sky that human eyes ever
beheld. Even Staff Officers stopped their cars and got out
to look. A series of accidents: a gorgeous sunset, a clear
sky, great visibility, all combined to make the empyrean
into an operatic "set" which Wagner might have envied
but could never have imitated.

In November, 1915, I also paid a visit to the front. I
had some exciting moments, but here again I want to give,
not war reminiscences which will seem very small beer
to half the population of the United Kingdom, but merely
to describe an incident which combined the picturesque
and the entertaining.

I was taken by my son-in-law, Captain Williams Ellis,
and a life-long friend, Lord Ruthven, then the Master of
Ruthven, and chief Staff Officer of the Guards Division,
into the first trench-line opposite the Aubers Ridge, and
incidentally to view some of the worst and wettest trenches
on the whole front, at the moment held in part by my son-
in-law's regiment, the Welsh Guards. My guides naturally took me up a communication-trench, named "Fleet
Street," where one was always up to one's knees in water
and sometimes over them. They brought me back,

however, by Drury Lane, which was a somewhat drier street, also appropriate to *The Spectator*. Here again I will quote from my Diary:

When we emerged from the end of the Drury Lane communication-trench upon the Route de Tilleloi, we proceeded down that excellent road, discoursing on a hundred war topics. Suddenly, however, we came upon a strange spectacle,—a row of men with their backs to the trench-line, walking with extreme slowness and seriousness, in the most strict alignment, both as regards their front and the distances between them, across a piece of muddy pasture. The sun was just about to set, but the light was good and we could see in this row of intent backs that there was a subaltern in the middle and about eight or nine men on each side of him. In solemn silence they went on their way. I was just beginning to think within myself how very worthy it was of the said subaltern to take out a section of his platoon and practise them in some particular type of advance in open order, when, looking more closely at the line of backs, I noticed that the men on the extreme right and left were carrying something slung over their shoulders. I then saw that these somethings were hares. The young devil of a subaltern, quite contrary to orders and at the risk of courtmartial, was indulging in a hare drive under shell-fire! His men, of course, were greatly delighted in the adventure. The whole proceeding was marked by that seriousness which Americans say is only shown by Britons when engaged in some form of sport. Light-heartedness is good enough for the trenches, but not to be thought of when on a predatory sporting expedition. Fortunately for my conductor, the subaltern and his party did not belong to his Division, and so he was able to turn a blind eye. My heart warmed to the young wretch, but the authorities are perfectly right to be very stern in such matters. All shooting is forbidden by the French law, and of course a French proprietor feels it a horrible outrage that while he is not allowed to shoot, some young English officer prances over his ground and bags his hares. That is more than flesh-and-blood can stand, and one is glad to think that it is being stamped upon. Still, when all is said and done, I wouldn't have missed the sight of shooting hares under shell-fire for anything in the world. It is correct to say that the drive was conducted under shell-fire, but no one must suppose that shells were exploding at everybody's feet. All the same, only a little time before a shell did drop the other side of the shooting party, and a very little time afterwards we saw one explode to the right, about two hundred yards from where we were. In fact, the general position was not unlike that described by Mr. Jorrocks: the shooters were having all the pleasures and excitements of war with only one per cent. of the risks.

After a very pleasant visit to General French at his headquarters at St. Omar, the visit ended with a touch of excitement.

On the morning of my departure, we received news that a hospital ship had been sunk in the Channel. At 10.30, I finished my talk with Sir John, got into a motor and drove to Boulogne. Having been told that all the mines had been swept up and that everything was perfectly right, I was to have started by the 12.15 boat, that is the boat which started an hour after the doomed hospital ship. We were all told, however, that we were not to cross by the said 12.15, or leave-boat, but must wait for the P. & O. mail-boat. I rather kicked at this, but as all sorts of generals and big wigs were placed under the same condemnation I saw it was useless to protest, and went and had lunch. I can only presume they had already had wireless news of the sinking of the hospital ship and also of the steam collier, and wanted to be sure that there were no more mines about. Accordingly we did not sail till 3.45, no one in the ship, of course, knowing anything about the disaster. I only heard of it coming up in the train to London, and then the news characteristically came—not from a general with whom

I was travelling—but from a subaltern who had somehow picked up the news on the Folkestone quay. . . . It was curious to reflect that if anyone had offered me the opportunity of going on a hospital ship as one of the sights, I should have closed with it unhesitatingly.   Luckily for me, however, I had not come across any R. A. M. C. people, and therefore am still in a position to sign my name to these notes.   I managed to get to Brooks's for some late supper at 9.30.   At first I was told that I could only have cold beef, but not being a Staff Officer, and not being afraid of being called a luxurious and self-indulgent pig, I insisted upon having some hot soup and some cold pheasant, and also a cup of hot cocoa.   After this warming supper I went to Garland's, and found awaiting me large packets of letters and proofs.   Next morning I was writing my Thursday leader at *The Spectator* office, "as usual."

My last and most exciting visit to the front took place on August 2, 1916, that is, just after the great attack on the Somme.   Most of my experiences, however, though very exciting to me at the time, would now make very dull reading.   Still, there were one or two impressive moments. During the visit I was for a night a guest at Lord Haig's advanced headquarters, and from a little hill above the château in which he lived, I was able to see the trench-line by night.

During dinner, the guns began to speak loudly, and after dinner I got one of the Staff to take me to the top of the down above the château to watch the lights of the battle-line.   It was a memorable sight.   The flashes of our guns on one side, and of those of the Germans on the other, made an almost continuous line of pallid light.   Besides, every minute or two, all along the front, one could see the German or British magnesium flares illuminating the trench-line.   These flares are used as one uses a bull's-eye on a dark walk.   Just as you turn the bull's-eye on any place which you are not quite sure of, so a flare-light is sent up when either side suspects evil designs on a particular part of their trench-line. The effect of the lights was very much like that of a distant firework display, but the continual roar of the guns gave a touch of anger and menace which made one realise that one was watching war and not a Brock's Benefit. The roar of the artillery lasted all night, and when I woke early in the morning it was still going on. Just about five o'clock, however, it suddenly stopped, and I realised with a thumping heart that the Australians and Kents and Surreys were going over the parapet at Pozières.

At breakfast the Commander-in-Chief showed us a telephone message he had just received from Pozières, saying that we had carried the piece of trench which we desired to carry, and had inflicted considerable losses upon the Germans without suffering too heavily ourselves. We had, besides, taken several hundred prisoners.

In the course of this visit, I had the good luck to go into the former German trenches at Notre Dame de Lorette, and also to see some of the German first-line trenches and dug-outs on the Somme at Fricourt, and Albert and its hanging statue. But although this was exciting, it was eclipsed by a visit to Ypres, which I was able to induce my friend, R——, to manage for me. Ypres just then was not considered a very healthy spot. I was General Hunter Weston's guest at the Château de Louvet.

I had once before been in Ypres. It was in the course of a bicycle tour in 1896 or '97, a fact which afforded me some very poignant points of comparison. The chief thing that is impressed on my memory was a curious and pathetic little idyll which is thus recorded in my Diary.

We left our car outside the walls, and entered Ypres close to the Menin Gate, now demolished—where my wife and I entered the town twenty years ago.

23

(We bicycled from Lille, where we had gone to see the Lille bust—a journey which the whole wealth of the world could not now buy one the right to take.)

I was glad to find that my memory was not in fault, and I recalled perfectly the great grey-brick walls and the wide moat which in June, 1896, was covered with white waterlilies. There seemed to be none now, but perhaps "they withered all" when the town died. I should not wonder if this were so, for shells must certainly have dropped in the moat, and in so doing must have disturbed them at the very roots. Crossing the moat by the bridge, we went to the *Place*, once bordered by one of the greatest and most magnificent examples of civic mediæval architecture the world had to show—the Cloth Hall of Ypres. Its walls now only stand some 20 or 30 feet high. The remains of the towers of the Cathedral are a little higher, and one of the pinnacles of the Cloth Hall points like a gaunt grey finger to the sky. I wandered alone into the Institute of St. Vincent de Paul, which stands to the north of the *Place* and is only partially ruined. The façade, a pleasant example of Louis XIV work, is still standing, and there are also pieces of the roof intact. One enters by the church or chapel door. I passed through this, with its desecrated altars and its ruined ecclesiastical finery, into the sacristies and other rooms behind, including one lofty room lined entirely with blue-and-white tiles. While there, I heard, to my surprise, a faint and very distant sound of a sweeping broom. It echoed through those empty, roofless halls with a weird sound, for at that moment there was only an occasional growl of artillery in the air. Everything else was strangely quiet. Needless to say, an uninhabited town is never noisy, and at five o'clock in the morning it is not merely not noisy but deadly still. Greatly astonished, I followed the sound through a long succession of ruined rooms, until I came upon a soldier with a broom, steadily sweeping the floor of a small empty room a little off the main sacristy. He had a steel helmet upon his head, like myself. Slowly and like a man in a dream he plied his work. He looked at me as if I too were part of the dream, and when

I asked him what his regiment was, he answered with a sort of shadowy salute and in faint, far-away tones, "The 52nd." I am bound to say I have never been more taken aback than I was by that answer. It literally left me speechless—a record, my friends tell me. The strangeness of the whole scene and the silence had made me prepared for mysteries, but it was a little too much to be told that I was face to face with a man from one of the most famous of the Peninsular regiments. It is unnecessary to say that no modern soldier, asked his regiment, would now give its old numeral. He would have described himself as belonging to, say, the 2nd Battalion of the Oxford and Bucks Light Infantry. I hastily retreated from this vision of the past, and recounted my experiences to R——. As much mystified as myself, he moved with me on the sound of the broom. The man gave him the same answer as he did to me, and produced the same sense of mystery. But then there came the prosaic explanation. He belonged, he added, to the Canadians. His far-away manner was soon accounted for by the fact that he was a French-speaking Canadian and only very dimly understood my question. So passed into prose a very pretty piece of mystery! He was no doubt a Roman Catholic and anxious to do anything he could to keep the sanctuary clean. From the Grande Place, with its air of Pompeian melancholy, we passed on to the ramparts. There, I was thrilled to see the guard being relieved in the dead silence of the dawn by helmet-clad men. Mounting or relieving guard on these ramparts is no empty pageant, for at any moment a German shell may drop and obliterate the post. . . . When we had gone what I judge to be about a mile along the canal, it being now seven o'clock, we turned off to the left into some fields, in order to take a path which led to a point in the road where our car had been sent round to meet us. When we were about half the way across the fields a shell came over our heads, and we could see it bursting upon the road almost exactly at the spot where we expected the car to wait. This was somewhat disconcerting, and R., after the manner of the British officer, whose first thought in reality as well as in fiction is for his man, showed a good deal of anxiety lest his chauffeur should have been in trouble. The shell was not a solitary one, and there was soon another bursting on our left and another in the air in front of us. Though I have, in the abstract, no desire for shellfire, even when very mild, I could not, in a sense, help being glad that I was obliged to get so excellent a view of what a shell bursting in the air looks like at fairly close quarters. To be truthful, it looks almost exactly like what I used to call an absurdly exaggerated picture in the illustrated newspapers! There was no great danger, but R.— who was no doubt slightly anxious about his charge, *i.e.* myself, just as one is anxious when showing sights to visitors when one is threatened by a hailstorm,—thought we had better sit down and wait till we saw whether the shelling was going to stop or possibly develop into something really unpleasant. Accordingly, we sat down on what had once been a rather neat piece of sandbag work, something in the nature of what an Irishman might have called a "built-up dug-out." Though the roof was off, I was glad to have a feeling of security in the small of my back. It rested against a double thickness of sandbags. While waiting here I was consoled by my companion by a story of what an artillery general had said to him under similar circumstances, *i.e.* that when one saw the shells not bursting near enough to do any harm, one was perfectly safe. The only trouble, he went on, was that "some infernal idiot in the German artillery positions might go and monkey with the sights." "In that case, there might be a nasty accident." Happily no interfering idiot in this case monkeyed with the sights, and very soon the battery which was attending to our part of the country "ceased fire," and it was soon pronounced safe for us to resume our walk. Altogether I was much impressed with R.'s complete indifference. Nothing could have been more reassuring for civilian nerves. When we emerged on the piece of road where we ought to have found our car and chauffeur, we were immediately plunged back from the solemnities of war into the normal picnic situation. Everyone knows how at a picnic the car is sent round another way, with clear directions to go to a perfectly familiar spot, a place where the host says he has made his chauffeur meet him a dozen times before, and to wait there. Yet the rendezvous when you reach it always turns out to be absolutely vacant and bereft, not only of the car but of any signs of human life whatever. No desert looks so forlorn as a place where one expects to meet somebody and does not meet them. This was exactly our case. Happily there were no signs of the car having been destroyed, and therefore our anxiety for the chauffeur's safety was relieved.

To cut a long story short, we wandered about till we found and commandeered another car, and drove up the main road. There we soon found the errant car, waiting behind a shed and some trees. It appeared that the chauffeur had found the rendezvous too hot for him, after two shells burst not a dozen yards away from the car, and he retreated therefore to a safe corner, where we found him talking to a fellow-soldier. He was very properly reprimanded for having moved from the place where he was told to wait, but all the same I was glad there was no accident.

During our return journey, we were not worried by bombardment of any kind, and got back to H. Q. for an excellent breakfast at 8.30. The morning I spent strolling about the grounds of the château. At luncheon, R. asked me what I would like to do, and I suggested a visit to the Belgian inundations. The arrangements required were somewhat elaborate, but thanks to the good offices of the Belgian *liaison* officer attached to the Corps Commander's staff, we got the necessary permits. I am exceedingly glad to think that we did pay this visit, for it was not only most picturesque but also most deeply interesting from a military point of view. The greater part of the Belgian line and the whole of the part we visited runs parallel to the course of the canalised river Yser, which empties itself into the sea at Nieuport. To reach it we had to pass through Furnes, most charming of old Flemish towns, with a ravishing Grande Place, surrounded by beautiful brick houses, some of them of the XVth century, some of them dating from the time of the Spanish occupation, and some again, of the epoch of Louis XIV. As the Belgian lines are on a dead flat alluvial plain reclaimed from the sea, it had proved impossible to manage communication-trenches. If they were dug into the ground they would instantly become full of water. No doubt they might have been built up with sandbag parapets, but this apparently was not thought necessary, owing, no doubt, to the fact that the inundation pushes back the German lines for nearly two miles. We (*i.e.* the two Belgian officers who accompanied us, R. and myself) all packed into one motor for this part of the drive, lest two motors should draw the attention of the enemy's artillery. Also the car was made to drive very slowly lest it should raise a cloud of dust and so give us away. We ran up a road parallel to the course of the Yser, and passed three brick chimneys belonging to a factory which had been much knocked about by the German artillery fire. One of the chimneys was pierced by the very neatest shell-hole you ever saw. It went straight through the shaft of the chimney, in at one side and out at the other, for all the world like two windows opposite each other. The fabric of the chimney remained secure. Needless to say, this eye was put into the needle of the chimney because it had been used as a Belgian observation-post. We soon got out of our car and walked across the fields to the old railway embankment, which was now being used as the bank of the inundation. On the land side of it the ground was marshy, but it was *terra firma*. On the other side there are two thousand yards of grey-brown water about three or four feet deep. The inundation was produced by reversing the process of reclamation. The gates of the Yser used to be shut against high tides, to prevent the sea-water coming up, and opened at low tides to let down the land water. Now they are opened at high tides, so that the tide can rush in and maintain the inundation, and at low tides they are closed, so that the fresh water of the Yser can overflow its banks. On the top of the railway bank is a fine series of sandbag parapets and parados. R., however, pointed out that the parados is so good as to be really another parapet. Therefore, if the enemy took those Belgian trenches they would, without any alteration of the premises, be able to open business on the south side. In the south face of the railway embankment a number of excellent dug-outs have been excavated, and strengthened with stone, brickwork, and concrete by the ingenious Belgian engineers. Those works showed what the world has always seen in the architecture of the Low Countries, namely, what wonderful constructors are the Flemings. Building seems to come as naturally to them as to the Italians, though their staple is brick, not marble.

Before I leave the subject of the inundations, I ought to say that across the stretch of muddy water the Belgians hold a good many little islets and pieces of ground, which, for some reason or other, are a few feet higher than the rest of the reclaimed plain. Communication with these is kept, not by boats, but by paths of duck-board which lie across the flooded lands. The Germans, however, recognise that they have been completely outwitted by the inundation, and that it is no use to attempt to attack the Belgians. Accordingly things are very quiet on this line. It happened, however, that as we walked back across the fields, having followed the same plan as in the morning of sending our car round to meet us at a safe place, the Germans chose to throw a few shells, and I had therefore, when I reached the place of safety, the feeling, good to the civilian heart, that I had been shelled both before and after luncheon in one day—though I admit that the shelling was not of a very serious description. It did, however, justify the steel helmet and the gas-mask.

I shall end my Idylls of the War with what I hope will not be called a frivolous note.

At the end of the war, when men had to be taken away even from the necessary work of agriculture, women, with that surprising capacity for work of all kinds, which seems to be their privilege, took on every sort of job and did them all remarkably well. Perhaps the most curious instance of this is that women at once took up the work of shepherds, and began to keep their flocks on bleak and lonely Downs; a function, remember, which no women had performed in England for two or three hundred years. Here is my account of the first shepherdess I ever saw, written on October, 1918, and on the day of my encounter.

I had always longed to see a shepherdess, keeping her sheep on the Downs, and watching them feed, in sober security. I think it was that desire that made me, when at Oxford, contemplate a learned study of Elizabethan pastoral plays—a work which, if I remember rightly, never got beyond a dedication to a damsel who, "perchance to soothe my youthful dreams," appeared too bright for common life and needed the crook and the wreath. And now today I saw, as I was riding along the Pilgrim's Way across the Downs, a shepherdess. Alas! *quantum mutata ab illa.* Even when I saw her, a long distance off, leaning on her crook, I did not desire to:—

> "Assume her homely ways and dress,
> A shepherd, she a shepherdess."

Still less, when I rode up closer, did I entertain any romantic ideas. I had not been so fantastic in mind as to expect a war shepherdess to wear a straw hat in December, wreathed with roses and forget-me-nots, or a mixture of all the flowers of spring, summer, and autumn, as is the wear of the pastoral Muse. Again, I did not look for a "Rogue in porcelain," with gold buckles on neat black shoes, and highly ornamented stays worn outside her gown. A stalwart young woman, in a khaki smock and sou'-wester, Bedford-cord breeches, and long leather boots, would have satisfied my utmost demands in 1918. Instead, however, my shepherdess was dressed, if her clothes could be called dress, like a female tramp. Long draggle-tailed skirts, some sort of a shawl, and the most appalling old cloth cap on her head, concealing a small quantity of grey hairs and shading a wrinkled, aged face! It was a bitter disappointment.

She would have done far better for a Norn or one of the Weird
Sisters.   Yet, when I stopped my horse to talk to her—I had
not forgotten that "the courtesy of shepherds" demands that
one should always exchange words with the folk of the lonely
trade—I found myself unconsciously dropping into the
language of pastoral verse.   Does not the Third Eclogue of
Virgil begin:

"Die mihi, . . . ? An Melibei?"

At any rate, I began: "Whose flock is this?"   She answered
as if out of the book: "It's Farmer Black's.   First the one-
armed shepherd had it.   Now I've got it," and her eyes looked
lovingly on as fine a flock of ewes as you could wish to see.
They were spread fanwise along the opposite side of the
sharply-defined chalk valley.   She went on to tell me that she
had also got the lamb flock, but not with her that day.   I asked
how she had come to take up pastoral work, thinking that
probably she was the widow of a shepherd.   But it seemed
that she had never done shepherd's work before, though, as she
said, she had "been brought up among them."   "Them" was
obviously the ewes and lambs.   One could see that she was
thoroughly competent, and that while she was in charge there
would be no straying or stealing, or over-feeding, or starving,
or any other ill.

Then we talked of her dog, who sat by her, vigilant and
confident, ready at her slightest word or nod to race round his
charges.   Yes, he was a good dog now, but when she had him
first he was wicked.   "He was that spiteful, you dursn't trust
him."   The one-armed shepherd had "used him cruel," and
made him savage with the sheep.   Now at last she had got him
quite right again, and she looked down lovingly upon the dog—
a bob-tail of the South Down breed—who sat at attention by
her side.   But, she ended, the work was very hard, and the
weather getting too cold for her to be up on the Downs much
longer.   She would have to give it up for this winter.

I wished her good luck and cantered off, a disillusioned man.

But as I turned my heard for one more glimpse of my one and only shepherdess, I saw the dog looking up with the utmost faith and affection into her poor, kindly, weazened old face. I could not wish her other than she was. I could well believe that the farmer was satisfied with her, and hardly regretted that she had not thought it worth while to dress the part with a little more attention. Perhaps in the time to come we shall develop a real race of shepherdesses,

> " Who without sadness shall be safe,
> And gay without frivolity."

If we do, I think they are pretty sure, whether young or old, to tie bunches of wild flowers to their crooks. But, after all, for a war shepherdess, garments such as my Downland Amoret had on were more appropriate. Anyway, the brave old thing was doing her war-work sturdily. She shivered, I am sure, for service not for hire. All honour to her and the thousands of women who did as she did!

CHAPTER XXIV

FIVE GREAT MEN

THERE are five men,—three of them close friends and the others good friends and men for whom I felt a warm admiration,—who stand out as prominent influences in my life. In the first group I put Lord Cromer, Colonel John Hay, and Mr. Theodore Roosevelt. They were men with whom I was, I think, in sympathy on every point in regard to the conduct of political life and to the spirit in which it should be carried on. The other two were Joseph Chamberlain and the Duke of Devonshire. Mr. Chamberlain I knew intimately and esteemed highly, having always a sincere admiration for him even when we differed most in politics. In regard to the other, the late Duke of Devonshire, I may say that although I was on much less intimate terms with him than with Mr. Chamberlain, I never felt any political difference, except in the matter of speed of action. Yet even when one was most impatient with the Duke's slowness in uptake, one often admired him most and felt at the back of one's mind that he was most in the right.

In selecting these five men from among my friends I must remind people that this does not show that they were my only close and intimate friends in public life. There were plenty of others, but I am thankful to say I am prevented from mentioning most of them because of my rule not to write of the living. Indeed, I have been so fortunate in my friends that but for this rule I could fill not a single volume but a series of vast tomes.

In moments of mental elation I had planned to direct my executors to place upon the tablet which will be fixed to the wall of the Strachey Chapel in Chew Magna Church, nothing but the words: "His friends were many and true-hearted." I admit that this is a piece of self-laudation that a man could hardly be justified in bestowing upon himself. If you can read their "history in a people's eyes," you can certainly best read a man's history by asking who were his friends and how did they treat him and feel towards him. Till lately, however, I have felt a difficulty in the matter, for, to tell the truth, these deeply moving words came in the first place not from some classical writer but from that nautical ditty, "Tom Bowling." They are the work of that amazing British Tyrteus Dibdin,—the broken-down poet actor who drew an annual salary from the Admiralty for maintaining the spirit of the British Navy through his songs! ["*We 'ires a poet for ourselves*" was, according to Byron, the boast of Mr. Rowland of oily fame. The Admiralty could make a similar claim.]

I felt that it would be rather much to ask one's executor to get a country vicar to pass a line of a nautical ditty for insertion in a church. If, in verifying the quotation, the parson should be arrested by the neighbouring line, "*His Poll was kind and true*," what then? There is no harm in the poem as a whole but somehow it has not quite the monumental air about it. Lately, however, I discovered to my great satisfaction and not a little to my amusement that, as so often happens, one of the Greeks of the great age had been before Dibdin. In that enchanting dialogue, "The Symposium" of Xenophon,

Hermogenes is asked by one of the persons of the dialogue: "On what do you plume yourself most highly?" *"On the virtue and the power of my friends,"* he answered, *"and that being what they are, they care for me."* I feel now that when the time comes, my complimentary self-determination may be shrouded in the veil of a learned language, and if the words, "His friends were many and true-hearted" are added in the vernacular they will pass with men of Hellenic culture as an allowable example of a free translation.

It will also have a certain support from one of the tablets with which my tablet will be colleague, the tablet that commemorates the first Sir Henry Strachey, the Secretary of Clive and a man who was for forty years and more a Member of the House of Commons. This epitaph has not the usual flowery pomposity that one would expect to find in the case of a man of his age and occupation and position. It is reticent, if conventional. One phrase, however, stands out. Henry Strachey is described as *"an active friend."* That is much too great praise for a man to claim for himself, but there is nothing that I should like better than to be able to think when I boasted that my friends, like the friends of Hermogenes, were many and cared for me, that I had helped to make them so because in a world so full of passive friends I had at any rate tried to be active.

I must begin with Lord Cromer, for I had a regard for him, and for his wise and stimulating advice, which touches the point of veneration. He was seldom out of my thoughts. He was in the habit of consulting me freely in regard to public events and on other great matters, and we either met and talked or else wrote to each other almost daily.　I was a much younger man than he, and I had not, as he had, come into personal contact with the problems of practical administration at first hand, but had been accustomed to see them and deal with them rather as abstractions.　It is true that the questions on which my opinion had to be expressed in *The Spectator* were often of vital importance and that I had to advise my readers thereon.　Still, I was never myself an executant.　I was, indeed, rather like the type of laboratory doctor who has of late come into being.　He does not himself come into contact with the patient though he is asked to investigate special points.　His opinion may have great weight and influence, but he does not carry out the physical cure of the patient.

Many of Lord Cromer's oldest and most intimate friends may perhaps be surprised to hear that Lord Cromer consulted me so often and on so many points.　If so, I shall not be astonished at their astonishment.　It would be most natural in the case of a man so self-reliant, so able to judge and balance things for himself—so little liable to be carried away by personal feelings, as Lord Cromer. Yet, it is true　The reason was, I think, that Lord Cromer found with me, as I found with him, that in response to, or in reaction from any particular series of events we almost always found ourselves *ad idem*.　We wanted the same good causes to win, and we wanted to frustrate the same evil projects.　In public affairs, we agreed not only as to what was injurious and as to what was sound, but, which is far more important, we agreed as to what was *possible*.

In economic matters, both in theory and practice, we moved on exactly the same lines.　Once or twice, when I most sincerely thought that I was differing from Lord Cromer and told him so, because I felt I might seem to be shifting my ground,—or rather, looking at things from a different angle,—I found that an exactly similar process had gone on in his mind.

As so often happens with a friendship of this kind, I foretold in my own mind almost from the first moment I saw him, the kind of tie that was going to unite us. I had not spent half an hour in his company before I realized that I had at last found a man dealing with great affairs in a great way,—not only a man who satisfied me absolutely in theory, but a man with whom I could act unreservedly because his mind was tuned to the same pitch as mine.

I well remember the day and the hour of our meeting. Always deeply interested in Imperial questions, and especially in the Egyptian problem, I determined, in the year 1896, to pay a visit to Egypt. Like most young men of my day, I admired Lord Cromer and his work, but I had no special cult for him. Naturally, however, I took out letters of introduction, for until the end of his occupation of the post of Consul General, he was "Egypt." One of these was from my chief, Mr. Hutton, one from my uncle, Sir Richard Strachey, and another, if I remember rightly, from another uncle, Sir John Strachey; the two uncles had been colleagues of Lord Cromer's on the Indian Council. Directly I arrived in Cairo, I left my card and my letters of introduction in the usual way, and expected, after a decent delay, to be asked to pay a semi-official visit at the Agency. Instead, Lord Cromer acted with his characteristic promptitude. Early on the morning of the day after I had left my letters of introduction and my own and my wife's cards, there came one of the beautifully dressed Syces from the Agency with an invitation to lunch with the Cromers that day. We went and to our great delight found them alone. Therefore,

I was able at once to get *en rapport* with my friend that was to be. I had not finished luncheon before we had plunged into the whole Egyptian question and had got to my own cherished point, one connected with the French occupation of Tunis, their promises of evacuation, and so forth. This, my first experience of I do not know how many hundred talks with Lord Cromer, was exactly like the last. In the art of unfolding his mind and his subject he was a master. I questioned and he answered, and I remember distinctly feeling that I had never before put myself so easily *en rapport* with any man. I had been told that he was gruff, nay, grumpy, and quite without any of the arts of the diplomatist, and that I should find him very different from the statesmen and politicians to whom I was accustomed. Instead, I found him plain and straightforward, but as kind as he was quick.

After luncheon, we had a very long talk which was at last interrupted by Lord Cromer having to go out to open something or to see somebody. As I was saying good-bye he suddenly said: "I suppose you can keep a secret?" I made a suitable reply, and added I had a lock to my portmanteau. With his quick step he was at the side of his bureau in a moment. Unlocking a drawer, he thrust into my hand a white paper. "That," he said, "is a memorandum which I wrote the other day for Lord Salisbury, giving a character of the Khedive and of all the chief Egyptian statesmen. It wouldn't do to lose it, and there are, I suppose, agents of the Khedive who might possibly look out for papers in your rooms if they heard you had been seeing me." He said this rather apologetically, for he hated anything sensational or melodramatic like the true Whig he was. He added however: "I think it would be better when you are not reading it if you kept it in your portmanteau. Don't trouble to return it till you have read it thoroughly. I think it will amuse you."

I was touched at the moment, but when I got back to my hotel and saw the nature of the document I felt pleased beyond words. I did not, of course, imagine that Lord Cromer would suspect me of wanting to betray his secrets, but considering the place, the Agent General's position, and the fact that he was then at the height of his quarrel with the Khedive and on the most delicate terms with half the men mentioned in the document, I felt that he had reposed a confidence in me which most people would have thought only justified in the case of a man they had known for years, a man who, they were sure, would not cackle about a subject of which he was naturally, as I was, quite ignorant. No doubt he knew there was no peril of my publishing anything, but if I had left these perfectly plain-spoken *dossiers* of all the big men in Cairo about in the hotel, the result might have been catastrophic. This exhibition of confidence was characteristic of Cromer. If he trusted you, he trusted you altogether. Though he indulged in no nonsense about being able to tell in a moment whether a man was trustworthy or not, and did not often act upon impulse, he was quite capable of doing so on occasion.

In itself the document was exceedingly brilliant and just the piece of work which a busy Prime Minister like Lord Salisbury would greatly value. It put him *au fait* with the exact position of the various players in the great game of intrigue which was always going on, and with the plots and counter plots made in the Khedive's Palace or in the houses of the various Pashas. They spent most of their time in those days in trying to trip up the Agency.

Lord Cromer not only exposed the motives of the men with whom he was dealing; he often gave the just apologies

24

for these motives. But he did more than this. Without being unduly literary or rhetorical he gave lively characters of the men described. What fascinated me about these analyses of character, however, was that though they were like the best literature, you felt that Cromer had never let himself be betrayed into an epigram, a telling stroke, or a melodramatic shadow in order to heighten the literary effect. The document was a real State Paper, and not a piece of imitation Tacitus or Saint Simon.

I found myself greatly admiring and even touched with envy. I wondered whether, in similar circumstances, I should have been able to resist the temptation to be Tacitean. One felt instinctively that Lord Salisbury must have been grateful to have such an instrument for dealing with a situation so delicate and so intricate and placing so great a responsibility on the man in charge.

During my stay in Cairo, my intimacy with Lord Cromer deepened from day to day. We talked and talked, and from every talk I gained not only knowledge of the East, but knowledge on a thousand points of practical and also theoretical politics. Cromer, like so many Imperial administrators before him, was an exceedingly well-read man, in modern and ancient history, in Economics, and in political theory. Above all, he was a devotee of Memoirs and he was always able to reinforce an argument with "Don't you remember what . . . said about that." I may say frankly that the great delight to me was the delight of confirmation. Inexperienced as I then was in public affairs, it was a matter of no small pleasure and of no small amount of pride to find my own special opinions, views, and theories as to political action plainly endorsed.

In not a single case was I disappointed or disillusioned either with what had been my own views or with what were Lord Cromer's. I soon saw, as I am sure did he, that we were capable of a real intellectual alliance; and so our friendship was made.

Considering the reputation that Lord Cromer had for masterfulness and for something approaching disregard of other people's feelings when he thought them foolish or in the wrong; for the irritability of extreme energy; or again for a fierce impatience with anyone who opposed his views, my experience surprised me not a little. I did not find a trace of these things in my intercourse with him, and this in spite of the fact that knowing what to expect in this way, I was keenly on the lookout. Moreover I was, with all a young man's prickliness, quite determined that I would not be treated as I was told Cromer was apt to treat people. But I seldom if ever found myself in disagreement with him on the merits and never as to manner of action. No doubt we were as a rule concerned with matters where I did not know the facts and he did.

Neither of us could, of course, differ as to conclusions when once the facts were agreed on. Each had his little inch measure of logic and both measures were scaled alike. Still, in intercourse so constant as that between us in letters and in talk, it is, I must confess, extraordinary that he and I never really differed and that this was certainly not due to either of us being prepared to give way upon essentials.

If anyone thinks that I occupied what the XVIIIth century people were wont to call the spaniel position to Lord Cromer, they are mistaken. He never attempted to bully me out of an opinion or even out of a prejudice. If, indeed, I had been a self-conscious man, I might have been a little worried by the fact that when I told him of some line that I had taken or was going to take in *The Spectator*, he would almost always say, with his cheerful and eager self-confidence: "You are perfectly right: of course, that's the line to take"; and so forth.

It was indeed, sometimes a subject of chaff in my family when Cromer was staying with us at Newlands that he would begin ten or twelve sentences in the course of a Saturday to Monday visit with: "Strachey, you and I have been absolutely right from beginning to end." And so I believe we were, though it may seem strange that I should have the hardihood to record it "between boards."

In view of Cromer's alleged testiness, I may record a very striking "contraindication." During the year and a half or nearly two years in which he wrote a review every week in *The Spectator* on some important book, I never had any difficulties with him whatever. He was, with the possible exception of my cousin, Lytton Strachey, the best reviewer I ever had. He not only took an immense amount of trouble with his reviews from his own point of view, but he also took immense trouble to realise and understand *The Spectator* view and to commit me to nothing which he thought I might dislike. It happened, however, that on one occasion I did have to use the editorial blue pencil and alter something, or at any rate get him to alter it. At first he seemed a little fussy about my objection, but when I was firm and explained my reasons he agreed, and in the end, with that attractive frankness that always went side by side with any testiness, he said that on reflection he thought I was perfectly right.

In this context I ought also to record that so clever a reviewer was he and so reasonable were all his views, that it was not only difficult but almost impossible to catch him out, I will not say in a mistake in facts, for in these he was always accurate, but in an over-statement or an under-statement.

A full balanced judgment of Lord Cromer and his work

for the country and the Empire is one which cannot be framed now. Again, I am not the man to frame it, for I admit that I loved the man too much to make a judicial estimate by me possible. Still, I want to say something of his character and his achievement. He stood for so much that is good in our national activities, and his example and inspiration are of such value, that I desire almost beyond anything else in politics to make people understand his point of view; and specially in what pertains to the Government of the Eastern races. In such questions the British people will, I am confident, find his principles the safest of guides.

I realise that Lord Cromer is now in the blind spot of politics. Sooner or later, however, there will be a revival in interest in this great man. People will begin to ask what it was that made his fame with his contemporaries so great. To such questions I shall venture to anticipate the answer.

The British people may be stupid, but they know a man when they see him. That is why they honoured Lord Cromer, yet I doubt if even one per cent. of the nation could have given true and sufficient reasons for the belief that was in them. It was certainly not because he had added, in fact if not in name, a great province to the British Empire. Plenty of countries richer and greater have been drawn within the magic circle of the *Pax Britannica* without the men who accomplished the task having received anything approaching the recognition accorded to Lord Cromer. Again, it was not Lord Cromer's administrative skill that won him his fame, great though that skill was. In India and in East and West Africa we have had examples of successful development by great officials that have passed almost unnoticed. Lord Cromer's financial ability, or shall I say financial judgment? for he himself was the last man to profess any special and personal knowledge of figures, was doubtless very great; but most of his countrymen were quite incapable of gauging its scope, or of understanding what he had done to produce order out of chaos, or how he had turned a bankrupt country into a solvent one.

Deftness, no matter how great, in the placing of a loan, or in evolving financial freedom out of the mass of hostile checks and balances sought to be set up by the Powers in Egypt, would by itself have entirely failed to win him the acclamations which greeted him when he retired from active duty. Even his work as a diplomatist, though so supremely skilful, was never properly understood at home. There was a vague notion that he had played a lone hand against all the Powers and had won out, but success here could not possibly have obtained for Lord Cromer that unbounded confidence which was shown him by the nation.

The respect and veneration which the British public felt for Lord Cromer would, if his health had permitted, have called him to power at the moment of worst crisis in the war; yet those who called him could not have said why they felt sure he would prove the organizer of victory. They were content to believe that it was so.

What was the quality that placed Lord Cromer so high in the regard of his fellow-countrymen throughout Britain and the Empire? What was it that made him universally respected,—as much by soldiers as by civilians, by officials as by Members of Parliament, by Whigs as by Radicals, by Socialists as by Individualists? The answer is to be found in the spirit in which Lord Cromer did his work. What raised him above the rank-and-file of our public men was his obedience to a very plain and obvious rule. It was this: *to govern always in the interests of the governed.*

This sounds a trite and elementary proposition, and yet the path it marks out is often a very difficult one to follow. It may be straight, but it is so narrow that only the well-balanced man can avoid stepping off either to the right or to the left. It is always a plank across a stream; sometimes it may be compared to a spear resting on the rocks in a raging torrent.

There are a hundred temptations, many of them by no means ignoble, to divert the Imperial administrator from keeping the narrow path exactly. In certain circumstances it may seem a positive virtue to exploit some province of the Empire for the Mother Country, or for the Empire as a whole—to forget the interests of the governed in the interests of the great organism of which that province forms only a part. Plentiful are the arguments for leaning a little to the one side or to the other. Yet if these were listened to, on the ground of the interests of the Empire as a whole (it must be admitted that the temptation to think of the interests of the people of these islands is one which has been steadily resisted by all our great Proconsuls) they might bring disaster in their train.

Strange as it may seem, nothing has proved a better or surer foundation of Empire, or has more helped even its material development, than the determination not to take advantage of the absolute power of the Mother Country over the Dependencies and subject States, but, on the contrary, to develop these as a sacred trust. We rightly asked for, and we took, far more help from the Daughter Nations during the war than from the Dependencies, for the very good reason that the Daughter Nations were their own mistresses and could do what they liked. They stood on an equality with us. In the case of the Dependencies, we are Trustees, and no temptation whatever, either for ourselves or for others, would allow us to budge one inch from the straight path.

Here, Lord Cromer was at his very strongest. He was an ideal Trustee. And what made this evident was the fact that he talked comparatively little about his trust, and never behaved in regard to it as a pedant or a prig. As long as the principle was firmly maintained, he bothered himself very little about matters of appearance.

If Lord Cromer kept the path successfully in this respect, he kept it equally well in regard to another temptation. The weak administrator is always liable to govern, not in the true interests of the governed, but in what the governed think is their interest—to do what they actually desire rather than what they would desire if they were better judges. Weak governors, that is, act as if they were servants and not trustees. To play the part of an obedient servant is right and necessary here, for we are over age, have no need of trustees, and govern ourselves. It is wrong when you stand *in loco parentis* to those whose affairs you administer. We all know what is the kind of government that an Eastern people establishes for itself. In spite of the suffering that it inflicts upon the people, there is good evidence to show that, judged by the test of popularity, the governed in the East prefer arbitrary personal rule to just and efficient constitutional government. In the same way a child will tell you, and honestly tell you, that he prefers raspberry-jam and heavy pastry at odd times to regular meals of brown bread and butter, and that he is quite willing, in the interests of the pastry system of nourishment, to brave the pains which Mary experienced when she consumed both jam and pastry. The wise guardian does not, however, in view of such statement, conclude that it is his or her duty to let the child have whatever he likes.

In the same way, Lord Cromer, though perfectly willing to admit that in a truly self-governing State it is the duty of the administrator either to resign or to carry out the will of his masters, the people, he would make no such admission in the case of an Oriental country. Yet this did not, as might be supposed, lead to a cold, harsh, or metallic system of government. Lord Cromer had far too much wisdom and moderation, was far too much of a Whig, as he himself would have said, to push to extremes the view that a native must have what was good for him, and not what he asked for at the top of his voice.

In small matters, indeed in all non-essentials, Lord Cromer strove of course to give the native what he wanted, and strove still more to refrain from forcing on him, because it was for his good, what he did not want. Lord Cromer was never tired of quoting what, in Bacon's phrase, he would call "luciferous" stories, to illustrate the folly of the administrator who thrusts physical improvements or the devices of European enlightenment upon the unwilling Oriental solely because they are good *per se*, or economical, or will make the governed richer or cleverer or happier. One of the stories of which Lord Cromer was particularly fond was that of the young Indian civilian who on his first day in a new district, and when he was entirely unknown, took a walk in the fields and saw an elderly ryot ploughing the land. Being good at the vernacular and full of zeal, the district officer asked how things were in that part of the country. The old man, like all tillers of the soil, replied with a kind of gloomy complacency that things were undoubtedly very bad, but that they might be worse. Anyway the only thing to do was to go on cultivating the land. "This year it is the cattle plague. Last year it was the Agricultural College. But since they are both the will of God, both must be borne without complaint." That story the present writer remembers Lord Cromer telling him on his return from the opening of a model farm or some such agricultural improvement. Such improvements ought, no doubt, as Lord Cromer said, to make the task of the fellaheen much easier, but nevertheless it was certain that the majority would regard them as pure evil—mere oppressions by wayward if not demented tyrants.

They wanted to be left alone, not taught how to get another fifteen per cent. of produce out of the land. Knowing this, Lord Cromer harried the native as little as possible. He was fond indeed of saying that there was very little you could do to make an Oriental people grateful.—"Why should they be grateful?" he would interject.—There was, however, one thing which they could and did appreciate, and that was low taxation. It was no good to say to the Oriental: "It is true you pay higher taxation, but then look at the benefits you get for it— the road up to the door of your house which enables you to save immensely in transport, the light railway not far off, the increased water for irrigation, a school for your children, and so forth and so on." To all these benefits the Oriental taxpayer is totally indifferent, or at all events he refuses to see any connection between them and the taxes paid. They come or do not come, like the rain from Heaven. All he is certain about is that the tax-collector is asking him double what he used to ask. So much for local improvements!

In fine, Lord Cromer, though he kept his rule to govern in the interests of the governed so strictly and was so exact a trustee, was always human—never pedantic, professorial, or academic, in the carrying out of his rule. He was above all things, a just man, and he realised that justice was not true justice unless it were humanised by

knowledge and the sympathy of comprehension. Yet
he knew and understood the benefits of strong government, though he always tried so to harness his administration that the straps would gall as little as possible.
That is why he won to such a strange degree the trust and
admiration, I had almost said the love, of the Egyptian
people. Peasant men and women who had never seen
him, and who had the dimmest and vaguest idea of what
he was and what he stood for, yet felt an unbounded belief in his desire that they should be justly treated. There
is a well-known story which exactly illustrates the point I
am making.

A young English officer engaged in sanitary work in the
Delta pointed out to a well-to-do farmer's wife in a
cholera year that she was running terrible risks by having
her cesspool quite close to the door of her house, and so
placed that it was contaminating all the drinking-water
used by her and her family. At last after many in-
effectual remonstrances he ordered the removal of this
sure and certain road to death by cholera. The woman
was furious, and ended up a battle royal by telling
him that though for the moment he could oppress the
poor and triumph over the Godly, it would not be for
long. "The man Krahmer" in Cairo would see her
righted. She would appeal to him and he would protect
her.

Lord Cromer felt, and felt rightly, that this invocation
was his best epitaph. Appeals, no matter how strange,
were never frowned down by him but encouraged. However ill-founded, they taught something. They were
often of an intimate character and couched in the wonderful language of the Babu, for Egypt has its Babus as well
as Bengal. One complaint which had to do with an
irrigation dispute began as follows: "Oh, hell! Lord-

ship's face grow red with rage when he hears too beastly conduct of Public Works Department."

Macaulay's splendid eulogy of Hampden may, with very little alteration, be applied to Lord Cromer. "The sobriety, the self-command, the perfect soundness of judgment, the perfect rectitude of intention," were as truly the qualities of the Ruler and regenerator of Egypt as they were of the great statesman of the Rebellion—the man who fought so nobly against the sullen tyranny of Charles and Laud.

For Joseph Chamberlain, I felt a very real and very warm affection as a man. Unfortunately for me, however, I was, except in the matter of Home Rule, out of sympathy with most of his later political principles, or, at any rate, his political standpoint. Mr. Chamberlain, though in no sense a man of extreme, wild, or immoderate views, was in no sense a Whig. To tread the narrow, uphill, and rather stony path of the *via media*, fretted him. He liked large enterprises and large ways of carrying them out, and, though it would be a great mistake to call him imprudent, he was distinctly a man of daring imagination in politics. He liked to prophesy and to help fulfil his prophecies. He was not content to wait and watch things grow. He was, indeed, one of the political gardeners who thoroughly enjoy the forcing-house. If he had been a grower of vegetables instead of Orchids, he would have dealt, I feel sure, almost entirely in "*primeurs*."

I can think of no man who used the imaginative faculty more in politics than he did, except Disraeli, and here, indeed, Mr. Chamberlain had the advantage. Disraeli was apt to let his imagination run so wild as to become vulgar, pompous, and ostentatious, whereas Mr. Chamberlain always kept his visionary schemes within the due bounds of seriousness and reason. Though I think he placed no limits to the capacity of the English people to meet and to overcome dangers and difficulties in the world of politics, and always held them, as, indeed, do I, capable to be of heroic mould, he never inflated himself or his countrymen on any subject, but spoke always weightily and with good sense. To take a concrete example, he, no more than Lord Cromer, would have intoxicated his mind with a fantastic idea like that of the Cape to Cairo railway as did Mr. Rhodes. That was at its best only a symbol and at worst the caprice of an Imperial egoist. Though Mr. Chamberlain had gained from his training and business success some of the best qualities of the statesman, that is, confidence in himself, and his sound practical sense, he was not, as I think his greatest admirers would agree, a deep political thinker.

He was, however, a great orator and a great parliamentary advocate, and, if properly briefed, there was no man who could state a case better or more persuasively than he did. This gift of advocacy, though an advocacy quite untouched by cynicism, was apt to raise doubts in the public mind as to his sincerity,—doubts which were due to ignorance of the man and to nothing else. It is true that he argued as the most convinced and most happy exponent of Free Trade during the first half of his political life and later as a convinced Protectionist. Yet I am certain that on both occasions he was perfectly sincere. In each case, though he did not realise it, he was speaking from a brief, but from a brief that for the time had thoroughly converted him and made him think of the policy advocated in the spirit of a missionary.

Mr. Chamberlain was a man of whom the nation was proud, and had a right to be proud. He was a good fighter and an unwearied worker, and he spent himself ungrudgingly in the service of his country. Above all things, he had that quality of vigour and daring which endears itself, and always will endear itself, to a virile race. He was not for ever counting the cost of his actions, but would as gaily as any hero of romance throw his cap over the wall and follow it without a thought of the difficulties and dangers that might confront him on the other side.

No one has ever asserted that Mr. Chamberlain left his comrades in the lurch, failed to support a friend in a tight place, or accepted help from others and then was careless about helping them in return or making them acknowledgment for what they had done. Remember that it is very rare in the case of a public man to find so total an absence of the complaint of ingratitude. The accusation of ingratitude, indeed, may be well described as the commonest of all those brought against the great by the small. "He was willing enough to take help from me when he needed it; now he has raised himself, the humble ladder is kicked down or else its existence is utterly ignored."—"While we were unknown men we worked together shoulder to shoulder and helped each other. When he grew big and strong, he forgot the colleagues of his early days, ignored their past services, and humiliated them with the cold eye of forgetfulness."—"I soon saw that, if he had not actually forgotten me, he would very much rather not be asked to remember me."—"It was evidently a bore to him to talk of old days, or to be reminded that even his prowess and strength had once been glad of 'a back up.'"—"He liked to think that he owed it all to himself and to no one else." These are the kind of criticisms that most winners in the Political Stakes have to bear. Such criticisms, very likely unfair in themselves, were, for example, constantly made in regard to Mr. Gladstone. But though my recollection carries me back to very nearly the beginning of Mr. Chamberlain's active career, I cannot recall a single instance of such grumbling, either in private or public, in regard to Mr. Chamberlain. On the contrary, the world of politics is filled with men who gratefully remember that, though their work for Mr. Chamberlain may have been humble in appearance or in fact, he never forgot the helping hand and the loyal service, but repaid them a hundredfold.

That genius for friendship of which Lord Morley once spoke, extended far beyond the ordinary limits of friendship. Mr. Chamberlain not only never forgot a friend, but never forgot any loyal or honest helper, and, what from the helper's point of view is equally important, never forgot also that it is not enough merely to remember the helper. You must try to help him in return.

This unwillingness to forget support, this instinct towards repayment of loyal service, was no piece of cynical calculation, no acting on the maxim that the way to get men to serve you well and support you is to make it clear to them that you always pay your debts with full interest. That Mr. Chamberlain was proud of the fact that no man could call him ungrateful I do not doubt; but I am sure also that his action was due to the impulse of a generous nature and to no sordid calculation.

He was a natural chieftain. He expected obedience and loyalty in the men who enlisted under his banner, but he felt in every corner of his being that it was the duty of the chieftain to succour, to help, and to advance those who stood by him. No labour and no self-sacrifice was too great to help a member of the clan he had constituted, and it was given quite as readily to the man who was never likely to be able to help again as to him from whom future favours might be expected.

This quality of gratitude and devotion may not be the greatest of moral qualities, but it is certainly one of the most attractive—a quality which will always secure a love and veneration similar to that with which Mr. Chamberlain was regarded, not only by his own people, but throughout the country. Cool and pedantic political philosophers may think that he carried the backing of his friends too far, but it was a generous fault and not likely to be resented in the workaday world. The man who has the instinct for comradeship will "bring home hearts by dozens" when the virtuous and well-balanced awarder of the good-conduct prizes in life's school will leave his fellows cold.

Because I have dwelt on this side of Mr. Chamberlain's character, it must not be supposed that I have forgotten, or that I desire to minimize, the splendid public services done by him, first in the region of municipal life—a priceless contribution—then in national politics, and last of all in the wider Imperial sphere. In every part of our public life he lit a torch which will not be extinguished. Men differ, and will continue to differ, as to his policy. None will differ as to the spirit in which he acted, or deny that he gave what nations most need—the stimulus of high endeavour.

However, I do not want to speak too much of his politics, partly because my aim is to be uncontroversial, and still more because his personal character is far more likely to interest my readers than any diagnosis of the politician.

The qualities of heart and head, which I have described, were not learned by me through Mr. Chamberlain's public form, but through a close study at first hand. From the year 1887 or '88 till the Tariff Reform controversy, I was on very intimate terms, social as well as political, with Mr. Cham-

berlain. I think he was fond of me. I know I was fond
of him. I expect he thought I was a little too cool, or, as
he might have said, not keen enough, just as I thought him
inclined to be too zealous a partisan,—too ready to push
party conditions to the uttermost. Yet both of us, and that
is after all the great thing in friendship, felt the sense of
personal attraction.

He was among other things one of the most delightful
of companions. To see him, as I so often did, in his house
in the country set at the edge of a great city,—that best
describes Highbury,—was a delightful experience. The
house-parties at the Whitsuntide and Easter recesses,
which lasted double the length of ordinary Saturday to
Monday parties, were most attractive. Chamberlain
was an expert at asking the right people to meet each other,
but if he had not been it would not have mattered.
Owing to his vigour of mind and the stimulating character
of his talk he would have turned a house-party of the
purest "duds" into a success. As a matter of fact, however, he was the last man to endure bores. People who
were asked to Highbury, were asked because he liked them,
not for any conventional reasons.

Another factor which made these visits to Birmingham
delightful was the hostess. Mrs. Chamberlain had as high
social qualities as the host. But I must not speak of
Mrs. Chamberlain as I feel, for to do so would break the
rule of not writing about living people. I will say, however, that even an interval of a quarter of a century—
the date in her case sounds utterly preposterous I admit—
has not dimmed my recollection of a fascinating and
gracious young woman. New to England, new to our
politics, and plunged into the midst of a party crisis of a
very bitter kind, she showed an unfailing instinct as a
hostess. She never said an unkind thing or made an

25

enemy. Besides her youth, her good-looks, and her charm of manner and her natural dignity she possessed the gift of making parties go. Though she always made herself felt in her parties, she was never formidable. She was always friendly and yet never gushing or affected. But I most sincerely ask Mrs. Chamberlain's pardon for I cannot conceal from myself that she will not like to be written about in terms of eulogy.

Mr. Chamberlain was indeed singularly fortunate in his family as supporters in the matter of entertaining. His two sons, Austen and Neville, evidently enjoyed the house-parties as much as did their father and his guests. Both inherited a liking for good company. Therefore, whether one went in the evening to the big or the little smoking-room one was sure of good talk.

Highbury was a house thoroughly well designed for entertainments, and the large gardens, or small park, whichever you like to call it, which surrounded the house, afforded plenty of sitting-out room. No one who shared in the parties will ever forget the long and good talks on the lawn on which the wicker chairs were set with brightly coloured rugs for the sitter's feet. Guests worthy of that honour were taken through the orchid house by Mr. Chamberlain himself, for his knowledge and love of his favourite flower was no pose, but a reality.

This absence of "pose" was, by the way, one of the most striking things about Mr. Chamberlain. He was an extraordinarily natural man. You cannot possibly imagine his taking up anything, from a new kind of cigar, a new form of hat, or a new type of novel, because he was told it was the right thing to do, or because he thought it was expedient for a politician with a future to encourage this or that fashionable craze. I have compared him to Disraeli in the matter of imagination. In the absence of "pose" he was, however, the exact opposite of Disraeli. For example, Lord Beaconsfield praised Lord Bolingbroke and talked about Lord Carteret, not because he really liked either of the statesmen mentioned, but because he thought it sounded well, and also because it amused him to look more learned historically than he was. You could no more expect Mr. Chamberlain to do that than to wear a particular flower, not because he liked it, but because it had been admired by say Mr. Pitt or Mr. Canning.

It must not be supposed from this, however, that Mr. Chamberlain was indifferent to, or ignorant of, the past. Though he was not going to let himself be dominated by old traditions, he was as distinctly well read in political history as in poetry. If he wanted to do so, he could quote freely and intimately from Browning, or Matthew Arnold. The latter was, I think, specially liked by him. But here again, any idea of his liking to prove himself a person of culture or learning cannot be entertained for a moment. He was much too sure of himself and much too sure of his own aims to want to be regarded as a man of cultivation. He liked what he liked, and he talked about what he liked. There was no "showing off." Again, there was not the slightest touch of snobbishness in Mr. Chamberlain. I don't think he was even amused by people expecting him, because he was not a man of great family or known as a great merchant prince, to be socially a kind of wild man to whom it must seem strange to eat a good dinner every day of his life "complete with the best of wines and cigars,"—in fact, to live exactly like men who had inherited their money, not made it. In truth, though the fact was unknown to the public and it never occurred to Mr. Chamberlain to talk about it, he was not a self-made man, but the son of a rich father. He belonged to a very old City family, for Mr. Chamberlain was not a Birmingham man, but a Londoner, through and through. His family had, however, remained in London even after it had grown rich and not retired to the country, like so many "warm men" to use the eighteenth century *argot*. I remember well Austen Chamberlain telling me that he had taken up his membership of the Cordwainers Company by right of inheritance. His family had been connected with that company in tail male, so to speak, since the time of Charles II.

This connection with the city companies had an interesting result. In the '70s and '80s it was a mark of a Radical to demand the abolition of the Livery Companies of London and to say hard things about the Corporation and the City. A Radical meeting was hardly complete without an attack on the City and its "fat and feasting Tories." When you were on a Radical platform you expected indeed as Shakespeare says:

> " . . . to hear the City
> Abused extremely, and to cry 'That's witty!'"

Mr. Chamberlain, however, whether in the House of Commons or on the platform, did not like his Colleagues to abuse the City Companies, but instead, gave them, as all sane people will now agree quite rightly, the benefit of his support. We should all be the poorer without the picturesqueness lent to London Municipal Life by its livery. Some of them may still want a little reform, but for the most part their wealth is well spent.

But Mr. and Mrs. Chamberlain were not only good country hosts. Nothing could have been more pleasant or more interesting than their London dinners. The talk was always good and Mr. Chamberlain was always the chief point of attraction. He was never cross, or moody, or depressed. Instead, he was always ready to talk. You could put up any game with him and he would fly at it with zest and spirit.

Time has not dimmed the warmth of my personal feeling either for Austen or Neville Chamberlain. And here I want to say one word of regret in respect of Miss Beatrice Chamberlain,—her father's eldest daughter who died during the first year of the Peace. She was a woman of great ability and inherited no small share of her father's power of talk and fondness for social life. Highbury house-parties owed much to her.

CHAPTER XXV

FIVE GREAT MEN (*Continued*)

IT was at one of Mr. Chamberlain's house-parties that I first met one of the five distinguished men who made a deep impression on my mind and so on my life. That man was Colonel John Hay, some time Ambassador of the United States to this country. I shall never forget going down, some thirty-two years ago, to Birmingham with my wife for a Saturday to Monday party, and finding that the chief guest was the new American Ambassador. When one is young and going to a pleasant house, there is nothing more delightful or stimulating than the moment of waiting at the side of a country-house omnibus consecrated to station work and wondering who are to be one's fellow-guests. On that occasion it was not long before we discovered that they were Colonel and Mrs. Hay and their daughter Helen. It did not take one long to see what a memorable man Hay was. It was indeed a case for me of friendship at first sight. Though it only took, even in pre-motor days, some twenty minutes to drive to High-bury, I had become, long before we reached the front door, a fervent admirer of the man who had been Private Secretary to the greatest man of modern times,—Abraham Lincoln.

The acquaintance begun at Highbury ripened for both of us into a true friendship. I was deeply touched to find that Mr. Hay met me half way in my desire to be friendly, for I knew enough about him to know that his reputation was that of a very reticent, very fastidious man—a person by no means inclined to fall into the arms of the first comer. But I don't want to flatter myself. Perhaps the passport to Hay's heart in my case was my love of Lincoln, for that he soon saw was real and not assumed. Anyway, Hay and I soon began to see a great deal of each other, and he paid me the compliment of confiding in me throughout the war between Spain and America. He would have liked to avoid that war and did his very best to do so, but I knew that all the time he felt it was inevitable. I remember well his saying to me that the positions of the United States and Spain were like two railway engines on the same track, neither of which would give way and both of which were advancing. You might delay the collision, but you could not prevent it, unless one train cleared out of the way of the other, and to this neither side in control would agree. Therefore, a collision had to come,—and come it did.

Hay loved his tenure of office in England and greatly regretted that he had to accede to Mr. McKinley's request that he should go back and become Secretary of State. He knew the work would be too much for him, and told me so quite simply and unaffectedly, but he was never a man to shirk a duty. During his term of office, he and I were constantly in touch with each other by letter. Though Hay did not write long letters, he contrived in his short notes to say many poignant things,— often in the form of comments on *Spectator* articles, for he was a diligent reader of my paper. One example is so curious and so interesting that I must set it forth. The War enables me to do so without any risk of doing injury in the diplomatic sphere. It concerns the memorable visit of Prince Henry of Prussia to the United States in the year 1902.

The Kaiser was alarmed at the good feeling growing up between Britain and the United States. He therefore made a special effort to capture American goodwill, largely in the hope of drawing off American sympathy from this country. Accordingly he sent his sailor brother to American to announce his august and Imperial satisfaction with the United States. The Americans—most kindly of hosts—gave him the best possible reception. At that time Mr. Roosevelt was President, and Hay was Secretary. Writing of Prince Henry's reception on March 1, 1902, *The Spectator* pointed out what delightful hosts the Americans had proved and were proving, but went on to express very grave doubt whether in the circumstances and with the men then at the helm, the Kaiser would "cut any political ice" or gain any material advantage by the visit or by the attempts at diplomatic bargaining sure to be connected with it. The article continued as follows:

American photographers are taking "snapshots" of the Prince at every turn in his progress; but the snapshots we should like to see would be those of the President and Mr. Hay just before and just after the Prince had made some political request. They would hardly look, if our view of the American temperament is correct, like the faces of the same persons. The infinitely courteous hosts will in a moment become hard business men, thinking not of the pleasantest sentences to say, but of the permanent interests of the United States. Only the humour might linger a little in the eyes.

The article took some six days to get to America, but as soon as it was possible for a return of comments I received from Hay the following characteristic and laconic note:

Spectator, March 1, p. 317, 2nd Column,
        half-way down.

MY DEAR STRACHEY,
    You are a mind reader.

                                        J. H.

I turned eagerly to the passage, for I could not at the moment recollect what we had said, and found what I have given above. By a guess, or (shall I say?) by a piece of thought transference, I had had the good luck to envisage exactly what had happened at Washington. Prince Henry was not merely a social but a political bagman. He had asked for something. He wanted a tangible "souvenir" of his visit. He had made proposals to the State Department of the usual Prussian type. By "usual Prussian type," I mean that he had asked for concessions of territory and engagements in which all the real, and most of the apparent, benefit was on the Prussian side. I do not now remember their exact nature, though later I learned from Hay something of their general scope and character. My only trustworthy recollection is that Hay referred to them with that patient, well-bred disgust with which he always received overtures of this kind. He was a man of a very fastidious sense of honour, and not amused by the low side of life, or by trickery even when foiled. And here I may perhaps be allowed to interpolate another personal recollection. I remember his telling me twenty years ago—that is, during the Spanish War—how the German Ambassador in London had approached him officially with the request that a portion of the Philippine Islands should be ceded—Heavens knows why—to the Kaiser. I can well recall his contemptuous imitation of the manner of the request. "You haf so many islands; why could you not give us some?" I asked Hay what he had replied. With a somewhat grim smile he answered: "I told him: 'Not an island—not one!'"

I shall perhaps be accused of indiscretion in what I have written, especially when I am dealing with a man so discreet, so punctilious in all official intercourse, as John Hay. I feel, however, that I am justified by the time which has elapsed, and by the events of the last few years.

I could fill, not one, but several chapters with the delightful talks about Lincoln which I had with Mr. Hay. He was always at his best when talking about Lincoln. It must not be supposed, however, that he was a man with one idea or that he was, as it were, eaten up by his great chief. Hay was a true statesman and a man with clear and consistent views of his own. I had the pleasure of bringing Hay into touch with Lord Cromer. Cromer was, of course, greatly impressed. I remember pointing out to him that Hay was really the best illustration that he could have had for one of his favourite theories,—that is, that the people who in their youth had been private secretaries were, other things being equal, the best people to whom to give big appointments. Cromer used to say that the reason for this was a very plain one. The difficulty with most officials, and especially with men in the Army, was that they so often did not attain to positions of real responsibility, and where they had to take the initiative, till their minds had been atrophied by official routine and by the fact that they had simply carried out other people's orders, and not to think or act for themselves. It was different with a young man who at the most impressionable time of life had not only been under the influence of a great man, but had seen great affairs absolutely at first hand and not dressed up in official memoranda. Again, the Private Secretary saw the whole of them and not merely departmental fragments.

It was no doubt this fact which made Hay a great Ambassador and a great Secretary of State. He had not only had the magnificent education which was received by the whole of Lincoln's personal staff, the inspiration, intellectual, moral, and political, which a man like Lincoln spreads around him, but he had seen at their very source the great affairs of home, war, and foreign politics.

He had seen how great questions arise and how hard it is to settle them; how they go wrong through accidents, or delay, or negligence, how necessary it is to prevent the rise of prejudice, selfishness, and folly in their handling. In a word, there could not have been a better proof of Lord Cromer's dictum than Hay's career. I remember talking on the general subject to Hay, who in effect agreed, and later I also said the same thing to President Roosevelt. I told him I thought it was a great pity that the Presidents of the United States and other holders of great offices did not encourage young men of brains and also of great possessions, coming from families with great influence, local or social, to become, when young, private secretaries. There would be a double blessing produced thereby. It would help to bind men of wealth and influence to the public service, and would get them trained to fill in later life the great offices of State—Cabinet Ministers, Ambassadors, and special commissioners. If a young man had been a member, say, of the President's official family for four or five years and had then gone into business or even into leisure, he would, granted that he was a man of intelligence, have received an insight into affairs which might be of great use to the nation later on. I even went so far as to dream that the President of the United States and the Prime Minister of Great Britain might have an occasional exchange of secretaries and so get a certain number of people on both sides of the Atlantic

who knew something about the arcana in each government. As it is, both halves of the English-speaking race
are apt to make official bogeys,—to spell Washington or
London as the case may be with a very big capital letter,
and then to envisage this impersonation as something dark,
mysterious, or even terrible. How useful it would be if,
when this sort of talk was in the air, someone could say,
"Honestly, they really are not a bit like that (in Washington, or in London). You picture them as hard-shell
Machiavellis with sinister reasons for not answering our
despatches or proposals promptly, or as going behind our
backs in this or that matter. Believe me, they are just
about like what we are here. They go out to lunch as we
do; they forget big things and trifle with small things, and
for fear of their trivialities being exposed, they talk big as
if they had some great and ruthless reasons of state for
their official misadventures. When you begin to ask,
'What are they up to? What is their game?' the answer
ninety-nine times out of a hundred is 'There is not any
game at all.'"

Before I take leave of Hay, I want to add a fact which
deeply touched me. It will be remembered that the Secretary of State, after a breakdown in his health at Washington, came over to Europe to try the Mannheim cure. The
treatment at first seemed to do him good; but he was in
truth a broken man. So precarious, indeed, was his condition that, passing through London, the only people he
saw were Lord Lansdowne, then Foreign Minister, and
King Edward VII. I was the only exception. He asked
me to come up and see him, telling me that I must not let
it be known or he would be killed with kindness. If I
was deeply touched by his thought of me, I was still more
moved to see how extreme was his weakness of body. His
mind, however, was as clear as ever and he talked almost

in his old way. He was the kind of man who was much too sensitive to say in words, what I knew he felt—that it was good-bye. I came away from that last talk, with my devotion to the man, high as it was before, greatly heightened.

Though I did not know the Duke of Devonshire, earlier known as Lord Hartington, nearly so intimately as the other four, I had for him a political admiration which was almost unbounded. When a young man as was only natural—I was twenty-six when I first came into contact with him—I rather chafed at what I thought was his impenetrability. This, however, I soon discovered was due to no want of intelligence, but partly to natural shyness, partly to his education, partly to temperament, and partly also to a kind of dumbness of the mind, which is by no means inconsistent with a real profundity of intellect.

It is this mental profundity which is the main thing to remember about the Duke of Devonshire. To speak of him as if he were merely a man of character and firmness is to mistake him altogether. The Duke impressed all who saw him at close quarters. It was only the people who did not know him who said that he owed his rise to high office solely to his birth and wealth. I remember Mr. Chamberlain once saying to me, "It's all nonsense to talk about Hartington being dull and stupid. He is a very clever man." What made this admission all the more memorable was that Mr. Chamberlain was at the moment in a condition of something like exasperation with his colleague's dilatory ways, and his constitutional unwillingness to tackle a question till it was almost too ripe; you simply could not hurry him. One of the difficult things about the Duke was that he never realised the full greatness of his position in politics, how much people depended on his lead, and how anxious they were to find out what he thought and then follow him without demur. But the more they wanted to get a lead out of him, the more he seemed determined to avoid if he possibly could the responsibility they had asked him to assume, and partly because of a certain lethargy of his mind, and partly because he never could be made to believe that anybody could really want to lean upon and follow somebody else, he often appeared to be utterly stubborn. I remember once, just before the election in 1905, urging him as strongly as I knew how to make a public statement and to give a public lead to the Unionist Free Trade electors as to how they should vote. He was more than loath to take my advice. He was all for letting the thing alone. He actually went so far as to say, and remember, this was without the slightest suggestion of pose, "I don't see why I should tell people what I should do if I had a vote. They will do what they think right and I shall do what I think right. They don't want me to interfere." It was no good to try and talk him round, as one would have been inclined to talk round any ordinary politician, by pointing out how very flattering it was to him for people to wait upon his words and to desire to follow him, or to paint in romantic language what he, as a leader of men, owed to his followers. Anything of that sort was unthinkable with the Duke, and, if it had been tried, would first of all have puzzled him utterly and when it had at last dawned on him, would have put him off more than ever.

I could only repeat then that it was his duty to give people a lead and when I said this once more I was met with the old tale that he would do what he thought right, and they—the voters—would do what they thought right. But what was wonderful in the Duke about a matter of this kind was that he did not in the least show any annoyance at being badgered by a man who was not only so much younger than he was, but also of so much less experience in politics or affairs.

He was essentially a good-tempered man and had not a trace of *amour propre* in his nature. I doubt if he had ever intentionally snubbed a man in his life, though, no doubt, he had often done so unintentionally, for he was plain-spoken. He hated to hurt people's feelings, but he sometimes thought that their feelings were like his own,— quite iron-clad. I remember an example of his imperturbability in this respect. Once, in the eagerness of pressing a plan of action for the Unionist Free Traders, to which he was disinclined, I expressed the wish to propose it to the Council of our group and see what they thought of it. He made no objection and I gathered that he thought it could do no harm to have the matter aired, which, of course, was all I desired. A day or two afterwards, however, the Duke casually and in the most good-humoured way happened to say to me that I, of course, no doubt realised that if people assented to my motion, he would have to resign as President of our Association. I was, horror-struck, for to have lost him would have meant utter destruction for our movement,—the movement, that is, to prevent the Tariff Reformers running away with the Unionist Party. I said at once that I would most gladly withdraw my proposal, and expressed my complete confidence in his leadership.

He was delightfully naïve about the whole matter and, here again, without any pose. He declared that he did not see why I should not go on with my scheme if I really thought it was a good one, and that he did not regard it as in the least hostile to himself. There was nothing in it that was in the least personally objectionable to him.

At a much earlier period of my acquaintance with him the Duke gave another example of his good nature and want of fussiness. When the split came in the Liberal party and the Liberal Unionist organisation was created under his leadership and that of Mr. Chamberlain, I was chosen as I have related elsewhere to act as Editor of the party organ, *The Liberal Unionist*. Each number was to contain an article by some man of importance, so I naturally asked Lord Hartington, as he then was, to supply the signed article for the first number. I was entirely new to the task of editing, and the Duke had never, oddly enough, written anything before for publication, though, of course, he had made plenty of speeches. The Duke was old-fashioned in his ways and did not have a type-writer or a secretary, but wrote with his own hand. It was a very good handwriting, but not quite printer-proof. Like all first numbers mine was late. The proofs of the Duke's article were not sent out early enough, with the result that we had to go to press without getting back a corrected proof from the Duke. The result was one or two bad misprints; the Duke was not angry—only sad, for he thought it might make him look ridiculous. I was told, however, by excited members of the Committee that I had made an awful blunder and must go and apologise for so bad a beginning. Naturally, I was eager to express my regret, and went down at once to the House of Commons and sent in for him. Now, as ill-luck would have it, he was in the middle of an important debate on Home Rule and just on the point of rising to speak when he received my message. However, in the kindest way he came out, to see, as he said, whether he could do anything for me, and apologised most profusely for having kept me waiting for ten or twelve minutes. It was not, indeed, till these apologies had been got over that I was able to make my apologies, which he received in the most delightful way. If he had been a pompous prig, he might so easily have lectured me (for I was not 26) on how important it was for a young man just entering political life, etc., etc. Of course, he had no thought of making me his special adherent by his good temper and easiness. Such things never entered his head. All the same, his courtesy, consideration, and evident determination not to take advantage of my slip, made a deep impression on me. A final example of the Duke's inability to realise that it mattered to anybody else what he did was shown when he let Mr. Balfour, then Prime Minister, persuade him to remain in the Unionist Ministry in 1905 when the rest of his Free Trade colleagues resigned. I felt none of the amazement mixed with indignation felt by some of the Liberal Unionists, because I knew my man, I felt, indeed, quite sure that what had happened was that the Duke imagined that nobody would misunderstand him and that perhaps, as he said, it was a pity when so many people were resigning that he should resign also. He wouldn't be missed and so why should he not just remain where he was? I felt equally sure, however, that in a very little time he would come to understand the importance of clearing up his position.

I was on manœuvres and riding with the Hampshire Yeomanry at a great sham fight on the Wiltshire downs, when I heard of the Cabinet crisis. I well remember that on a hill-top, which was finally carried by our side, I met the present Lord Middleton, then Mr. St. John Broderick, Secretary of State for War and learned from him what had happened. That night I went home to write on the crisis. When I got home I said to my wife, "The Duke has not resigned, but it is all right. I will write an article in *The Spectator* which, while perfectly sympathetic, will set forth

26

the situation in a way which will be certain to bring the Duke out." The result was as I expected.

I was interested some time afterwards to hear from one of his relatives that my article was largely instrumental in determining him to follow his followers in the matter of resignation. Almost the last time I saw the Duke of Devonshire affords another example of his good-nature, of his plain-spokenness, of his humanity, and of his public spirit. I had always been, and still am, deeply concerned in the housing question. We cannot be a really civilised nation unless we can get good houses and cheap houses for the working-classes. Not being a philosopher, I had always supposed that one way of getting good and cheap houses was to find some improved form of construction. I have been informed, however, by my Socialist friends that this is an entire mistake and that there are much better ways. Though admitting that this was possible, and hoping that it might be, I was always inclined to add, though I made no converts,—"However good the other scheme, cheap construction, granted it is also adequate construction, must be a desirable premium upon any and every other scheme, financial or rhetorical, of getting good houses." Therefore, I advocated and carried out by the joint action of *The Spectator* and another paper I then owned, *The County Gentleman*, a scheme for an exhibition of good cottages, in which a prize was given for the best cottage. The novelty of my plan was that the exhibits were not to be models of cottages, but were to be real cottages. The Garden City were almost as glad to lend me their ground as I was to avail myself of it, and by a well thought out arrangement we were able, as it were, to endow the Garden City with some £20,000 worth of good cottages without their having to put their hands into their pockets. It was quite easy to guarantee to find pur-

chasers or hirers of the cottages put up by competitors.
The competitor, therefore, could not lose his money or tie
it up for very long, and he was very likely able to win a
prize in one of the various categories. The greater number of cottages were planned for competitions in which the
cost was limited to £150, for that was my ideal of the price
for a cottage; and if a competitor was sure to get his £150
back and might also get a prize either of £150, or £100, or
£50, he was in clover.

But I am not out to describe the success of the Cheap
Cottages Exhibition, but only to throw light on the character of the Duke of Devonshire. I asked the Duke to
open the Exhibition for me, and this he did in a speech
full of excellent good sense. He obeyed *ex animo* my
direction of "No flowers by request." I remember, however, being somewhat disconcerted as we went down in the
special train by a remark which he made to one of the Directors of the Garden City, who was saying, very properly,
the ususal things about how pleased the Company had
been to help with my scheme. The Duke, with a loud
laugh, replied with what was meant to be a perfectly
good-tempered joke, "And a jolly good advertisement for
your company you must have found it. Ha! Ha!" The
Director, as was perhaps not to be wondered at, looked
somewhat flabbergasted at this sally. Fortunately, I over-
heard it and was able to prevent any risk of wounded feelings by explaining how helping to spread information in
regard to the good work being done by the Garden City was
a thing which I and those who were helping me were
specially glad to do. If we had been able to provide a
useful advertisement for the Company we should feel almost as well pleased as by the success of our own venture.
The Duke at once fully assented, but I don't think he in
the least realised that his original way of putting the re-

mark might easily have given umbrage. If it had been said to him and not by him it would not have caused any annoyance and he no doubt assumed that other people would feel as simply and as naturally as he did.

It would be impossible to give any account of the Duke and his character and actions without noticing his devotion to the Turf. It was that devotion which made Lord Salisbury once say with humorous despair that he could not hold a most important meeting "because it appears that Hartington must be at Newmarket on that day to see whether one quadruped could run a little faster than another." The Duke was quite sincere in his love of racing. There was no pose about it. He did not race because he thought it his duty to encourage the great sport, or because he thought it would make him popular, or for any other outside reason. He kept racers and went to races because he loved to see his horses run, though oddly enough I don't think he was ever a great man across country, or was learned in matters of breeding and trainers. He just liked racing and so he practised it and that is all that is to be said about it.

In this combination of sport and high political seriousness he was extraordinarily English. Pope described the Duke's attitude exactly in his celebrated character of Godolphin; the words fit the Duke of Devonshire absolutely. They may well serve as a peroration to this chapter.

> Who would not praise Patricio's high desert,
> His hand unstained, his uncorrupted heart,
> His comprehensive head! all interests weigh'd,
> All Europe sav'd, yet Britain not betray'd?
> He thanks you not,—his pride is in piquet,
> Newmarket fame, and judgment at a bet.

But I am dwelling too much on the picturesque side of
the Duke and so getting too near the caricature view of the
man. What I want is to give in little a true picture of a
really great man, for that is what he in truth was.

Instead of tracing the Duke's political actions and political opinions, I prefer to attempt an analysis of his political character. The first and most obvious fact about the
Duke was his independence, and what I may call his
inevitableness of action. Knowing the Duke's views on a
particular subject, you could always tell in any given circumstance what would be his line of conduct. With most
politicians explanations have to be found at some point
of their career for this or that action. Everything seemed
to point to their taking a particular course, and yet they
took another. In the case of one man this was due to influence exerted over him by a friend. In that of another it
was due to hostility to some colleague or rival. The personal element deflected the course of history. In the case
of the Duke of Devonshire such explanations are unthinkable. It is impossible to imagine him a Home-ruler out
of devotion to Mr. Gladstone, or a Free-trader out of
jealousy or distrust of Mr. Chamberlain. The Duke had
no dislikes or prejudices of this kind. Certainly he had
none in the case of Mr. Chamberlain. All the efforts of
the Tapers and Tadpoles and paragraph-writers in the Press
failed to produce the slightest sense of rivalry between
them. The Duke, to use a racing phrase, went exclusively
on men's public form, and gave his contemporaries credit
for the same public spirit which he himself showed.

He was the last man in the world to think that he had
a monopoly of patriotism. His high-mindedness was, he
assumed, shared by others. He never betrayed a colleague, and he never thought it possible that a colleague
could think of betraying him. The result was that

throughout his career he was never once the victim of any intrigue or conspiracy. He kept his mind fixed always on questions and not on men, and just as he always endeavoured to solve the real problem at issue rather than secure a party triumph, so his aim was to bring advantage to the nation, not to gain a victory over an opponent. I should be the last to say that in this the Duke of Devonshire was unique. What, however, was unique about his position was the fact that no one ever attributed to him unworthy motives or insinuated that he was playing for his own hand. If any one had ventured to do so, the country would simply have regarded the accuser as mad.

Another striking quality possessed by the Duke of Devonshire was his absolute straightforwardness of conduct and clearness of language. No one ever felt that he had a "card up his sleeve." He told the country straight out exactly what he thought, and his reticence—for reticent he was in a high degree—was due, not to the fact that he did not think it advisable at the moment to let the country know what he was thinking, but simply and solely to the fact that he had not been able to come to a determination. He did not like meeting questions half-way, but waited till circumstances forced them on his attention.

The late Duke of Argyll once said of him at a public meeting: "Oh, gentlemen, what a comfort it is to have a leader who says what he means and means you to understand what he says." Here in a nutshell was the quality which the country most admired in the Duke of Devonshire. They always knew exactly what he stood for, and whether he was a Unionist or a Home-ruler, a Free-trader or a Protectionist. He was never seeking for a safe point to rest on, one which, in the immortal language of the politician in the *Biglow Papers*, would leave him "frontin' south by north."

In spite of the independence, straightforwardness, and clearness of the Duke's attitude, he often showed a curious diffidence, and seemed unable to realise that he had so absolutely the confidence of the country that no explanations were ever necessary in his case. For example, after the secession of the Unionist Free-traders from Mr. Balfour's Administration spoken of above, the Duke thought it necessary to explain—in his place in the House of Lords—how it was that he remained for a few days longer in the Cabinet than did his Unionist Free-trade colleagues. I have reason to know that the Duke found such an explanation a painful and trying one to make. Nevertheless he insisted on making it, and this though on the day he spoke he was suffering from the beginnings of a severe attack of influenza. It will be remembered that he then declared, with a sincerity which in one sense deeply touched, and in another sense might almost be said to have amused, the nation, that his mind was not so clear as it ought to have been during his negotiations with Mr. Balfour, and that he had not at first completely grasped the situation. As a matter of fact, is it safe to say that no one, least of all his Unionist Free-trade colleagues, thought there was the slightest need for such an apology. If the thought of the nation on that occasion could have been put into words, it would have run something like this:—"There was not the least reason for you to say what you have said. Every one recognised that you would in the end do exactly what you did—that is, leave the Ministry—and the fact that you took four or five days longer than your colleagues to realise that this was inevitable was looked on as the most natural thing in the world. It was a proof to the British people as a whole that a Free-trader could do nothing else.

If you had acted as quickly as others, it might possibly have been thought that there was something not absolutely necessary in your action."

The Duke of Devonshire was often spoken of as a great aristocrat and as a representative of the aristocratic interests in the country. Nothing, however, could have been further from the truth. Though no doubt the Duke was in a sense intensely proud of being a Cavendish, and though he felt in his heart of hearts very strongly the duty of *noblesse oblige*, he had nothing of that temperament which people usually mean when they use the word "aristocrat." He was the last man in the world whom one could associate with the idea of the noble who springs upon a prancing war-steed, either real or metaphorical, and waves his sword in the air. His represented rather what might be called the old-fashioned English temperament, the possessors of which in effect say to the world:—"I'll mind my own business, and you mind yours. You respect me, and I'll respect you. You stand by me, and I'll stand by you; and when we have both done our duty to ourselves and each other, for heaven's sake don't let us have any d——d nonsense about it."

But though this is true in a sense, one would lose touch altogether with the Duke's character if one insisted on it too much, or gave the impression that the Duke's nature was one of surly defiance such as Goldsmith describes in the famous line on the Briton in *The Traveller*. No doubt one of his colleagues, Robert Lowe, once said of him: "What I like about Hartington is his 'you-be-damnedness.'" But though this element was not wanting in the Duke's character, it did not in any way prevent him from being at heart as kindly, as sympathetic, and as courteous as he was reasonable, straightforward, and plain-spoken.

One may strive as one will to draw the character of the Duke, but in the end one comes back to the plain fact that he was a great public servant,—one who served, not because he liked service for its own sake or for the rewards it brought in sympathy and public applause, but solely because he was mastered by the notion of duty and by the sense that, like every other Englishman, he owed the State a debt which must be paid. Pope said of one of his ancestors that he cared not to be great except only in that he might "save and serve the State." That was exactly true of the late Duke of Devonshire.

This tradition of public service is one which has long been associated with the house of Cavendish, and it is cause for national congratulation to think that there is no risk of that tradition being broken. The present Duke possesses the high character and the sense of public duty which distinguished his predecessor. It may safely be predicted of him that the ideals of public duty maintained by his uncle will not suffer in his keeping.

Of the five great figures in England and America, who were known to me and who are dead, I find by far my greatest difficulty in writing about Theodore Roosevelt. Though I saw very much less of him than I did of Lord Cromer, my feeling of regret at his death was specially poignant. Mr. Roosevelt was almost my exact contemporary. Therefore, I could look forward, and did look forward, to enjoying his friendship for many years to come. Lord Cromer was ten or fifteen years my senior, and, though my intimacy with him was of the very closest, far closer than that which I enjoyed with Mr. Roosevelt, I did not feel myself on the same plane with him. To put the matter specifically, Lord Cromer was engaged in most important and most responsible public work when I was little more than a child, and by the time I left Oxford he had already finished the first three or four years of his great task in Egypt. Again, when Roosevelt's death came, it came without warning. I did not know that his health had in any way been failing.

Roosevelt and I were always so much in accord and our friendship through the post was of so intimate a kind that I am sometimes amazed when I think of the comparatively small number of days, or rather hours, that I actually passed in his company. For several years before I saw him in the flesh I had exchanged constant letters with him, and so much did he reveal himself in them that, when we did meet, he appeared to me exactly the man I had envisaged. Naturally I wondered greatly whether this would be so, and took a strict inquisition of the impression made on me in seeing him face to face. In similar cases, one almost always finds surprises in minor, if not in major, differences; but Roosevelt needed no re-writing on the tablets of my mind.

I shall never forget my visit to the White House. If I had slept under that roof alone, and without any guide or interpreter, I should have been deeply moved. My readers then may imagine what my feelings were when I, who had read and thought so much of Lincoln, found that my dressing-room was the little sanctum upstairs into which Lincoln, in the crises of the war, used to retire for consultation with his Generals, Ministers, and intimate friends. At that time the ground floor of the White House, other than the great ceremonial rooms, had been almost entirely absorbed by the various officials connected with the Presidency.

Our train from New York was nearly an hour late, and, therefore, when we arrived, we had only bare time to dress for dinner. Yet when we reached the room where guests assembled before dinner we found the President alone. Though it was through no fault of ours that we were late, my wife had fully realised the necessity of being down in time. Dinner was if I remember rightly at eight, and we were shaking hands with the President by five minutes to.

I have already described how Lord Cromer at first sight showed himself willing to tell me everything and to trust wholly to the discretion of his visitor. Mr. Roosevelt exhibited an equal confidence. In the long talk which I had with him on my first evening at the White House, throughout the Sunday and during a long ride on the Monday, in pouring rain on a darkish November evening, we talked of everything under the sun, and had our talk out. Mr. Roosevelt was one of those very busy men who somehow contrive to have time for full discussion. After breakfast on the Monday morning,—we did not move to other quarters in Washington, till late on the Monday,— Mr. Roosevelt asked me whether I would like to see how he got through his work. I accepted with avidity. Accordingly we went from the White House to the President's office, which had been built, under Mr. Roosevelt's directions, in the garden and was just finished. We first went into Mr. Roosevelt's special room. There he put me in a window seat and said I was quite free to listen to the various discussions which he was about to have with Cabinet Ministers, Judges, Ambassadors, Generals, Admirals, Senators, and Congressmen.

It was very remarkable to see the way in which he managed his interlocutors,—who by the way apparently took me either for a private secretary or else as part of the furniture! I recall the clever manner in which Mr. Roosevelt talked to an Ambassador, and kept him off thorny questions, and yet got rid of him so skilfully that his dismissal looked like a special act of courtesy. The interview with a leading Western or Southern Senator, who had got some cause of complaint, I forget what, was equally courteous and dexterous, though the President's attitude here was, of course, perfectly different. Roosevelt was a man, for all his downrightness, of great natural dignity and of high breeding, though he had the good sense never, as it were, to *affiché* this good breeding to any man who might have misunderstood it and thought that he was being patronised. In this case the Senator was a self-made man, who would, no doubt, have been suspicious if he had been talked to in the voice and language used for the Ambassador. Mr. Roosevelt had no difficulty whatever in making his change of manners as quick as it was complete. A Judge of the Supreme Court, who came for a short talk, demanded yet a third style and got it, as did also one of the members of the President's Cabinet.

"The President's Cabinet" remember, is not only a piece of official style. It represents a fact. The American Cabinet Ministers are not responsible to Congress, as ours are to Parliament, but are the nominees of the President and responsible only to him. In a word, they are *"the President's Cabinet."* Communications between them and the House of Representatives and the Senate come always theoretically, and largely actually, through the President.

After an hour, or rather more, had been spent in these interviews, the President took me into another room, which was the Cabinet Room, and very soon the Members of the Administration began to assemble and to take their seats round the big table in the centre. I felt as the children say, that this was getting "warm." Even though I had the President's general leave to stop, I thought I had better not take advantage of it. As soon as I saw my friend Colonel Hay enter, I went up to him and asked him whether he did not think that though I had been honoured by the President's invitation, I had better not remain during the Cabinet. I could see that this relieved him not a little. Though devoted to Roosevelt, he was a little inclined to think that the President's ways were sometimes too unconventional. Therefore, I slipped quietly out of the room.

It is amusing to recall that when at luncheon, I apologised half whimsically for my desertion, Mr. Roosevelt told me that I had acted *"with perfect tact."* Anyway, I look back to the incident with interest. I hold that I probably got nearer to seeing the United States Cabinet actually at work than do most people. Business had actually begun before I completed my retreat.

I won the approval of the President not only for my discretion here, but, as I afterwards found out, for my complete willingness, nay, pleasure, in going out for a ride with him in a flood of rain on a dark November evening. That was not a very great feat, but apparently some of his visitors had shown themselves anything but happy in such rides. He was indeed inclined to use his afternoon winter rides as a test of men. Accustomed, however, as I was to the English climate and always, not only willing, but intensely eager to get on the back of a horse, it never occurred to me to think that our ride would either be put off because it poured or its accomplishment counted to me for righteousness.

Certainly it was a curious kind of ride. I was mounted on a superb Kentucky horse procured for me from the Cavalry Barracks—a creature whose strength and speed proved how well deserved is the reputation of that famous breed. We were a party of four, with General Wood and a young aide-de-camp. No sooner were we mounted—I on a McClellan saddle—than we set off at a fast pace which very soon became a gallop. I remember, as we dashed through the rain on the hard pavements, thinking that our horses' hooves sounded like an elopement on the stage—"heard off." The lovers' ardour is usually marked by the vivid manner in which their horses wake the thunders of the King's highway.

We crossed the well-known creek or torrent in the park near the city, which meant putting our horses through a fairly swift and broad though not deep stream, and then passed through what had once been a largish plantation. The trees had, however, been cut down a year or two before. This we negotiated at a gallop, the President leading. I admit that it was an exciting performance. Not only was it almost dark when we reached the wood or ex-wood, but the wood-cutters had left the stumps of innumerable small trees or saplings, standing up about six inches from the ground. You could hardly imagine anything better devised for catching a horse's foot. But even worse than the risk of a horse stumbling over a stump, was the thought of his putting his hoof down on one of the more sharply pointed stumps, often not more than the thickness of a big walking stick. It would have pierced like a spear.

However, I felt that the honour of my country and of my profession as a journalist were at stake. Therefore, I made my horse, who was not at all unwilling, keep well alongside the President. Under such conditions steering was impossible; and we galloped along at haphazard. I was consoled to feel that if the President's horse could pick his way, mine could probably do the same. As it happened nobody's horse made a blunder, and we all four emerged quite safely from the ordeal and soon turned homeward, but by a different way. Our pace, however, did not slacken. We galloped along a main thoroughfare, which was not made safer by tram lines. All the same I thoroughly enjoyed myself, and was proud to bring my big horse of nearly seventeen hands home without a slip. It was in truth a delightful experience. My horse proved well able to keep up with the President's very fine charger—needless to say, I knew enough to know that one does not attempt to out-ride persons in the position of sovereigns—and we talked as hard as we rode, for a whole hour without interruption.

The President's remark as we dismounted was characteristic,—"Don't you think, Strachey, I am quite right, as I can only get an hour's exercise a day, to go while I am at it, as hard as I can?" That remark was really meant as a kind of rebound argument for General Wood.

I assured the President in the enthusiasm of the moment that he was perfectly right, but General Wood in a ride, which I subsequently took with him, shook his head over the President's way of galloping fast on the hard roads and declared that he shook his horse's legs all to pieces. Some day there would be an accident. "I try to get him to give up the practice but I am afraid I don't have much success, though he takes it very well. No, he's not a careful rider!"—a comment, by the way, which I had so often heard about myself that it sounded quite familiar. Need I add that this was anxious affection on the part of General Wood, one of the ablest of military and civil administrators alive today—and a man whom I am proud to say has honoured me with a friendship as warm and as generous as that of his great Chief and friend.

Some day my correspondence with Mr. Roosevelt will, I hope, see the light; but not yet. The President's powers in the matter of letter writing, however, deserve a special comment. He was probably one of the greatest letter

writers in the matter of quantity who ever lived.   He was
also high up in quality.   He liked letter writing, and he
certainly expressed himself not only with vigour but with
ease and distinction.   If not a faultless writer, he wrote
well enough for his purpose, and showed his largeness and
fineness of character.   Though a well-educated man, with
a strong tradition of culture behind him, and, further, with
a very marked love of good literature, he was too busy and
too practical to find time to turn or tune his phrases.   His
letters are very readable and from many points of view
very attractive, but they do not possess the kind of fascination which belongs to the correspondence of some of the
elder statesmen of England or America—the kind of
fascination which we may feel sure will be exercised whenever Lord Rosebery's letters are given to the world—may
the event be a long way off.   Finally, they have not that
inspiration in word and thought of which the history of
personal and political correspondence affords us its best
example in the letters of Abraham Lincoln.

One of the delightful things about Roosevelt's correspondence is, that he touched life at so many sides.   He
struck the hand of a great gentleman, a great statesman,
and, in the best sense, a man of the world, into the hands
not only of kings and emperors, ministers and soldiers, but
of authors, poets, artists, men of science, explorers,
naturalists, and last, but not least, of men of action in all
ranks of life.   He attained to this freedom of the Great
World early in life.   He had in effect that singular advantage which belongs to kings.   For twenty years of his
life at least he had always at his command the best brains
in the world.   He had only to make a sign to get *en rapport* with the man who knew most on the subject that was
interesting him.   Besides this, as his Biographer, Mr.
Bishop, has pointed out, Roosevelt had the essential

mark of a great man. Emerson truly said, "He is great who never reminds us of others." Certainly Roosevelt stood alone. Though he touched many men of the Old World and the New, and of the old age and the new, he was intensely individual.

As to his personal characteristic. One of the most memorable of his personal characteristics was that, in spite of the fierce conflicts of his political life, no one ever seriously accused him of a mean or ignoble act. Though, not professing to be a political saint, he ran as straight as any statesman of whom we have record. Not Pitt nor Lord Grey here, nor Washington nor Lincoln in America, had a finer sense of honour and of political rectitude. He preached the square deal; he practised it.

To do that in party politics and with a democracy so vast and so full of cross-currents and stormy elements as that of America is not nearly as easy as it sounds. Roosevelt was of course no plaster saint. He dared to look at life as a whole, and without its trappings and disguises, and yet all the time he made men feel that it was not only right but quite possible, in Burke's phrase, "to remember so to be a patriot as not to forget that you are a gentleman."

I shall not touch upon Mr. Roosevelt's political views or political acts. They are too well known for comment. Nor, again, is there, I am glad to say, any necessity to make clear in these pages how strong was the sympathy between Roosevelt and the English people, and how anxious he was to keep together the whole of the English-speaking race,—not, of course, by any sort of alliance, but by mutual understanding, and through adherence to common aims and common ideals.

These things are public property. What I would rather dwell upon is a certain boldness of attitude in which

Roosevelt set a wonderful example to the leaders of a democracy. Though Mr. Roosevelt was in many ways an exceedingly astute and practical politician, he was not the least awed by rumour, not the least afraid of touching questions because they were thorny. His attitude towards Labour when questions of public order were involved, is well shown in the letter to Senator Lodge in which Roosevelt gives an account of a visit which he paid to Chicago during a strike, accompanied by disorder in the streets.

When I came to Chicago I found a very ugly strike, on account of which some of my nervous friends wished me to try to avoid the city. Of course I hadn't the slightest intention of doing so. I get very much puzzled at times on questions of finance and the tariff, but when it comes to such a perfectly simple matter as keeping order, then you strike my long suit. The strikers were foolish enough to come to me on their own initiative and make me an address in which they quoted that fine flower of Massachusetts statesmanship, the lamented Benjamin F. Butler, who had told rioters at one time, as it appeared, that they need have no fear of the United States Army, as they had torches and arms. This gave me a good opening, and while perfectly polite, I used language so simple that they could not misunderstand it; and repeated the same with amplifications at the dinner that night. So if the rioting in Chicago gets beyond the control of the State and the City, they now know well that the Regulars will come.

Commenting on the President's visit to Chicago, Mr. Secretary Hay said: "It requires no courage to attack wealth and power, but to remind the masses that they, too, are subject to the law, is something few public men dare to do." That of course is perfectly true. But it is equally true that when a public man does dare speak the truth it always turns out to be the best and most paying policy that he could have adopted. Roosevelt did not lose popularity with the mass of his countrymen but gained it by his honesty.

Another example of Roosevelt's political honesty was the way in which he treated the question of negro-lynching in the South. This is delicate ground, and as I have been accused by a Southern newspaper most absurdly, as I am certain all reasonable Americans will agree, of attacking America and the American people because in *The Spectator* I have spoken out in regard to lynching, I will quote without comment the account of Roosevelt's plain speaking, given by Mr. Bishop:

The President gave another illustration of his courage in October, 1905, when he made a tour of the South, speaking at various points in Virginia, North Carolina, Georgia, Arkansas, and Alabama, including a visit to the home of his mother at Roswell, Georgia. At Little Rock, Arkansas, on October 25th, he was introduced by the Governor of the State to a large concourse of citizens in the City Park. In his introductory remarks, the Governor made a quasi defence of the lynching of coloured men for supposed outrages upon white women. In opening his speech the President declared that he had been fortunate enough to have spoken all over the Union and had never said in any State or any section what he would not have said in any other State or in any other section. Turning a few minutes later directly to the Governor, he said: "Governor, you spoke of a hideous crime that is often hideously avenged. The worst enemy of the negro race is the negro criminal, and, above all, the negro criminal of that type; for he has committed not only an unspeakably dreadful and infamous crime against the victim, but he has committed a hideous crime against the people of his own colour; and every reputable coloured man, every coloured man who wishes to see the uplifting of his race, owes it as his first duty to himself and to that race to hunt down that criminal with all his soul and strength. Now for the side of the white man. To avenge one hideous crime by another hideous crime is to reduce the man doing it to the bestial level of the wretch who committed the bestial crime. The horrible effects of the lynchings are not for that crime at all, but for other crimes. And above all other men, Governor, you and I and all who are exponents and representatives of the law, owe it to our people, owe it to the cause of civilisation and humanity, to do everything in our power, and unofficially, directly and indirectly, to free the United States from the menace and reproach of lynch law."

I have never gone, and do not want to go, one hairs-breadth beyond what Mr. Roosevelt said in condemnation of the lynchers. Further, I fully realise that the best men in the South detest lynching and are as anxious to put down lynching as indeed were the best men in the South to get rid of slavery. I want, however, to say with Roosevelt that whatever else is right, and whatever ought to be the relations between white men and black, lynching must be wrong, and must tend to make the difficulties of a mixed population even greater than they were already. Whatever may be the vices of the black man, burning negroes alive at the mandate of an irresponsible mob, who are acting on rumour and hearsay, cannot but be the very acme of human depravity. And it is as stupid as it is wicked.

Though there was a distinct strain of austerity as well as authoritativeness in Mr. Roosevelt's nature, there was also a deep strain of sentiment. He was a man easily moved, not only by "the sense of tears in mortal things," but by all that was generous and noble. A delightful example of how deeply and quickly his feelings could be touched when a child is given by Mrs. Douglas Robinson, his sister, in the account of her brother.

The Roosevelt family were in Rome at the end of the

"sixties" and played, like other English-speaking children, on the Pincian Hill. While they were playing at leap-frog word was suddenly passed round that the Pope was coming.

"Teddie" whispered to the little group of American children that he didn't believe in Popes—that no real American would; and we all felt it was due to the stars and stripes that we should share his attitude of distant disapproval. But then, as is often the case, the miracle happened, for the crowd parted, and to our excited, childish eyes something very much like a scene in a story-book took place. The Pope, who was in his sedan-chair carried by bearers in beautiful costumes, his benign face framed in white hair and the close cap which he wore, caught sight of the group of eager little children craning their necks to see him pass; and he smiled and put out one fragile, delicate hand towards us, and lo! the late scoffer who, in spite of the ardent Americanism that burned in his eleven-year-old soul, had as much reverence as militant patriotism in his nature, fell upon his knees, and kissed the delicate hand, which for a brief moment was laid upon his hair. Whenever I think of Rome this memory comes back to me, and in a way it was so true to the character of my brother. The Pope to him had always meant what later he would have called "unwarranted superstition," but that Pope, Pio Nono, the kindly, benign old man, the moment he appeared in the flesh, brought about in my brother's heart the reaction which always came when the pure, the good, or the true crossed his path.

That is almost as good a papal story as that of the Pope whom the great Napoleon brought a virtual captive from the Vatican to grace his coronation as Emperor. The Pope, while moving about Paris, was accustomed to give his blessing freely, for he soon became a very popular character. It happened, however, that one day, while going through the galleries of the Louvre, he unwittingly gave his blessing to a little crowd that contained a fierce, anti-clerical Jacobin and revolutionary. The man showed the greatest disgust and contempt at receiving the Pope's blessing, and retorted with curses on the man who dared implore for him Heaven's grace and favour. The Pope, with his Italian grace and good manners, easily got the best of the scowling brows and the muttered imprecations. He apologised simply and humbly to the man whom he had blessed by mistake and added, "I do not think, sir, that after all an old man's blessing can have done you any harm." Quite as little could Roosevelt's boyish kiss make him a votary to superstition.

I feel for the reasons that I have already given that I am not managing to express my personal feeling about Roosevelt. Yet he is the last man of whom I want to write perfunctorily or even ceremoniously. Therefore, for the time I shall bring my recollections of him to a close by merely noting certain characteristics of the statesman.

The essential quality in Roosevelt was the spirit of good citizenship. He was a very able politician and party leader. He was also no mean orator in a nation where the arts of the rostrum are specially cultivated and understood. He was a skilled and powerful administrator. He had a soldier's eye for country and a soldier's heart. What is more, he understood the soldier's spirit as well as did Cromwell. Though a strict disciplinarian, he knew that if you are to get the best out of a soldier, you must make him feel a free citizen and not a fighting slave. Roosevelt, again, was a man highly qualified to be the personal representative and head of a great nation. He had the dignity of demeanour, the sense of proportion, the knowledge of the world, the instinct for great affairs, together with that universality of comprehension which is necessary to the efficient discharge of high office.

Yet, great as was Roosevelt in all these matters, it was not so much the qualities just enumerated which make, and will continue to make, his memory live in America. Others could rival him or surpass him on the political stage. He made good citizenship an art. He never tired in enforcing by precept and example the duty which men and women owe to the community. No man, as his life and work showed, can be allowed to keep his good citizenship in watertight compartments. He must not say that he had done his best in his district or city or State, or at Washington, and that no more was to be required of him. He must do his duty to the State in all capacities. Duty accomplished in one sphere would not relieve him of responsibility in the others.

Though Roosevelt was a Whig, an individualist, and a man who hated over-centralisation, abhorred administrative tyranny, and loathed *Etatism*, he never failed to pay due homage to the nation personified. To him the Government as representing the community, was something sacred and revered, not merely a committee to manage tram-lines, roads, and drains. Treason to the State was to him the greatest of crimes. When he talked of the National Honour, he meant something very real and definite, and was not merely indulging in a rhetorical flourish. Good citizenship was indeed to Roosevelt a religion, as in a rougher and less conscious way it was to Cromwell and to Lincoln.

CHAPTER XXVI

MY POLITICAL OPINIONS

THOUGH I have been engaged in politics all my life, I have deliberately left my political views, aspirations, and actions to almost the last chapter in my autobiography. That will seem strange to all except my most intimate friends, for I know well that the majority of people who know anything of me regard me as altogether given over to politics.

My reason for assigning so small a place in my memoirs to what has occupied so much of my life is a double one. In the first place, I was most anxious not be polemical. Politics are synonymous with strife, and if I had written a political biography, it would have become the record of a battle, or rather, of many battles, in which I could hardly have avoided saying hard things both of living and dead people. But that was what I most wanted to avoid. The veteran who tells of his old fights is always apt to become a bore. People who disagree with the view put forth think him prejudiced and unforgiving, while those who are with him yawn over a twice-told tale. Further, though I confess to being as deeply interested and as deeply concerned in politics as ever, I have greatly enjoyed a rest from strife. To suffer my mind to turn upon the poles of literature and the humanities is a pure delight. No doubt Marcus Aurelius in his autobiography says that

J. St. Loe Strachey at Newlands Corner. Ætat. 45.

life is more like a wrestling-match than a dance. That was like a Stoic. Instead, I can say *ex animo* with Mrs. Gamp, "Them that has other natures may think different! They was born so and can please themselves." Therefore, I have chosen the point of view of the dance rather than the dust, the oil, and the sweat of the athlete.

But though I do not want to fight my political battles over again, either in regard to Home Rule or the fiscal controversy, I realise that my readers will, at any rate, expect me to say something about my political views. Further than that, there are one or two things which, if unsaid, would undoubtedly give a false impression of the writer of this book.

The pivot of my politics is a whole-hearted belief in the principles of Democracy. I mean by this, not devotion to certain abstract principles or views of communal life which have had placed upon them the label "Democratic," but a belief in the justice, the convenience, and the necessity of ascertaining and loyally abiding by the lawfully-expressed Will of the Majority of the People. By using the phrase "lawfully expressed" I do not mean to suggest any pretext for evasion. On the contrary, I use the words in order to prevent and avoid evasion. A good many people who call themselves Democrats, or believers in the Popular Will, such, for example, as the leaders of the French Revolution, the apologists for the Russian Soviet, and the men from whose lips the words "Proletariat" and "Proletarian" are constantly falling, do not, when it comes to the point, want to obey the Will of the Majority of the whole People, but only the majority of a certain arbitrarily selected section of the people. They are, in fact, willing to recognise the Will of the People only when this accords with their own will—that is, with what they believe ought to be the Will of the People. When I use the expression "the Will of the People lawfully and constitutionally expressed," I use it to avoid this false democracy.

To put it quite frankly, I am willing to bow to the maxim, "Vox populi, vox Dei" as long as the "vox populi" is the genuine thing and not obtained by falsity or fraud, by corruption or coercion.

Though I am prepared to bow loyally to the Will of the People, whether I personally agree with it or not, I, of course, have a right, nay, a duty, to do my best to bring the Will of the People in accord with what I hold to be right, just, and likely to promote the welfare of the nation. I retain, that is, the right to convert, if I can, a minority view into a majority view. If any section of the people try to prevent me from exercising this right of conversion, then I believe that the sacred right of insurrection arises.

It is possible that it arises also in the attempt to prevent me from exercising the rights of conscience, that is, the right to think and to express my views. The rights of conscience are not, in my opinion, pooled and placed at the command of the majority, as are the *actions* and *behaviour* of the units that make up the State. The Will of the People even cannot command the minds of men and women. That region is under an eternal taboo, which even the majority must not attempt to violate. If they do make the attempt, they must expect resistance. Christ taught us to "render unto Cæsar the things that are Cæsar's," but a man's conscience is not one of Cæsar's perquisites.

So much for the abstract basis of Democracy. Of the convenience of following out and obeying the Democratic principle I have as little doubt as I have of the moral obligation involved. What, in my view, is wanted in the State is homogeneity. Such homogeneity, or, shall I call it completeness of the admixture of the elements which constitute the State, is essential. The fullest and strongest sanction for the laws is the security of a State, and where can you get a sanction fuller and stronger than the Will of the Majority?

The point is best seen in a simple illustration. Suppose that among seven people in a railway carriage the question arises as to whether the window is to be put up or down. As it must be settled one way or the other, if order is to be preserved, the only just way is to go by the Will of the Majority. If five people want it shut and only two want it open, the will of the five must prevail. That, of course, does not prove that the five have given a sound decision from the hygienic point of view. They have, however, come to a settlement, and it is obvious that the maximum of convenience rests in respecting that settlement. It has the superior physical power behind it. If, however, any gentleman or lady in the carriage can give a discourse upon the advantage of fresh air, which will bring over three of those who originally voted in the majority, then the policy can be changed.

With these views, it is no wonder that I have always found it impossible to feel much sympathy with the people who say that Democracy is on its trial and must be judged, like any other form of government, by its results. This either means too much or too little. No doubt it may be argued that, if the Will of the People properly expressed was to elect a single man as dictator and invest him with the power of deciding in all matters of detail, you might still have a Democracy, though it looked like a Monarchy. But these are abstract points. For practical purposes in a European community there can, in my opinion, be no doubt as to the convenience of basing, in the last resort, your system of government upon the Will of the People, as it is based, in theory, at any rate, in England and in America.

I admit, however, that when you come to apply your principles in practice the problem alters. Nothing is more obvious in our great modern communities than the fact that the people cannot rule themsevles directly. Though they could meet in the Agora of Athens and decide the fate of the Athenian Republic, or in the meadow of the Gemeinde at Appenzell, or any of the other small Swiss cantons, in a country with even only a couple of million of people, you must rely on the Representative System. In other words, though the many must will the direction in which the State shall move, it is only the few who can make that will executive.

Now comes the difficulty. As the advocates of Proportional Representation have been telling us for so many years, the Representative System may actually place the control of the Government in the hands of a minority. Again, though men may be elected to do one thing, they may in practice do another. Representative assemblies are often swayed, not merely by the voice of the orator, but, what is even a more serious matter, by the voice of the minority. Also, as Mill pointed out, under the party system applied to the Representative System, you are liable to be ruled not by a majority, but by a majority of a majority. Your Parliament is split up into two parties—the lefts and the rights. The lefts are not completely homogeneous. Therefore they have to decide on their course of action by a vote within their party. But if the party is nearly divided, it may well be that the majority of the majority is a small minority of the whole. But things are even worse than that when party loyalty is maintained, as is usually the case. Then, a minority within the lefts may be so powerful through its persistency, or, again, through its fanatical obsession on a particular point, that it is able to force a majority within the party to act in the particular way the minority wants. In short, there are a dozen different ways, under a Representative System, of making operative, not the Will of the Majority of the People, but the Will of a Minority.

It is because of this that since the Anglo-Saxon peoples have had representative institutions they have sought some system under which the people as a whole could exercise a veto on the legislative vagaries of their "deputies" or "select men." The people, in moments of tension, have yearned for the right to veto the work of their representatives when such work is obviously based upon the decision of a minority. The only substantial result of that yearning in Great Britain up till now has been the *ad hoc* General Election.

At the time of the destruction of the Monarchy of Charles I, the Army of the Commonwealth, a very democratic body, actually demanded the Referendum, or Poll of the People, for all important changes in the Constitution. Their descendants in the United States, though they did not insert the Popular Veto in the Federal Constitution, have in each State decreed that all fundamental legislation, *i.e.*, all changes in the Constitution, shall be passed subject to the veto of the whole mass of the electors. Switzerland is generally regarded as the home of the Referendum, though in reality that honour belongs to the individual States of the American Union. In Switzerland every Federal Act is either submitted *automatically* or else is submittable "on demand," to the veto of the People.

Favouring, as I do, real Democracy, and so believing that the Will of the People alone should prevail, and that we should get complete and unchallengeable sanction for the laws, I have always regarded the Referendum, or Poll of the People, as an essential corrective to the incon-

veniences and anomalies of the Representative System.
The Popular Veto is, in my view, the essential antiseptic
of the Constitutional Pharmacopeia.

*To put it with brutal plainness, I desire the Referendum
in order to free us from the evils of log-rolling and other ex-
igencies of the kind which Walt Whitman grouped under the
general formula of "the insolence of elected persons."*

I am told by my horrified Radical friends that my proposal is politically odious—a Tory device that would stop
all reforms. This I doubt. But if it is really the Will of
the People that we should not have reforms, then we must
do without them. Till we can convert the Will of the
People, we must abide by it. Anyway, I have always
thought this objection (which, by the way, is not, as
Artemus Ward would say, "writ sarkastic") an exceedingly illuminating fact. It shows how skin-deep is the
democratic principle in the minds of many men who think
themselves strong Radicals. They do not really believe
in submitting to the Will of the People. They want to
do what they think is good for the People, but they have
no true sense of freedom. They do not realise that if you
are to give a man true freedom, you must inevitably give
him the right to do wrong as well as the right to do right.
If you do not do that, he is no freeman, but merely a
virtuous slave—a creature, as Dryden said, "tied up
from doing ill." For such compulsory freedom I have
no use. I want to convert people, not to force them, or
cajole them. Of course, I cannot banish force altogether,
because if the Will of the Majority is not obeyed, we shall
never arrive anywhere. We shall spend our time in
fruitless and so futile discussions. What we can avoid
by the Poll of the People is coercion by the minority.
Curiously enough, the minority, *teste* Lenin, seem to have
no sentimental objection to coercion. They fly to it at

once. As a rule, however, the show of power is quite
enough when the will of the majority is expressed. So
great is the impact of its declaration that men will not
fight against it.

Having got so far, a great many of my readers will, no
doubt, rub their eyes and say, "Why on earth is this man
letting forth this torrent of rather obvious, well-known,
elementary, political stuff? It might do for a Fourth
Form in a public school, or for a lecture on the duties of
persons on the new Register of Electors, but one really
thought that the adult citizen had got beyond this sort of
thing."

I apologise humbly for being so elementary; but, after
all, I have an excuse. It seems to me that the real danger
of the moment is minority rule. Therefore, though all I
have said may be condemned as unoriginal, I hold it
worth while to bring people's minds back to the fact that
they *are* in danger of minority rule, in spite of the fact
that they have the very strongest moral reasons for
refusing to be ruled by a minority.

Perhaps some of us have not yet observed that in almost
all countries the so-called Labour Parties are copying the
brutal frankness of Lenin and Trotsky and saying openly
that it is only the Proletariat, or, as the wiser of them put
it, the manual workers who have the right to decide in
what direction the Ship of State shall be steered, and how
she shall be worked on the voyage. Now, though I have
no desire to substitute any other section of the community
for the manual workers, and hold most strongly that such
workers have as great a right as University professors, or
members of the Stock Exchange, or even members of the
bureaucracy, to say how we are to be governed, I will never
admit that they have a prerogative right to rule, and that
I and other non-manual workers have only the right to

obey. That is, however, the Proletarian claim. The so-called capitalist or bourgeois is, in effect, to be outlawed.

In such a context I cannot help thinking of the carman and Uncle Joseph in *The Wrong Box*. Uncle Joseph makes a remark about the lower classes, to which the carman replies, "Who are the lower classes? You are the lower classes yourself!" I claim an inalienable right to be regarded as one of the people, and I do not mean, if I can help it, to have that right taken away from me, either by a Cæsarian Dictator, an Oligarchy of manual workers, a Federation of Trade Unions, Combined Guild Socialists, or a Soviet of Proletarians.

I will yield anything to the members of these Societies in their capacity of citizens possessing each the same rights as mine, but I will yield nothing to them as the possessors of privilege. I hope I shall not be considered arrogant when I say that I am sure that in the maintenance of this view I shall find myself with the majority both in England and in America. But, of course, the rub is, shall we be able to awaken the Will of the Majority? May not a group of subtle and skilful demagogues, acting with the manual workers' Oligarchy or the Soviet of Proletarians, contrive to prevent me and my fellows in the majority coming together? That, I admit, is a real danger, and that is why I want to amend our Constitution in such a way as to place in the hands of the People themselves a right of veto over the work of the House of Commons. I want legislation of a vital description referred to a Poll of the People. Needless to say, I do not want to see every petty Bill referred to the people, but I do want all laws affecting great issues to obtain the popular sanction. Let Bills be discussed and threshed out in Parliament, and then put to the people with this question, "Do you or do you not desire that this Act shall come into operation? Those in favour of the Act will mark their papers 'Yes'; those against it will mark their papers 'No.'" In my opinion, we shall not be safe from minority rule until we get this acknowledgment of the right of the people to say the final word. Let us loyally obey the will of the majority, but let us be sure that it is the majority.

I have been at pains to make my position clear on the point of Democracy, but being a whole-hearted believer in the Democratic principle does not, of course, prevent one having strong views on specific and particular points of policy, or having affinities with particular schools of political thought. By inclination and conviction I belong to the Moderates. Whether they are called Independents, or Whigs, or men of the Left Centre, or Anti-revolutionaries, does not greatly matter. I prefer the Whig variety when the Whigs were at their best, that is, in the days of the Revolution of 1688, the days of Halifax and Somers. No doubt the Whigs, like every other party, became corrupted by too easy and too prolonged possession of power, for power, when it is too easily attained and too securely held, is a great corrupter. Lord Halifax gives a description of The Trimmer, by which term he meant, of course, not a man of vacillation or timidity, but the man who deliberately "trims" the boat of State and endeavours to keep her on an even keel. When he sees that there are too many people, or too much cargo, on one side, with the result that the boat is heeling over, he trims her by throwing his weight, or his portmanteaus, to the other side. The trimmer does not want to stop the progress of the boat, but he wants her progress to be safe and not risky. He does not object to things being done, but he does object to them being done in a wrong way, or in an ineffective way.   But, though the true Whig is a man of compromise, he is not afraid of working for specific objects of which he approves, in company with people who perhaps disagree with him on fundamentals.   He makes no lepers in politics, except of those who favour corruption and demoralisation; but will work honestly for a good cause with any honest man, no matter what his abstract opinions.   For example, I have always loved the old saying about the Whigs and the Republicans.   The Whig leader says to the Radical extremist, "You want to go the whole way to Windsor.   We want to go only half-way; but, at any rate, we can keep together as far as Hounslow."

The mention of Monarchy suggests a word or two about my own personal position on a point which, though not now of practical importance, may conceivably become so in the near future.   I am one of those people who might without error be described as a theoretical Republican and a practical Constitutional Monarchist.   I feel that in theory nobody could in these days set up an hereditary Constitutional Monarchy.   At the same time, there are a great number of practical advantages in a limited and Constitutional Monarchy, and when it exists only fools and pedants would get rid of it.   We possess, in fact, all the advantages of a Republic and also all the advantages of a Monarchy, and these are by no means small.

In a word, I have always agreed with Burke on this matter.   Burke, quoting from Bolingbroke, says somewhere— I forget where for the moment, but I think in one of his Speeches in the House of Commons—that he prefers a Monarchy to a Republic for the following reason: "It is much easier to engraft the advantages of a Republic upon a Monarchy than it is to engraft the advantages of a Monarchy upon a Republic."   That is obviously true, though I admit that the drafters of the American

Constitution made an attempt—in some ways very successful—to implant some of the advantages of a Monarchy upon their Republic. The reason behind the aphorism of "Burke out of Bolingbroke" is obvious. The stock on which the graft is made is not the thing which you wish to fructify. It is the inactive base. Constitutional Monarchy is just the stock you want. In the first place, it is permanent—that is, its roots are in the ground. But though the stock does not need to be changed, you can change and renew your graft as much and as often as you like. You get through the Monarchy stability and continuity, and you can make as much or as little of your Monarch as occasion requires. If he is a specially vicious or untrustworthy man, you can get rid of him. If he is an imbecile, you can, have a Regency. If he is a nonentity, you can, through the Constitutional principle that the King reigns but does not govern, see that your system is not interfered with. If, on the other hand, the King is a sensible man with a high sense of public duty and of fine personal character, as, for example, the present occupant of the Throne, there gradually grows up a power and influence in the State which is of the very greatest use. The King gets for the whole nation a position analogous to that which the permanent official gets in a great Department of State. He has not the power of the Secretary of State, but his knowledge and experience give him immense weight. In a word, a monarch, after fifteen or twenty years of experience, in which he had seen Ministries go up and down, parties blossom and wither, develops an instinct for government which is very valuable. He becomes an ideal adviser for his advisers.

I well remember being immensely struck by the emergence of this point of view in the speech which Lord Salisbury made in the House of Lords on the death of

Queen Victoria. Without exactly using the phrase, he described how the Queen advised her advisers. He spoke of the occasions on which the Queen had tendered her admonitions to the Cabinet, and went on to say that the Queen knew the English people so thoroughly and so sympathetically, and had such an instinct for interpreting their wishes, that it was always with grave anxiety and doubt that her Ministers refrained from taking her advice or finally decided to disregard her warnings on some specific matter of policy, which involved possibilities of a clash with public opinion.

No one who has studied the law of the Constitution and the history of its growth can but feel a kind of instinctive awe for the happy series of accidents, tempered by human wisdom, which has given us the Constitution we possess. Under the Act of Settlement and the various Declaratory Statutes regulating the powers of the Monarch and promulgated at the time of the Revolution of 1688, for example, "The Bill of Rights," we have a crowned Republic with a royal and hereditary President. We talk about the King being Sovereign "by Divine Right" and "by the Grace of God," but, of course, in fact, the King's title is a purely Parliamentary one, and is derived from an Act of Parliament—an Act of Parliament which settles the Throne upon "the heirs of the body of the Electress Sophia," who shall join in communion with the Church of England and who shall not be a member of the Roman Catholic Church or intermarry with a Roman Catholic.

Therefore, when the Sovereign dies and a new Sovereign succeeds, he succeeds in virtue of an Act of Parliament, and in no other way. He is the choice of the people. The repeal of the Act of Settlement would put another man in his place, and, again, an amendment of the Act of Settlement might secure the selection of some other member of the Royal Family, instead of the person previously designated to succeed by the Act of Settlement.

But these, of course, are legal technicalities. The British Monarchy is an early example of Whiggism. The theory may be pedantic, or, if you will, ridiculous, but the result is excellent. It is a practical working-out of the national determination, partly conscious and partly subconscious, to obtain for our use the best features of a Monarchy and of a Republic. This, no doubt, would horrify the acute, analytical minds of the Latin races. Again, the philosophic Teuton would despise it as incomprehensible. Only those possessed of the Anglo-Saxon temperament by birth or training—that is, only English-speaking persons, whether British or American, can appreciate fully the British political and constitutional system. Indeed, it sometimes has the effect of producing in foreigners a sense of desperation. Old Mirabeau, surnamed "The Friend of Man," the father of the great Mirabeau, and a political philosopher of no mean order, was reduced to a paroxysm of incoherent rage by the mere contemplation of our Constitution. "Those miserable islanders do not know, and will not know until their whole wretched system comes to its inevitable destruction, whether they are living under a Monarchy or a Republic, a Democracy or an Oligarchy." A wit with a penchant for the vernacular might well reply, "That's the spirit!" It is this that will last, while what delights and soothes the well-balanced mind of the clear-thinking Academicians of the Constitutional Law flaunts and goes down an unregarded thing. As Sir Thomas Browne said long ago, nations are not governed by ergotisms (or as we should say syllogisms) but by instinct and common sense.

Natural parts and good judgments rule the world. States are not governed by ergotisms. Many have ruled well, who could not, perhaps, define a commonwealth; and they who understand not the globe of the earth command a great part of it. Where natural logick prevails not, artificial too often faileth. Where nature fills the sails, the vessel goes smoothly on; and when judgment is the pilot, the insurance need not be high.

Though one may be both a Democrat and a Whig, and yet think there is no better function for the good citizen than to trim the boat, this does not necessarily mean that one cannot be a party politician. Party, in spite of all the very obvious objections that can be raised against it, is, it seems to me, absolutely necessary to representative government. If you choose out of the body of the population a certain number of men to rule, those men are sure to have divergent views and aims. As Stevenson said about our railway system, "Wherever there is competition there can also be combination." The first instinct of a body of men with number of divergent opinions is for those who have similar or allied aims to get together and take combined action. But the moment that has happened you have got a party system. The party system is, indeed, first a plain recognition of these facts, and then an organization of the common will.

As the party system grows and intensifies, it alters its phenomena, but its essentials are always the same. The main objection to the party system lies in the closeness and strictness of its organisation. The best party system is one in which the organisation is not too perfect, and from which it is comparatively easy to break away. The really bad party system is that in which a man is caught so tightly and becomes so deeply involved in party loyalty, or what may be called the freemasonry side of politics, that he grows into feeling a kind of moral obligation to stick to his party, right or wrong. Party tends, that is, to become a kind of horrible parody of patriotism. Oddly enough, the less clear are the dividing-lines between parties and the less real the distinctions between the views that they wish to carry out, the more intense the party spirit seems to become, and the more impossible it is for the members to break away. Though they disagree at heart with the proceedings of their leaders and disapprove of the party's action as a whole, they seem condemned to adhere to the platform.

I remember a luciferous story which was told to me by Colonel John Hay to illustrate the frenzy of party. A murderer was supposed to have entered the house of a great Republican politician and, holding a dagger over him, to have told him that his hour was come and that he must die. The politician tried every appeal he could think of. "Consider," he said, "my poor wife and the misery she will feel at my death." "I am sorry for her, but it cannot be helped. You must die." "But think of my poor innocent children who will be left helpless orphans." "I am sorry for them too, but you must die." "Think of the evil effect on the country at this moment of crisis." "Yes, I know, and I am sorry; but that cannot move me. You must die." And then came the final appeal, "But think of the effect on the Republican Party!" Across the would-be murderer's face came a quiver of irresolution. The dagger dropped from his hands, and with the cry, "Good heavens! I never thought of that," he rushed from the room.

But though this is the danger, there is, happily, no need for us to carry the party system quite so far as that. Party discipline there must be, but it can be kept well within bounds. Nothing is more wholesome than for party leaders to know that if they push things too far and too often ask their followers to condone doubtful acts, their followers will leave them.   Clearly, as the Irishman said of the truth, this spirit of independence must not be dragged out on every paltry occasion.   It must, however, always remain in the background as a possibility, and, what is more even those who do not themselves revolt would be well advised to prevent extreme penal measures being applied within the party to a man who breaks away on a particular point.

For myself, curiously enough, I never felt any dislike of party, and was, indeed, I fondly believe, designed by Providence for a good and loyal party man, with no inconvenient desire to assert my own views.   A perverse fate, however, has forced me twice in my life to break with my party, or, to put it more correctly, it has twice happened to me that the party to which I belonged adopted the policy that I had always deemed it essential to oppose. To begin with, I left the Liberal Party, to which my family had always belonged ever since the time of the Commonwealth, over Mr. Gladstone's sudden conversion to Home Rule and the abandonment of the Legislative Union. Whether I was right or wrong I am not going to discuss here.   At any rate I followed Lord Hartington, Mr. Chamberlain, Mr. John Bright, the Duke of Argyll, and a host of other good Liberals and Whigs and became, first a Liberal-Unionist, and then an unhyphenated Unionist, and a loyal supporter of Lord Salisbury, Mr. Balfour, and their administration.

In the Unionist Party, which has become quite as thoroughly Democratic as its opponent, I had hoped to live and die, but unfortunately, there came the one other question upon which I felt it my duty to take as strong a line as I did in opposing the very injurious and unjust form of Home Rule which first Mr. Gladstone, and then Mr. Asquith, advocated.

People who have forgotten, or who are not aware of the actual conditions, may think it strange that I, who proclaim myself so strongly in favour of obeying the Will of the Majority, should have become so strong a Unionist. A little reflection will show, however, that not only was there nothing contradictory in my attitude, but that it was natural and inevitable from my democratic premises. I held the Union with Ireland to be as much an incorporating union as the union between the several States of the American Republic. I held that the Will of the Majority must prevail within the United Kingdom. The area in which the votes were to be counted was, in a word, to be the whole national area, and not a small portion of it. As I have argued for the last thirty-five years, in public and in private, and as I still feel, the Home Rule Question is and always must be a question of area.

The area which I took for the decision, and which I still think was the right area to give the decision, was the United Kingdom. If any other were adopted, you might very soon fritter away the whole United Kingdom. Again, if we are to make a great financial present, as the Irish claim we must do, from the taxpayer of the centre to the detached fragments of the circumference, the process becomes a tragedy. If Ireland may go at the wish of her electors, so, of course, may Scotland, and so may Wales, each with their subsidy from England. Next, outlying portions of England may want to break away. The result would be a veritable apotheosis of political fissiparousness.

In spite of this, I admit that you cannot fight a political battle on the principle of the *reductio ad absurdum*. The people of England might hold that for special reasons Ireland would have a right to separate, but that this must not be a precedent to be applied to the rest of Britain.

Assuming, however, that Ireland shall have exceptional treatment, I saw, as of course, did many other people, for I am not so foolish as to make any claim to seeing further than my neighbours, that the question of area again controlled the event. Ireland was not a homogeneous country. There were two Irelands—the Ireland of the North and the Ireland of the South, the Ireland of the Celt and of the Teuton, and, above all, the Ireland in which Roman Catholics formed a large majority of the population, and the Ireland in which the Protestants formed the local majority. In a word, the twenty-six counties of the South and the six counties of the North differed in every respect. Neither could justly be put in control of the other; though both might be united through a Union with England, Scotland, and Wales.

From these premises I drew certain inferences, which I believe to be entirely sound. One was that you could not say that Ireland, as a whole, might claim to break away from the United Kingdom, and then refuse the claim of the Six-County Area to break away from the rest of Ireland. Arguments against the diversion and disruption of Ireland would be exactly the same as those used by the Unionists to forbid the destruction of the United Kingdom. Feeling this, as I did, when Mr. Gladstone introduced his second Home Rule Bill, I took an early opportunity of going over to Belfast and ascertaining the facts on the spot. I was confirmed in my view that there could be no solution of the Irish Question which would be either just, or reasonable, or efficient, that did not recognise the existence of the two Irelands—which did not, in effect, say to the Nationalists, "If you insist on your pound of flesh and break up an arrangement which has done so much for Ireland as a whole, that is, the Legislative Union, you must also yield the pound of flesh to the

people of North-East Ulster, a community which does
not want the United Kingdom to be partitioned, any more
than you want Ireland to be partitioned." In this faith
I have remained. I believe that the breaking-up of the
Legislative Union with Ireland was bad for England, bad
for Ireland, and bad for the Empire; but if it should be the
Will of the People of the United Kingdom, then that Will
could only be equitably applied by a recognition of the
existence of the two Irelands. Yet this simple fact
Liberal party politicians like Mr. Gladstone, Mr. Asquith,
and their followers either absolutely ignored, or else
sapiently admitted that it was a serious difficulty and
then passed on to the purchase of the Southern Irish vote
for other purposes!

Perhaps it will be said, "But you are getting away from
your main premise—the Will of the Majority. If it
should be the will of the Majority of the United Kingdom
not to recognise the existence of the two Irelands, you are
bound, according to your theory, to submit to that view."
I admit that I may be bound, but I do not believe, and
never have believed, that the people of North-East Ulster
are bound. You can turn Northern Ireland out of the
Union if you will, but you have no moral right to place
them under the dominance to which they object—the
dominance of a Dublin Parliament. To do that is to call
into existence that rare but inalienable, right, "the
sacred right of insurrection" against intolerable injustice.

As far as I know, no State has ever yet seriously claimed
the right to deprive any portion of itself of the political
status belonging to its inhabitants, except when compelled to do so by foreign conquerors. That is why I,
though a Majority Democrat, have always felt that the
people of Belfast and of North-East Ulster were loyal, and
not disloyal, citizens, when they declared that if they were

to be turned out of the United Kingdom they had an inalienable right to declare that they would not be placed under a Dublin Parliament. The Parliament of the United Kingdom, of which their representative formed an integral part, though it had a right to make laws for them, had no right to hand them over to the untender mercies of the Southern Irish. *Delegatus non potest delegare*—the delegate cannot delegate. But the representatives of the United Kingdom are delegates for the people of the United Kingdom. They have a right to govern it, but they cannot hand over their power of government to some other body. My contention is triumphantly supported by what happened during the attempt, happily unsuccessful, to break up the United States of America. When Virginia seceded from the Union, the people of what might be called the Ulster Virginia, a group of counties in the west of Virginia, declared that the Richmond Legislature had no right to deprive them of their inalienable right of citizenship in the American Republic. Therefore they not only refused to secede, but, as they were physically unable to control Virginia as a whole, they formed themselves into the Loyal State of West Virginia, just as the Ulster people were prepared, if they had been forced out of the Union by Mr. Asquith's Bill, to set up a State for themselves.

At the end of the Civil War, the legal pedants of Washington were inclined to say that, right or wrong on the merits, the people of West Virginia had not acted legally in setting up their State, and that therefore, when the Peace came, they must be put back into Virginia and under the Richmond Government. The self-made State of West Virginia naturally objected at this intolerable and unjust decision. When the matter came before Mr. Lincoln and his Cabinet, that great and wise man acted with a firmness not outdone even in the list of his magnificent achievements. He would hear nothing of the technical pedantries and legal sophistries submitted to him. West Virginia, he declared, must remain detached from Virginia, and it remains to this day a State of the Union. Here are the concluding words of the memorandum which Mr. Lincoln circulated to his Cabinet:—

Can this Government stand, if it indulges constitutional constructions by which men in open rebellion against it are to be accounted, man for man, the equals of those who maintain their loyalty to it? . . . If so, their treason against the Constitution enhances their constitutional value. . . . It is said, the devil takes care of his own. Much more should a good spirit—the spirit of the Constitution and the Union—take care of its own. I think it cannot do less and live. . . . We can scarcely dispense with the aid of West Virginia in this struggle; much less can we afford to have her against us, in Congress and in the field. Her brave and good men regard her admission into the Union as a matter of life and death. They have been true to the Union under very severe trials. We have so acted as to justify their hopes, and we cannot fully retain their confidence and co-operation if we seem to break faith with them. The division of a State is dreaded as a precedent. But a measure made expedient by a war is no precedent for times of peace. It is said that the admission of West Virginia is secession, and tolerated only because it is our secession. Well, if we call it by that name, there is still difference enough between secession against the Constitution and secession in favour of the Constitution.

I shall never forget the profound impression made upon me when I first read those words. They gave what to me was the support of the highest moral and political authority to the view at which I had arrived instinctively. I had, as was natural, some doubts about my position, for

I saw that my theories might lead to encouraging resistance to the apparent Will of the Majority. But after finding a supporter in Lincoln, I had no more doubts or fears.

I have dwelt so long on this matter because I want to show what, rightly or wrongly, was my guiding principle: —I objected to Home Rule as bad for the Empire, bad for the United Kingdom, and bad in an even extremer degree for Ireland herself. If, however, it should be determined that some measure of Home Rule must be passed, then the existence of the two Irelands must be recognised in any action which should be determined upon. Therefore, when the support which the Unionist Party determined on giving to Mr. Lloyd George at the end of the War made some form of Home Rule seem almost inevitable, I strongly advocated the division of Ireland as the only way of avoiding a civil war in which the merits would be with Northern Ireland. I would personally have preferred to see the Six-County Area incorporated with England and become one or two English counties. As that seemed for various reasons unobtainable, the setting up of the Northern Legislature and the Northern State became the inevitable compromise.

That accomplished, I should have preferred to see Southern Ireland detached from the Empire. I have no desire to be a fellow-citizen with Mr. de Valera, Mr. Michael Collins, or even Mr. Griffiths, or, again, with the hierarchy of the Roman Church in Ireland. They have perfectly different views of the crime of murder from mine. I believe murder to be the greatest of crimes against the community, and, granted that we should give up any attempt to teach Ireland better, I would rather detach her altogether from the Empire. I hold that to be included in the British Empire is one of the highest and greatest privileges obtainable by any community, and I am not going down on my knees to beg an unwilling Southern Ireland to enjoy this privilege.

Further, I hold that if we let the Southern Irish go, we have a duty to the Protestants and Roman Catholic loyalists, of whom, of course, there are a very great many in the South. We have no right to force them to forfeit their citizenship of the British Empire. They must be allowed to come away from the South with full compensation for their disturbance if they so desire. If circumstances force you to denationalise a certain part of your country, you must give the loyal inhabitants an opportunity to leave, and as far as possible must not allow their material interests to suffer. It would be perfectly easy to have exempted all persons in the South who were loyal to Britain and to have put the burden of their migration where it ought to have fallen—that is, on the Southern enemies of England and Scotland who, by their policy, had made human life for the Protestants and Loyalists a veritable hell.

If the South had refused to pay, we should ourselves have taken on the burden and imposed a duty on agricultural produce coming from the South of Ireland into England sufficient to find the interest on a loan raised to compensate the Southern refugees. That would be a perfectly possible way, a very easy fiscal transaction.

I am not going to argue further whether these views on the Irish problem are *per se* right or wrong. I can only adopt with variation the party-politician's peroration: "These, gentlemen, are my principles; if they don't suit, they can't be altered."

CHAPTER XXVII

MY POLITICAL OPINIONS (*Continued*)

I HAVE described how the policy of Home Rule adopted by the Liberal Party made me, as it did so many other people in the United Kingdom, first a Liberal-Unionist and then a Unionist without a hyphen. Unfortunately, however, the Unionist Party did not for very long offer me a quiet and secure political haven. Like the Duke of Devonshire, whom I always regarded during his life as my leader in politics, I had to weigh my anchor during the tempest caused by Mr. Chamberlain's scheme of Tariff Reform, and then seek safety in the ocean of independence. I am not going at length into the merits of the fiscal question, except to say that, though it was the only point on which I differed from the bulk of the Unionist Party, it was, unfortunately, the one other matter of policy in which I could not play the good party man and bow my head to the decision of the Party as a whole. I felt as strongly about the Tariff Reform as I did about the dissolution of the United Kingdom. Rightly or wrongly again, my opposition was based very much on the same essential grounds. I believed that the policy of Tariff Reform, if carried out, would end by breaking up instead of uniting the British Empire, which I desired above all things to maintain "in health and strength long to live." I held that to give up Free Trade would do im-

448

mense damage to our economic position here and intensify our social conditions by impoverishing the capitalist as well as the manual worker; and, finally, that there was very great danger of any system of Protection introducing corruption into our public life. If four or five words, or sometimes even a single word and a comma, added to or taken away from the schedule of a Tariff Act can give a man or group of men a monopoly and tax half the nation in order to make them rich, you have given men too personal a reason for the use of their votes.

I can summarise my position in regard to Tariff Reform very easily. I am no pedant about Protection, and if it could be shown that the security of an island kingdom like the United Kingdom could only be made complete by Protection in certain matters, I should be perfectly willing to vote for measures to give that security. In other words, I would have voted for what has been called "a state of siege" tariff. I should have regarded it as an economic loss which must be borne just as must the charges of the Army and Navy, in order to ensure the safety and welfare of the realm.

But Mr. Chamberlain and his followers, though there was an occasional word or two about national security, did not base their appeal to the nation on the ground of national security. They based it on quite different grounds. They told us in effect, "If you want to maintain and develop your industries, if you want to prevent them gradually dying out, if you want to get the greatest amount of employment for workingmen, and also for capital,—in a word, if you want to increase the wealth of the nation, you must go in for Protection, *i.e.*, Tariff Reform." Tariff Reform thus became a national "get-rich-quick" political war-cry. That, to my mind, was an appeal which had to be counter-attacked at once as the most dangerous delusion from which any people could suffer, and a delusion specially perilous to a country like England—a nation living, and bound to live, by trade and barter rather than by agriculture or the satisfaction of her own wants.   England is a country to which the encouragement of every form of exchange is vital.   But you cannot encourage exchanges under a system of Protection.   Protection sets out to limit Exchange by forbidding half the exchanges of the world, that is, exchanges between persons of different nationalities and different locations.

If your object is to increase the national wealth, you must be a Free Trader.   There is no other way.   If, however, your object is national security—if you say, "I would rather see the nation safe than wealthy," then I fully admit there is a good case, not merely in theory, but very possibly in practice, for a certain amount of Protection.   The existence of arsenals in which rifles, explosives, and other material of war can be made are obviously necessary, and no nation could safely see such essential industries depart from these shores on the ground that we could more economically make something else to exchange for rifles, guns, ammunition, and armour-plate made elsewhere.   Again, since the existence of dye industries is so closely connected with the manufacture of explosives, I am perfectly willing to admit that it may be necessary to give Protection in this special matter.   Again, it is possible, though I think it less clear than is generally supposed, that there may be one or two key industries which the experience of the War shows us it is worth while to maintain here, even if a subsidy is required for such maintenance. Finally, I think the experience of the War proved that we must see to it that our ability to feed ourselves, though it may be at short commons, for at least six months of the year, ought to receive due consideration.

I am as much opposed to war and as much in favour of peace as my neighbours, but I do not want my descendants some day when called upon to resist a threatened wrong to have to decide on peace, not on its merits but because they are at the mercy of an international bully; and remember we are not going to get rid of international bullies till we have got educated and reasonable democracies established throughout the world.

The world will be safe only when rid of populations so servile by nature that they are willing to allow themselves to be governed by men like the ex-German Emperor. True education and true democracy are the best anodynes to war.

But, as I have said, Mr. Chamberlain and the Tariff Reform Leaguers, though, of course, they occasionally spoke about security, really made their appeal on the old Protectionist ground that "Day by day we get richer and richer"—provided we limit our exchanges instead of extending them. When the Tariff Reform agitation had made me, as I have said, find safety in sea room with men like the Duke of Devonshire, Lord Cromer, Lord George Hamilton, Mr. Arthur Elliott, Lord Hugh Cecil, Lord Robert Cecil, and a number of very distinguished *Conservative* Unionists was well as *Liberal* Unionists, I experienced the full disadvantages, or rather the weakness, of independence in politics. We Unionist Free Traders, as we called ourselves, were not really strong enough to organise a party for ourselves, nor, indeed, did we think it advisable to do so, for, except in the matter of Tariff Reform, we were strongly opposed to the Liberal and Free Trade Party, and strongly in sympathy with the bulk of the Unionist Party. In a word, we Unionist Free Traders could not form a whole-hearted alliance with either of the two old parties. We detested the Irish policy followed by

Mr. Asquith, its truckling to the Nationalists and its apparent determination to shed the blood of the people of Ulster, if that was necessary to force them under a Dublin Parliament. Again, we hated, and no man more than I, the socialistic legislation which the Asquith Government were willing to adopt at the bidding of the Labour Party. The mixture of coercion and cajolery which Mr. Lloyd George knew so well how to employ in his Radical days, in order to induce the House of Commons to accept his various measures, was particularly abhorrent to us.

It was not only the bad Irish policy of the Government, their flirtation with Socialism, and the Marconi business, that made me strongly opposed to Mr. Asquith's pre-War administration. I greatly disliked the foreign policy of the Liberal Government. It was a weak and timid compromise between half-hearted pacificism and inadequate preparation. I was confident, as must have been anyone who kept his eyes open, that Germany was preparing for war with this country as part of her world-policy, and I felt it likely that as soon as the widening and deepening of the Kiel Canal was finished, and so the effective strength of the German Fleet doubled, the first excuse would be taken to bring on the "inevitable" world-war. Therefore, I held that preparation for war was absolutely necessary. Adequate preparation might indeed avert war. The German Emperor wanted not so much war as victory, and the more we were prepared the more we should be able to say that we would not allow the conquest of Europe by arms, though we were quite ready to let Germany conquer by good trading, *if she could*. The British people, as a whole, had no jealousy of her splendid trade organisation and power of manufacture, and nothing could ever have induced them to make an unprovoked attack on Germany.

If we had adopted universal military service here; if we had even, as I wanted and urged in public, kept a couple of million of rifles in store here, ready for the improvisation of great military forces, Germany, however anxious to strike her blow, would probably have held her hand. We were tempting her to war by our want of preparation.

Unfortunately, Mr. Asquith and his Government, though full of anxiety and trembling at the prospect of what might happen, came to the disastrous decision not to make whole-hearted, but only half-hearted, preparations. They decided that, though they would not do enough in the way of preparation to make war impossible, they would do enough to give an excuse to the Potsdam war-party. For the rest, they would trust to the peace party— or alleged peace party—in Germany. In reality, there was no such peace party, or, if there was, it was an impotent thing. The servility of the German people rendered it quite unimportant! True democracy may be trusted in the matter of peace. Your tyrant whether he speaks with a popular voice, or whether he professes to be a God-given autocrat, is always a danger.

It was the slavish spirit of the German people and their willingness, though so intelligent and so highly organised, to let themselves be governed by a blatant Emperor of second-class intellect, which constituted the real danger to European peace. If Mr. Asquith had said to the people of this country, or, indeed, to the world, "We are going to be vigilant in our preparations till the German people have freed themselves and so given hostages for the peace of the world," he would, I believe, have had the support of all the best elements in English political life. He would not have used such crude language, but he could have made his meaning clear in courteous phrases. Instead of which, he took a line which, in effect, encouraged France, and so

Russia, to stand up against Germany, and not to take her threats lying down, and yet did not insure against the obligations he was, in effect, incurring.

To say that preparation, as is sometimes said, would have precipitated war is a delusion. It might, I well believe, have precipitated it if the preparations had been delayed till 1913, but not if they had been undertaken, as they could have been quite easily, several years earlier, *i.e.*, after the Agadir incident and when the trend of events was quite clear. Yet in January, 1914, Mr. Lloyd George thought it advisable to say that we had reached a period when we could safely reduce our Army and Navy. His speech was as provocative of war as any public utterance recorded by history.

Finally, I had a quarrel with the Liberal Government over Mr. Lloyd George's famous first Budget, which I thought, and still think, a thoroughly bad measure. But even here Fate did not allow me to range myself with my old party, the Unionists. I could not, any more than could Lord Cromer and many other of my political Unionist Free Trade associates, believe that it was wise from the constitutional or conservative point of view to try and fight the so-called "People's Budget" by invoking action in the House of Lords over a financial matter. I think the action of the Lords was bad from the legal point of view. I am sure it was bad from the point of view of political convenience. The country instinctively recognised that the Lords were indulging in a revolutionary action, and, though the English people are, I am glad to say, not frightened by the mere word "revolution," they have a feeling that, if revolutionary action is to be taken, it ought never to be taken by the representatives of Constitutionalism. That is just the kind of inappropriateness which always annoys English people. The result, of course, was that at the inevitable General Election the Unionists did not gain enough seats to justify their action, and thereupon Mr. Asquith and his followers undertook in the Parliament Act the abolition of the power of the House of Lords to insist on the people being consulted in matters of great importance. The Lords in recent times never claimed the veto power but only this right to see that the country endorsed the schemes of its representatives.

Then came another break with the Unionists for me and for those who thought like me. Lord Halsbury, Mr. Austen Chamberlain and their followers, chiefly the right, or Tory, wing of the Unionists, were strongly in favour of the Lords throwing out the Parliament Bill. It was known that if the Lords did throw the Bill out, Mr. Asquith would advise the King to create sufficient Peers (four hundred was the number calculated to be required) to pass the measure. Though it was unpleasant to be associated in this matter with the people who were most keen about Mr. Lloyd George's Budget, I had not the slightest hesitation as to what line of action I ought to take, and in *The Spectator* I urged with all the strength at my command that the Unionist Party had no business to set up as revolutionaries, which they in effect were doing by insisting that the Bill should only be passed by the creation of four hundred Peers. They, I urged, would appear before the public as the wreckers of the Constitution. The result of the line I took in *The Spectator*—a line not supported by the rest of the Unionist Press, or, at any rate, by only a very small section of it—was to call down a vehemence of denunciation on my head more violent than I, accustomed as I was to abuse from both sides, had ever before experienced. Happily, I am one of those people who find a hot fight stimulating and amusing and who, like Attila, love the *certaminis gaudia*, the glories and delights of a rough-and-tumble scrap. I and *The Spectator* were, I remember, denounced by name by Mr. Austen Chamberlain at a banquet of Die-Hards. Mr. Garvin in *The Observer* abused *The Spectator* in perfect good faith, I admit, but with characteristic intensity. I received dire threats from old readers of *The Spectator*, and finally I received gifts of white feathers to show what the country Die-Hards thought of me!

I felt quite certain, however, that not only was I right to speak my mind, but that in the last resort the common sense of what the Anglo-Saxon chronicler called "*miletes agresti*," and the new journalism "the backwoodsman peers," would turn out to be not for but against revolutionary action. And so it happened.

I did not actually go to the House of Lords to hear the debate, as I am one of those people who confess to be easily bored by what Lord Salisbury called "the dreary drip of dilatory declamation." I waited, however, pen in hand, to hear the result of the division, which was not taken till late on a Thursday night. A relative in the House had undertaken to telephone the event to me at the earliest moment, so that I should have plenty of time to chronicle a victory for common sense, or deplore the first step in an ill-judged constitutional revolution. When the telephone-bell rang and the figures of the division were given, they showed a majority against the rejection of the Bill. It was not a large majority, but it was sufficient, and I at once turned with a sense of real relief to write the funeral sermon on a round in the great political game which had been as badly played as possible by the Unionist leaders. I am still proud to think that *The Spectator* had taken a considerable share in preventing the crowning blunder. Throughout the crisis I had acted in the utmost intimacy and complete accord with Lord Cromer. He worked as hard with the Unionist chiefs in private as I did with the rank-and-file in public.

There were several curious episodes in this fierce quarrel of which I was cognisant; but these events, and also those connected with the Conferences on the Home Rule Bill, which was in progress when the War broke out, cannot be fully dealt with. In fifteen or twenty years' time either I or my literary executors may be able to disclose that portion of them with which I was specially concerned. Till then the memoranda and letters in which they are set forth must remain sealed books. For fear of misconception I ought perhaps to add that they disclose nothing dishonourable in any sort of way to any of the participants. Instead, they bear out Lord Melbourne's aphorism. A lady is reported to have addressed him in the following terms: "I suppose, Lord Melbourne, that as Prime Minister you found mankind terribly venal." "No, no, Ma'am; not venal, only damned vain." I might, during my inspection of the Arcana of the Constitution and my first-hand knowledge of our leading politicians, have been inclined to vary it, "Not venal, not self-seeking—only damned foolish, or damned blind."

Before I leave off reviewing my political views and actions, in which there are many things which I am exceedingly sorry not to print at full length, I desire a word or two in regard to my position towards the War. I want to say quite plainly and clearly that, though it would be out of place and wearisome to discuss the War and its origin here, I refuse absolutely and entirely to apologise for the War, or to speak as if I were ashamed of it, or of the part which, as a journalist, I played in regard to it before it came or while it was in progress. The War was not only necessary to secure our safety, but it was, I am as fully convinced as ever I was, a righteous war. Unless we had been willing to run the risk of being enslaved by Germany, or, if you will, unless we had been prepared to fight for our lives and liberties at the most terrible disadvantage, we were bound, both by reasons of safety and by reasons of honour, to prevent France being destroyed by Germany.   If after all that had happened in the ten years before the war we had remained neutral, France and Russia would have felt, and with reason, that we had deserted them.   It is, therefore, quite possible that, if Germany, after a rapid initial success, had proposed very generous terms, they might have patched up a peace at our expense, and in effect told Germany that she might have as much of the perfidious British Empire as she required. Germany would almost certainly have been willing to agree to such an arrangement.   Her rulers, like Napoleon, knew that they could not rule Europe unless the naval supremacy of the British Empire was destroyed.   In a word, it was quite clear that if we, France, and Russia did not hang *together*, we should hang separately.

That was the argument of convenience.   The argument based on honour and justice was stronger still.   The notion of allowing Belgium and France to be exposed to the risk of destruction while we watched in fancied security was absolutely intolerable.   We could not say to France, though some people actually thought it possible, "This is not our quarrel.   You must decide between Russia and Germany as best you can.   We refuse to fight Russia's battles; though we would fight yours if you were wantonly attacked."   But that was as foolish as it was selfish.   France and Russia were bound to support each other against the foe they found so potent and so menacing;—a foe willing, nay, eager, to support that "negation of God erected into a system" called the Austrian Empire.

To be concise, France was bound in honour not to leave

Russia in the lurch when she was attacked, and we were also bound in honour not to desert France. We had pursued, in the past, a policy which directly encouraged France, not only to make a stand against Germany, but to commit herself more and more to her Russian Allies and to regard, indeed, that alliance as part of the security of the world, part of the insurance against a German domination of Europe, part of the joint peace premium. First to back up France, as we did at Agadir and afterwards, and then suddenly to step aside with the cry of "Angela, there is danger. I leave thee," would have been so base that, had we perpetrated it, we could never have recovered our national self-respect. But self-respect is as essential to the welfare of nations as it is to the welfare of the individual.

The War was a terrible evil, and we have suffered very greatly, but I refuse absolutely to be apologetic in regard to our method of carrying it through. On the contrary, I think there is nothing in human history more magnificent than the way in which people in the British Empire steadily kept to their purpose and were willing to make any and every sacrifice to maintain the right. Here I appeal to a contemporary judgment which happens to be as impartial as the judgment of any future historian is likely to be. I mean the judgment passed on us by the firm if friendly hand of the American Ambassador, Mr. Page. Wonderful and deeply moving are his descriptions of the way in which the English people of all classes and of all political creeds and temperaments withstood the shock of the declaration of war and of its first dreadful impact. Speaking generally his descriptions of the years '14, '15, and '16—"Years which reeled beneath us, terrible years" —are as great and as memorable as anything ever recorded in human history. As a picture of a people undergoing. the supreme test and seen in the fullest intimacy and absolutely at first-hand, it is equal to anything even in Thucydides. A noble passion inspires and consecrates the narration—vibrant with the sense not only of sorrow but also of exaltation and complete understanding. It was the happiest of accidents that one of our own race, and blood, and language should have been able to view the nation's sacrifice as he viewed it, and yet be able to speak as could only a man who was not actually participating in the sacrifice, and was not actually part of the nation. An American citizen of pure English language and lineage, like Mr. Page, could say things, and say them outright, which no Englishman could have said. The Englishman would have been checked and tongue-tied by the sense that he was plucking laurels for his own brow. *Page's immortal letters—I am using the words with sober deliberation and not in any inflated rhetoric—stand as the best and greatest national monument for Britain's dead and Britain's living.*

That noble attitude of the British people, that gallantry without pose or self-glorification, that valour without vain glory, that recognition that pity and truth must be shared by the conqueror with the conquered all were maintained by our people in war as in peace. There were tears for the sons of the enemy as well as for our own. In spite of endless provocations we kept our humanity and so our honour.

If our battle spirit became us, our spirit since then has been as worthy of the best that is in mankind. It is true that while making the Peace, we said and did many foolish things, both as far as the rest of the world is concerned and also in regard to our own interests; but we have a perfect right to say that all was done in honour and nothing in malice, in selfishness, or in that worst of all crimes and follies, the spirit of revenge. There is no justice in revenge. It is a hateful and premeditated negation of justice, the creature of ignoble panic, and not of faith and courage. It is pure evil.

I even refuse to bemoan the legacies of the War. The War has left us in poverty and in peril. But even though that poverty and that peril are largely the result of the mismanagement of those to whom we have entrusted the work of reconstruction, I am not going to sit down by the international roadside and rave about it. The way in which that social peril and that poverty have been borne by the vast majority of our population has been wholly admirable. I am optimist enough to see and salute a nobility of sacrifice in all classes which to my mind is earnest that the future of our half of the English-speaking race—of the other half no man need have any doubts—will be as great as was its past.

Could anything have been better than the way in which the rich, opulent, well-to-do classes of this country have taken the tremendous revolution in their lives and fortunes accomplished by the War? The economic and social change has been as great and almost as shattering as those wrought by any social revolution in the world's history. Yet they have hardly caused a murmur among those who have had to endure them.

The great country-houses of England, only some eight years ago its architectural and social glory, are passing rapidly out of the hands of their old owners. Some are destined to fall actually into ruin, some to become institutions, schools, hospitals, or asylums, and a few—but only a few—to pass into the hands of the new possessors of wealth —a body much smaller in numbers than is usually represented. There are thousands of families whose members, once rich, have now passed into a condition so straitened that only ten years ago they would have regarded it as utterly insupportable—a position to which actual extinction was preferable. Yet, Heaven be praised! this great social revolution has not caused one drop of blood, and very little bitterness or complaint. Coming, as it has come, as the result of a great national sacrifice, it has been accepted with a patriotism as great as that which accepted the sacrifice of the War. English people of all classes are tenacious of their rights, and one may feel certain that the class of which I am speaking, if they felt an injustice was being done them, would not have forfeited their property without a struggle. Of such civil strife, however, there has never been a thought. In a word, our revolution has come in the guise of a patriotic duty and sacrifice.

It was accompanied, strange to tell, by a sudden, and therefore unsettling, temporary great increase of material prosperity among the poorer part of the community. The sacrifices, moral and physical, though not material, made by the manual workers were, though not greater, every bit as great as those made by the rich and the well-to-do. They were borne by the working-classes with what one must admit showed, in one sense, an even greater nobility of conduct. Education made matters explicable to the prosperous, and especially to their women, whereas the greater part of the women of the manual workers, and a very large part of the men, had to take the reasons for the War wholly on trust. They had not been sufficiently forewarned of the danger, and the War burst upon them literally as a horrible surprise—a surprise which so soon meant for the women the sacrifice of all they held most dear.

Though there seems a likelihood that proportionately the material sacrifice may remain less great for the manual workers than for those who are above them in the economic scale, the loss caused by the world's destitution is bound to be great, even though it will not be revolutionary. Still, I am convinced that it will be met with equal courage, provided our rulers, through panic or through false ideas of expediency, do not feed the manual workers of the nation on a diet of mere flattery, sophistry, and opportunism, but rather instruct and inspire them to play a worthy part.

But, though I see how many and how great are the dangers that surround us, I believe that as a nation and an Empire we shall pass through the fiery furnace with unsinged hair. It has been said that the Almighty must favour the British Empire, for again and again some event which it is difficult to regard as a mere accident has saved it from destruction, or turned its necessity to glorious gain. I find no difficulty in agreeing and also have no desire to apologise for calling it the Will of God that our nation shall not perish. I admit, however, it would be more in the philosophic fashion to describe it as the resultant of the Life-Urge, or of "the Something behind the Somebody"—a formula which is possibly destined to take the place of Matthew Arnold's more polished "stream of tendency making for righteousness."

But when I say this of the new voices, I hope that no one will imagine that I speak cynically or even in sympathetic irony. It may well be that those who use the phrase "Life-Urge" in reality mean very nearly what I mean when I speak of "the Grace of Heaven." They, indeed, may be more honest and more sincere than I am in their reticence of language and in their determination not to deceive themselves, even by an iota. Their fierce preservation of the citadel of agnosticism, till they are sure, may make them unhappy and hard-pressed in spirit. It can never make them ignoble.

For myself, I am convinced that there is no better way

of serving God, or of acknowledging the greatness of the issues of life and death than that splendid devotion to truth which will not allow even the minutest dilution,—which demands, not only the truth, and the whole truth, but nothing but the truth. Who dare blame these young "Knights of the Holy Ghost" who make their Gospel a demand for an absolute purity, who ask for the thing which has no admixture?

Does not our Lord Himself tell us, "*Blessed are the pure in heart, for they shall see God*"?   And does not purity of heart mean no mixed motives, no substitutes, no easy concessions, no compromises, no arrangements, but only the truth and the light, single and undefiled?

But I fear I may seem to be losing touch with that of which I speak, or claiming some sort of monopoly of Divine guidance for my race and country. Nothing could be further from my thought. All that I do is to cherish the belief that the trend of events is towards moral and spiritual progress, and that the chief instrument of salvation will be the English-speaking race.   In speaking thus, as a lover or a child, I am certainly not pointing to the road of selfishness.   If the English-speaking kin is to take the lead and to bring mankind from out the shadow and once again into the light, it can only be through care, toil, and sacrifice—things little consistent with national selfishness or national pride.

CHAPTER XXVIII

UNWRITTEN CHAPTERS

THE writing of memoirs is a pleasant exercise. At any rate, I have found it so. It has led me back to many curious and delightful things which I had wholly forgotten. They came unbidden in the train of events which I had always remembered "in principle" and was at pains to evoke in detail. But though the process has obvious advantages, it has had one drawback. My recollections, and still more my reflections, and what I may call my self-comments Conscious and Subconscious, have been so many that at times I have felt like a man struggling in a mighty torrent.

The result has been that, though I have written more than I intended to write, I have not covered anything like the amount of ground which I hoped to cover. I am left staring at a list of unwritten chapters. A list as long as that of those chapters included in my book or else eliminated lest the volume should swell to the size of the London Directory or to one of those portentous catalogues which Mr. Bernard Quaritch used to put forth in the days when I first began to love books, not merely for their contents, but as books.

The titles of the unwritten chapters have, however, so fascinated me, and seem so necessary to my life and, therefore, to my book, that I must, at any rate, put their names on record, together with some faint indication of their nature, lest my readers should think there is some deep reason why I do not touch them.   It is, I feel, only natural that people should think the worst of an Autobiographer.

The unwritten chapter which I most deeply regret is that chapter on the War Hospital which we opened in the house in which I am writing—a Hospital which my wife, though I suppose I ought not to say this, managed, in spite of ill-health and many difficulties, with extraordinary success.   Though physically disabled, she, for nearly five years, maintained practically single-handed, the organisation and direction of a well-equipped surgical and medical institution in a house not built for that purpose, though, oddly enough, one which in certain ways lent itself to hospital purposes.   The Newlands Corner Hospital had an average of forty beds.

Four and a half years is a long time to be out of one's house.   It is a still longer time in which to turn your home into an institution and yourself into a matron.   Altogether some eight or nine hundred men passed through the hospital.   The doctors of the Royal Herbert Hospital, Woolwich, with which we were affiliated, and Colonel Simpson, the A.D.M.S. of that Hospital,—a man of marked ability in his profession and with a natural gift for administration,—soon found out that Newlands air and Newlands care were excellent things for difficult and anxious cases.   Therefore we had our full share of bad, or, as the Sisters and nurses put it, good, cases.

As I had nothing to do with the hospital except on the proprietory side—I was very busy with war-work of my own—I cannot be accused of self-laudation if I say that my wife won the praise, not only of the Medical Authorities, but, which was still more to her and to me, the confidence and gratitude of her patients.   No small part of her success was due to a very simple fact. She early saw the necessity of dividing the administrative side of the hospital from the nursing side. Nursing is so fascinating in itself that many Commandants were drawn from their proper sphere of administration into surgical and medical work. My wife, partly from an instinct for sound administration, and partly also because at the moment she lacked the physical strength, confined herself strictly to her own side. In a hospital in which the patients were continually changing, which was four miles from a town and two miles from a railway station, that side was in war-times and during the period of rationing, by no means a light job. But the fact that there was one person, and that the person in supreme charge of the institution, who did nothing else except attend to the smooth running of the machine, meant that there were no arrears of correspondence, that all Army forms were filled up exactly and not, as many Commandants were inclined to think was far better, in accordance with what they themselves judged to be reasonable and necessary. Indeed, I was wont to tell my wife that I was appalled at the bureaucratic spirit which she developed! I believe I am right in saying that she never got an Army form wrong, though on several occasions she was able to point out to her official superiors that they had mistaken, or at any rate forgotten, their own elaborate rules.

The result was an extremely easy functioning of the official engine. While other Commandants could be heard complaining that they could not get answers from the authorities, or get the Army payments made properly, my wife, I believe, never once failed to get the War Office cheque, on the day it was due. There were never any complaints that she was in arrears with her correspondence or with necessary information. But then, instead of raging, as no doubt, she might have been quite as much inclined to do as anyone else, at the absurdities of "red tape" and so forth, she accepted them as necessary evils, like hailstorms and the "all dreaded thunder-stroke."

Six months before the War, believing the catastrophe was coming, she took instructions from an R.A.M.C. staff sergeant-major in all the intricacies of yellow, blue, and red tickets, and of forms from A to Z, or rather, from the first wound to the burial, required by the R.A.M.C. The result was that when the War broke out she knew a great deal more about the details of the Army Medical system than did many Staff or Regimental Officers, and even more than many Medical Officers.

But I am breaking my rule of not writing about living people, and I must stop. I may, however, say something about my own place in the hospital, for my position was curious, and of very great interest to me. During the four and a half years that the hospital was open, I lived in it as what might be called a parlour-boarder. I kept my own bedroom, but my house contained, as it were, forty guests, and guests of a very fascinating kind. Our family life was embedded in the hospital. My daughter was working in the wards, and my son used to come back from Eton to spend his holidays in his hospital home. I was working at the time, not only at *The Spectator*, but also at recruiting for the Regular Army, which I regarded as my special duty, for I happened that year to be Sheriff of my county. In addition I was at the head of a curious little corps called the Surrey Guides and further was a member of the Executive Committee for the Volunteer Training Corps—a body whose activities alone would be well worth a chapter.

But though my work lay outside Newlands, and though I always spent two nights a week in London, conducting, besides my editorial duties at *The Spectator* office, the duties I have already described in connection with the American Correspondents, I gained a most valuable experience from the hospital. In the first place, I did something which was almost unique. I lived for four and a half years in a community of women—the only man amongst nine. The house, of course, was full of male patients, but I lived with the staff.

Besides my wife and daughter, there was a Sister-in-Charge, and, when needed, an additional professional nurse, a staff of *masseuses* which varied in number in accordance with the nature of the cases sent to us, and four or five resident V.A.D.'s, including the night nurses. In a house in such an isolated position as ours it was not possible for the V.A.D.'s to live at home and come in for their duty hours.

I suppose the conventional cynic will expect me to say that I found out how much more quarrelsome, jealous, and feline is a community of women than one of men. Though I amused myself very much by watching how women work in association, I am bound to say that I saw nothing which led me to any such conclusion. I have seen plenty of men's quarrels in offices, in clubs, in the common rooms of colleges, at schools, and still more, perhaps, in mess-rooms and barracks, and I am bound to say that, according to my experience, my sex is quite as bad as, and, on the whole, rather worse than, women at the communal quarrel. Women are a little less noisy in their quarrels, and little more ingenious, but that is as far as I should care to generalise.

"They did not let you see."—That will not do as an explanation, for I am sure that after the first seven or eight months, the ladies of the staff came to ignore me completely, or to regard me rather as a part of the furniture. Consequently, I saw them in what, if they had been men, one might have called their shirt-sleeves. When you see hard-worked and anxious people, as they come down to breakfast in the morning, when they rush in to lunch, and when they sink, tired, into their chairs at dinner, you have a pretty good opportunity for finding out all about them. Under such conditions they cannot keep up the veil of convention and of company manners. However, I cannot go into all these details, much a I should like to, but must give only a general verdict.

I ended up my four and a half years as a parlour-boarder in a semi-convent with a respect for women and their work, which had always been very high, made still higher. If perhaps I found women a little less sensitive than I thought, I certainly found them a great deal more sensible, and, of course, as I suppose is the universal experience, a great deal less easily shocked by things that ought not to shock them than they are supposed to be. I mean by this that women are much less afraid to look life full in the face and much more willing to understand and to pardon, than is supposed. Also, I came to the conclusion that women, though great disciplinarians, and often hard upon each other, are not essentially merciless.

They are certainly, on the whole, less lazy than men, which is probably a misfortune. I think Matthew Arnold was right when he spoke of women being "things that move and breathe mined by the fever of the soul." The fever of the soul, especially in a Sister, who, as is the case with most of them, was grossly overworked in the hospital where she was trained, is apt to prove a great evil.

If I learned a good deal about women at the hospital and if the result of that learning was respect and admiration, I acquired an equally great respect and admiration for the British soldier. I had always loved those "contemptible regiments" who, as Sir Thomas Browne says, "will die at the word of a sergeant," but I loved them still more when I saw their good-natured, unostentatious way of life. They were, above all things, easy and sympathetic livers. Almost the only thing that shocked and disgusted them was being treated as heroes. Dr. Johnson talked about the "plebeian magnanimity of the British common soldier" and meant the right thing, though, in truth, there was nothing plebeian in the said magnanimity,—nothing which would not have been worthy of the highest birth and the highest breeding.

But the hospital did not raise my admiration merely for the soldier. It raised it equally for the British working-man, who composed by far the larger part of our patients. Ours, remember, was a soldiers' hospital, not an officers'. We had, I think, in the whole course of our hospital not more than four men who had been public-school boys or University men. All the rest were labourers or artisans. When the hospital doors closed, I respected the English working-man as much as ever, and added to that respect a love and sympathy which I may record, but shall not attempt to explain or to express in detail. I could fill a book with stories and studies of our friends, for so they became, and so they still remain.

My wife is constantly in touch with her old patients, and this does not mean applications for help or for work, but letters and visits of pleasure. That is good, but what is even better is that we constantly come across references to the Newlands feeling, for around it quickly grew up an indefinable *esprit de corps*. For example, on the day on which I write these pages, one of our local newspapers contains a letter from a Yorkshireman who had somehow seen an article in the aforesaid paper in regard to some Red Cross work done by my wife. He talks of the happy hours he spent at Newlands Corner, "hours which will live for ever in my mind." That, of course, is commonplace enough and sounds trivial, but it is repeated often enough to provoke a sense of true communal fellowship.

One of the things with which I think my wife and I were specially pleased about the hospital was the rapid way in which this sense of *esprit de corps*, *i.e.*, the public-school feeling, grew up. After the first month or two, patients talked quite seriously and candidly about "the old hospital." Again and again men told us that they should never forget Newlands. Like the true Englishmen they were, they partly loved Newlands because of the beauty of the scenery. The Englishman, though generally insensible of, or at any rate irresponsive to, the arts, is never irresponsive to a view. (John Stuart Mill's Autobiography contains, by the way, a curious passage in regard to this point.) I remember my wife telling me, the day after she had admitted a very bad case, that the patient had said to her, "I am sure I shall get well here, Commandant. It's such beautiful scenery."

But no more of the hospital here. I live in the hope that some day I may write its history, and may be able to say something which will not be open to the charge of, "Oh! Another boring book about the War!" As I conceive it, my hospital book will be an analysis of the mind and character of the British working-man with his defensive armour off, and not an attempt to give any views on military or medical reform and so forth.

One word more. My position in the hospital with the men was a strange one. They soon saw that I played the game, and that if I saw them breaking rules, met them, when I was riding, out of bounds, or discovered them at any other of their wicked tricks, I never told tales, or got them into trouble, or evoked any disciplinary reprisals.

This intensive cultivation of the blind eye raised me to the position of a friendly neutral and gained for me their confidence. Besides, I believe it soothed them to think that I, too, had to endure the regiment of women to which they were exposed. They suspected that I also quailed, as they must, before "the Sister in charge."

Their manners, by the way, were always perfect without being formal or absurd. They seemed to have an instinct for absolute good breeding. Yet they were all the time what Whitman called "natural and nonchalant persons." Neither my wife, nor her staff, nor I ever made any pretence to ourselves that they were plaster saints because their manners were good. They were as wicked as demons and as mischievous as monkeys, and seized every occasion for natural wrong-doing. In fact, they were just like schoolboys, but they observed always the schoolboy law. Quarrel they might, and dislike each other as they often did very bitterly, they never told tales of each other. The Belgians, of whom we had some at the beginning, were very different. They, curiously enough, gave each other away quite freely, and complained of each other to the Commandant. But, as one of our men said to me in excuse for the bad behaviour of the Belgians, "They was never taught any better. They hadn't the training we've had."

Another unwritten chapter, which I desire particularly to write, is a chapter on Newlands, the history of the house which I love only less than I love Sutton Court,— the house which I and my wife built, if not with our own hands, at any rate with our own heads,—the house in which my children were born, and two of my grandchildren,—the house from which my daughter was married,—the house which I have seen grow like a tree out of the ground,—finally, a house sanctified by the sufferings of brave men, who had fought for a great cause and laid us all under an obligation never to be expressed in words. Newlands, with its keen, almost mountain, air, its views, its woodlands, its yews, its groves of ash, and oak, and thorn, its green paths winding through the greyer and deeper-toned gorse, heather, and bracken, is a thing to live for. If one can be grateful, as certainly one can, to things inanimate, I am grateful for the health and strength which Newlands has given me. But this must be told, if I ever write it, in the history of the house. Still, I regret not to have done more honour to Newlands here, as I regret not to have been able to make my salute to the wounded in better form.

Another chapter "arising out of" Newlands, which I should like to have written, would have been on my work as Chief of the Surrey Guides. My readers need not be afraid of some burst of amateur militarism. I should have treated the Surrey Guides simply as a kind of "new model" version of Cobbett's *Rural Rides*. It was my duty to explore all the paths and roads of the county, and delightful work it was. My experiences must certainly be put on record somewhere and sometime, for, alas! the horse is dying out and with him will die the bridle-paths and the pack-roads. The night-riding part of my Surrey Guide work was to me particularly attractive. No one who has not tried night-riding across country will realise how fascinating it is and, comparatively speaking, how easy. Provided you ride a pony, instead of a huge, long-legged, heavy-weighted, badly-balanced horse, there is neither danger nor difficulty.

I will not say that the secret of night-riding is to give yourself up to your horse, for your horse may be as big a blunderer as you, and become a mixture of stupidity and anxiety. What I advise is, give yourself up to your subconsciousness, if you can, and this will lead you through the darkest places and the roughest roads in ample security.

Another chapter which I believed I was going to write in this book was to be devoted to inscriptions. I have always loved the art of the epigraphists, and I wanted to quote some examples, including (1) an inscription for a sun-dial, (2) an inscription for a memorial to Lord Halifax, the trimmer, the greatest of Whig statesmen, (3) another to William Pitt, and (4) an inscription to the Quakers who fought and died in the War,—men whose noble combination of patriotism and self-abnegation impressed me profoundly.

> Their ashes in a peaceful urn shall rest,
>   Their names a great example stand to show
> How strangely high endeavour may be blest
>   When Piety and Valour jointly go.

Another Surrey chapter might have dealt with my activities as Sheriff and my conceptions of that office.

Still another chapter ought to have centred in my personal life at Newlands. It was at Newlands that my health broke down and I saw, or thought I saw, as did my doctors, the advance of the penumbra, the shadow of eclipse which was to engulf my life. I wanted very much, when I began this book, to put on record a description of how utterly different than is commonly supposed are the feelings of the occupant of the condemned cell. I should also like to have recorded certain reflections upon how a serious illness becomes a kind of work of art, a drama or film in real life, in which the patient, the doctors, the nurses, the friends, and the relations all play their appropriate parts, and contribute each in his order to the central theme. But this and "The Adventure of Dying," a theme which has never yet been adequately treated, but ought some day to be, must await not, of course, the actual coming of the Gondolier, for that is too late, but that interval between life and death which the Emperor Diocletian boasted that he had created for himself.

Another unwritten chapter on a subject which may sound dull, but which might very well have been one of the best, was to be called "The Consolations of the Classics." It would have told how in his later years new stars had risen for the adventurer in the voyage of life, while many of the planets that were in their zenith in his youth have suffered decline.

As a boy, and even in the prime of life, I knew nothing of Racine. I now bend my head in adoration. Again, I knew little or nothing of Balzac. I now think of him as one of the greatest of the analysts of human conduct,—not as great as Shakespeare, but, all the same, very great, and almost as terrible as he is great. If ever a man fascinates and is intolerable, it is Balzac.

I should have liked, but that is not a thing which can be compressed or sandwiched into any chapter, to have written quite frankly and fully about my religious beliefs. Here, indeed, I had planned with some care. I wanted to say not what I thought other men ought to believe, nor what I thought I ought to believe myself, or, again, what I ought not to believe in order to make my *credo* look reasonable and "according to plan." What I wanted to do was to say frankly, fairly, and truthfully what I do believe as a matter of fact and not as a matter of ought or ought not. I wanted to record an existing set of actualities, not to write a piece of philosophy or metaphysics. *I wanted, in fact, to photograph my soul.* But this, again, must wait, though I hope it will not wait very long.

If I write such a paper I shall certainly take for my motto Lord Halifax's words to Bishop Burnet: "I believe as much as I can: and God Almighty will, I am sure, pardon me if I have not the digestion of an ostrich."

I will neither be put off on the one side by making an effort to express belief in more than I can believe, nor, again, refuse to record my honest belief in some "fact of religion" because it will not be thought creditable for me, or because certain people will think me superstitious and unreasonable, just as other people will think me too rationalistic. I will yield nothing to the demand, "You cannot possibly believe *this*, when you have just said that you don't believe *that*. The two things must hang together. You cannot pick and choose like this at your fancy."

My answer is, I can, I do, and I will. My endeavour is not an attempt to reconcile beliefs, but to say for good or for evil what I do believe. I believe that London lies to the Northeast of the place at which I am dictating these words. Faith is a fact, not a fragment of reasoning, and I mean to put down the said fact for what it is worth.

How I wish I could write my chapter on the odd things that have happened to me in life, and record the strange and inexplicable things that I have heard of from other people. I don't mean by this that I have a number of second-hand ghost-stories to tell. All the same I could tell of certain things much more impressive because they are so much less sensational. It was my habit as a young man, a habit which I wish I had not abandoned, to ask everybody I came across, who was worth interrogating, what was the oddest thing that had happened in their lives. One would have supposed that I should often have got for my impertinence a surly answer, or, at any rate, an elegant rapier-thrust, or some other form of snub.

Strangely enough, I never found anyone "shy" at my question, but I did get many curious answers, and some of these I have a perfect right to record. A section of this chapter should deal with accidental conversations and accidental confessions. It has been my good luck once or twice to listen to the most strange talk in trains and other public places, and again, by straight questions I have sometimes elicited very crooked answers.

For example, when I was a young man I once heard an old gentleman in a third-class railway carriage remark vaguely and yet impressively to the company at large, as follows: "I once saw six men hanged in a very rustic manner." That, I think everyone will agree with me, was an excellent conversational opening. The full story, though I cannot tell it here, was quite as good. So was the story of William Harvey, *the girt big Somersetshire man,*" and what he did in a fight with Spanish Pilots in the Bilbao River. Of this story, told to me in the broadest Somersetshire dialect by a Somersetshire boatman who was present at the fight, I cannot resist quoting one passage: "They were all dressed in white and fighting with their long knives. But William Harvey, who was six feet six high, got hold of the axe we always kept on deck for cutting away the mast if it went in a storm, and he knocked them over with that. And as fast as he did knock them over, we did chuck the bodies into the water."

Another of my accidental conversations opened with these words: "And she never knew till she followed her to her grave that she was her own mother." The personal pronouns are slightly mixed, but the story might well develop like a Greek play.

Again, I planned a chapter to describe the four most beautiful human beings seen by me in the course of my life. Strangest of all, and perhaps most beautiful of all, using beauty in rather a strained sense, was the man alluded to in my dedication,—the man my wife and I saw in the Jews' Garden at Jahoni. We were resting in the garden after a very long ride in very hot weather, when there entered a young man in a white tunic, with bare feet and legs. On his head was a wide hat of rough straw, and across his shoulder a mattock. His face and form could only be described in the famous words, "Beauty that shocks you." Why his beauty shocked us, and must have shocked any other seers possessed of any sensibility, I cannot say. Thinking he was a gardener, we asked our Dragoman to ask him some simple question but he could not, or did not, obtain any information. The creature was like the figures of Faunus or Vertumnus, or one of those half-deities or quarter-deities that one sees among the marbles in public collections. "Græco-Roman School, of the late Antonine Period; probably representing a Rural Deity, or God of Spring or Agriculture in the Latin mythology." Certainly the more decadent side of late Greek or Roman art seemed in some strange way to be living again in this amazing being.

Far more really beautiful, far more interesting, and far more impressive was a woman whom I and my younger brother met with in a tram-car outside the Porta del Popolo in Rome. Up till then I had spent much time in wondering why the Italian population had declined in the matter of good-looks and why one never saw anyone like a Bellini or a Raphael Madonna. And then I looked up after having my ticket clipped and saw the perfect youthful mother of the Cinquecento painters sitting opposite me. A more exquisitely harmonious face and expression were never vouchsafed to my eyes. She was a countrywoman of the richer peasant class, and was apparently making her first visit to the city accompanied by her husband. One would gladly have taken oath at first sight that she was the perfect wife and mother, and yet there was no sentimental pose about her—only the most naïve and innocent delight told in smiles, laughter, and blushes. The things she saw from the tram window seemed to make her whole being ripple with pleasure. Happily I cannot here be judged as a sentimental visionary for my companion will avouch the facts.

Curiously enough, though I think English women, as a whole, far surpass the Italians in their looks, the other perfectly beautiful woman whom I have seen was also an Italian. I was taking an early walk, with my younger brother, from Baveno to the summit, or at any rate, to the shoulder of the Monte Moteroni. The time was between five and six o'clock in the morning, and the place a small peasant's farm just at the fringe of the land between the open mountain and the cultivated slopes. I looked over the hedge or wall, I forget which, and there was a bare-legged girl of some seventeen or eighteen working in the field with her father and her brothers, hoeing potatoes. Here, indeed, was something worth writing home about— a figure like the Lombard girl in Browning's "Italian in England,"—a face gentle, simple, kind, but, above all, beautiful, and a figure worthy of the face.

The fourth figure in my gallery of the visions that the turn of the road took from my eyes and "swept into my dreams for ever" was seen during a purely prosaic walk in South Kensington. Unsuspecting, unperturbed, I was bent on a constitutional, or maybe a shopping expedition, when there suddenly arose before my astonished eyes, out of a man-hole in the middle of the street—I honestly believe it was the Cromwell Road—a young workman with flaxen hair and a short beard,—a man with something of the face and figure which the Italian painters gradually came to attribute to the Christ. But here again, as in the case of the Madonna of the tram-car, the man evidently had never been told of, or thought of, the resemblance. He seemed perfectly unconscious and natural. Though the trained eye might notice a resemblance in the outline of the face, the happy smile and negligent air showed nothing of the Man of Sorrows. He was just an ordinary Englishman.

When I think of those four figures of resplendent beauty —and especially of the two women, for the Syrian had something sinister and uncanny about him and the young Englishman was too prosaic in essentials—I recall the passage which I know is somewhere in Sir Thomas Browne, though I am quite unable to find it, in which the Physician Philosopher declares that when he sees specially beautiful persons he desires to say a grace or thanksgiving to Heaven for the joy that has been vouchsafed him.

As to the strange stories and strange things told me, I should have liked particularly to chronicle two at length. One is the story of a tiny Indian spindle that spun by itself in the dust, and the other, though it had no marvel in it, except the marvel of maternal feeling, is the story of a chamois and her young one on a glacier-pass. The English mountaineer who told it me, was on a difficult climb. Suddenly he saw to his astonishment a chamois, the shyest of all animals, standing stock-still on a steep glacier. She actually let him come so close to her that he could have touched her with his hand, and then he saw the reason. The chamois stood at the very edge of a deep crevasse, and up from its cold, blue depths came the cry of a terrified and agonised creature—cries that were answered by the mother chamois. The little chamois had fallen through the ice-bridge and lay some hundred feet or so below and beyond all recovery. The narrator was an

31

ordinary *table-d'hôte* Smoking-Room tourist, but he could hardly recount the story without tears. He tried, but it was impossible to effect a rescue, and he had to leave the wretched mother where she was. As he said, "Considering what chamois are, it sounds absolutely incredible that the mother should have been able to overcome her shyness of mankind and stay by the young one. I wouldn't have believed it if I hadn't seen it. She took no more notice of me and my guide than if we had been rocks. Poor brute!"

Another chapter would have recorded the influence upon my life of great writers, great poets, great painters, great sculptors, and great musicians. Next, I should have loved to give in detail accounts of my travels, not in strange or dangerous parts of the earth, but through some of the most beautiful scenery of Europe and in the fringes of Africa and Asia. As a young man, I journeyed in sledges over most of the Alpine passes in the winter, for, owing to my uncle John Symonds being one of the discoverers of the High Alps in winter, I was early, so to speak, in the snow-field. To this day nothing attracts me more than the thought of a long day or night spent in a sledge.

I crossed the Splügen by day in the winter, and by moonlight in the summer. I crossed the St. Gothard (before the tunnel was made) in a Vetturino carriage. I have crossed the Simplon, and I have many times crossed the Bernina and all the other passes of the Grisons in the snow in mid-winter. For those who like, as I do, sharp cold, and ardent sunlight, there is nothing more delightful, and if as sometimes happens, one can see or hear an avalanche really close, without getting into it, a pleasant spice of danger is added. But I did not love the Alps merely in the winter. Though no expert climber, I was fond of the mountains to the point of fanaticism, and though I never got higher than 11,000 feet, or a little over, I had the extremely interesting experience of falling into a crevasse. Fortunately I was well held by the rope against the white grey edge of the blue abyss, while my legs kicked freely in the illimitable inane.

Is there anything in the world like being aroused in the grey of dawn by the man with the axe and the rope? Can anything equal that succession of scenes, the Alpine village in sleepy silence, the pastures and the cultivated land, the inevitable little bridge on the inevitable stream, then the belt of pines, then the zone of rocks and flowers, best and gayest of all gardens, and last the star gentians and the eternal snows? A holiday heart, twenty years of age, a friend, a book of poetry, and a packet of food in one's pocket!—Truly, "If there is a Paradise, it is here, it is here!"

Horses that I have known and liked, and on whose backs I have felt supremely happy—rides on mules in Spanish or African mountains, rides in the Syrian or Libyan Deserts on true Arabs, or, perhaps most thrilling of all, night rides on the Downs, would make a tale, whether delightful to read by others I know not, but certainly delightful to be recorded by me.

"Projects Fulfilled and Unfulfilled" would have made a good chapter, as would also "Quotations and the Effects of Poetry on Everyday Existence."

Another chapter which I have not written, but should like to have written, would have been "Some Uncles"—I use the word "some" in both the common and the slang sense—for I may be said to have been specially rich in this relationship. Two of my Indian uncles were well known to the public. One was Sir John Strachey, for six months acting Viceroy of India, owing to Lord Mayo's assassination and the delay in his successor taking up the post. The other was Sir Richard Strachey, who began his Indian life as a subaltern in the Hon. East India Company's Corps of Sappers and Miners. He had a horse killed under him at the Battle of Sobraon, and afterwards became one of the greatest of Indian Civil Engineers, a Member of Council (Public Works Department), and one of the greatest of canal and railway constructors. Henry Strachey, another uncle, commanded a battalion of Gourkhas, and died over ninety years of age. Though little known to the world, he was a man of memorable character and in his youth accidentally and temporarily the talk of London as a Thibetan explorer. William Strachey, a fourth uncle, was the strangest of men. Like the "Snark," he breakfasted at afternoon tea and lived by candlelight instead of sunlight,—a wholly fantastic man, though one of great ability. At one time he was what our forefathers called "a man about town,"—a member of Brook's Club during the Fifties and Sixties, a friend of Thackeray and of "Flemming, theF lea," and a clerk in the Colonial office. He was often selected by Lord Palmerston for special work. Later, however, he developed such strangely nocturnal, though by no means noisy habits, that he almost disappeared from the ken of his family. He, by the way, once spoke to me of Lady William Russell, of whom I have already written, describing her as one of the most beautiful and in later years one of the most delightful people he had ever seen, and the best of all hostesses—"You used to look up at the fanlight over the door of her house in South Audley Street, and if you saw the gas-jet burning you knew that she was at home, expecting the company of her friends, and needed no further invitation. Whatever the hour was, if the light was burning you could go in and finish your evening in talk with her and her other guests." She was thus at home almost every evening to the people favoured enough to have the entry of her house.

Another uncle was Mr. George Strachey, a diplomat, and for some thirty years Her Britannic Majesty's representative at Dresden,—a man of great ability, but with a nature better fitted to a man of letters than to an official. Of Strachey great-uncles I could tell many a curious and entertaining tale, and especially of the man whom my father succeeded,—the man we called "the second Sir Henry." It has been said of him that he was "odd even for a Strachey," and I could prove that up to the hilt. Almost as odd, from many points of view, though much more human, was his brother, Richard Strachey, one of the prize figures of the Military and Diplomatic Service of the East India Company. He is still commemorated in Persia on the leaden water-pipes of Ispahan, but how and why is too long a story for a chapter of apology.

Dearly should I have loved to write a chapter on "The Art of Living," for unquestionably "life demands art,"—an aphorism, by the way, not, as most people think, of Pope but of Wordsworth. (Wordsworth, remember, had a great deal of the Eighteenth Century in him.) That chapter, however, would easily become a book or a serpent, as says the Italian proverb.

Last of all, how many are the men and women, now dead, whom I should like to have mentioned and of whom I have something worth saying. They are included in a rough list which I drew up when I first thought of writing my autobiography. I give these names written down just as they occurred to me. Some of them have been referred to in the body of this book, but most of them are not even mentioned. Lord Roberts; Watts the painter; Sir John Millais; Sir William Harcourt; Lord Houghton;

Walter Bagehot; Lord Carlingford; Lord Goschen; the Duke of Argyll of Gladstone's Cabinets; Mr. Macmillan, the publisher; Mr. George Smith; Lady Stanley of Alderley; Lord Carlisle; Lord Morpeth; Sir Edward Cook; Lord Kitchener; the late Duke of Northumberland; Admiral Dewey; Mr. William Arnold; Lord Burghclere; Sir William Jenner; Miss Mary Kingsley; Lord Glenesk; the late Lord Grey; the late Lord Astor; Sir William White, the naval constructor; the late Lord Sligo; Dean Beeching; Bishop Perceval; Archbishop Temple; my uncle, Professor T. H. Green; Professor Dicey; Professor Freeman; Bishop Stubbs; Mr. Lecky; Mrs. Humphry Ward; Lord Bowen; Mr. Baugh Allen, the last of the Special Pleaders; Professor Henry Smith, the mathematician; Lord Justice Fry, and Lord Balfour of Burleigh.

There was another man, too little and too lately known, with whom I wanted to deal at length, for he exercised a distinct and special influence on my life. I mean Donald Hankey, "The Student in Arms." I had, indeed, designed to speak of him in a special chapter on the effect of the War on my life, but that chapter did not get written, or, rather, remains over to be written when the perspective is easier and better, and the world has given up its last, and to me very futile and foolish, mode of talking as if we ought to be ashamed of the War, or, at any rate, as if we ought to treat it as an utterly tiresome subject.

Here, then, I shall say only that the essential thing about Hankey was that he was one of the true saints of the world, or, rather, one of the saints who matter. Yet never was there a less saintly saint. He was a man you could talk to rationally on any subject. I, who really knew him, would not have called him a man of the world, because it would have been in essence misleading; but I should have quite understood someone else saying it and should have known exactly what he meant. Not only had he not the temper of the zealot or the fanatic, but he was a kindly man, with no fierceness about him. Yet somehow, and this was the miracle, he contrived to have none of the easy unction of the pushing man of holiness who realises that if he is to succeed in accomplishing what he wants accomplished, he must assume a certain cunning suavity of manner which is really foreign to his character. Hankey had no pose. He was at bottom what Walt Whitman calls a "natural and nonchalant" person, who happened to be made all through of sweetness and light, though never the superior person, and never, as it were, too good for this world. Not for one moment did you find in him the chill of sanctity. In the phrase of John Silver, "he kept company very easy."

I should imagine that confession was the very last thing that Hankey would ever have encouraged in anyone, for it is the most debilitating of the virtues. All the same, a penitent would have found him an extraordinarily easy occupant of the box. He was warm-hearted, sympathetic, and full of the victorious spirit. One felt with Hankey that he was born for whatever was arduous. In truth he was "God's soldier." What gives the extreme characteristic impression of Hankey is that last vision of him set forth in a letter by the soldier who, happening to look into a trench, saw him kneeling in prayer with his company gathered round him, just before they went over the parapet.

If he had lived, he would, I am sure, have talked about the scene. I never saw a man so natural and so little embarrassed in discussing such matters as prayer or other spiritual experiences. He had in a marked degree that absence of *mauvaise honte* which marks the good man at all times, in all places, in all religions, and in all races.

There is a man, now dead, who told me something which I want to record in this very convenient chapter. His words impressed me out of all proportion to their intrinsic importance. I feel indeed that there must be something in them which I cannot analyse, but which makes them worth preserving. The vitamines of food, we know, are not strictly analysable, though their presence can be detected. No one knows of what they consist, but, nevertheless, we know two things about them. They exist, and they have a great influence upon metabolism. So in the food of the mind there are vitamines which we can recognise, but not analyse, and, therefore, cannot wholly understand. My readers, if they will look into their own memories, will, I am sure, recall experiences of these mental vitamines, trivial or ordinary in themselves, and yet holding a place so clear and often indeed so vehement as to suggest that they contain some quickening quality of their own.

The man with whom I connect certain of these vitamines of the mind was Sir George Grove, the compiler of the *Dictionary of Music*. I did not know him well; but, as a boy, he did me a kindly service. He accepted the first poem of any length that I ever published. When I was seventeen, that is a year before I went to Oxford, I sent him a poem, alluded to in another chapter of this book, called "Love's Arrows." He liked it and published it in *Macmillan's Magazine*, of which he was then Editor. Macmillan's was a magazine given up to good literature, and to get a place in it was considered no small honour.

Grove possessed a keen sense of literature, and he had known many of the famous people of the Victorian era. True to my plan of asking questions, I asked him whether he had ever seen Cardinal Newman. He replied by a story which was revealing as to a certain fierceness in

Newman's character and mental configuration. In any case, it had both rhetorically and intellectually a considerable influence on my mind.

Here is a *précis* of our conversation.

"Did you ever see Newman?"

"Only once, and then I heard him preach."

"Was he in a big sense eloquent?"

"Yes. Though he had none of the airs and graces of the orator, he had somehow in a high degree the power of thrilling you. I heard him in Lent preaching in a small Roman Catholic chapel in London. He was a gaunt figure, extremely emaciated and hollow-cheeked, with a very bad cough, and as he stood in the pulpit, coughing hoarsely, he beat his breast with his hand and forearm, till it sounded like the reverberation of a huge cavernous drum." Grove went on to describe how the time was one of great spiritual excitement in the Church of England and in the Roman Church,—a time when people thought that Rome was going to reassert her ascendancy over English minds. During the very week or month in which the sermon was preached, Stanley's *Life of Arnold* had appeared. "At the end of that book Stanley describes how when Arnold lay dying, he had, one evening, a very long talk with him about the Sacraments and the part they played in the religious life. He records that conversation and the Broad Church view of Arnold, and then tells how he rose next morning and went to enquire as to Arnold, and how he found that Arnold had died in the night. Newman was preaching on the old, old maxim, '*Nulla salus extra ecclesiam*,' and dwelt, as a preacher with his views naturally would, on the contrast between the covenanted and uncovenanted mercies of God. Those who were in the Church were absolutely safe. For those who could trust only to the *uncovenanted* mercies of God there could be no such safety. 'But,' he went on, 'it is not for me to deal with them and their prospects of salvation and of life eternal.' And then, with great feeling and emotion, 'Nor shall I presume to canvass the fate of that man who, at night, doubted the efficacy of sacramental wine, and died in the morning.'"

Though the words, of course, had no spiritual effect on Grove, he dwelt upon the difficulty he had in conveying the profound emotional force of these phrases when they were spoken by this strange figure in the pulpit. Grove need not have made any apology. He amply managed, and this was a proof of the preacher's power, to transfer the emotion of the moment to me. The words in the spiritual sense mean nothing to me. Indeed, they disgust, nay, horrify me as utterly irreligious. Yet I am bound to say that I feel, and always have felt, their emotional appeal urgently and deeply. Here, if anywhere, are the vitamines of oratory.

Again, I should like to have had a chapter on the links of the past, because I have been fortunate in that respect. Some of these I have recorded in other chapters, but I should like to put on record the fact that I actually knew and spent several days in a country house with a lady who actually received a wedding-present from Keats and also one from Shelley. That lady was Mrs. Proctor, the widow of Barry Cornwall, the poet. When I first saw Mrs. Proctor, who, by the way, was well known to my wife and Mrs. Simpson, she was a fellow-guest with me and my wife at a house-party at the Grant-Duffs'. Though, I suppose, nearly ninety years old at that time (it was three or four years before her death), there was not a trace of extreme old age in her talk. She was neither deaf nor blind, but enjoyed life to the full. She did not seem even to suffer from physical weakness, but was capable of

hours of sustained talk. She had known everybody
worth knowing in the literary world and had vivid recollections of them. For example, besides mentioning the
wedding-presents from Keats and Shelley, she was also
proud to remember that she had received a present from
the murderer, Wainwright, Lamb's friend,—who wrote
under the name of Janus Weathercock—the man who
insured his step-daughter's life and then poisoned her.
Owing to the extraordinary way in which things were
arranged in those days, the murderer, though found guilty,
had his sentence commuted to transportation—apparently
as a kind of recognition of his literary ability.

Oddly enough, this was not the only time that accident
put me in touch with this singular and sinister figure,—
the man too who first talked about the psychological
interest of colours and cared, as Mrs. Proctor said, for
strange-looking pots and pieces of china. My friend
Willie Arnold told me that when his mother was a girl,
or a young married woman, I forgot which, in Tasmania,
she had her picture drawn by a convict, and that convict was the celebrated Wainwright. According to Willie
Arnold, his character was not supposed to be of the
best even in those days, and great care was taken that
during the sittings someone else should always be in the
room!

Another link with the past, which is worth recording, is
that I knew well a man, Sir Charles Murray, who told me
that he had seen Byron. When I cross-questioned him,
he told me something that I think must have been an
error of memory. He said it was at a ball in Paris that
he saw the poet. Now, I feel pretty sure that Byron
never was in Paris. In the earlier part of his life he
could not have got there because of the war, and after the
peace, as we all know, he began his travels at Antwerp,

and journeyed up the Rhine into Switzerland and then crossed the Alps by the Simplon into Italy.

Perhaps, however, my most sensational link with the past was as follows. When I first came into Surrey, the old Lord Lovelace—the man who married Byron's daughter, and who built Horsley Towers—was still alive and could be seen, as I saw him, driving about our Surrey lanes in a pony-chaise. Lord Lovelace is reported to have made the following entry in his diary about the year 1810, that is, when he was a boy some ten or twelve years old—"Today I dined with the old Lord Onslow [a neighbour then, presumably, of about ninety years of age], and heard him say that as a boy he had known one of the Cromwellian troopers—Captain Augustine—who was on guard round the scaffold when Charles I was executed."

Oddly enough, I have another link with the Cromwellian Wars. I remember, some forty years ago, my uncle, Sir Charles Cave, of whom I am glad to say I can speak in the present tense, told me that he was shooting on one of his farms below Lansdowne, the hill that rises above Bath. The tenant of the land was a very old farmer, and he informed my uncle that his grandmother, who lived to a great age, but whom he had just known as a boy, used to say that she remembered how, when a girl, the soldiers came into the village after the Battle of Lansdowne and took every loaf of bread out of the place.

An even more personal link with the past was afforded by my mother's aunt, Miss Sykes, and my great-aunt. She had seen George III walking on the terrace at Windsor, old, blind, and mad, with his family and courtiers curtseying to those poor blind eyes and vacant wits every time he turned in his constitutional. Another of her recollections, however, was far more thrilling to me as a lad. Miss Sykes, sister of my mother's mother, belonged to a naval family, and her mother's sister had married Admiral Byron, the seaman uncle of the poet. Therefore, Byron and Miss Sykes were in that unnamed relationship, or pseudo-relationship, which belongs to those who have an aunt or an uncle in common. It happened that my aunt was on a visit to the Byrons when the poet's body, which was consigned to the Admiral, was brought to London. The Admiral, who lived near Windsor, posted up to receive the barrel of spirits in which the remains were preserved. When he returned from his gruesome visit the ladies of his family, and none more so than my aunt, then a girl of fifteen or sixteen, were very anxious to know what he had seen and what the remains of the most-talked-of man in the Europe of his day looked like. "What did he look like, my dear? He looked like an alligator," said the Admiral, who did not mince his words. It is strange that men should prefer to put their kin in what, in the naval records after Trafalgar, is called "a pickle" rather than give them a burial at sea or in "some corner of a foreign field"! But on such matters there can be no argument. It is a matter of feeling, not of reasoning.

So much for unwritten chapters and unwritten books, though, perhaps, I ought to add a postscript upon the writing of memoirs, describing how pleasant, though arduous a task it is. At any rate, it has proved so in my case. I began these memoirs with the feeling that, though it was quite worth while to record my part in the general adventure of living, I must expect that, even if I were to contrive to give pleasure to my readers, the part of the writer must be hard, laborious, and ungrateful. "Why," I asked myself, "should I munch for others the remainder biscuit of life?" Yet, strange to say, what I had looked forward to almost with dread, turned out to be by far the pleasantest literary experience of my life. I have never been one of those people who dislike writing, or find it, as some people do, agonising; but I was not in the least prepared to find how pleasant it could be to dive into the depths of memory and let, what the author of the anonymous Elizabethan play, *Nero*, calls "the grim churl" of memory lead you through the labyrinth of the past.

But, though the path was pleasant, nay, exhilarating and stimulating, I must confess to the fact that I have had no psychological experiences, regrets, or disillusionments. I have had no temptation to write as to the shortness and precariousness of human existence, or to reflect how base I had found mankind, or, again, to deplore the past, curse the present, and dread the future. Life to me, in looking back, seems on the whole a very natural and simple show. No one, in one sense, feels more strongly than I do that we are being swept along by the mighty current of a vast river, without any clearer indication of what is the outlet of the river than of what is its source. But though these things may be an excuse for a great deal of rhetoric, they somehow seem to me, if I may use the word again, natural and non-inflammatory. It is far easier to trust what those who, liking the vagueness of theology, call "the larger hope," but which I should be content to call plainly the mercy of God—a mercy which I, for one, make bold to say I would rather have uncovenanted than covenanted. Covenanted mercies are a kind of thing which may do very well at an insurance office or for business purposes, but they are not the mercies one would ever dream of asking for or accepting from an earthly father. Then how can one dare to speak of them in the same breath with God?

"But this," I hear some readers say, "is the illusion of

faith and has nothing of the permanence of fact." Well, I, for one, am content to rest on faith, honest and instinctive. Faith, to my mind, is a fact and a very palpable fact,—a fact as vital as any of the other great incommensurables and insolubles of our existence.

If I am asked to treat of the river, or rather, the ocean of life and the adventure of its voyage in terms that will satisfy those not fortunate enough to have faith, let me commend to them that memorable dream set forth by that most honest and exact of agnostics as of jurists, Mr. Justice Stephen. The dream, published some fifty years ago, is as noble a piece of literature as it is a monument of intellectual insight.

I dreamt [he says, after Bunyan's fashion] that I was in the cabin of a ship, handsomely furnished and lighted. A number of people were expounding the objects of the voyage and the principles of navigation. They were contradicting each other eagerly, but each maintained that the success of the voyage depended absolutely upon the adoption of his own plan. The charts to which they appealed were in many places confused and contradictory. They said that they were proclaiming the best of news, but the substance of it was that when we reached port most of us would be thrown into a dungeon and put to death by lingering torments. Some, indeed, would receive different treatment; but they could not say why, though all agreed in extolling the wisdom and mercy of the Sovereign of the country. Saddened and confused I escaped to the deck, and found myself somehow enrolled in the crew. The prospect was unlike the accounts given in the cabin. There was no sun; we had but a faint starlight, and there were occasionally glimpses of land and of what might be lights on shore, which yet were pronounced by some of the crew to be mere illusions. They held that the best thing to be done was to let the ship drive as she would, without trying to keep her on what was understood to be her course. For the strangest thing on that strange ship was the fact that there was such a course. Many theories were offered about this, none quite satisfactory; but it was understood that the ship was to be steered due north. The best and bravest and wisest of the crew would dare the most terrible dangers, even, from their comrades, to keep her on her course. Putting these things together, and noting that the ship was obviously framed and equipped for the voyage, I could not help feeling that there was a port somewhere, though I doubted the wisdom of those who professed to know all about it. I resolved to do my duty, in the hope that it would turn out to have been my duty, and I then felt that there was something bracing in the mystery by which we were surrounded, and that, at all events, ignorance honestly admitted and courageously faced, and rough duty vigorously done, was far better than the sham knowledge and the bitter quarrels of the sickly cabin and glaring lamplight from which I had escaped.

Was there ever a nobler parable more nobly expressed? It may well end the last page of the last chapter of *The Adventure of Living*.

INDEX

Index

A Selection from the
Catalogue of

G. P. PUTNAM'S SONS

Complete Catalogues sent
on application

EMINENT VICTORIANS

By LYTTON STRACHEY

8vo.   With Portraits

A selection from a host of reviews of this brilliant and extraordinarily witty book :

The New York Times—"There is every temptation to quote from this volume, for it abounds in striking stories and brilliant interpretations. . . . Mr. Strachey has not written history in the usual fashion, but he has made a notable contribution to that prodigious undertaking, the history of the Victorian Age."

The Outlook—"Brilliant."

The Metropolitan—"It is one of the few current books that I would specially recommend as worth reading. He is a refreshing, brave, witty, and large-minded biographer."—*Clarence Day, Jr.*

The Chicago Daily News—"Lytton Strachey can write circles around any living biographer; can give handicaps to any living essayist and match the most touted workers in the language with one hand tied behind his back. . . . When you have read the last line of these soul-portraits you are aware of the stark truthfulness of the work. It is not only art—it is reality."

The New York Tribune—"We receive Mr. Strachey's volume with gratitude and joy. . . . Profound sincerity of both constructive and destructive criticism, sanity of judgment and splendor of spirit make this volume a memorable tribute to one of the most memorable eras in the history of the human intellect."

The Chicago Tribune—"One of the outstanding biographical works in English literature. . . . In a generation that produces one Strachey there bob up several thousand professional mourners, who model their style and general appreciation of the truth upon epitaphs. . . . Strachey wields one of the most engaging pens now employed in literature. His humor is unfailing, but always smooth, unforced, ironic. He knows the satiric value of hyperbole and antithesis. His book is altogether a remarkable performance. . . . In his gallery are portraits of familiar personages wearing new expressions, and the manner of presentation is that of a cultivated and penetrating artist. The volume is recommended eagerly to all lovers of vivid and daring biography."

The Springfield Republican—"Mr. Strachey's wit gives stimulating piquancy to a style at once brilliant and pure. His power of illuminating the figures which he presents is matched by his ability to interest the reader in his craftmanship."

The Hartford Times—"Under his pointed, facile, and illuminating pen dry-as-dust facts become of absorbing interest. It is astonishing what he can do to make a 'life' worth reading."

The Indianapolis News—"Mr. Strachey has succeeded notably in making biography more dramatic and fascinating than fiction."

New York　　　　**G. P. PUTNAM'S SONS**　　　　**London**